SECOND EDITION

VMware Cookbook

Ryan Troy and Matthew Helmke

O'REILLY®

Beijing • Cambridge • Farnham • Köln • Sebastopol • Tokyo

VMware Cookbook, Second Edition
by Ryan Troy and Matthew Helmke

Printed in the United States of America.

Published by O'Reilly Media, Inc., 1005 Gravenstein Highway North, Sebastopol, CA 95472.

O'Reilly books may be purchased for educational, business, or sales promotional use. Online editions are also available for most titles (*http://my.safaribooksonline.com*). For more information, contact our corporate/institutional sales department: 800-998-9938 or *corporate@oreilly.com*.

Editor: Andy Oram
Production Editor: Rachel Steely
Copyeditor: Absolute Service, Inc.
Proofreader: Absolute Service, Inc.

Indexer: BIM Publishing Services
Cover Designer: Karen Montgomery
Interior Designer: David Futato
Illustrators: Robert Romano and Rebecca Demarest

June 2012: Second Edition.

Revision History for the Second Edition:

2012-06-06 First release
2012-12-14 Second release

See *http://oreilly.com/catalog/errata.csp?isbn=9781449314477* for release details.

ISBN: 978-1-449-31447-7

[LSI]

1355331642

Table of Contents

Preface

VMware is one of those products that many of us, including this book's authors, have been reading about for years. Ryan has had the opportunity over the years to become involved with and architect many virtualized environments, ranging from small- to large-scale cloud deployments using VMware technology. As time passes, Ryan has grown fond of the VMware product suite and continues to discuss it daily.

Matthew and Ryan have worked together on several projects in the past. In the summer of 2008, the two of us decided we would like to write a book together. We tossed around ideas and decided to write on VMware's ESX platform, because it impressed us so. Since Matthew was already an established writer and also technologically proficient, although new to this specific software, we decided that Ryan would do the technical writing and Matthew would concentrate his efforts on making sure it all came across clearly and accurately.

We are genuinely delighted by VMware as a company, and have found its employees very kind and helpful. We have also become sold on its products. Using VMware's platform in a production environment has been everything it is advertised to be: it has made system administration easier, made the use of resources more efficient and cost-effective, and quite frankly, been a lot of fun. If this weren't the case, like all true geeks (in the best sense of the word), we would find something else to play with. So far, we haven't.

This book encompasses many of the most useful and interesting recipes we have discovered while using the platform in production, as well as some cool tricks we encountered while testing and playing. We believe that anyone who's using the VMware platform will find this book useful, and we hope it helps you enjoy VMware as much as we do.

Audience

This book is intended for system administrators who have some experience with VMware ESX, ESXi, vCloud Director, or vSphere. Throughout the book we have not only tried to appeal to beginners, but we also include a generous amount of complex recipes for advanced users. We believe this book will be a solid reference guide for any system administrator, regardless of his or her level of knowledge. We hope you enjoy it!

Organization of This Book

This book is made up of nine chapters:

- Chapter 1, *VMware Infrastructure Installation*, covers installation details for ESXi 5 and vCloud Director.
- Chapter 2, *Storage*, covers partitions, iSCSI and NFS configuration, and other choices reflecting local or external data storage.
- Chapter 3, *Networking*, covers communications at multiple levels, including configuration of virtual switches, software and hardware adapters, Ethernet frame sizes, and more.
- Chapter 4, *Resource and vCenter Management*, shows you how best to apportion memory and CPU resources through clustering, shares, hot add/hotplug support, and other options.
- Chapter 5, *Useful Tools and References*, presents miscellaneous commands that can rescue you in a pinch and help you keep apprised of your servers' functioning.
- Chapter 6, *General Security*, covers a range of access issues, such as how to control which users have access to each level of the system and how to set up firewalls, networking, and remote access to your desired level of security.
- Chapter 7, *Automating ESXi Installations*, introduces the configuration files used to control basic networking options, startup activities, and other aspects of the system you'll want to automate in order to make it easier to replicate virtual machines.
- Chapter 8, *vCloud Director Overview*, introduces features for moving into the cloud and allowing configuration by end users.
- Chapter 9, *vSphere Storage Appliance*, shows how to create virtual storage and reclaim unused disk space through vSphere Storage Appliance.

Along the way, you'll also find plenty of pointers and advice on good programming practices and tips that may help you find and solve hard-to-detect programming errors. There are also plenty of links to websites containing further details on the topics covered.

Font Conventions

This book uses the following typographical conventions:

Italic
: Used for email addresses, URLs, filenames, pathnames, and emphasizing new terms when they are first introduced

`Constant width`
: Used for the contents of files and for commands and their output

`Constant width bold`
: Used in code sections to show commands or text that would be typed by the user, and, occasionally, to highlight portions of code

`Constant width italic`
: Used for replaceable items and some comments in code sections

Indicates a tip, suggestion, or general note relating to the nearby text.

Indicates a warning or caution relating to the nearby text.

Using Code Examples

This book is here to help you get your job done. In general, you may use the code in this book in your programs and documentation. You do not need to contact us for permission unless you're reproducing a significant portion of the code. For example, writing a program that uses several chunks of code from this book does not require permission. Selling or distributing a CD-ROM of examples from O'Reilly books *does* require permission. Answering a question by citing this book and quoting example code does not require permission. Incorporating a significant amount of example code from this book into your product's documentation *does* require permission.

We appreciate, but do not require, attribution. An attribution usually includes the title, author, publisher, and ISBN. For example: "*VMware Cookbook*, by Ryan Troy and Matthew Helmke. Copyright 2012 Ryan Troy and Matthew Helmke, 978-1-449-31447-7."

If you feel your use of code examples falls outside fair use or the permission given above, feel free to contact us at *permissions@oreilly.com*.

Safari® Books Online

Safari Books Online (*www.safaribooksonline.com*) is an on-demand digital library that delivers expert content in both book and video form from the world's leading authors in technology and business.

Technology professionals, software developers, web designers, and business and creative professionals use Safari Books Online as their primary resource for research, problem solving, learning, and certification training.

Safari Books Online offers a range of product mixes and pricing programs for organizations, government agencies, and individuals. Subscribers have access to thousands of books, training videos, and prepublication manuscripts in one fully searchable database from publishers like O'Reilly Media, Prentice Hall Professional, Addison-Wesley Professional, Microsoft Press, Sams, Que, Peachpit Press, Focal Press, Cisco Press, John Wiley & Sons, Syngress, Morgan Kaufmann, IBM Redbooks, Packt, Adobe Press, FT Press, Apress, Manning, New Riders, McGraw-Hill, Jones & Bartlett, Course Technology, and dozens more. For more information about Safari Books Online, please visit us online.

We'd Like to Hear from You

Every recipe in this book has been tested on various platforms, but occasionally you may encounter problems. The information in this book has also been verified at each step of the production process. However, mistakes and oversights can occur and we will gratefully receive details of any you find, as well as any suggestions you would like to make for future editions. You can contact the author and editors at:

O'Reilly Media, Inc.
1005 Gravenstein Highway North
Sebastopol, CA 95472
800-998-9938 (in the United States or Canada)
707-829-0515 (international or local)
707-829-0104 (fax)

We have a web page for this book, where we list errata, examples, and any additional information. You can access this page at:

http://oreil.ly/VMWare_CB

To comment or ask technical questions about this book, send an email to the following address, mentioning the book's ISBN (9781449314477):

bookquestions@oreilly.com

For more information about our books, courses, conferences, and news, see our website at: *http://www.oreilly.com*.

Find us on Facebook: *http://facebook.com/oreilly*

Follow us on Twitter: *http://twitter.com/oreillymedia*

Watch us on YouTube: *http://www.youtube.com/oreillymedia*

Acknowledgments

Ryan: I would like to thank my wife, Holly, for her continued support and always-sound advice while I work on projects, which require me to be engulfed in concentration. Without her dedication and interest in my projects, they probably wouldn't become realities. I want to thank my son, Hayden, for helping me realize just how precious life is. I want to thank my coauthor, Matthew Helmke, for his words of wisdom, great ideas, and neverending copyediting; you are a true rock star. I'd also like to say thanks to my family, friends, and coworkers for supporting me during the writing of this book—your consistent interest helped keep me motivated.

Matthew: I would like to thank my wonderful wife, Heather, for her consistently supportive attitude and encouragement. I want to thank my wonderful kids—I love you, Saralyn, Sedona, and Philip! I want to thank Ryan Troy for the opportunity to collaborate on this and other projects and also for the hospitality he and Holly have shown me. I freely and gratefully acknowledge that there is no way this book could/would have been written without Ryan. Finally, I would like to thank all my computer geek friends around the world who were genuinely excited with me when they discovered I was involved in a book project with O'Reilly—I'm so glad to have people like you in my life with whom I can share my joy as well as my enjoyment of this topic.

Together, we would like to thank all those who helped us make this a better book than it would have been without their assistance: our editor, Andy Oram, and all of the staff at O'Reilly, who have been kind and attentive from the moment we first submitted our book proposal; additionally we would like to thank our tech editors for their hard work and efforts during the review process.

CHAPTER 1

VMware Infrastructure Installation

This book aims to be useful for both new and seasoned VMware ESXi users. Because of the intermediate-to-advanced nature of this cookbook, we will assume from time to time that you have advanced knowledge and understanding of how the products work. Before we begin serving the main recipes of our cookbook, we define several terms we will use throughout the rest of the book, and make sure that you have all the necessary components installed.

Virtualization provides a way for multiple operating systems to be installed on the same physical hardware. By using virtual technology, we can consolidate hardware and instantly build production, quality assurance, and test environments. This is a tremendous breakthrough, as it allows underutilized equipment to do more than sit around idly, and allows developers and administrators to test and use multiple software configurations and packages that require different operating systems on the same piece of equipment, without having to purchase, set up, and maintain multiple computers. This savings makes the accounting department and managers happy and gives the technology lovers an opportunity to do all the things they want or need to do at the same time.

A typical IT scenario goes something like this: you have lots of servers in your rack or collection of racks. Most of them run at only about 10%–15% of their capacity the majority of the time, but you let that happen because you want to keep their various functions and operating systems isolated from one another. This provides some security, both because if one server is compromised it does not necessarily mean that access has been granted to others, and because a problem with one piece of software will not cause other parts of your IT infrastructure to go down as you deal with it.

Virtualization helps you make better use of those physical resources, without compromising the original intent of keeping services isolated. Instead of installing your operating system directly on your hardware, you instead begin with a *virtualization layer*: a stripped-down OS designed to schedule access to network, disk, memory, and CPU resources for guest OSs, the same way that those guest OSs control that scheduling for their applications. Most virtualization platforms limit themselves to specific hardware and present a specific set of virtual components to the operating systems installed on top of them. This provides a very stable and consistent presentation to the operating systems you install and allows them to be moved much more easily.

Once you've installed and configured the virtualization layer, you can partition the physical hardware and assign it to discrete operating system instances that you install on top of the virtualization layer. These virtual installations operate exactly as they would normally. They are not aware of the presence of other virtual installations that exist on the same hardware. Each acts as if it is installed on a predefined piece of equipment by itself, with the virtualization layer controlling what the virtual installation sees and how it interacts with other equipment outside of its control. Basically, the virtual installation looks, feels, acts, and is administered exactly the same as a standard installation from the inside, but it may be manipulated and configured easily and alongside others from the outside.

Here is the coolest part: virtualization, as provided by sophisticated systems like VMware, also allows you to pool the resources of several physical machines and then divide them up however you want or need. If you have 10 physical servers, each with 4 processors, 4GB of RAM, and an 80GB hard drive, you can segment those resources to provide a small and low-powered server for your in-house email, a powerful and high-memory processor for the number crunchers in accounting, multiple load-balanced servers for your web server, a separate server for your database, and so on, each with a configuration of memory, disk space, processor power, and so on, specific for its needs. Then, if you discover that one virtual server has more resources than it really needs and another doesn't have enough, you can change the configuration quickly, easily, and without taking your servers offline! You can take a physical server offline for maintenance without losing access to any of your virtual servers and their functions. You can move resources in and out and around your pool as needed, and even automatically. These are the sorts of things we will discuss in this book.

There are many companies that provide powerful and stable virtualization platforms, but we have found VMware's offerings to be wonderfully stable, flexible, easy to set up, maintain, and well supported. We like VMware. If you are reading this book, you probably do, too, but chances are you want to make better use of its potential than you are doing now—either that, or you have been asked to set it up or maintain it and you are wondering how to get started. Whatever your reason, if you use VMware at all, we hope you will find this book useful and practical.

1.1 What Is VMware Infrastructure 5?

VMware, Inc., is a company headquartered in Palo Alto, California, with over 11,000+ employees and about 300,000 customers, including 100% of the Fortune 100. In 2007, it had revenues of over $1.33 billion. In 2010, that number was up to $1.4 billion. VMware is a rapidly growing company that began in 1998 and now has more than 300,000 customers and over 25,000 partnerships with companies ranging from somewhat small to extremely large.

VMware vSphere 5 is easily the most widely used virtualization platform today. It is well tested and has been used in applications ranging from very small, localized installations with just a handful of servers to exceptionally large server farms in major corporations. It is robust, scalable, easy to administer, and flexible. It is also small and fast, which means the virtual installations running on top of it have more processor power and other resources available to them than they would if they were using some of the more resource-heavy virtualization software available.

Unlike some of the other hosted virtualization products you may be familiar with, including the company's well-known VMware server, VMware vSphere 5 does not require any other operating system. Most virtualization platforms begin with a Linux/Unix, Mac OS X, or Windows platform; install their product on top of it; and then begin segmenting the resources from there. This is how a developer may run a copy of Windows on top of her laptop's base installation of Linux, perhaps using a product like VMware server, Xen, or VirtualBox. vSphere is designed to be installed on bare metal, as the base operating system. This design choice eliminates a layer of software between the virtual installations and the hardware and results in faster, smoother performance.

1.2 What Is VMware vSphere 5.0?

In August 2011, VMware launched ESXi 5.0, which now falls under the vSphere 5.0 suite of products. vSphere 5.0 encapsulates both vCenter Server and ESXi 5.0, along with other products that we don't discuss in this book. This new release not only brings incremental improvements, but also takes the virtualization platform to a whole new level by letting you think in terms of complete installations or deployments instead of managing your site server by server. It's worth mentioning that ESXi 5.0 has some really great features, such as:

- vSphere 5.0, which is now based on the ESXi platform, eliminating the old ESX platform
- Updated Virtual Machine functionality, including more CPUs, RAM, support for USB 3.0, and 3D graphics
- Support for OS X, larger file systems, 512 virtual machines per physical host, and Metro vMotion

For a complete list of new features, please visit:

> *http://www.vmware.com/support/vsphere5/doc/vsphere-esx-vcenter-server-50-new-features.html*

Here are 10 features we feel are worth highlighting:

Metro vMotion
: Metro vMotion allows the end user to move a running virtual machine between two physical locations when certain circumstances allow; there is a minimum of 5

ms latency between the two remote ESXi servers. However, the maximum latency is supported up to 10 ms.

Improved SNMP support
: vSphere 5 now allows you to convert CIM indications to SNMP traps. vSphere 5 supports a larger set of vendors and equipment, but we still recommend you check with your vendor to ensure your vendor supports these features.

VMFS 5 filesystem
: VMFS 5 will allow scaling up to 64TB per datastore using one extent. This is a massive improvement over the VMFS 4 filesystem, which could only scale up to 2TB using one extent.

Storage distributed resource scheduler
: Storage distributed resource scheduler (DRS) allows the storage system to take advantage of resource aggregation, automated placement, and the ability to avoid bottlenecks. By creating datastore clusters, you can create a load-balanced scenario that allows the VMDK files to be placed on the storage system with less I/O load.

Enhanced network I/O control
: Administrators can now create user-defined network resource pools, giving the ability to create multitenant environments and the ability to bridge virtual and physical infrastructures with QoS per resource using 802.1 tagging.

vSphere auto deploy
: Administrators with large ESXi installations can simplify their deployments by creating a set of rules. These rules can be used to upgrade ESXi versions by simply rebooting the physical server.

Virtual machine hardware improvements
: Virtual machines can now scale up to 32 virtual SMP processors and up to 1TB of RAM. There is also support for 3D graphics, UEFI virtual BIOS, and USB support.

Physical node improvements
: Physical hosts can now have up to 2TB of memory, 160 logical CPUs, and 512 virtual machines.

Distributed switch improvements
: With the improvements in the vSphere 5 distributed switches, administrators now have a deeper and more granular view into the virtual machine traffic using Netflow. Additional troubleshooting is now available via SPAN and LLDP.

Storage profiles
: Allows for streamlining the storage provisioning process and allows for the VMware administrator to mass scale the storage within the environment.

1.3 Convergence from ESX to ESXi with vSphere 5.0

VMware started to get the community familiar with ESXi back with ESXi 3.5 and has continued to develop and evolve the product over the course of the past few years. In 2010, VMware stated that it would be moving to the ESXi platform in 2011, thus eliminating the older ESX version. Here, we outline the changes and benefits from this convergence.

A smaller and more efficient platform
: Older versions of ESX were based on the Red Hat Linux operating system. VMware utilized this as the OS layer in which its VMkernel and application stack lived. Today, by removing the Red Hat OS, VMware was able to remove 2–3GB of OS that wasn't required to run ESXi, so the installation size is now around 100MB. This switch means that less security and update patches need to be applied to the ESXi server.

Simple deployment
: Because the installation is only around 100MB, the complex setup routine has been removed. Now the installation can be done within minutes.

Improved management and API
: ESXi has a built-in API that allows third-party application vendors to build plug-ins. No longer do you need to install each plug-in on the ESX console, which was required with previous releases of ESX. VMware has also developed a remote command line interface (RCLI) to run the familiar commands that were present on the ESX 3.x and 4.x consoles.

1.4 VMware ESXi 5.0 Configuration Maximums

VMware's vSphere (ESXi 5.x) has limits within which it can operate. We feel it is important to include this information so that you have it at your disposal prior to installing ESXi 5.0 or vCenter. These values are crucial when planning your virtual environment, and we suggest you read through them to become familiar with the different limits. We've included all relevant, publicly provided values from VMware for reference (Tables 1-1 through 1-23).

Table 1-1. Virtual machine maximums

Value/Item	vSphere 5.x maximum
Number of virtual CPUs per virtual machine	32
RAM per virtual machine	1TB
Virtual machine swap file size	1TB
Virtual SCSI adapters per virtual machine	4
Virtual SCSI targets per virtual SCSI adapter	15

Value/Item	vSphere 5.x maximum
Virtual SCSI targets per virtual machine	60
Virtual disks per virtual machine (PVSCSI)	60
Virtual disk size	2TB - 512 bytes
Number of IDE controllers per virtual machine	1
Number of IDE devices per virtual machine	4
Number of floppy devices per virtual machine	2
Number of floppy controllers per virtual machine	1
Number of virtual NICs per virtual machine	10
Number of serial ports per virtual machine	4
Number of remote consoles to a virtual machine	40
Number of USB controllers per virtual machine	1
Number of USB devices connected to a virtual machine	20
Number of parallel ports per virtual machine	3
Number of USB 3.0 devices connected to a virtual machine	1
Number of xHCI USB controllers	20
Maximum amount of video memory per virtual machine	128MB

Table 1-2. Compute maximums

Value/Item	vSphere 5.x maximum
Logical CPUs per physical ESXi host	160
Virtual Machines per physical ESXi host	512
Virtual CPUs per physical ESXi host	2,048
Virtual CPUs per physical ESXi core	25
Fault tolerance virtual disks per physical ESXi host	16
Fault tolerance virtual CPUs per physical ESXi host	1
Maximum RAM per fault tolerant virtual machines	64GB
Maximum Fault Tolerant virtual machines per physical ESXi host	4

Table 1-3. Memory maximums

Value/Item	vSphere 5.x maximum
RAM per physical ESXi host	2TB
Number of swap files per physical ESXi host	1 per virtual machine
Maximum swap file size	1TB

Table 1-4. Virtual disk storage maximums

Value/Item	vSphere 5.x maximum
Virtual disks per physical ESXi host	2,048

Table 1-5. iSCSI physical storage maximums

Value/Item	vSphere 5.x maximum
LUNs per physical ESXi server	256
Qlogic 1Gb iSCSI HBA initiator ports per ESXi server	4
Broadcom 1Gb iSCSI HBA initiator ports per ESXi server	4
Broadcom 10Gb iSCSI HBA initiator ports per ESXi server	4
NICs that can be associated with or bound to the software iSCSI stack	8
Number of total paths on a physical ESXi server	1,024
Number of paths to a LUN (software and hardware iSCSI)	8
Qlogic iSCSI: dynamic targets per adapter port	64
Qlogic iSCSI: static targets per adapter port	62
Broadcom 1Gb iSCSI HBA targets per adapter port	64
Broadcom 10Gb iSCSI HBA targets per adapter port	128
Software iSCSI targets	25

Table 1-6. NAS storage maximums

Value/Item	vSphere 5.x maximum
NFS mounts per physical ESXi host	256

Table 1-7. Fibre Channel storage maximums

Value/Item	vSphere 5.x maximum
LUNs per physical ESXi host	256
LUD ID per physical ESXi host	255
Number of paths to a LUN	32
Number of total paths on an ESXi host	1,024
Number of HBAs of any type	8
HBA ports per physical ESXi server	16
Targers per HBA adapter	256

Table 1-8. FCoE storage maximums

Value/Item	vSphere 5.x maximum
Software FCoE adapters	4

Table 1-9. VMFS storage maximums

Value/Item	vSphere 5.x maximum
Volumes per ESXi host	256
Physical hosts per volume	64
Powered on virtual machines per VMFS volume	2,048

Table 1-10. VMFS 3 storage maximums

Value/Item	vSphere 5.x maximum
Volume size	64TB
Raw device mapping size (virtual)	2TB - 512 bytes
Raw device mapping size (physical)	2TB - 512 bytes
Block size	8MB
File size (1MB Block Size)	256GB
File size (1MB Block Size)	512GB
File size (1MB Block Size)	1,024GB
File size (1MB Block Size)	2,048GB
Files per volume	~30,720 files

Table 1-11. VMFS 5 storage maximums

Value/Item	vSphere 5.x maximum
Volume size	64TB
Raw device mapping size (virtual)	2TB - 512 bytes
Raw device mapping size (physical)	64TB
Block size	1MB
File size	2TB - 512 bytes
Files per volume	~130,960 files

Table 1-12. Storage DRS maximums

Value/Item	vSphere 5.x maximum
Virtual disks per datastore cluster	9,000
Datastores per datastore cluster	32
Datastore clusters per vCenter	256

Table 1-13. Storage concurrent operations

Value/Item	vSphere 5.x maximum
Concurrent vMotion operations per datastore	128
Concurrent storage vMotion operations per datastore	8
Concurrent storage vMotion operations per ESXi host	2
Concurrent non-vMotion provisioning operations per host	8

Table 1-14. Networking physical NICs

Value/Item	vSphere 5.x maximum
e1000 1Gb Ethernet ports (PCI-x)	32
e1000 1Gb Ethernet ports (PCI-e)	24
igb 1Gb Ethernet ports (Intel)	16
tg3 1Gb Ethernet ports (Broadcom)	32
bnx2 1Gb Ethernet ports (Broadcom)	16
forcedeth 1Gb Ethernet ports (NVIDIA)	2
nx_nic 10Gb Ethernet ports (NetXen)	8
ixgbe 10Gb Ethernet ports (Intel)	8
bnx2x 10Gb Ethernet ports (Broadcom)	8
be2net 10Gb Ethernet ports (Emulex)	8
Combination of 10Gb and 1Gb Ethernet ports	6x 10Gb Ports & 4x 1Gb Ports
Infiniband ports (refer to VMware Community Support)	N/A - third-party drivers available from Mellanox Technologies

Table 1-15. VMDirect path limits

Value/Item	vSphere 5.x maximum
VMDirectPath PCI/PCIe devices per host	8
VMDirectPath PCI/PCIe devices per virtual machine	4

Table 1-16. vSphere standard and distributed switch maximums

Value/Item	vSphere 5.x maximum
Total virtual network switch ports per host (VDS and VSS ports)	4,096
Maximum active ports per host (VDS and VSS)	1,016
Virtual network switch creation ports per standard switch	4,088
Port groups per standard switch	256
Distributed virtual network switch ports per vCenter Instance	30,000
Static port groups per vCenter Instance	5,000
Ephemeral port groups per vCenter	256
Hosts per VDS switch	350
Distributed switches per vCenter instance	32

Table 1-17. Networking concurrent operations

Value/Item	vSphere 5.x maximum
Concurrent vMotion operations per host (1Gb/s network)	4
Concurrent vMotion operations per host (10Gb/s network)	8

Table 1-18. Cluster, High Availability (HA), and DRS maximums

Value/Item	vSphere 5.x maximum
Physical ESXi hosts per cluster	32
Virtual machines per cluster	3,000
Virtual machines per host	512
Maximum concurrent host HA failover	32
Failover as percentage of cluster	100%
Resource pools per cluster	1,600

Table 1-19. Resource pool maximums

Value/Item	vSphere 5.x maximum
Resource pools per ESXi host	1,600
Children per resource pool	1,024
Resource pool tree depth	8

Table 1-20. vCenter Server maximums

Value/Item	vSphere 5.x maximum
Hosts per vCenter server	1,000
Powered on virtual machines per vCenter server	10,000
Registered virtual machines per vCenter server	15,000
Linked vCenter servers	10
Hosts in linked vCenter servers	3,000
Powered-on virtual machines in linked vCenter servers	30,000
Registered virtual machines in linked vCenter servers	50,000
Concurrent vSphere clients	100
Number of host per datacenter	500
MAC addresses per vCenter server	65,536
USB devices connected at vSphere Client	20

Table 1-21. vCenter VASA maximums

Value/Item	vSphere 5.x maximum
Storage providers	10

Table 1-22. vCenter update manager maximums

Value/Item	vSphere 5.x maximum
Host scans in a single vCenter server	1,000
Virtual machine scans in a single vCenter server	10,000
Cisco VDS update and deployment	70
VMware Tools scan per ESXi host	90
VMware Tools upgrade per ESXi host	24
Virtual machine hardware scan per host	90
Virtual machine hardware upgrade per host	24
VMware Tools scan per VUM server	75
VMware Tools upgrade per VUM server	75
Virtual machine hardware scan per VUM server	75
Virtual machine hardware upgrade per VUM server	75
ESXi host scan per VUM server	75
ESXi host remediation per VUM server	71
ESXi host upgrade per VUM server	71
ESXi host upgrade per cluster	1

Table 1-23. vCloud director maximums

Value/Item	vSphere 5.x maximum
Virtual machine count	20,000
Powered-on virtual machine count	10,000
Organizations	10,000
Virtual machines per vApp	64
vApps per organization	500
Number of networks	7,500
Hosts	2,000
vCenter servers	25
Virtual data centers	10,000
Datastores	1,024
Catalogs	1,000
Media	1,000
Users	10,000

See Also

Recipes 1.7 and 1.11

1.5 VMware ESXi 5.0 Server Overview

VMware's ESXi server is the foundation for every other piece of the virtualization package. It's the *hypervisor* or main software layer that installs on the bare metal and allows everything above it to communicate with the hardware to allow virtualization. It used to be that when you installed VMware ESXi, you were actually installing two main components: the VMkernel and the Service Console. This has changed slightly, as we will now explain.

The VMkernel is the base on which all other software in the package is built: the operating system. For those familiar with Linux, this would be the equivalent of (and is built from) the Linux kernel, without any other software.

The changes in ESXi 5.0 have removed the Service Console that existed in ESX 3.x and 4.x. Today, a minimum configuration can be done at the provided console within the ESXi hypervisor or using the RCLI tools. For everything else, VMware has provided a large and useful collection of utilities that can be run from the command line on *any* server. These tools are called the RCLI. The RCLI provides the same tools that were once available via the service console. Typically, management will be done via the vCenter client; however, there may be cases where you find you can accomplish things more easily with the command line or need to use it because you can't access vCenter.

VMware has designed the ESXi server to run only on specific pieces of hardware and has removed support for any kinds of devices it is not interested in, thereby reducing the kernel code. What remains is a stripped-down, fast kernel and tool package with little to no extra overhead. This is one of the things that gives VMware an advantage over other virtualization technologies that require installation on top of a standard operating system, which will be filled with drivers and features you won't need.

It is important to verify the hardware on which you will be running your virtualized environment, because VMware does not directly support smaller desktop-related hardware. However, everything that a server needs is well supported. This is a sleek operating system designed to put as little as possible between the virtual machines and the hardware.

Refer to the VMware Hardware Compatibility list for ensure support for your hardware: *http://www.vmware.com/resources/compatibility/search.php*

1.6 VMware ESXi 5.0 Overview

ESXi is a newer form of the technology that strips down the ESXi server even further, to the absolute bare minimum possible. It does not include or rely on a service console and it can perform its hypervisor duties with an installation that takes up a mere 32MB of disk space. In the ESX server, the service console runs on top of the hypervisor alongside the installed virtual machines. In ESXi, the hypervisor is all you install on your hardware. This allows for very fast hardware additions to existing pools. Want to add a new server to your rack? No problem. Hook it up, power it on, install ESXi, set your root password and networking details, take a minute or two to configure the virtual network, and you're all set. This is an amazingly quick way to create or expand an existing ESXi hardware cluster.

Even more exciting than the installable version of ESXi is the embedded version. It is now possible to buy hardware that is preconfigured with ESXi installed on it. This completely eliminates the installation step and speeds up the configuration process. Companies such as Dell, which graciously allowed us to borrow some of its equipment as we were writing this book, are now selling servers that require only a little more than racking, cabling, and powering on to expand your VMware cluster.

The benefits of using ESXi over the standard ESXi product are that it's extremely lightweight and installs quickly, it can be purchased on some servers from Dell and other vendors as an embedded option, it has no service console, and it requires less patching and maintenance. ESXi is also available for free and includes the basic functions needed to start a virtual environment.

1.7 VMware ESXi 5.0 Installation

VMware customers who have received a preinstalled OEM version of ESXi may have vendor-specific customizations and drivers. These versions will be different from the downloadable version on VMware's website.

Before you get started installing ESXi, you should verify that your hardware is fully compatible by visiting the following URL, because VMware's ESXi product has a much smaller compatibility list than its older ESXi model:

http://www.vmware.com/resources/compatibility/search.php

ESXi 5.0 can also be installed and virtualized within the VMware Workstation and VMware Fusion. This allows you to install, test, and get a feel for the products before implementing them on physical hardware.

ESXi 5.0 has the following CPU requirements: it will run and install only on 64-bit x86 CPUs, it requires at least two cores, and it supports only LAHF and SAHF CPU instructions.

VMware ESXi 5.0 has the following requirements:

- Supports all AMD Opteron processors
- Supports all Intel Xeon 3000/3200, 3100/3300, 5100/5300, 5200/5400, 5500/5600, 7100/7300, 7200/7400, and 7500 processors
- 2GB of RAM minimum
- One or more gigabit or 10Gb Ethernet controllers; check hardware compatibility matrix (*http://www.vmware.com/resources/compatibility/search.php*)
- Basic SCSI controllers such as Adaptec Ultra-160 or Ultra-320, LSI Logic Fusion-MPT, or most NCR/Symbios SCSI
- RAID controllers such as Dell PERC (Adaptec RAID or LSI MegaRAID), HP Smart Array RAID, or IBM (Adaptec) ServeRAID controllers
- SATA disk drives connected behind supported SAS controllers or supported on-board SATA controllers
- Dedicated SAN disk on Fibre Channel or iSCSI
- USB devices

This list represents the minimum requirements to install ESXi, but many more devices are available. To ensure complete compatibility, search for your specific hardware at the aforementioned URL.

You can download the ESXi ISO image from a VMware site (*http://www.vmware.com/download/esxi/*) or use an alternative method such as PXE boot, Kickstart or VMware Auto Deploy. VMware has done a great job of streamlining the installation of ESXi. If you are familiar with installing older versions of ESX, this will be a breeze. After booting to the installation CD-ROM, you'll notice a blue screen titled "ThinESXi Installer" that looks similar to the bootloader in Linux.

Once the initial boot has completed, the installer will present a couple of options: you can choose to cancel the installation, upgrade an existing installation, or perform a fresh ESXi installation (Figure 1-1). Once you have selected the appropriate installation type, you will be shown the end user license agreement (EULA). Press F11 to accept and continue the installation.

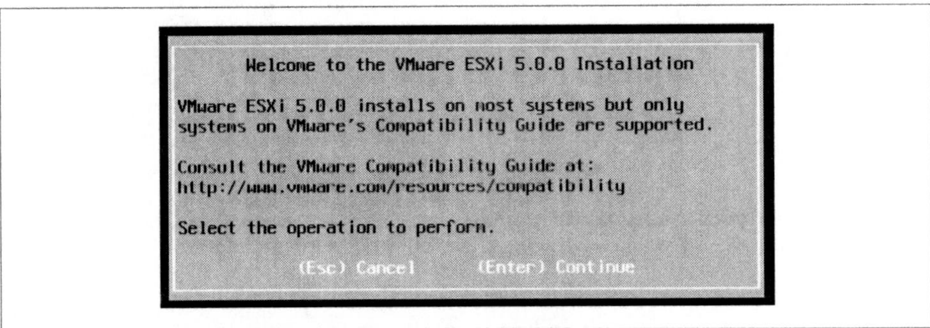

Figure 1-1. ESXi initial installation

Select the disk on which you wish to install ESXi. Typically, this will be a local disk. Also, make sure you have disconnected all your Fibre Channels or iSCSI SANs and direct-attached storage, if connected, to prevent any accidental data removal. Once you've selected the disk, the installation will begin and will take only a few minutes. When it is complete, remove the CD-ROM and reboot the system. If you are installing with PXE or another automated tool, reboot once the installation is completed.

ESXi requires a little more configuration after the initial install, because the only thing being configured during installation is the disk on which the hypervisor is going to be installed. Once the new ESXi server has been rebooted, you will notice a screen that is similar to the ESXi console screen but with two new options: F11 to reboot the system and F2 to manage the system.

1. To begin configuration, make sure you have a keyboard and monitor plugged into the ESXi server. Press F2 to access the menu-based configuration utility, which will be the main screen in which all ESXi configurations will take place (Figure 1-2).

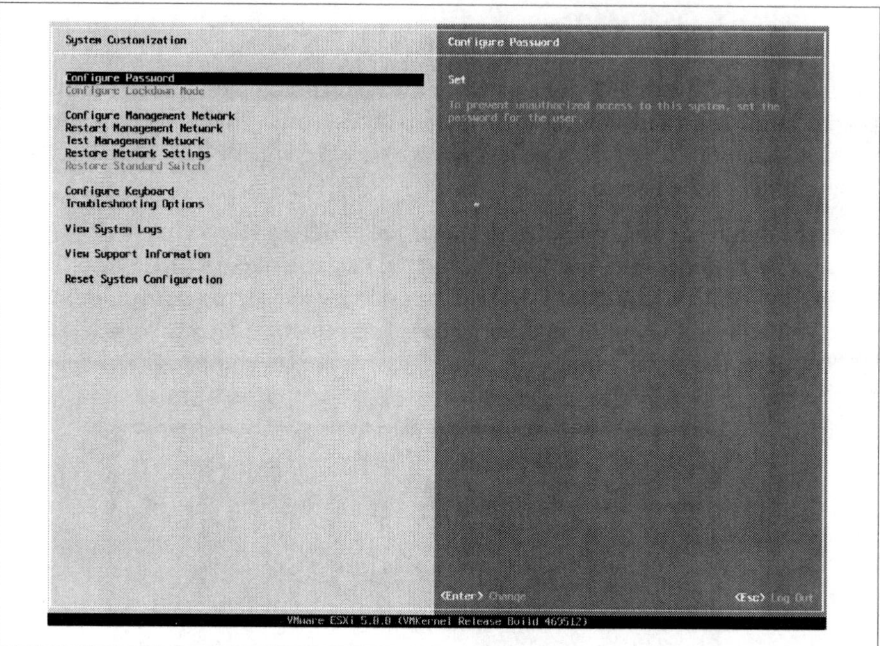

Figure 1-2. ESXi management menu

2. This is the first option that will need to be configured, because it is not set by default. The password you set here will be the default for the "root" user account (Figure 1-3).

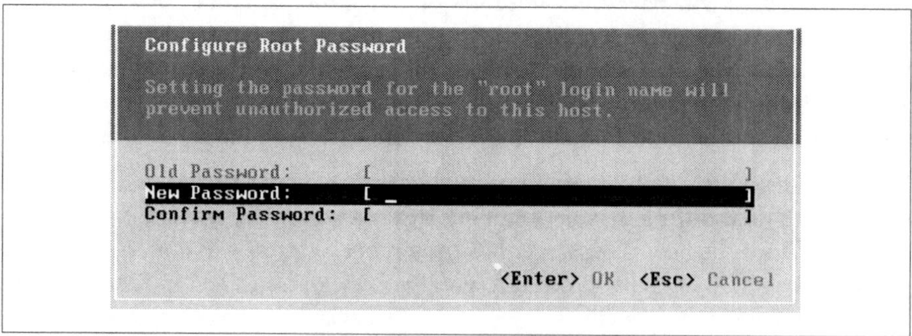

Figure 1-3. Changing the password

3. By default, ESXi will be configured to use the Dynamic Host Configuration Protocol (DHCP) and will automatically attempt to configure the IP address. However, you can bypass this and set your network to use a static IP address using the tools provided in the management network interface. Using a static IP address is recommended.

As shown in Figure 1-4, the management network offers a few options to configure your ESXi server.

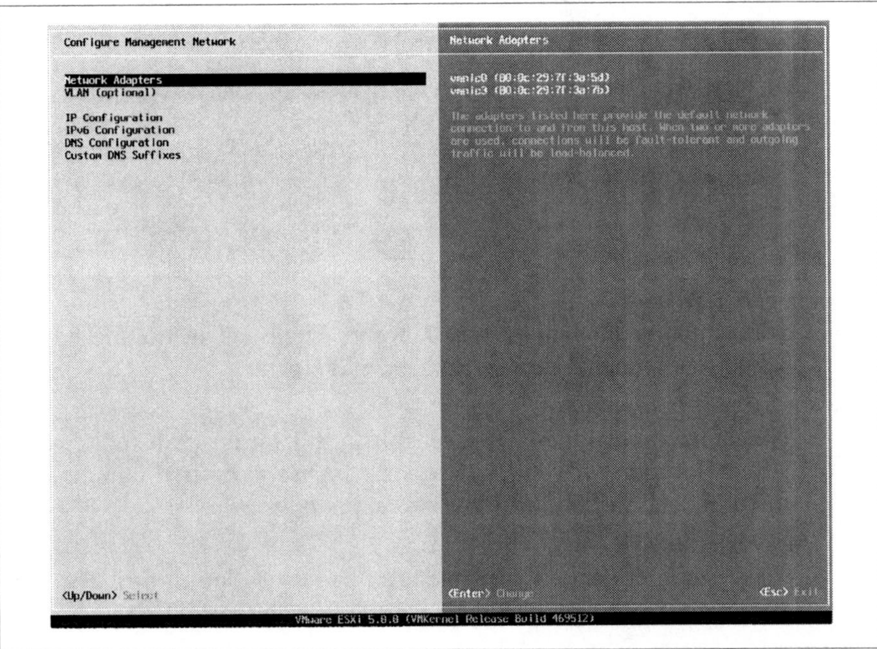

Figure 1-4. Management network configuration

The Network Adapters option allows you to select which network adapter to use for the service console IP address if you have more than one interface available; the interfaces will be labeled *vmnic0*, *vmnic1*, etc.

You also have the option to configure your service console IP address to use a specific VLAN. This is an optional setting.

The next option on the list is IP Configuration. Here, you have the option to configure a DHCP or a static IP address. Choosing the latter will allow you to enter the basic information needed, such as the IP address, subnet mask, and gateway (Figure 1-5).

Restart Management Network
: Making changes to a static IP address or renewing a DHCP lease on the network may require a restart of the management network.

Test Management Network
: Testing the management network will bring up a menu allowing you to perform ping tests to resolve DNS entries.

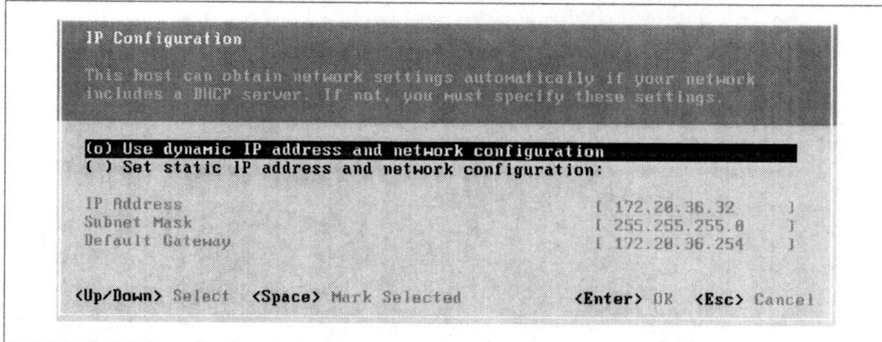

Figure 1-5. IP configuration screen

Configure Keyboard
: ESXi supports different keyboard layouts. English is the default, but you can select from French, German, Russian, and Japanese.

View Support Information
: No configurable options are available in this menu; however, it provides a general location for your ESXi server's license key, serial number, and SSL footprint, and the URL to VMware's support website.

View System Logs
: There are three options available here for viewing log entries. You can view system messages, config, and management agent (*hostd*) logs.

Restart Management Agents
: From time to time, it may be necessary to restart the management agents on the ESXi host without restarting the server itself. If the management agents are restarted, all remotely connected clients (such as vCenter clients and the vCenter server) will be disconnected.

: It's important to note that in your vCenter server, the host will show as disconnected while the management network restarts; however, your virtual machines will continue to be unaffected.

Reset Customized Settings
: Resetting the customized settings will reset all the variables on the ESXi server to factory defaults.

4. The DNS servers and hostname will need to be configured as well. Select the DNS Configuration menu as shown (Figure 1-6).

   Primary DNS Server
   : This will be the primary DNS server inside your network.

   Alternative DNS Server
   : This will be the secondary DNS server inside your network.

   Hostname
   : This will be the hostname of this ESXi server.

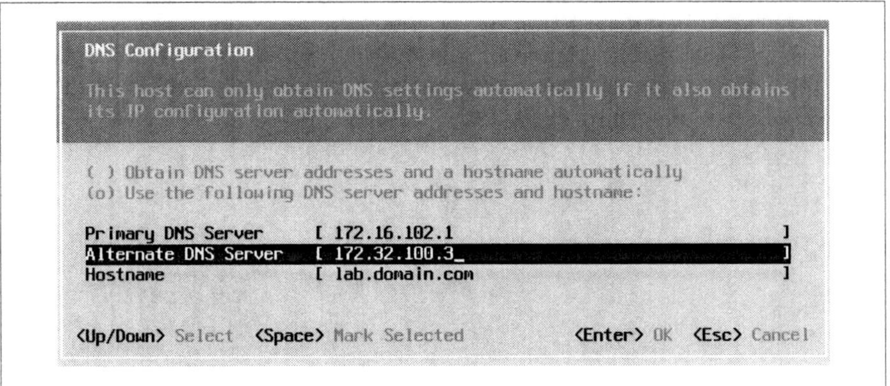

Figure 1-6. DNS configuration

5. You will now be able to manage this ESXi server via the vCenter client directly or add this host to an existing vCenter server for additional management.

See Also

Recipe 1.4

1.8 VMware vCenter Server 5.0 Overview

As virtual environments grow, there comes a point when it becomes unwieldy to manage each ESXi server individually. For some of us, that happens right around the time the second ESXi server is added, because we want to use our time for more interesting things rather than for repetitive procedures and maintenance. VMware vCenter Server provides a central location for managing all of the virtual machines deployed inside the VMware vSphere infrastructure. It is licensed and sold separately and requires a dedicated Windows server or a Windows virtual machine and a database (Oracle or Microsoft SQL Server). Once installed and configured, it will make the system administrator's life much easier. VMware vCenter Server provides a way to distribute resources, manage users, move virtual machines from one piece of physical hardware to another (while still running!), schedule tasks, and much more.

1.9 vCenter Server 5.0 Installation

To get started, download vCenter Server from the VMware site (*http://vmware.com/download/vi/*).

The vCenter Server installation is pretty straightforward. During the course of the installation you will be asked to enter some required information and make some crucial decisions about your environment. We will walk you through those steps in this section.

The vCenter server can be installed on a physical server or, as an alternative, inside a virtual machine. As infrastructure is consolidated into virtual environments, it often makes sense to utilize the high availability of the vSphere platform. The benefits of installing your vCenter server inside a virtual machine include taking advantage of HA inside the environment, moving the virtual machine to new hardware without outages, and using snapshots. There are many opinions about installing inside a virtual machine; we feel it makes sense.

It's worth mentioning that if you plan to install your vCenter database on the same server as your vCenter server, the system server requirements will be larger. However, it is best practice to separate the vCenter server and the database server.

VMware vCenter 5.0 Server Requirements

The vCenter server 5.0 requires a 64-bit operating system and will not install on a 32-bit operating system. The supported 64-bit operating systems are Microsoft Standard, Enterprise, or Datacenter 2003 (SP2/R2 SP2) or 2008 (SP2/R2). Minimum requirements are:

- A 2.0GHz or faster Intel or AMD X86 processor with two or more logical cores
- 4GB or more of RAM
- Minimum 6GB of disk space (this includes vCenter and SQL if on the same server)
- 10/100/1000 Ethernet adapter (gigabit recommended)

VMware vCenter 5.0 Server Database Requirements

The vCenter server requires one of the following databases:

- IBM DB2 9.5
- IBM DB2 9.7
- Microsoft SQL Server 2005 32-bit Standard with SP3
- Microsoft SQL Server 2005 64-bit Enterprise with SP3
- Microsoft SQL Server 2008 64-bit Express R2 (5 hosts and 50 virtual machines)
- Microsoft SQL Server 2008 R2
- Microsoft SQL Server 2008 32-bit or 64-bit Standard/Enterprise
- Microsoft SQL Server 2008 32-bit or 64-bit Standard/Enterprise with SP1
- Oracle 10g 32-bit Standard, Enterprise, One R2 (supported with version 10.2.0.3.0 or higher)
- Oracle 10g 64-bit Standard, Enterprise, One R2 (requires version 10.2.0.4)

- Oracle 11g 32-bit or 64-bit Standard, Enterprise, One R1
- Oracle 11g 32-bit or 64-bit Standard, Enterprise, One R2

The vCenter server offers a few download options: you may download an ISO image that can be burned to DVD, or a ZIP file that can be extracted on the server on which you wish to install vCenter Server. Once you have chosen your installation method, follow these steps:

1. Either insert the CD-ROM and let *autorun.exe* start the installation, or manually run the *autorun.exe*, which is located in the ZIP file that you downloaded (Figure 1-7). Click Next to continue.

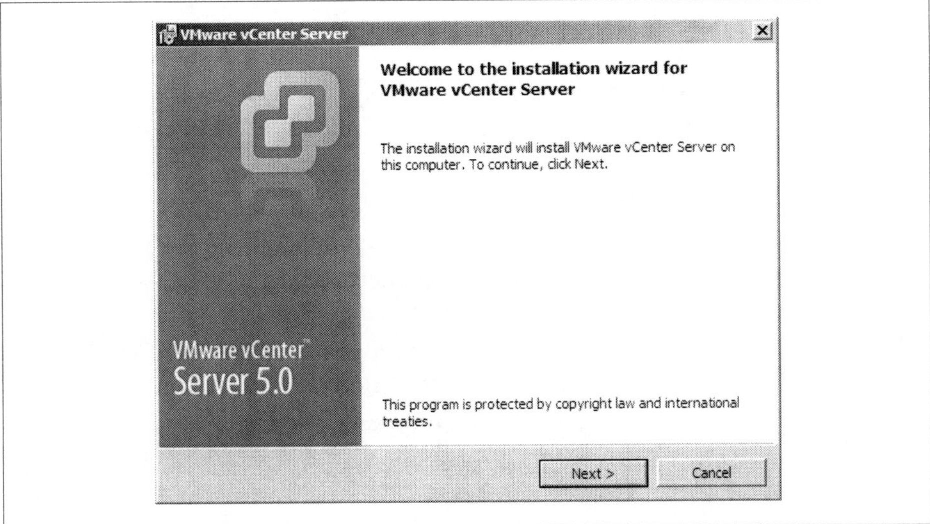

Figure 1-7. vCenter Server installation

2. The introduction page tells you the benefits of vCenter Server. Once you have read these, click Next to continue.
3. Read the license agreement and accept it by clicking "I accept the terms in the license agreement." The radio button next to this statement will now show a dot. Click Next to continue the installation.
4. You will now be prompted to enter information about your user account and company (Figure 1-8). When you're done, click Next to continue.
5. You are now ready to choose the database method (Figure 1-9). Refer to the database requirements list for the exact databases and versions that are supported.

   For production installations, VMware recommends that you do not use the Microsoft SQL Server Desktop Engine (MSDE) that is included with the installation because it's suitable only for sites containing, at most, 5 hosts and 50 virtual machines.

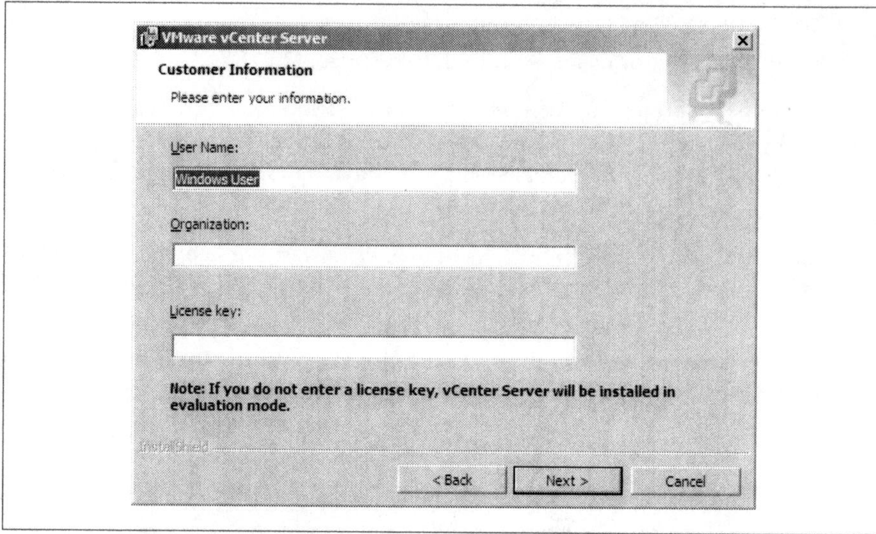

Figure 1-8. Entering customer information

Assuming the installation will be in a production environment, select the "Use an existing database server" option and fill in the necessary fields with your database's information, keeping in mind the following:

- You must set up ODBC connections before you use Microsoft SQL Server or Oracle. This can be accomplished in the Control Panel on Windows.
- The data source name (DSN) must be a system DSN.
- If you are using a local SQL server with Windows NT authentication, make sure to leave the username and password fields blank. Otherwise, enter the username and password of the remote SQL server to which you are connecting as shown in Figure 1-10.

Once you have entered your information successfully, press the Next button to continue the installation are connecting (Figure 1-10).

6. Next, select the destination folders for the vCenter server (Figure 1-11). Click Next to continue.

7. Now that the basic elements of the installation have been taken care of, you must decide what pieces of the application to install. You have two different options (Figure 1-12).

   Create a standalone VMware vCenter Server
   : This option will install vCenter server in standalone mode, or if this is the first installation, select this option.

   Join a VMware vCenter Server Group using linked mode to share information
   : Select this option if you will be joining the vCenter server to an existing vCenter server to create a linked group.

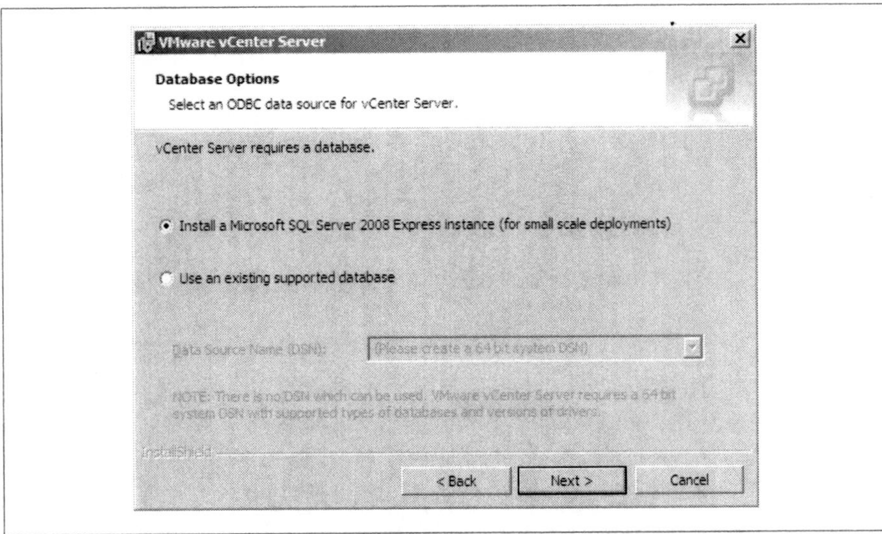

Figure 1-9. vCenter Server Database selection

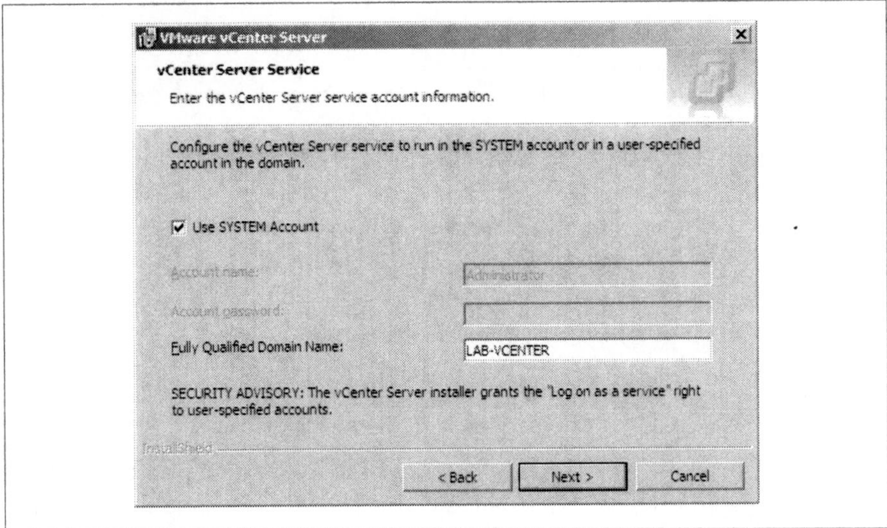

Figure 1-10. vCenter Server Database credentials

Once you have chosen the method of installation you wish to use, click the Next button to continue.

8. Next, configure the ports that vCenter Server will use (Figure 1-13) and click Next to continue. The default ports will be acceptable here unless you have specific requirements for your vCenter Server installation.

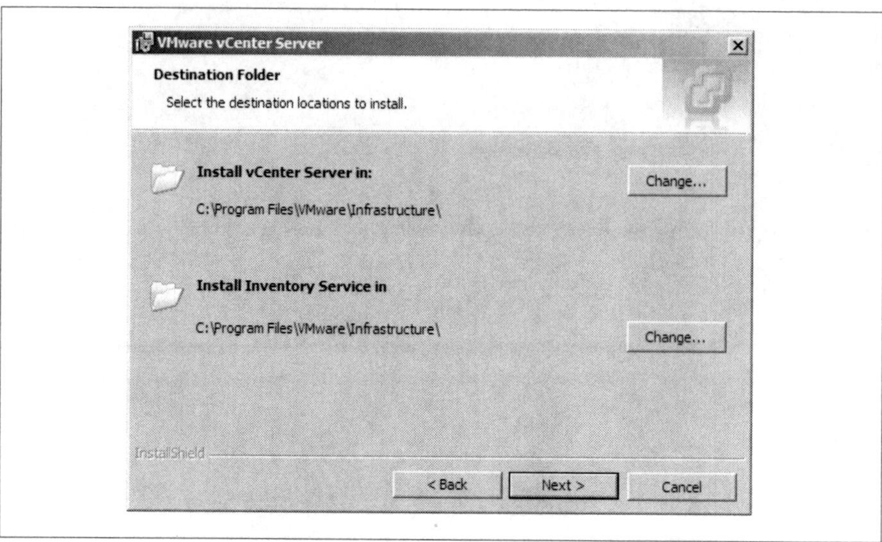

Figure 1-11. vCenter destination folders

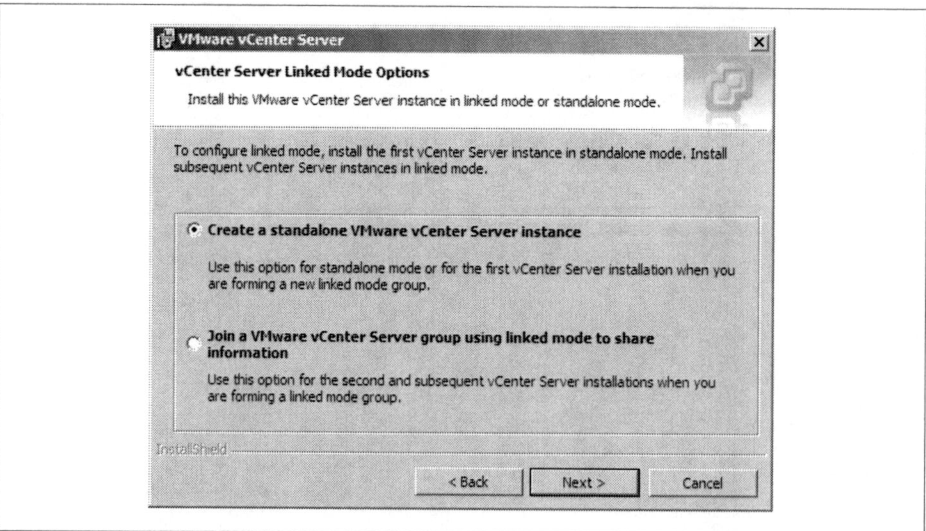

Figure 1-12. Choosing the vCenter installation type

9. Next, configure the vCenter Server inventory ports (Figure 1-14). Again, the default ports will be acceptable here unless there are specific requirements for your vCenter Server installation. Click Next to continue.

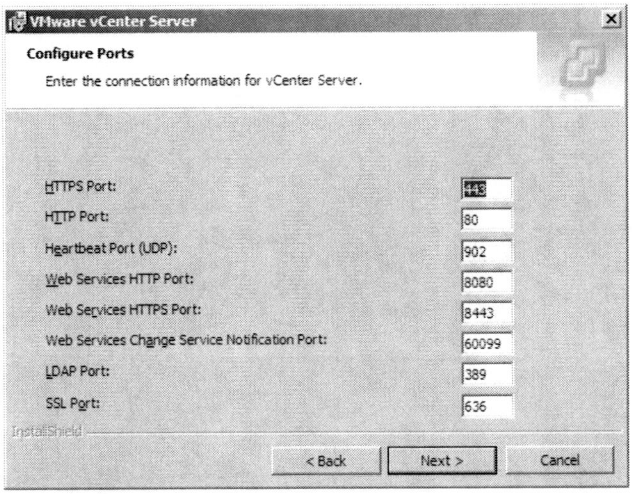

VMware vCenter Server

Configure Ports

Enter the connection information for vCenter Server.

HTTPS Port: 443
HTTP Port: 80
Heartbeat Port (UDP): 902
Web Services HTTP Port: 8080
Web Services HTTPS Port: 8443
Web Services Change Service Notification Port: 60099
LDAP Port: 389
SSL Port: 636

InstallShield

< Back | Next > | Cancel

Figure 1-13. Configure vCenter Server ports

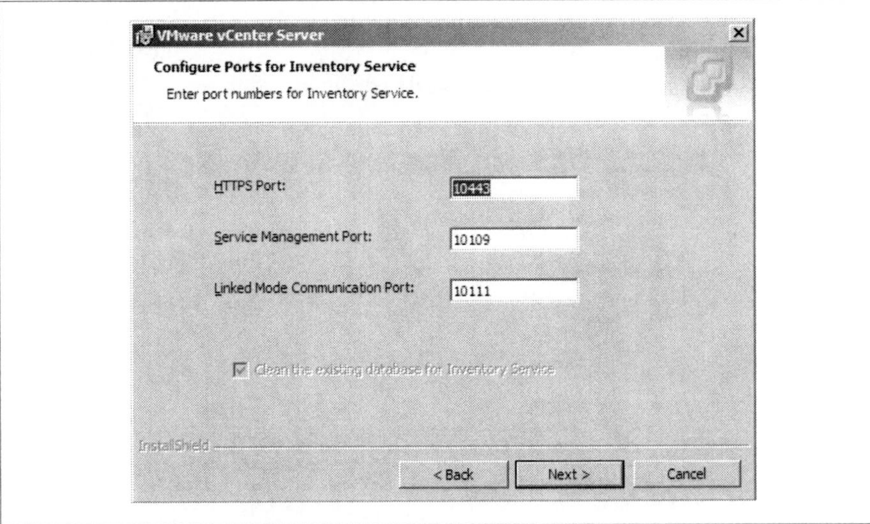

Figure 1-14. vCenter Server inventory ports

10. Next, set the Java JVM web server's memory configuration (Figure 1-15). This setting will allocate a specific amount of memory on the vCenter server for Java. If there is enough memory available on the vCenter server, select the large install option to prevent issues in the future if your environment will grow. For most installations, the small or medium option will be fine.

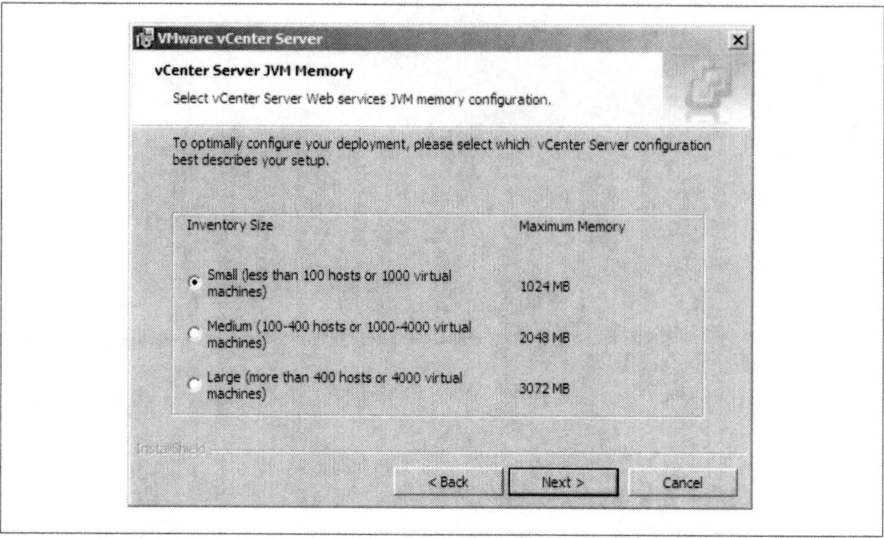

Figure 1-15. vCenter Server JVM configuration

11. Finally, click Install to begin the installation (Figure 1-16). If the vCenter server will be handling more than 2,000 virtual machines, click the check box to increase the number of ephemeral ports available within vCenter Server.

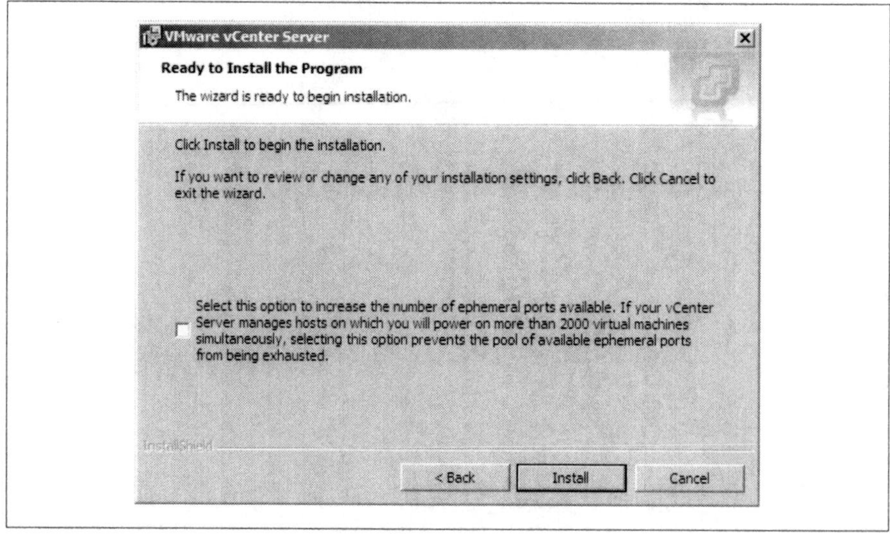

Figure 1-16. vCenter Server install summary

1.10 VMware vCenter Client 5.x Overview

The vCenter client is used to manage individual ESXi hosts as well as to provide an administration interface to the vCenter server. It is included with the vCenter server download.

1.11 vCenter Client 5.x Installation

vCenter Client requirements are:

- One of the following 32-bit or 64-bit operating systems:
  - —Windows 7
  - —Windows 7 SP1
  - —Windows 2003 Server with SP2
  - —Windows 2003 Server R2
  - —Windows 2008 R2
  - —Windows 2008 R1 with SP1
- .NET Framework 3.5 SP1 (this is included with the vCenter Client installer)
- 1 CPU, 500MHz Intel or AMD X86 processor, 1GHz CPU recommended
- 1GB RAM minimum (2GB recommended)
- 2GB storage space for the basic installation
- 1Gb network connection

The vCenter client is normally installed along with the vCenter server installation. However, it is possible to install the vCenter client by itself on other computers by going to *https://youresxserver/client/VMware-viclient.exe* and downloading the client installer. Once you've downloaded it, run the application. The installation is very intuitive.

1.12 vCenter 5.0 Web Client Installation

The release of vSphere 5.0 has brought some exciting changes to the way you can manage your VMware environment. Former web consoles weren't user friendly and administrators had to utilize the vCenter client install. However, with vSphere 5.0, this has changed. Today, there is a functional and useful interface that was written using Adobe Flex, allowing for cross-platform and browser compatibility. We'll outline the steps here to install the web client on your vCenter server or an additional server if you wish.

1. Insert the vCenter installation disk or mount the ISO image. Once the installer appears, select the vSphere Web Client (Server) option.
2. Follow the installation steps. After you complete them, additional options will need to be configured so the server can connect to your vCenter server.
3. Navigate to *https://127.0.0.1:9443/admin-app* inside your browser (from the server you installed the Web Client on).
4. Next, you'll need to register the Web Client with your vCenter Server. Click the Register vCenter server link in the upper right hand corner.
5. A new window will appear. Enter the credentials and click Register.

   vCenter Server URL
   : Enter the fully qualified name to the server on which you have vCenter Server installed.

   Username
   : Enter an administrator account inside vCenter.

   Password
   : Enter the password you have chosen for your administrator account.

   vSphere Web Client URL
   : This will be the URL used to access the web client.
6. You can now log in to the interface at *https://`webclientserver`:9443/vsphere-client/*, which allows you to log in with your vCenter credentials and start managing your virtual machines.

1.13 vSphere 5.0 License Changes

VMware has made some modifications to its license model with the release of vSphere 5.0. In this section, we'll take a look at those changes and what will be required to upgrade from vSphere 4.x or ESX 3.x.

vSphere 5.0 is still based on the per-socket license, but now also includes a vRAM entitlement. This means the license scheme will take a holistic approach, removing all CPU and memory limitations and then taking all the servers managed via vCenter into consideration when calculating the available licenses. This change allows customers to purchase servers with different CPU socket configurations without having to purchase expensive licensing if they do not plan to use the additional sockets or memory. Instead, the available resources inside vCenter will be used to create a pool of resources that each ESXi server will use.

VMware has implemented a compliance policy to maintain an accurate license model. Each physical CPU must be licensed, and will calculate a 12 month average of consumed vRAM rather than a high water mark. If the amount of vRAM is over the amount in the pool, additional licenses will be required. If an upgrade is required, a customer can upgrade all the CPU licenses to a license with a higher vRAM allotment.

In the following, we will take a look at the changes and how they will affect each part of the vSphere environment.

CPU restrictions
: The new license model requires at least one CPU in the physical server.

vRAM entitlements
: vRAM is the amount of RAM allocated to a virtual machine. For example, if you create a virtual machine with 2GB RAM that will translate into 2GB of vRAM. It is possible to overallocate vRAM on a single ESXi server regardless of the amount of physical RAM, as long as the resources are available from a vRAM perspective.

vRAM per VM
: RAM that is allocated to a virtual machine will pull from the vRAM license pool, which allocates a maximum amount of 96GB to each virtual machine. Thus, if a virtual machine was allocated 128GB of vRAM, it will only take 96GB from your license pool.

1.14 vConverter

vConverter is a free application available from VMware that allows you to transform your physical servers into virtual servers easily, moving them from their own machines into your VMware system. There are two ways this can be done. In a *cold migration*, you power down a server and convert it while it is offline. With vConverter, however, you can also perform a *hot migration*, which allows you to convert and migrate a live operating server while it is in use. VMware Converter also allows you to take older virtual machines and migrate them into a new network while upgrading them to the current version.

The installation of vConverter is pretty straightforward. vCenter Converter Standalone 5.x components (client, server, and agent) can be installed on the following platforms:

- Windows XP Professional (32-bit and 64-bit)
- Windows Server 2003 SP2, R2 (32-bit and 64-bit)
- Windows Vista (32-bit and 64-bit)
- Windows Server 2008 (32-bit and 64-bit)
- Windows Server 2008 R2 (64-bit)
- Windows 7 (32-bit and 64-bit)

vConverter can be downloaded from the following URL (registration is required to download):

> *http://vmware.com/download/converter*

To install vConverter on Windows:

1. Download the Windows executable file.
2. Run the installer and click Next at the introduction screen.
3. Accept the license agreement by checking "I accept the terms in the license agreement." Click Next to continue.
4. Choose the directory in which to install the files. The installer will default to *C:\Program Files\VMware\VMware vCenter Converter Standalone*. Once you're satisfied, click Next to continue the installation.
5. Select the type of installation you want to do. There are two options here (Figure 1-17):

   Local installation
   : This installs vCenter Converter on the server. It allows you to create and manage conversion tasks from this local server only.

   Client/Server installation (advanced)
   : This option sets up a client/server model for vCenter Converter. Here, you can install the individual client, server, and/or agent pieces on the local server (Figure 1-18).

   If you choose Local installation, jump to step 7; otherwise, continue to step 6.

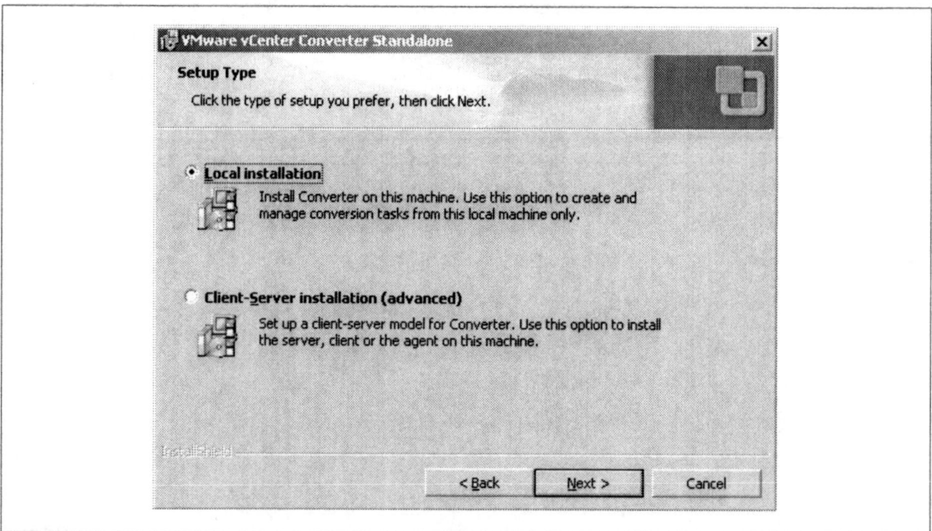

Figure 1-17. vCenter Converter setup types

6. The advanced installation choice gives you the option to specify which ports vCenter Converter will use (Figure 1-19). The defaults are:

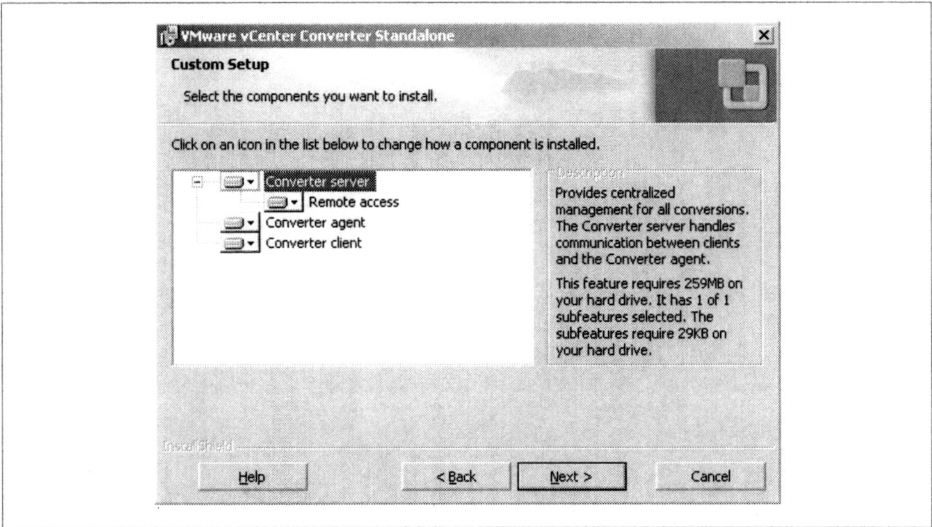

Figure 1-18. vCenter Converter custom setup

- HTTPS Service Port: 443
- HTTP Service Port: 80
- Agent Service Port: 9089

When you are satisfied with the ports, click Next to continue the installation.

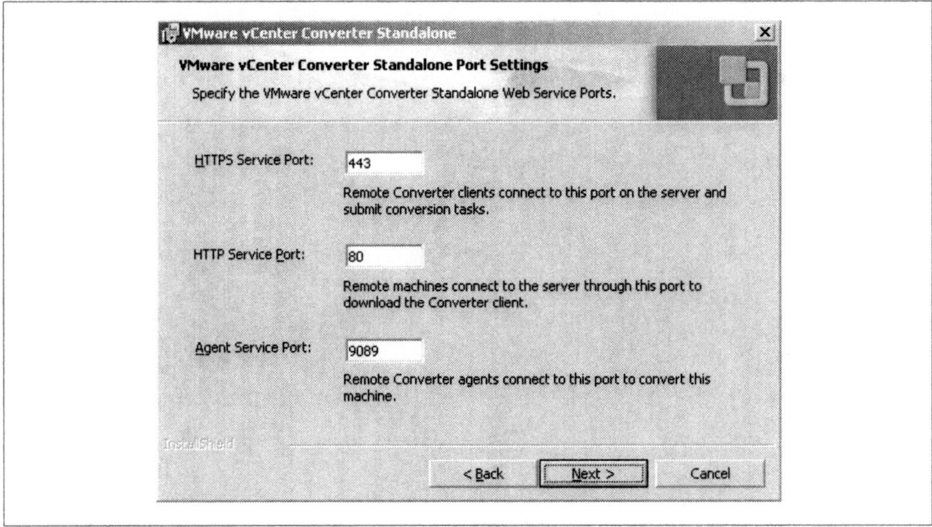

Figure 1-19. vCenter Converter custom ports

7. You are now ready to proceed with the installation. Click Install to continue.

8. When the installation has completed, you will have the option to automatically launch the vCenter Converter client. Click the Finish button to complete the installation.

CHAPTER 2
Storage

Storage will be one of the key components in your virtualized environment. In this chapter, we will look at the different types of storage and ways to successfully configure and use them within the ESXi environment.

2.1 Comparing ESXi Storage Options

Problem

You want to know which network storage types ESXi supports and what each type offers.

Solution

Review the comparison tables in this recipe.

Discussion

Table 2-1 lays out the types of storage ESXi supports. Table 2-2 lists the features of different storage types that can be utilized in ESXi. It's important to understand the technologies and their capabilities and limitations when setting up your ESXi environment.

You will achieve higher success and performance within your environment when using VMware with a SAN, regardless of which type of SAN you use.

Let's take a look at each technology and the benefits of each.

Fibre Channel
: Fibre Channel has been around for years and gives you 2, 4, or 8Gbps of throughput from your ESXi servers to the SAN. People who are using Fibre Channel tend to have dedicated storage administrators and larger environments that require its robust feature set. Fibre Channel, however, can be more difficult to set up because

of the switch zoning that needs to take place. However, zoning is a requirement if the SAN is directly connected to the servers.

Local storage
: Local storage implies exactly that. It's a local disk or disks inside a server or JBOD that are either in a single or RAID configuration. This is the least beneficial type of storage to use in a virtualized environment because VMware requires a SAN to use some of the high-end features.

iSCSI
: iSCSI, which stands for SCSI over IP, has also been around for years. This technology is robust and allows flexibility, while giving good performance for the price. Many people are starting to gravitate toward iSCSI from Fibre Channel when it makes sense. It's easier to configure and maintain and doesn't require a dedicated SAN administrator. iSCSI can be set up on either 1GB or 10GB connections depending on the host bus adapter (HBA) and SAN vendors.

Network attached storage (NAS)
: NAS, often using the network file system (NFS), is also popular among the VMware community. Most of the SAN vendors today will provide some type of NFS- or CIFS-type connectivity. Performance can vary on NFS, but it's still very usable in small- to medium-sized environments.

Fibre Channel over Ethernet (FCoE)
: Fibre Channel over Ethernet is a converged protocol that emulates Fibre Channel and is generally set up and configured in the same way as a normal Fibre Channel. The benefit to FCoE is you generally have a higher bandwidth connection, for example, 10GB or greater in which you isolate the Fibre Channel traffic from normal network traffic that flows over the link. This is beginning to become a popular option because it allows end users to eliminate cables inside their racks.

Table 2-1. Storage options for VMware ESXI servers

Technology	Protocols	Transfer	Interface
Fibre Channel	FC/SCSI	Block access/LUN	FC HBA
Local storage	SCSI/SAS	Block access	Local SCSI or SAS controller
iSCSI	IP/SCSI	Block access/LUN	iSCSI HBA for hardware iSCSI Ethernet card for software iSCSI
NAS	IP/NFS	File level	Ethernet card
FCoE	FCoE/SCSI	Block access/LUN	Converged network adapter or NIC with FCoE enabled

Table 2-2. Storage features offered by types of storage on VMware ESXi Servers

Type	Boot VM	VMotion	RDM	VMCluster	Datastore	Storage API/ Data Protection	HA and DRS
SCSI (local storage)	Yes	No	No	No	VMFS	Yes	No
Fibre Channel	Yes	Yes	Yes	Yes	VMFS	Yes	Yes

Type	Boot VM	VMotion	RDM	VMCluster	Datastore	Storage API/ Data Protection	HA and DRS
iSCSI	Yes	Yes	Yes	No	VMFS	Yes	Yes
NAS/NFS	Yes	Yes	No	No	NFS	Yes	Yes

2.2 Selecting the Virtual Machine Datastore Location

Problem

You need best practice guidelines for placing your virtual machines on specific types of storage.

Solution

In this recipe, we have put together some industry standard best practices for placing virtual machines on certain types of storage.

Discussion

Before we begin, it's important to mention that a lot of factors are involved when placing your virtual machines on storage. As the industry expands and new technologies come out, there is a standardization on *storage tiering*, which allows the SAN or storage array to automatically move data between different types of disks. For example, you might have a mix of 15,000 RPM and 7,200 RPM drives in a SAN. The goal of tiering is to place each type of data on a disk with a speed appropriate to the need and use for the data. The software on the SAN will automatically move work loads between the different types of disks, generally on the block level. It's important to note that each SAN vendor does things slightly differently.

Here we will take a look at the different tiers and what might be placed inside those tiers from a virtual machine perspective.

Fast/High-tiered storage
: This tier includes SSD or 15,000 RPM drives. This tier will be the most expensive disk you purchase and will generally house databases, fast transactional applications, exchange services, and other data where response time is noticeable from the user's perspective.

Mid/Performance-tiered storage
: The midrange includes 10,000 RPM drives. This tier will represent a mixed environment that might include web servers, small databases, and exchange services, among others.

Low/Slower-tiered storage
: The low/slower tier of storage includes 7,200 RPM drives. This tier will represent the "rest" of your environment, which might include web servers, utility servers, terminal services with low usage, FTP services, and the VM Template Storage.

As you can see, there is no real best answer for virtual machine placement. It's a best effort based on your knowledge of the workloads in your environment. Because virtualization allows you to easily place virtual machines on different datastores, you can pick and choose until you find a suitable storage location. However, VMware has additional tools like vCenter Operations Manager that can help ensure specific metrics can be met inside your virtualized environment.

2.3 Storage Runtime Naming Scheme

Problem

You wish to understand how ESXi names its devices when working with storage devices in ESXi.

Solution

This recipe breaks down the naming scheme so you can understand how it works.

Discussion

Figure 2-1 shows a typical list of volumes and their device names. In this figure we've listed multiple iSCSI volumes arranged them by the identification fields, followed by their device names, capacity, free space, and the type of filesystem on the volume.

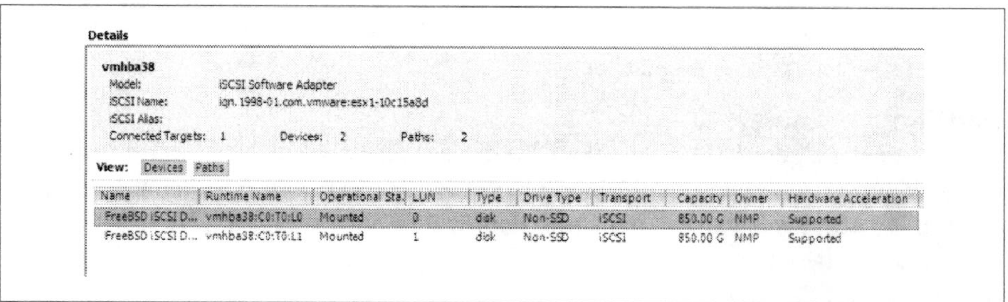

Figure 2-1. Datastore device names

The format of a storage device name in ESXi consists of three or four numbers separated by colons. As an example, in Figure 2-1, the device name for the first volume is *vmhba38:C0:T0:L0*. The numbers have the following meanings:

```
HBA:Adapter:Channel:Target:LUN
```

Our first volume's datastore HBA has a device ID of 38. The second number, 0, is the storage channel number, the third number indicates that the target of the LUN is 0, and the LUN number is 0.

The third value—the target number—is incremented for each volume added to the HBA. It should be noted that if the same target is shared across multiple ESXI servers, this value can be different.

The first and third numbers may change for the following reasons (if they are changed, they will still reference the same physical device to which they were originally connected):

- The first number belonging to the HBA can change if an outage occurs on the Fibre Channel or iSCSI network. In this case, ESXi will assign a different number to access the storage device. The first number can also change if the card is moved to another PCI slot in the server.
- The third number will change if any modifications are made to the mappings on the Fibre Channel or iSCSI targets that are visible to the ESXI server.

2.4 Creating a Network for the Software iSCSI Initiator

Problem

You want to create a separate iSCSI network to isolate storage traffic for servers when communicating with the storage device.

Solution

Using vCenter, create a network and VMkernel port on which the iSCSI device can communicate. Because we are using software iSCSI, we will create one vSwitch assigned to *vmnic1*.

Discussion

Before ESXi can communicate with an iSCSI device, a VMkernel network port must be created within the network component of the vCenter server.

The VMkernel port can be configured on an existing network, but we strongly advise you to put your iSCSI traffic on its own network and port group, isolated from all other traffic. This ensures maximum performance for your virtual machines. Follow these steps:

1. Log in to vCenter Server and select the server from the inventory list.
2. Select the Configuration tab from the right window pane, navigate to Networking on the lefthand side, and click the Add Networking link in the upper right corner.

3. Under Connection Types, select VMkernel and click Next. The VMkernel option allows you to set up VMotion, iSCSI, or NAS in your ESXi environment.
4. Under Network Access, select an unused network adapter (see Figure 2-2; we've selected *vmnic1* for our VMkernel port) to set up your VMkernel on a separate network (recommended), or select an already existing vSwitch and Ethernet adapter to share iSCSI traffic with other traffic. Your options will be displayed in the lower portion of the screen, in the Preview section (Figure 2-2). Click Next.

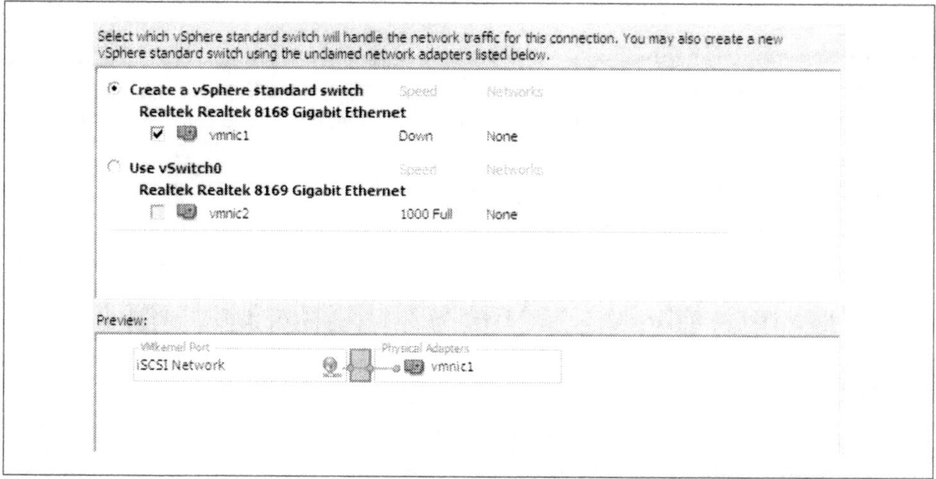

Figure 2-2. Adding an iSCSI VMkernel, selecting vmnic1

5. You will be required to enter some information about the VMkernel port on the Connection Types screen (Figure 2-3).

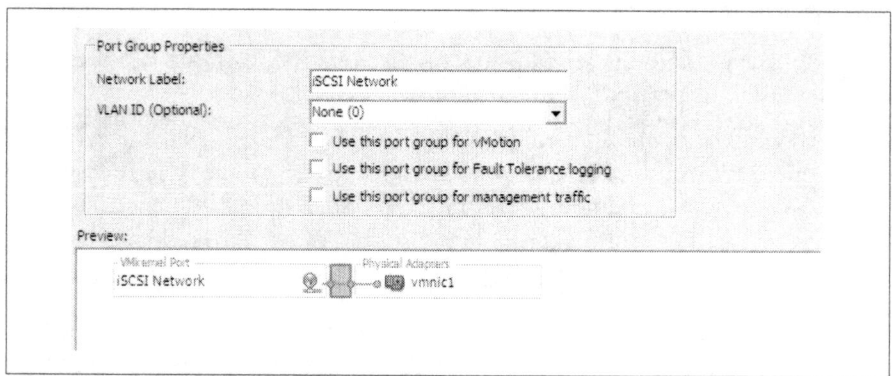

Figure 2-3. Setting information for the iSCSI VMkernel

First, configure the port group properties:

Network label
: The label by which the port group will be recognized within the virtual environment. It's important to give this port group the same name on all physical ESXi Servers to ensure that VMotion and other aspects of the ESXi environment will work.

VLAN ID (optional)
: The network VLAN your port group will use to communicate. This should be specified only if you are using VLANs in your network infrastructure.

Use this port group for VMotion
: This option should not be selected when configuring a VMkernel for iSCSI or NAS traffic because this port group will not include VMotion traffic.

Use this port group for Fault Tolerance logins
: This option should not be selected when configuring a VMkernel for iSCSI or NAS traffic because this port group will not include VMotion traffic.

Use this port group for management traffic
: This option should not be selected when configuring a VMkernel for iSCSI or NAS traffic because this port group will not include VMotion traffic.

Configure the IP settings. Generally, you will want to use a static IP address here and not use the Obtain IP settings automatically; however, this may depend on your network configuration.

IP address
: The IP address of the VMkernel. This is a required field.

Subnet mask
: The subnet mask of the network. This is a required field.

VMkernel default gateway
: Enter a gateway if your IP address resides on a network other than the one on which you are configuring the port group.

To configure additional options, such as DNS and advanced routing, click the Edit button.

6. Click Next to view the summary, and then Finish to create the port group.

2.5 Configuring Software iSCSI on ESXi

Problem

You want to use iSCSI connections to store area networks on an ESXi without an iSCSI host bus adapter.

Solution

Configure the software iSCSI initiator using vCenter.

Discussion

Because SCSI is an efficient, low-cost interface and many systems use the popular iSCSI protocol to reach network storage over a TCP/IP network, VMware ESXi allows iSCSI to connect ESXI servers to SANs. It is strongly recommended that you create a dedicated network for this traffic, as described in Recipe 2.4.

ESXi supports two different types of iSCSIs out of the box: hardware iSCSI and software iSCSI. Both are very powerful, but they're set up differently and require different components to work. Each uses a different kind of software translation, called an *initiator*, to send traffic from the ESXI server to the network.

Hardware iSCSI uses third-party HBAs to transmit iSCSI traffic over the network. Typically, if you can afford the iSCSI HBA cards, you will benefit from faster data transfers. These cards also offer configuration options for fine tuning and can allow you to boot your ESXI server off the iSCSI SAN. Booting an ESXI server from the iSCSI SAN can be helpful in a situation where you have limited local disk space or are utilizing blade servers.

Software iSCSI uses built-in code in ESXi, specifically the VMkernel, to run the iSCSI protocol over standard Ethernet cards. This eliminates the cost of HBAs, but it puts a significant load on your ESXI server's physical CPUs, which will affect system performance under high I/O loads. However, a lot of enterprise-grade systems will have TCP/IP offload engine-enabled Ethernet ports that can handle this offload and act like HBAs.

This section explains the basic configuration for a software iSCSI. By default, the iSCSI initiator is disabled, so you must enable it and indicate which SAN volumes you are communicating with:

1. Log in to vCenter Server and select the ESXi host you are configuring from the inventory list.
2. Select the Configuration tab from the right window pane. Click the Storage Adapters link on the lefthand side. Click Add and then select Add iSCSI Software Adapter (Figure 2-4). Click OK.

Figure 2-4. Enable software iSCSI support

3. A confirmation dialog box will appear. Click OK (Figure 2-5).

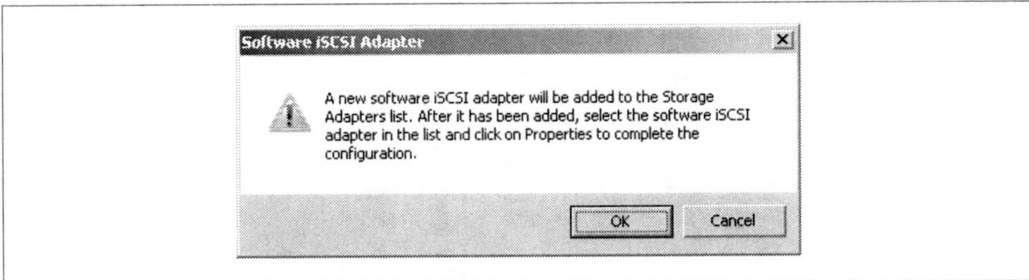

Figure 2-5. Software iSCSI confirmation

4. In the Storage Adapters configuration screen, right click the iSCSI Software Adapter (Figure 2-6) and choose Properties.

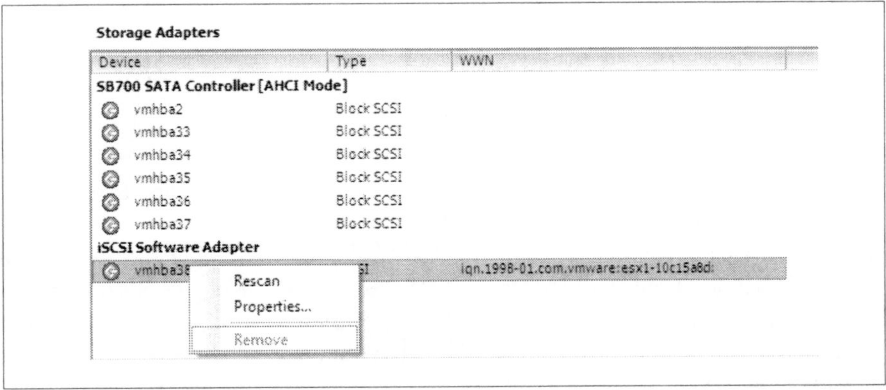

Figure 2-6. Software iSCSI properties

The iSCSI Initiator Properties window will appear (Figure 2-7). Enable software iSCSI by clicking the Configure button, putting a check in the Enabled box under Status, and clicking OK (Figure 2-7). A VMkernel port will be required for software-based iSCSI to work within the ESXI server; see Recipe 2.4 for more information.

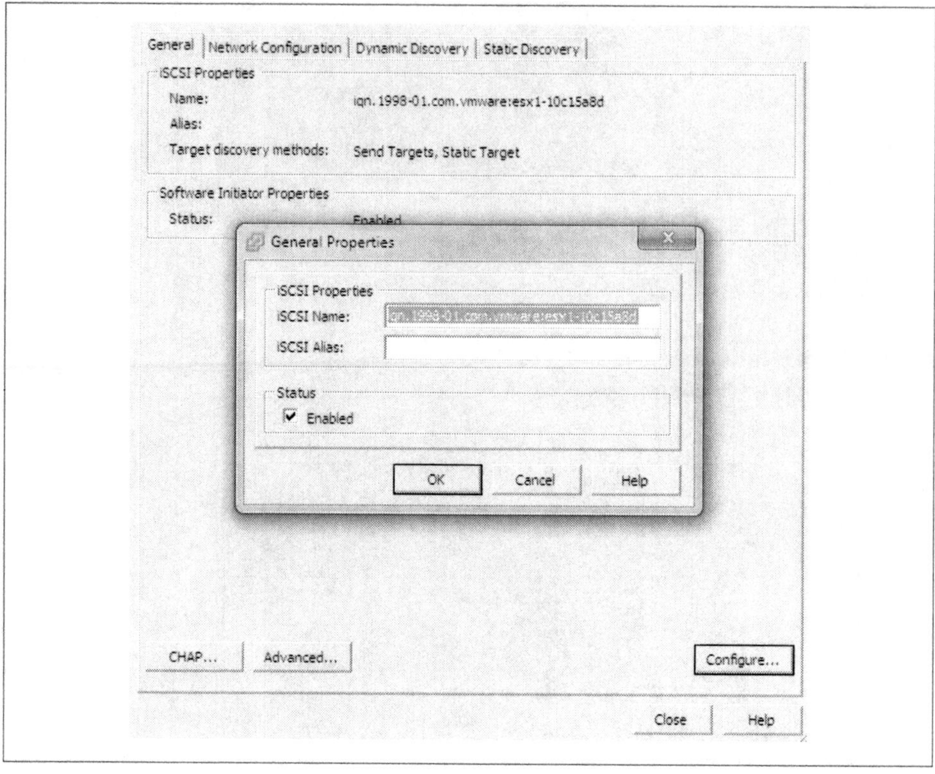

Figure 2-7. Software iSCSI status

5. Click OK to return to the iSCSI Initiator Properties window. From here you can begin to configure the initiator to see the iSCSI SAN volumes. Click the Dynamic Discovery tab, and then the Add button. In the dialog box that appears, enter the IP address and port of your iSCSI storage array—the default is 3260 (Figure 2-8).

   If your iSCSI SAN infrastructure requires use of the Challenge Handshake Authentication Protocol (CHAP), click the CHAP Authentication tab and enable and configure CHAP. Some iSCSI SANs, such as Dell's EqualLogic PS series, will allow you to set three different authentication methods, including IP address matching, iSCSI initiator name matching, and CHAP authentication. It's important to mention that CHAP authentication in ESXi 5.0 is one-way, allowing the array to identify the ESXI server.

   Click OK to finish (Figure 2-8).

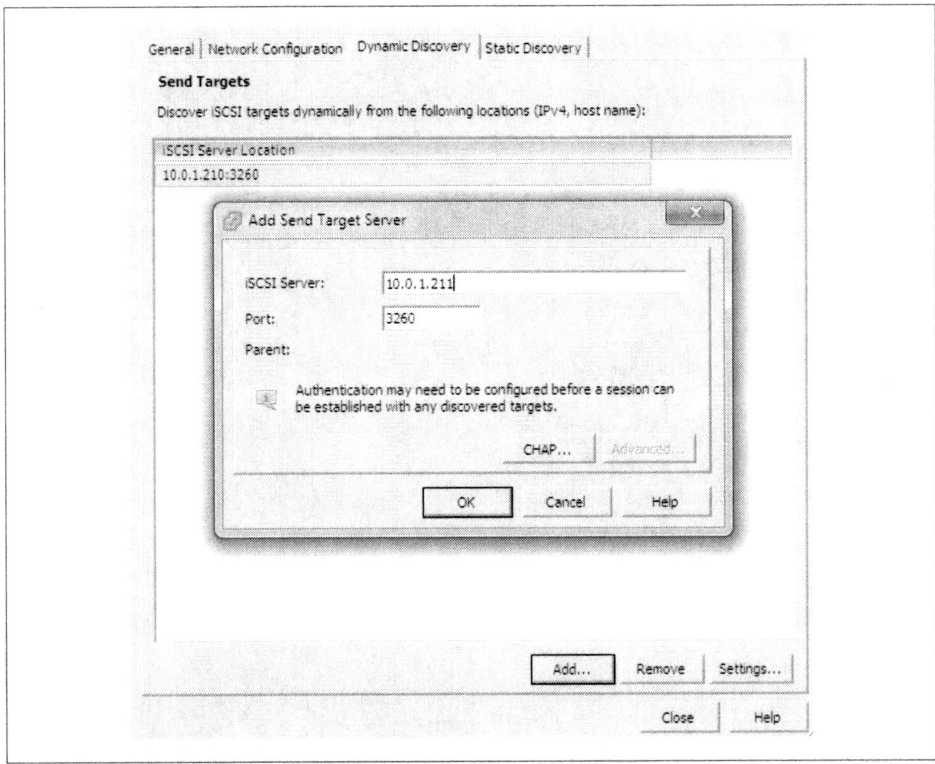

Figure 2-8. Adding an iSCSI target

6. Next, to bind a physical NIC port to the VMkernel, select the Network Configuration tab and Click *Add*. Select the iSCSI networks that were created in Recipe 2.4 (Figure 2-9) and click OK.

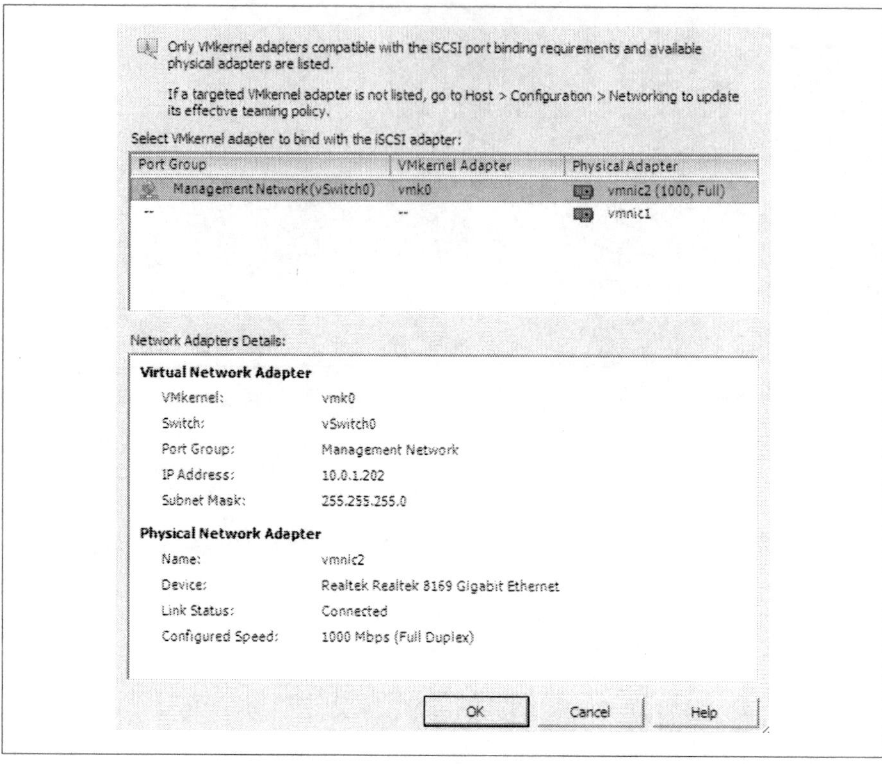

Figure 2-9. Adding networking to software iSCSI

7. After clicking Close, you will be asked whether you wish to rescan for new disks. Click Accept, and ESXi will rescan. When the scan is complete, the new target will appear in the iSCSI software initiator's Details window (Figure 2-10).

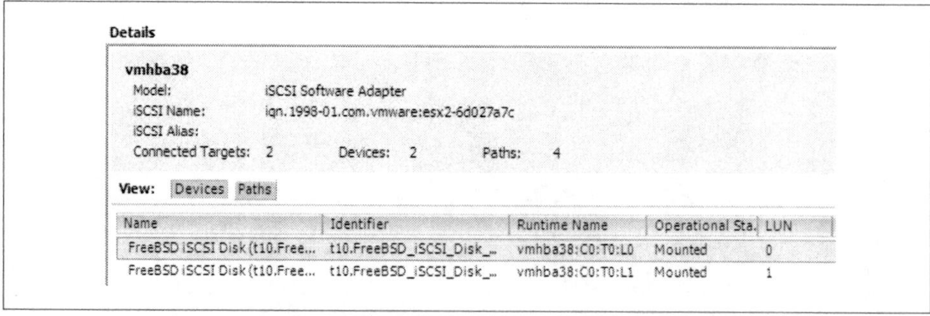

Figure 2-10. Showing the iSCSI target

See Also

Recipes 2.6 and 2.14

2.6 Configuring Hardware iSCSI with an HBA

Problem

You want to make iSCSI connections to storage area networks on ESXi with an iSCSI host bus adapter.

Solution

Use vCenter to configure the iSCSI HBA cards.

Discussion

Hardware-based iSCSI HBAs, such as a QLogic HBA, provides a dedicated and specially designed processor to send and receive iSCSI traffic. Before you purchase any iSCSI HBA cards, you should check the VMware HCL. It requires a hardware iSCSI initiator, which you can set up using the instructions in this section:

1. Log in to vCenter Server and select the server from the inventory list.
2. Select the Configuration tab from the right window pane and navigate to the Storage Adapters link on the left-hand side. Select the iSCSI HBA and click Properties. A new window will appear.

   Unlike with the software iSCSI Initiator, a separate network inside ESXi is not required. You will generally create a separate physical network outside your ESXi environment and set the IP address and network information directly on the iSCSI HBA.

   The iSCSI HBA we are using for our example is a QLogic QLE4062c, which has dual 1GB interfaces. If your iSCSI HBA has only one port, the model and device name (*vmhbaN*) will differ from those in our screenshot (Figure 2-11).

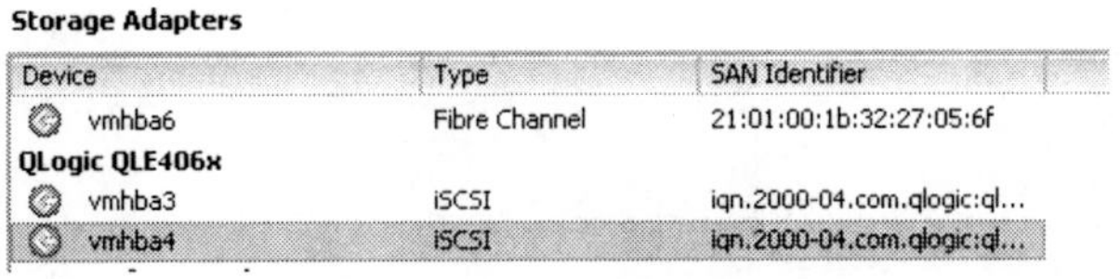

Storage Adapters

Device	Type	SAN Identifier
vmhba6	Fibre Channel	21:01:00:1b:32:27:05:6f
QLogic QLE406x		
vmhba3	iSCSI	iqn.2000-04.com.qlogic:ql...
vmhba4	iSCSI	iqn.2000-04.com.qlogic:ql...

Figure 2-11. Displaying the QLogic QLE4062c iSCSI HBA

3. Click the Configure button to configure the IP address, subnet mask, default gateway, and optional iSCSI name and iSCSI alias (Figure 2-12). Once you're finished, click OK to continue.

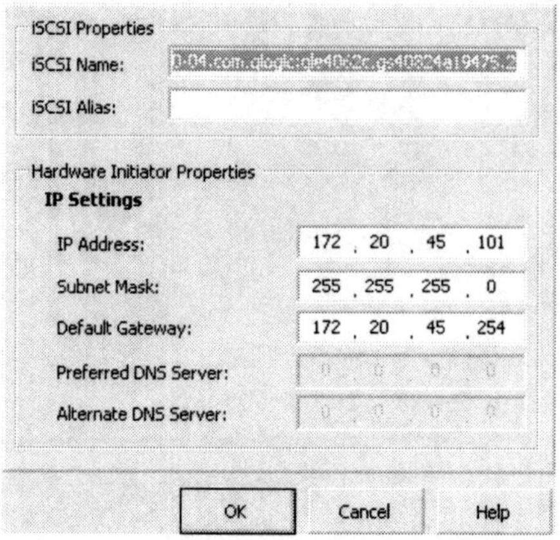

Figure 2-12. Configuring the IP settings for an iSCSI HBA

4. Click the Dynamic Discovery tab, then the Add button. Enter the IP address of the iSCSI server and, if necessary, change the default iSCSI port from 3260 to your customized value. Click OK, then click Close. The ESXI server will begin to scan for new devices.

New LUNs will appear in the Details window of the selected HBA card (Figure 2-13). The server can have a maximum of 64 LUNs, numbered SCSI Target 0, SCSI Target 1, and so on. In our example, the server has four targets, as identified in the Details window under *vmhba4*.

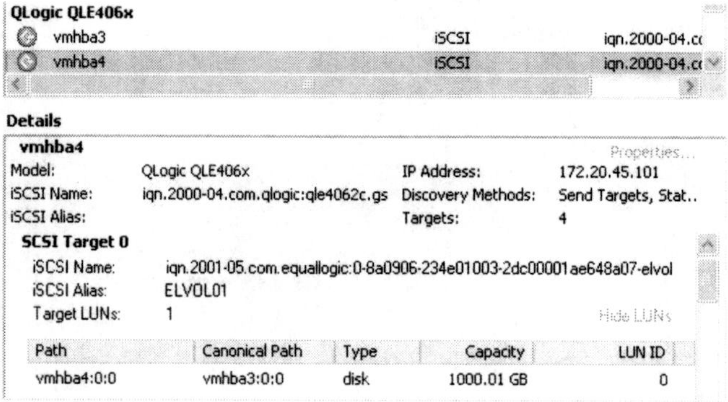

Figure 2-13. Showing the LUN after rescan

On the SCSI Target 0 LUN (Figure 2-13), notice that the path and the canonical path differ. This is because we are looking at the *vmhba4* path view on the second port of the HBA, and the canonical path is set to route all traffic through the first port of the HBA, which is *vmhba3*.

See Also

Recipe 2.5

2.7 Configuring iSCSI in Windows Virtual Machines

Problem

You want a Windows virtual machine to communicate directly with a SAN over your iSCSI connection.

Solution

Using the Microsoft iSCSI Initiator, you can configure your virtual machine to talk to your iSCSI SAN directly.

Discussion

Using Microsoft's iSCSI Initiator, you can directly connect a volume that resides on a SAN directly to a virtual machine that is running Windows. This recipe assumes you have set up a separate network for the ESXI server and a virtual machine to use for iSCSI traffic, and that you have assigned a dedicated Ethernet port on the virtual server for ESXi traffic. This section explains how to download and install the initiator.

Allowing your virtual machine to directly connect via iSCSI to your SAN will allow you to use features from the SAN directly, for example, snapshots done on the SAN or other types of backups that require access to a specific LUN. Additionally, some software vendors might require the storage live outside a VMFS volume and this method can provide RDM-like capabilities.

If you are running Windows Vista or Windows 2008, the iSCSI Initiator is already included and no download is necessary. However, if you're using Windows XP, 2000, or 2003, you'll need to download the initiator from Microsoft's website. Microsoft provides both 32-bit and 64-bit versions of the application.

Users who are required to download the application can install it by double-clicking the executable file and following the on-screen instructions. You will be presented with a new window giving you a set of options that include the following user-selectable options. However, we suggest leaving them checked by default.

Virtual port driver
: This is required and cannot be changed after installation.

Initiator service
: This service handles the behind-the-scenes communication of iSCSI traffic.

Software initiator

This will handle all the iSCSI traffic and works in conjunction with the initiator service to complete requests.

Microsoft MPIO multipathing support for iSCSI

MPIO increases throughput by utilizing multiple interfaces. If you have a target that supports this, such as a Dell EqualLogic iSCSI SAN, you may wish to utilize this technology if performance becomes an issue for you. This option is not available on Windows XP.

Continue the installation of the initiator by accepting the license agreement. When the installation has completed, you will have a new icon on your desktop called Microsoft iSCSI Initiator. You'll use this application to manage your iSCSI connections in Windows.

1. When you launch the application, you will be presented with a screen of options to configure the iSCSI connections. On the Discovery tab, click the Add button in the Target Portals section (Figure 2-14).

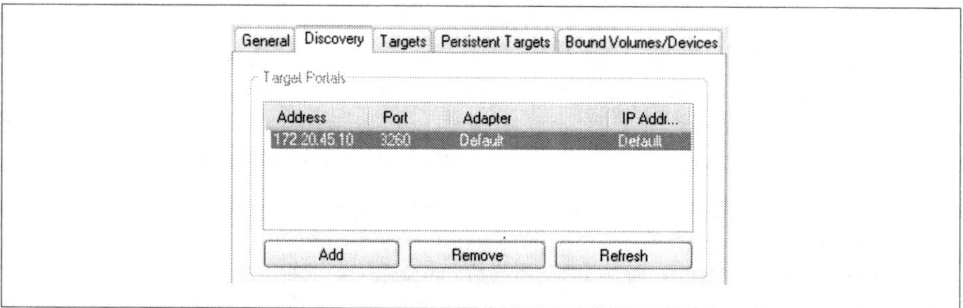

Figure 2-14. Adding a new target

2. The Add Target Portal dialog box allows you to enter the IP address or DNS name of your iSCSI SAN or array. The default port is 3260; you should change this if you're using a different port on the array. If you need to configure CHAP authentication or will be using IPsec for communication between the initiator and the iSCSI array, click the Advanced button and configure the necessary options.
3. Once you are satisfied, click the OK button to make the connection to the iSCSI array. The IP address or DNS name of the target will show up in the Target Portals area of the Discovery tab.
4. After creating the initial connection to the iSCSI array, you need to specify which volume you will connect to and mount on the Windows machine. Click the Targets tab to see the list of targets that are available for you to use (Figure 2-15).

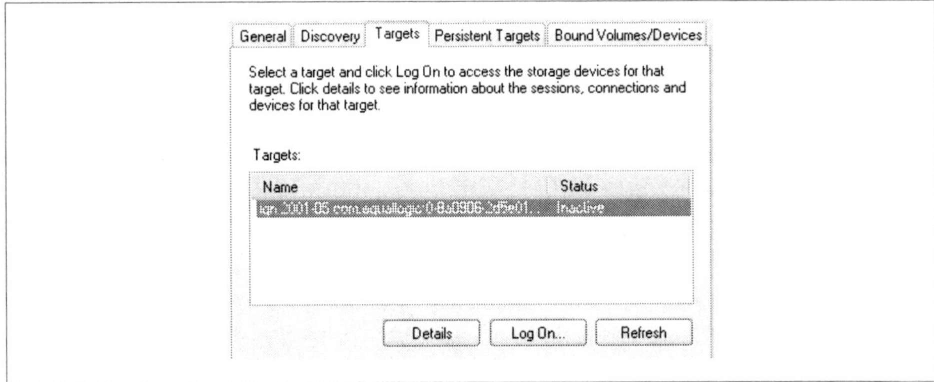

Figure 2-15. Available iSCSI targets in Windows

5. Select the volume to which you will be connecting and click the Log On button. A new window will pop up with the target name and two options (Figure 2-16). The options are:

   Automatically restore this connection when the system boots
   : Selecting this option will make the system automatically reconnect to the volume each time Windows reboots. Unless you have a very good reason not to, you should always check this box. If this option is not selected, the volume will need to be manually reconnected each time the system boots.

   Enable multipath
   : This option should be checked only if you plan on using multipathing for better reliability and performance. It requires multiple Ethernet cards dedicated to the iSCSI task.

     It can be valuable if you have the necessary hardware, need high availability, and previously configured multipathing when installing the initiator.

   Once you are satisfied, click the OK button. The status for the target under the Targets tab will switch to Connected, showing that the volume is connected.

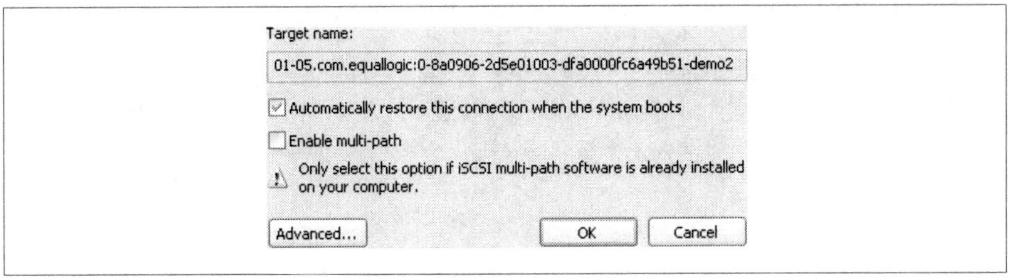

Figure 2-16. iSCSI target options

6. Now that the Windows machine can see the volume, you need to make, configure, and format the volume in Windows. Windows will treat the new iSCSI volume the same as if you had added a physical hard drive to the server.

   Right-click on My Computer and select Manage. Choose the Disk Management option. Because the volume is presumably a new volume with no data, Windows will pop up a new window with the Disk Initialization wizard.

7. Follow the steps presented by this wizard and select from either a basic disk (recommended) or a dynamic disk (this is not recommended for Windows iSCSI). Once the disk has been initialized, you will need to create a partition and format the new volume by right-clicking on the new disk in the Disk Management window.

2.8 Opening Firewall Ports for an ESXi iSCSI Software Initiator

Problem

Your firewall is blocking your ESXI server from communicating with storage over its iSCSI connection.

Solution

Use vCenter to open the necessary firewall port.

Discussion

In order for the iSCSI software initiator to communicate with its targets, port 3260 needs to be opened for outbound traffic on the ESXi Server's firewall. In ESXi 5.0, this port will be opened for you automatically when software iSCSI is enabled. However, for troubleshooting, or if there becomes a need to disable and reenable this service, follow the directions that follow.

Using vCenter, this task is easy. For each ESXI server that is part of your cluster or will be using the iSCSI Software Initiator, follow these steps:

1. Log in to vCenter Server and select the ESXi hosts from the inventory list.
2. Select the Configuration tab from the right window pane. Navigate to the Security Profile link on the left-hand side, and click the Properties link in the lower right corner under the Firewall section to display the Firewall Properties window. Look for the Software iSCSI Client service and select the box next to it to open the firewall on the ESXI server (Figure 2-17). Click OK when you're done.

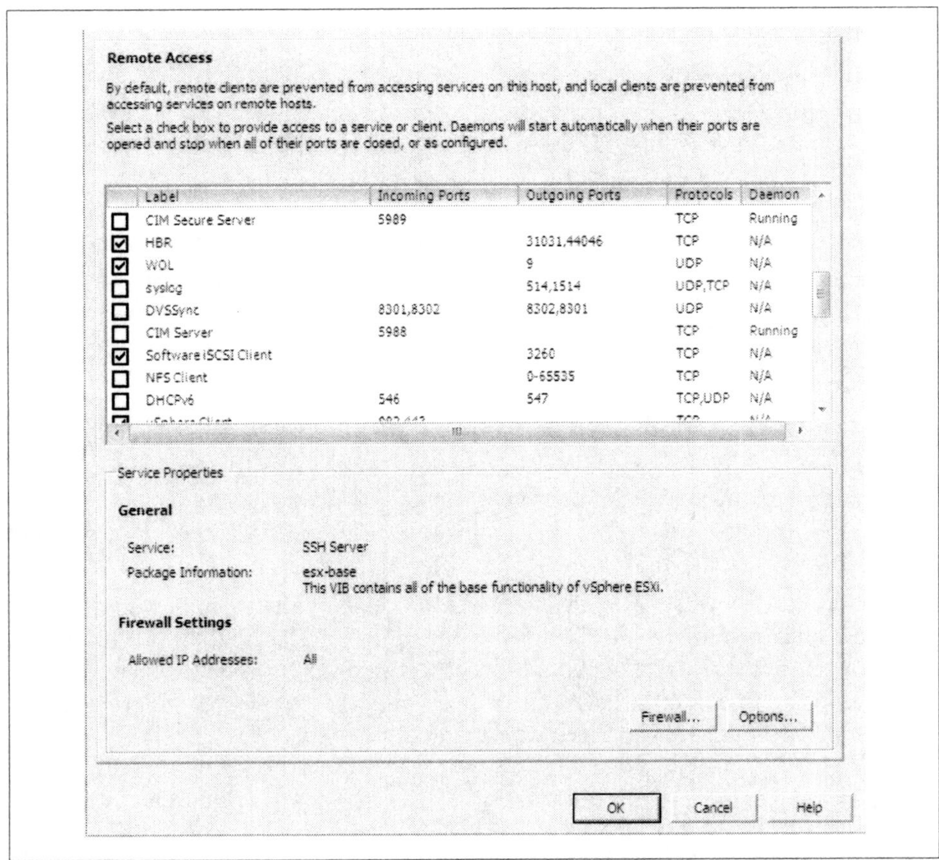

Figure 2-17. Enabling software iSCSI client firewall rules

See Also

Recipe 2.5

2.9 Multipathing with iSCSI

Problem

You want to route iSCSI traffic from an ESXI server over multiple paths for speed or redundancy.

Solution

Use vCenter to view and change multipath settings.

Discussion

One of the nice things about iSCSI is that it is IP based, so it already has built-in support for multipathing using IP routing if you are using dynamic routing protocols on your network. This configuration of iSCSI represents a simpler alternative to Fibre Channel.

The steps for configuring multipathing are as follows:

1. Log in to vCenter Server and select the server from the inventory list.
2. Select the Configuration tab from the right window pane and navigate to Storage. Then select the datastore you wish to modify and click Properties under the Datastore Details section of the screen.
3. In the properties window, click the Manage Paths button (Figure 2-18).
4. Path selection and paths will be displayed (Figure 2-19). The path selection will be Fixed, most recently used (MRU), or round robin. You may see third-party options as well if you have installed custom multipathing drivers from your SAN manufacturer. If you are using a SAN, it's highly suggested to use their multipathing drivers, if available.

   The ESXI server will automatically decide the default path depending on the make and model of your SAN. If the array is not an ESXi supported device, the default path will be set to active/active and the other options may not be available for you to use. Please refer to the hardware compatibility list found at *http://www.vmware.com/go/hcl* to ensure your hardware is fully supported.

   Failover is handled using one of the following policies:

   MRU
   : Uses the last access path for your storage traffic. For example, if you were using path 1 and it failed over to path 2, the device will continue to use path 2 even after path 1 comes back online.

   Fixed
   : Tries to use a specific path. For example, if you set your path policy to Fixed on path 1 and it has a failure, the device switches to path 2 until path 1 is restored, then switches all traffic back to path 1. This is the default policy for active/active storage devices such as Dell EqualLogic iSCSI SANs.

   Round robin
   : This method uses an automatic path selection algorithm that will rotate through all active paths when connecting to active/passive arrays, or if you are using an active/active SAN, it will use all the available paths.

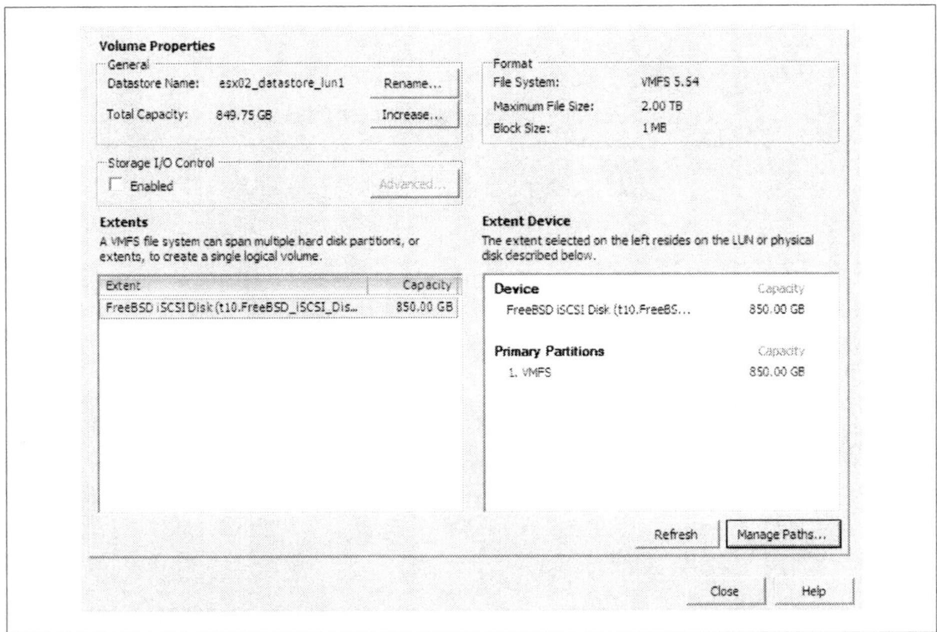

Figure 2-18. Showing hardware iSCSI paths

5. Click the Manage Paths button to configure the path settings (Figure 2-19).

   From the Path Selection drop-down menu you will be able to select the available pathing options available to you. Select the multipathing option you desire and click the Change button. Then click the Close button to save the configuration.

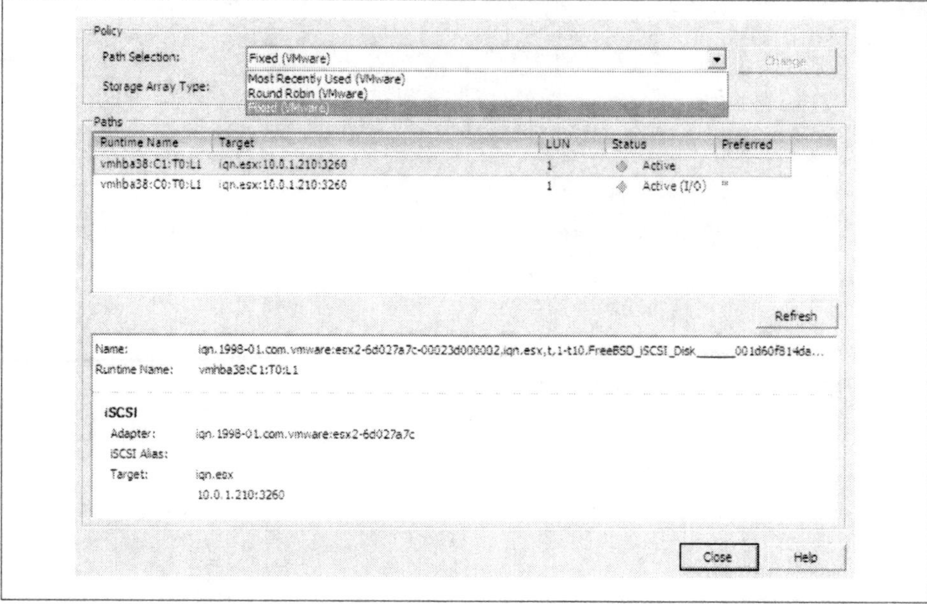

Figure 2-19. Managing paths

2.10 Adding Fibre Channel Storage in ESXi

Problem

You want to give your ESXI servers access to additional storage on a Fibre Channel SAN.

Solution

Use vCenter to configure the new storage and present the LUN to the ESXI servers.

Discussion

Before you can configure the Fibre Channel disks on the ESXI server, you must first create the LUN on the disk array (SAN) and set up the specific Fibre Channel zoning permissions. Normally, this is done in a utility that is provided by the SAN manufacturer. Fibre Channel zoning will take place on your Fibre Channel fabric on your switching environment. That is outside the scope of this recipe, so please refer to the documentation from your SAN and Fibre Channel switch manufacturers.

VMware has some best practice guidelines in place when using Fibre Channel storage. We'll outline the VMware best practices in the following before we look at adding new VMFS datastores via the Fibre Channel fabric.

House only one VMFS datastore per LUN
: An example to avoid would be creating a 1TB LUN and creating two 500GB datastores on that volume. Instead, create a 1TB datastore on the 1TB LUN.

Multipathing is generally set to support your SAN
: VMware has specific multipathing policies depending on the SAN vendor and the type of SAN you are using, for example, active/active, active/passive, etc. It's best practice to not modify the datastore pathing unless you understand the implications. However, some SAN vendors provide their own plug-ins that utilize the vSphere API and are acceptable to use.

Document everything
: As your environment grows, it's really important that you document every detail. This will help troubleshoot later and, additionally, it will help keep your VMware environment cleaner.

When the SAN-side configuration is completed, you can use vCenter to add the new disk to your ESXI servers:

1. Log in to vCenter Server and select a ESXi host from the inventory list.
2. Select the Configuration tab from the right window pane and navigate to Storage. Click the Add Storage link.
3. Select the Disk/LUN storage type and click Next to proceed.
4. Select the Fibre Channel device that will be used for your VMFS datastore. Click Next to continue. If the disk you are formatting is blank, the entire disk space is presented for configuration.

   If the disk is not blank, review the current disk layout in the top panel and select the appropriate configuration method from the bottom panel (this will erase and remove all data from the disk):

   Use the entire device
   : Selecting this option will dedicate all the available space to the VMFS datastore. This is the suggested option for VMware access, and selecting this option will remove all data currently on the LUN.

   Use free space
   : Selecting this option will use the remaining free space to create the VMFS datastore.

   When you are satisfied with your decision, click Next to continue.
5. In the Disk/LUN properties page, enter the name by which you want to refer to this datastore. Click Next to continue.
6. If you need to adjust the block sizes, do so and click Next to continue.
7. Review the summary and click Finish to add the new datastore.

You do *not* need to add the same datastore to multiple ESXI servers. After it has been added to one, the others will see it if the correct zoning has been configured or if no zoning is present on your fibre switch.

8. After the datastore has been created, you may need to click the Refresh link to see the new datastore. If multiple ESXI servers connect to the same datastore, you will need to refresh the storage on each one to see the new datastore.

2.11 Creating a Raw Device Mapping for Virtual Machines

Problem

You want direct access, without going through the virtual filesystem, from a virtual machine to a disk on your storage network.

Solution

Use vCenter to configure raw device mapping (RDM) for the virtual machine.

Discussion

RDM allows virtual machines to have direct access to a LUN on a physical storage system without the use of a VMFS datastore.

VMware generally suggests that you store your virtual machine files on a VMFS partition. However, certain situations may require the use of RDM, such as MSCS clustering that spans over physical hosts, or the use of SAN technologies inside your virtual machine. RDM is supported only over Fibre Channel and iSCSI at this time.

RDM has two different modes:

Virtual compatibility mode
: This mode allows the RDM to act like a VMDK (virtual disk file) and allows the use of virtual machine snapshots within ESXi. Virtual compatibility mode is also compatible when initiating a vMotion.

Physical compatibility mode
: This mode allows direct access to the device, but gives you less control within ESXi. For example, you will not be able to snapshot the data using ESXi. However, if your SAN supports snapshot technology, you will be able to use it on this volume.

To add an RDM disk to a virtual machine that has already been created:

1. Log in to vCenter Server and select the virtual machine to which you wish to add the RDM.
2. From the Summary tab on the virtual machine, click Edit Settings.

3. When the new window appears, click the Add button.
4. The Add Hardware wizard will open. Select Hard Disk, then click Next.
5. You will be presented with a list of options. Select Raw Device Mapping and click Next.
6. Select the LUN you wish to use for your RDM (Figure 2-20) and click Next.

Adapter:Target:LUN	Capacity
/vmfs/devices/disks/vmhba5:0:0:0	408.697 GB
/vmfs/devices/disks/vmhba5:0:1:0	500.000 GB

Figure 2-20. Selecting the LUN for the RDM

7. From the available list of disks, select the LUN you wish to use for your virtual machine.
8. Select the datastore for your RDM mapping file. You can store the mapping file on the same datastore as the virtual machine files (described in Recipe 2.17), or on another datastore. If you have N-Port ID Virtualization (NPIV) enabled, ensure that the RDM mapping files are on the same datastore as the virtual machine files. Once selected, click Next to continue.
9. You will be presented with a choice of two compatibility modes, detailed earlier in this recipe. Make your selection and click Next to continue.
10. Select the virtual device node and click Next to continue.
11. If you selected virtual compatibility mode, you will need to choose between the two following modes:

    Persistent
    : Changes are immediately and permanently written to the disk.

    Nonpersistent
    : Changes written to the disk are discarded when the virtual machine is powered off or when the virtual machine is reverted to a previous snapshot image.

Once you have made your selection, click Next to continue and click Finish to add the RDM to the virtual machine.

2.12 Creating a VMkernel Port for Access to NFS Datastores

Problem

You want to connect an NFS file share to an ESXi Server.

Solution

Create a VMkernel port to allow ESXi to communicate with NFS.

Discussion

Although a lot of larger ESXi environments use Fibre Channel or iSCSI, ESXi also supports the use of NFS. As with software-based iSCSIs, you will need to create a VMkernel on the ESXI server for NFS traffic to pass over. It is recommended that you configure the VMkernel to use a dedicated network, but you can configure it on an existing network if necessary. Here are the steps:

1. Log in to vCenter Server and select the ESXi host from the inventory list.
2. Select the Configuration tab from the right window pane and navigate to Networking on the left-hand side. Click Add Networking in the upper right corner.
3. Under Connection Types, select VMkernel and click Next.
4. If you are going to set up your VMkernel on a separate network (recommended), you will want to select an unused network adapter; alternatively, select an already existing vSwitch and Ethernet adapter. The options will appear in the lower portion of the screen, in the Preview section (Figure 2-21). After making your selection, click Next.

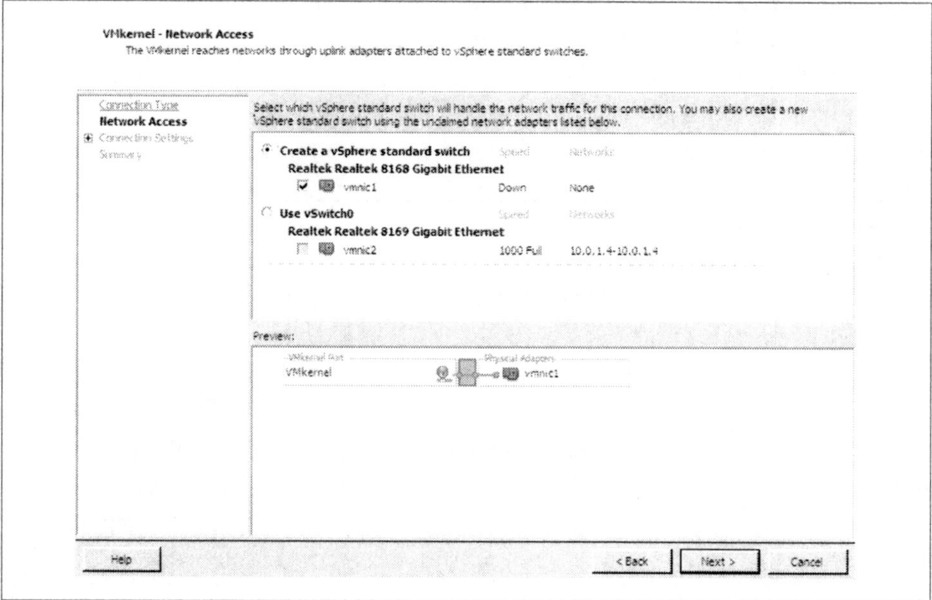

Figure 2-21. Adding the VMkernel port

5. You will be required to enter some information about the VMkernel port on the Connection Settings screen (Figure 2-22). Click Next once the Network Label is set.

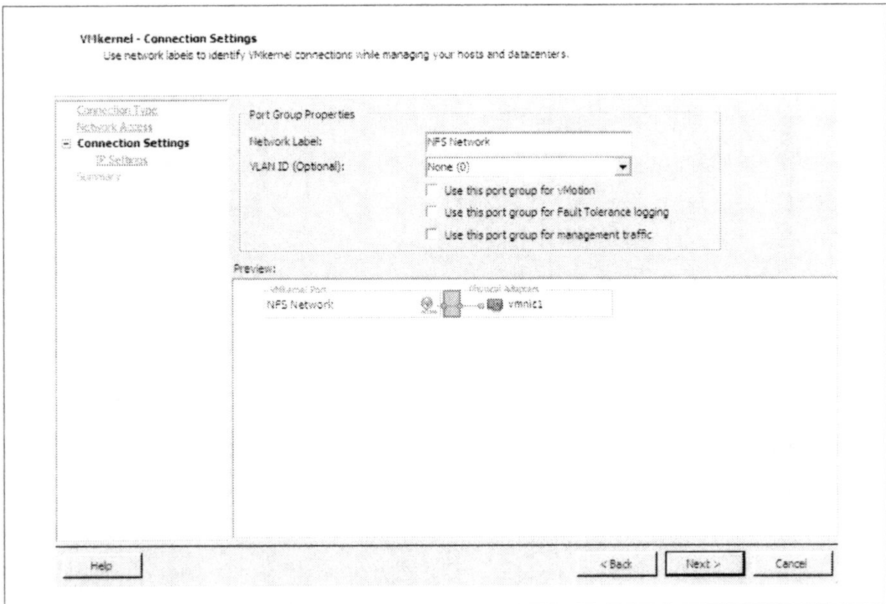

Figure 2-22. Setting NFS port group properties

First, set the port group properties:

Network label
: The label by which the port group will be recognized within the virtual environment. It's important to give the port group the same name on all physical ESXi Servers.

VLAN ID (optional)
: The network VLAN your port group will use to communicate. Specify this if you are using VLANs in your network infrastructure.

Use this port group for VMotion
: Because the VMkernel also handles VMotion traffic, this option is available when configuring the NFS VMkernel. However, you should leave it unchecked because it is not recommended to run VMotion traffic over the same network as your storage traffic.

6. Next, configure the IP settings as shown in Figure 2-23:

IP address
: The IP address of the VMkernel. This is a required field.

Subnet mask
: The subnet mask of the network. This is also required.

VMkernel default gateway
: Enter a gateway if your IP address resides on a network other than the one in which you are configuring the port group.

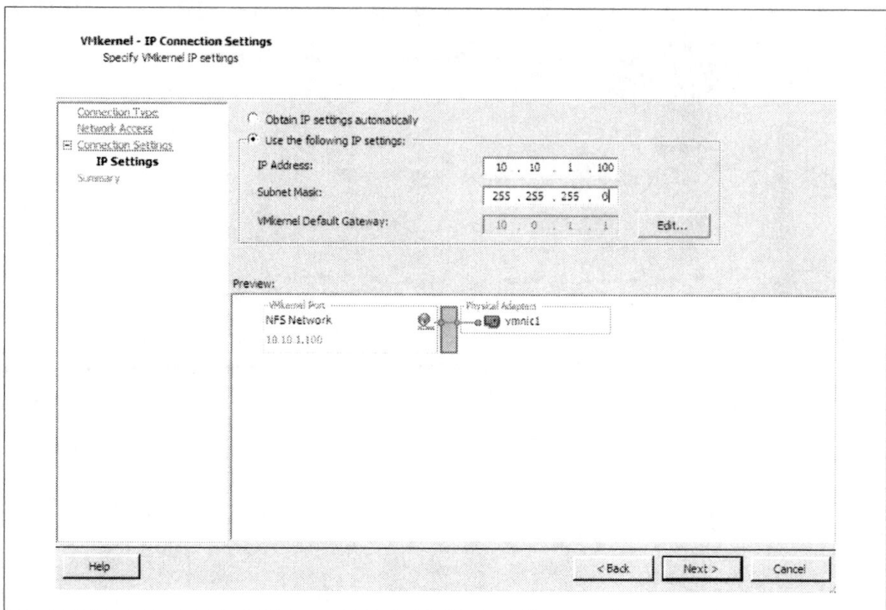

Figure 2-23. Specifying VMkernel port/IP settings

Further options, such as DNS and advanced routing, can be configured by clicking the Edit button.

7. Click Next to view the summary, and then click *Finish* to create the port group.

Before ESXi can communicate with the NFS datastore, you have to configure it to use the storage, as described in the next section.

2.13 Configuring ESXi to Use NFS

Problem

You wish to add an NFS datastore to your ESXi Server.

Solution

Use vCenter to configure the ESXI server so it recognizes the NFS device.

Discussion

NFS is becoming a popular storage tier because it is cost-effective and provides reliable speed. VMware supports HA, DRS, vMotion, and virtual machine snapshots on NFS datastores.

Before you follow this recipe, set up a VMkernel port to communicate with the NFS datastore, as described in Recipe 2.12. Then configure the ESXI server as follows:

1. Log in to vCenter Server and select the server from the inventory list.
2. Select the Configuration tab from the right window pane, navigate to the Storage link on the left-hand side, and click Add Storage in the upper right corner.
3. A new window will appear with two options: Disk/LUN or Network File System (Figure 2-24). Select Network File System and click Next to continue.

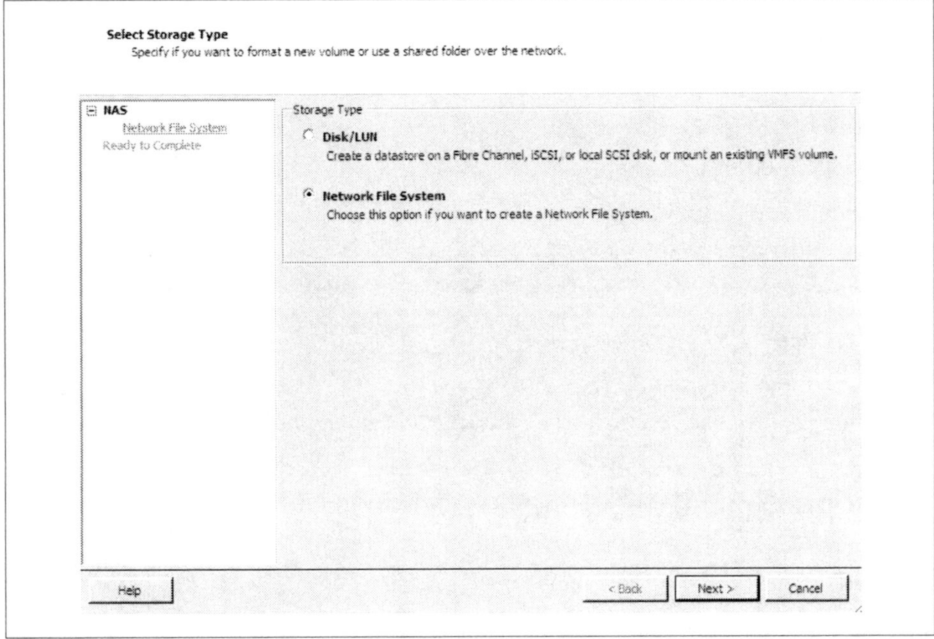

Figure 2-24. Selecting NFS to create a datastore

4. You will now be asked to enter some information about the NFS share (Figure 2-25). When finished, click Next.

   Server
   : The name or IP address of the device that is serving the NFS share

   Folder
   : The directory on the NFS device you are going to mount

   Mount NFS read only
   : This allows the NFS datastore to be read only.

   Datastore name
   : The name you wish to give the new datastore (for example, *NFS01*)

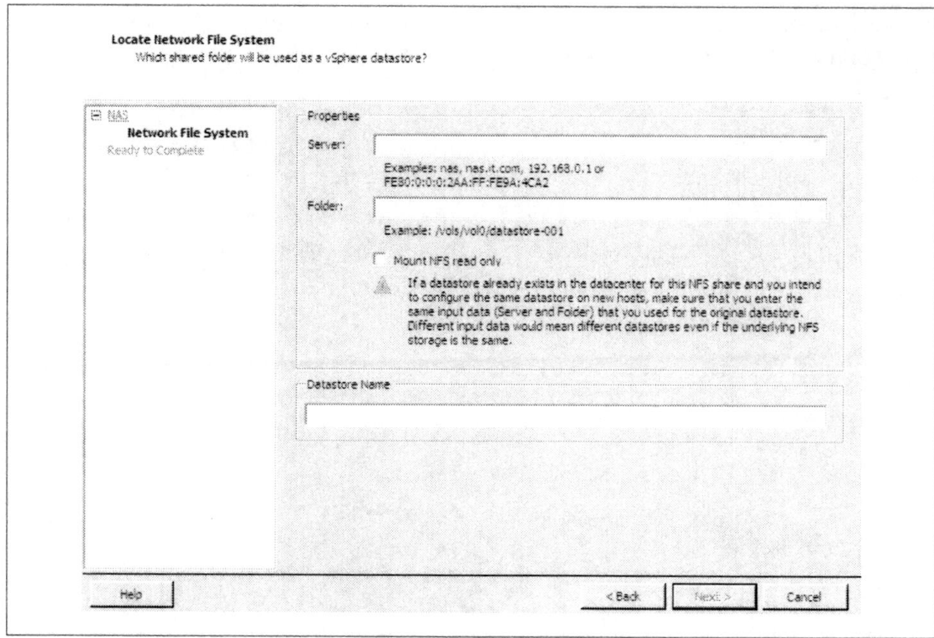

Figure 2-25. Entering NFS device properties

5. When you're done, click Finish. ESXi will proceed to add the new datastore.

2.14 Creating a VMFS Volume in vCenter

Problem

You want to add a new VMFS volume to an ESXi Server.

Solution

Using vCenter, you can easily create and attach new VMFS volumes.

Discussion

Adding an additional VMFS volume to your ESXI servers is pretty straightforward for all aspects of storage. For example, once configured on the SAN side, Fibre Channel and iSCSI disks will be visible to your ESXI server, and local disks will be detected automatically.

When adding a new disk to your ESXI servers in a clustered environment, where multiple ESXI servers will be accessing the SAN LUN/datastore, you only need to add it to one ESXI server. After the datastore is created, you can rescan or refresh the existing servers and the datastore will appear.

ESXi 5 allows you to have 256 VMFS datastores per host, with a maximum size of 64TB. The minimum size for a VMFS datastore is 1.3GB; however, VMware recommends a minimum size of 2GB.

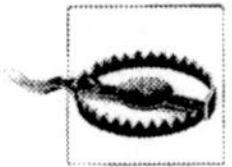

If you try to add the same datastore to each individual ESXi Server, you will get data corruption and configuration problems.

Follow these steps to create the VMFS volume:

1. Log in to vCenter Server and select the ESXi host from the inventory list.
2. Select the Configuration tab from the right window pane, navigate to Storage, and click the Add Storage link.
3. Select the Disk/LUN storage type and click Next to proceed.
4. Select the device to use for your VMFS datastore (Figure 2-26). The device may be a local, iSCSI, or Fibre Channel disk. Click Next to continue. If the disk you are formatting is blank, the entire disk space is presented for configuration.

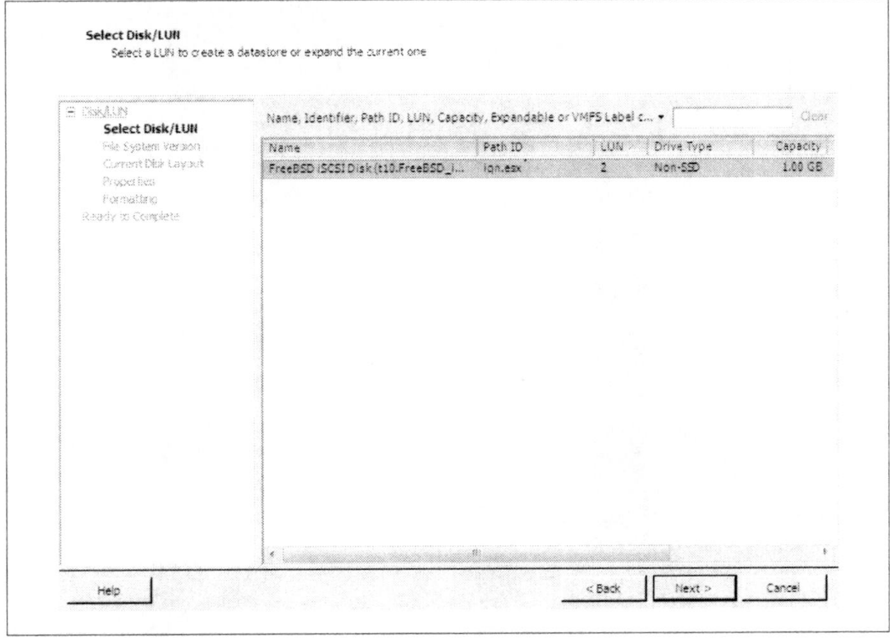

Figure 2-26. Select disk/LUN

If the disk is not blank, review the current disk layout in the top panel and select the appropriate configuration method from the bottom panel:

Use the entire device
: Selecting this option will dedicate all the available space to the VMFS datastore. This is the suggested option for VMware servers, and selecting this option will remove all data currently on the LUN.

Use free space
: Selecting this option will use the remaining free space to create the VMFS datastore.

After making your choice, click Next to continue.

5. Select the File System Version that you wish to use (Figure 2-27). In ESXi 5, you have the option to create VMFS-5 and VMFS-3 file systems. VMFS-3 limits the size of each datastore to 2TB, whereas VMFS-5 allows you to create datastores that can scale up to 64TB. Generally, you will select VMFS-5, unless you have a mixed environment of older ESX versions that share the datastore. Click Next to continue.

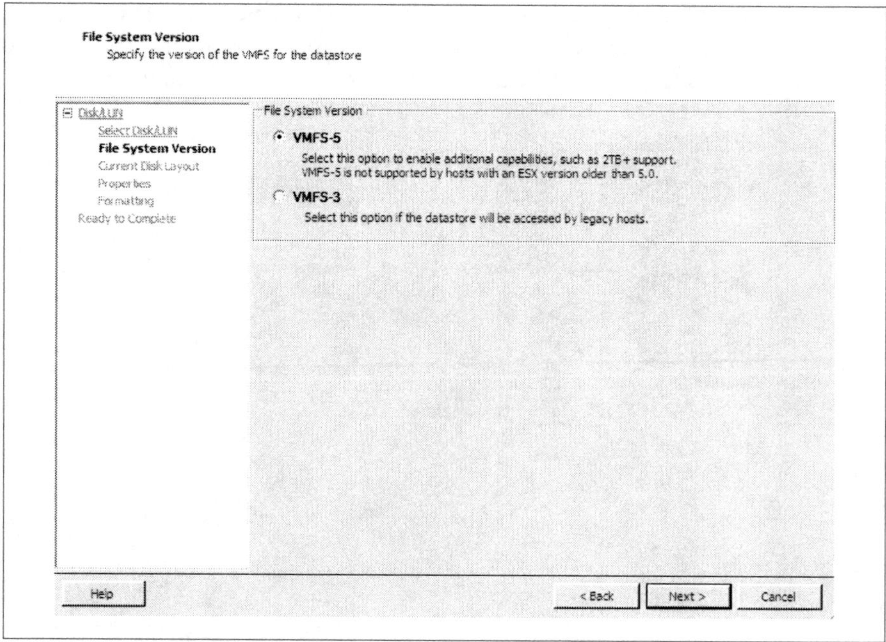

Figure 2-27. Select filesystem type

6. Review the disk layout (Figure 2-28). If you are satisfied, click Next to proceed.

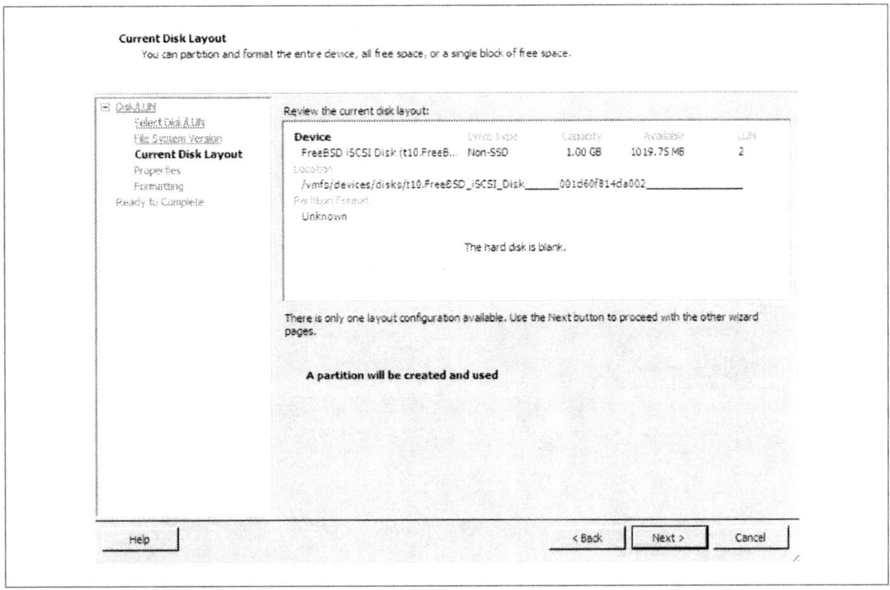

Figure 2-28. Review disk layout

7. On the Properties page, enter the name you want to give this datastore (Figure 2-29). Click Next to continue.

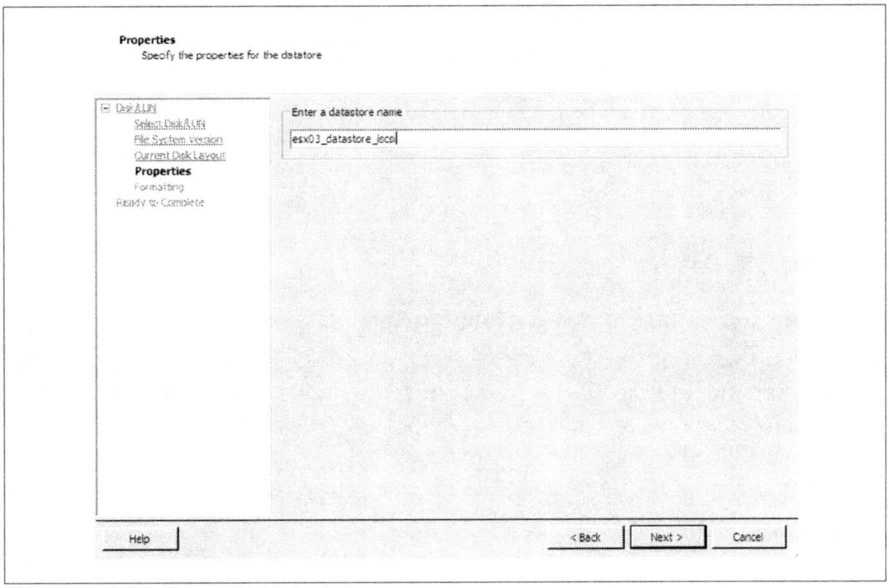

Figure 2-29. Enter the datastore name

8. On the Capacity/Formatting screen, select either Maximum available space or choose a Custom amount of space to allocate to the datastore (Figure 2-30). Generally, you will want to use the maximum amount of space. Unlike with ESX 3 and 4, version 5 will standardize on a 1MB block size for the datastore when using VMFS-5. However, if you selected VMFS-3, you will need to choose a block size as well. The block size will determine the amount of individual files you can store on the datastore.

   Click Next to continue once you have selected the capacity option that fits your needs.

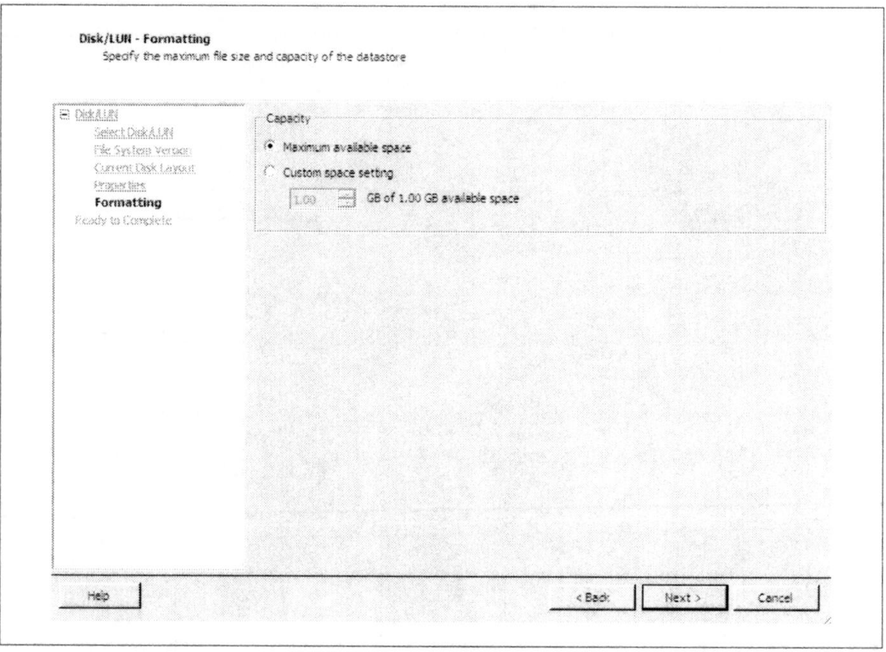

Figure 2-30. Disk formatting options

9. Review the summary and click Finish to add the new datastore.
10. After the datastore has been created, you may need to click Refresh to see the new datastore. If multiple ESXI servers connect to the same datastore, you will need to refresh the storage on each one to see the new datastore.

See Also

Recipe 2.16

2.15 Performing a Storage Rescan

Problem

You need to Rescan your storage adapters.

Solution

Use the rescan feature in vCenter Server.

Discussion

There may be times when it is necessary to rescan your ESXi Server's storage devices. These situations include:

- When changes are made to the disks or LUNS available to the ESXI server
- When changes are made to the storage adapters in the ESXi Server
- When a new datastore is created or removed
- When an existing datastore is reconfigured, for example, by adding an extent to increase storage

To rescan a server's storage adapters:

1. Log in to vCenter Server and select the ESXi host from the inventory list.
2. Select the Configuration tab from the right window pane, navigate to Storage Adapters on the left-hand side, and click Rescan.

   Alternatively, to rescan a specific adapter, you can right-click on that adapter and select Rescan.
3. If you wish to rescan for new disks or LUNs, select Rescan in the upper right corner and then choose the Scan for New Storage Devices option. If new LUNs are discovered, they will appear in the disk/LUN view.
4. To discover new datastores or update existing datastores after a configuration change, select the Scan for New VMFS Volumes option. If a new datastore is found, it will be displayed in the datastore view.

2.16 Creating a VMFS Volume via the Command Line

Problem

You must create a new VMFS volume but you do not have access to vCenter Server, or you want to create an automation script.

Solution

Using the `vmkfstools` command on your ESXI server allows you to create new volumes.

Discussion

The `vmkfstools` command creates a new VMFS volume. It also assigns it a unique UUID, which is a hexadecimal value that incorporates the SCSI ID and label name into the volume's metadata. Run this command on the ESXi host's service console:

```
vmkfstools --createfs vmfs5 --blocksize 1m disk_ID:P
```

The `--createfs` option tells the command which type of VMFS volume to create. In our case, we created a VMFS-5 volume. The `-S` option allows you to specify a label for your volume, which should be a simple name.

See Also

Recipe 2.14

2.17 Viewing the Files that Define a VMFS Volume

Problem

You need to find information about a VMFS volume, but this information is contained in files on that volume rather than in the vCenter.

Solution

Each virtual machine has a directory with files that define and control the virtual machine. You can view the contents of this directory and read the files themselves, because they're text based.

Discussion

Many files make up a virtual machine. Understanding the purpose of each one helps you keep your virtual machine environment running at top performance:

.vmx
: Holds the configuration for the virtual machine.

.vmss
: Present when the virtual machine is suspended.

.vmdk
: Holds the operating system and data for the virtual machine. This file is based on the *.vmx* file.

.vmem
: Virtual machine memory is mapped to this file.

.vmsd
: The dictionary file for snapshots and associated disks. If you have snapshots or multiple disks, this file keeps track of them.

.nvram
: Holds the BIOS for the virtual machine.

.vmx.lck
: A lock file is created when the virtual machine is powered on.

-flat.vmdk
: A single preallocated disk that contains data.

f001.vmdk.filepart
: The first extent of a preallocated disk that has been split into 2GB files.

s001.vmdk
: The first extent of a growable disk that has been split into 2GB files.

-delta.vmdk
: Holds the differences between the actual virtual machine and snapshot differences. This allows you to roll back your virtual machine to a previous state or merge the current state with the old state.

-Snapshot#.vmsn
: The configuration of a snapshot.

These files are located within the virtual machine's directory on the storage volume, which is typically */vmfs/volumes/`DATASTORE`/`VIRTUALMACHINE`*. For example, our server, which is named *W2KStandardBase*, is on the *ELISCSI01* database store, and its path is */vmfs/volumes/ELISCSI01/W2K3StandardBase*.

2.18 Increasing the VMFS Volume Capacity

Problem

One of the datastores on your ESXI server is running out of space.

Solution

Using the vCenter server, you can add an extent to your existing datastore to add more space.

Discussion

An extent is a physical hard drive partition on a physical storage device, such as a Fibre Channel, iSCSI SAN, or local disk. These partitions can be dynamically added to an existing VMFS-based datastore, allowing you to grow as needed. Datastores can span multiple extents and will be presented to ESXi as a single volume.

Adding new extents can be done while the existing VMFS datastore is online. This makes adding new space really easy. Each datastore can span up to 32 extents.

It should be noted that the first VMFS datastore (disk) in the extent holds the metadata for the entire datastore, including all new extents. If the first extent is corrupted or damaged, you are at risk of losing all the data on the entire extent set.

Add an extent as follows:

1. Log in to vCenter Server and select the ESXi host from the inventory list.
2. Select the Configuration tab from the right-hand window pane, navigate to Storage on the left-hand side, and select the datastore to which you wish to add the extent.
3. Once the datastore is highlighted, right click and select the Properties link (Figure 2-31).

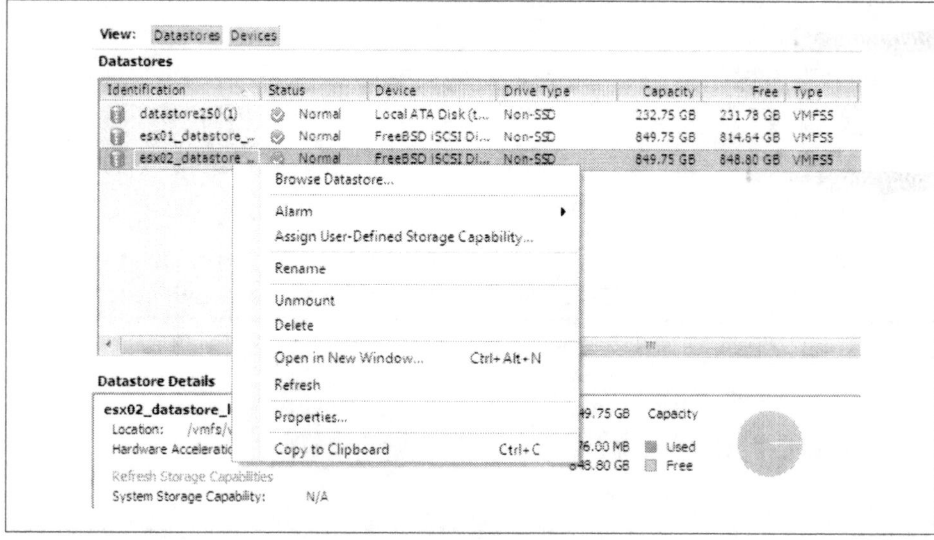

Figure 2-31. Showing the storage volume that will get an extent

4. A new window will appear with information regarding the datastore. Click the Increase button, which appears under the General section (Figure 2-32). A new window will pop up.

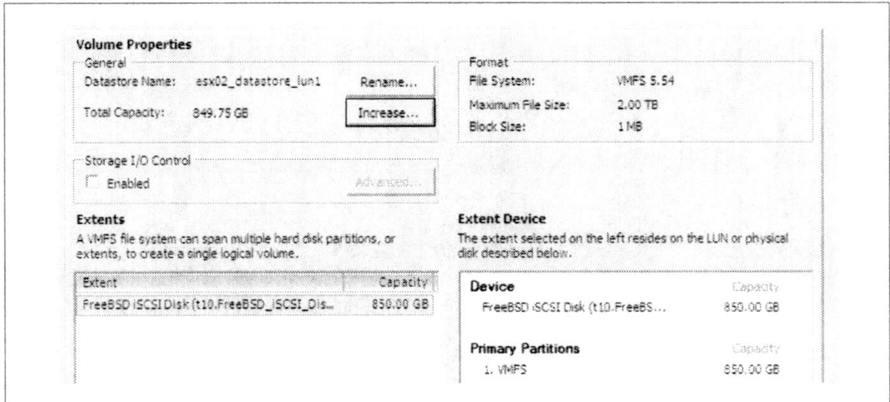

Figure 2-32. Increase a datastores space

5. Select the device from the list of available storage devices (Figure 2-33) and click Next.

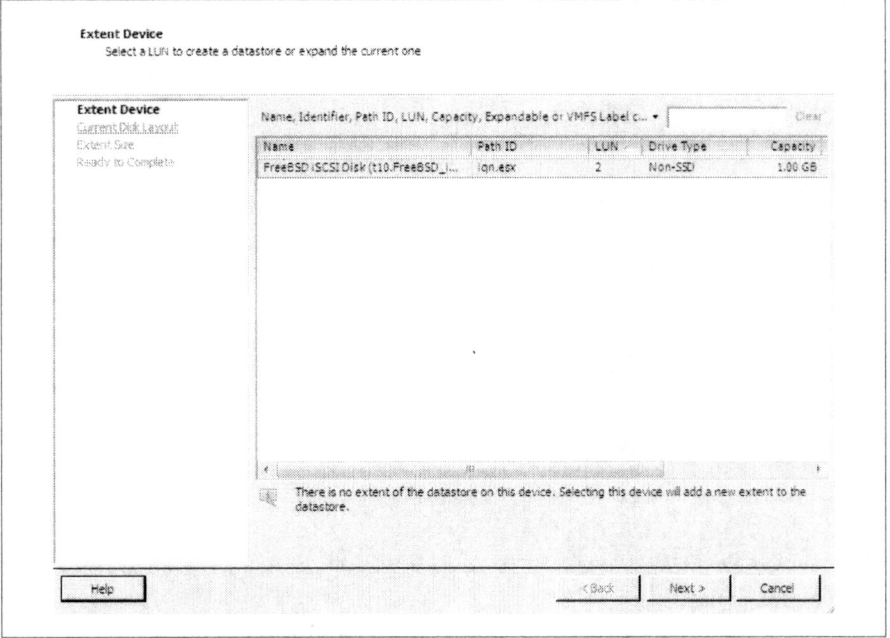

Figure 2-33. Selecting a device for the extent

6. Review the disk layout. When you are satisfied, click Next.
7. Select how the space should be used on the extent. You will have one or many of the following options from which to choose. Set the capacity for the extent. If using the custom setting, the minimum size is 1.3GB. When you are done setting the size, click Next.

Maximum available space
: Allows all the available space on the device to be used in the extent.

Custom setting
: Allows a custom amount of space to be used on the extent.

8. Finally, once you are satisfied, click Finish and the process to increase the datastore will begin.

Once the datastore has been expanded, you can click on the datastore to view the new extent in the lower Details window. You will also need to refresh the datastore on each host so the new capacity will be reported correctly.

You cannot remove individual extents after they have been added to a datastore; you can only remove the entire VMFS datastore, which will result in losing all of its data.

See Also

Recipes 2.5, 2.6, and 2.16

2.19 Reading VMFS Metadata

Problem

You wish to view the metadata for a specific VMFS volume.

Solution

Use the `vmkfstools` command.

Discussion

The metadata in a VMFS volume is made up of six parts:

- Block size
- Number of extents
- Volume capacity
- VMFS version
- Label
- VMFS UUID

The `vmkfstools` command lets you view the metadata in a specific VMFS volume:

```
vmkfstools -P -h pathname
```

The -P option allows you to read the metadata, and the -h option tells the `vmkfstools` command to display amounts in megabytes, kilobytes, or gigabytes, instead of the default bytes. The *pathname* is the pathname of your VMFS filesystem. For example:

```
VMFS-5.54 file system spanning 1 partitions.
File system label (if any): esx02_datastore_lun1
Mode: public
Capacity 849.8 GB, 848.8 GB available, file block size 1 MB
UUID: 4f546274-32257e8a-132c-5404a64c91b1
Partitions spanned (on "lvm"):
    t10.FreeBSD_iSCSI_Disk_____001d60f814da001_______________:1
Is Native Snapshot Capable: NO
```

2.20 Creating a Diagnostic Partition

Problem

Your ESXI server is missing a diagnostic partition.

Solution

Use the vCenter to create a diagnostic partition.

Discussion

ESXI servers need to have a diagnostic or dump partition in order to run. These partitions store core dumps for debugging and are used by the VMware technical support team. Diagnostic partitions can be created on a local disk, on a shared LUN on a Fibre Channel device, or on a device accessed by a hardware-based iSCSI initiator connection. Diagnostic partitions are not supported on software-based iSCSI initiators.

The diagnostic partition must be at least 100MB in size. If you use a shared storage device, each ESXI server must have its own separate diagnostic partition.

If you choose the Recommended Partitioning scheme when installing your ESXI server, the installer automatically creates the diagnostic partition for you. The following steps create a diagnostic partition if your ESXi installation lacks it:

1. Log in to the vCenter server and select the ESXi host from the inventory list.
2. Select the Configuration tab from the right window pane, navigate to Storage, and click Add Storage.
3. A new window will appear allowing you to select the storage type. Select the Diagnostic option and click Next to continue. If you do not see the Diagnostic option, your ESXI server already has a diagnostic partition. If your ESXI server already has a diagnostic partition, you can access it by issuing the `esxcli system coredump` command at the command line.
4. Select the type of diagnostic partition you wish to create. You have three options:

Private local
: Create the diagnostic partition on a local disk.

Private SAN storage
: Create the partition on a nonshared storage LUN using the Fibre Channel or hardware-based iSCSI.

Shared SAN storage
: Create the diagnostic partition on a shared LUN that is accessible by multiple ESXI servers and may store information for more than one ESXI server.

After making your selection, click Next.

5. Select the device on which to create the partition and click Next.
6. Finally, review the partition configuration and then click Finish to create the diagnostic partition.

2.21 Removing Storage Volumes from ESXi

Problem

You wish to remove an old datastore from your ESXi Server.

Solution

Use the vCenter to remove a volume from ESXi.

Discussion

The steps to remove a volume follow:

1. Log in to the vCenter server and select the ESXi host from the inventory list.
2. Select the Configuration tab from the right window pane and navigate to Storage. Right-click on the datastore you wish to remove, and choose Remove.
3. A pop-up window will appear asking you to confirm the removal of the datastore. It's very important to make sure you know which datastore you want to remove, because this window provides no details on the datastores.
4. Click Yes if you are positive the correct datastore has been selected, and the datastore will be removed. All of the data will be deleted.

2.22 Determining whether a VMFS Datastore Is on a Local or SAN Disk

Problem

Using the vCenter, find if a specific VMFS datastore is on a local disk or connected to a SAN or NFS device.

Solution

Through vCenter, you can determine the physical location of a VMFS datastore.

Discussion

To find out where your VMFS datastore is located:

1. Log in to the vCenter server and select the ESXi host from the inventory list.
2. Select the Configuration tab from the right window pane and navigate to Storage.
3. Find the datastore you want to check. Look for the Device column (Figure 2-34). This will identify if the datastore is Local or if it's connected to a Fibre Channel or iSCSI SAN. In the example, we can see that *datastore250* is a local disk datastore specific to the ESXi host.

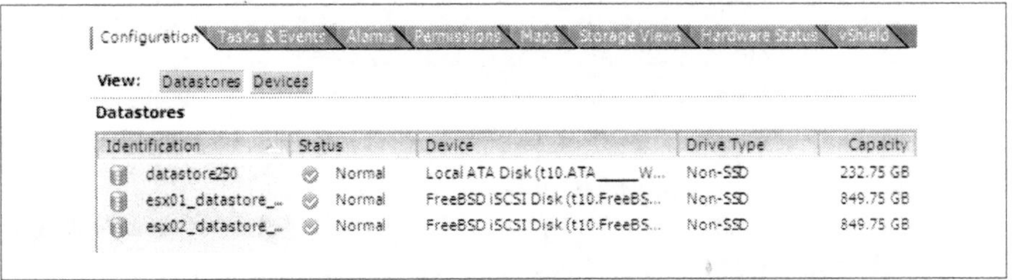

Figure 2-34. Checking for local/SAN disks

2.23 Adjusting Timeouts When Adding Storage in vCenter

Problem

When you try to add new storage in the vCenter, you receive timeout errors.

Solution

Adjust the timeout value in the vCenter.

Discussion

timeouts can occur for various reasons when adding new storage via the vCenter. It may be simply that the timeout values are just too short, but be aware that lengthening these values is not a fix-all solution; there may be a larger underlying problem in networking or I/O that you should investigate.

To lengthen the timeout in the vCenter client, navigate to Edit→Client Settings→Remote Command timeout→Use a custom value. The value is shown in seconds. Adjust it to a higher number (perhaps two times what is already set).

2.24 Setting Disk Timeouts in Windows

Problem

A Windows guest operating system will sometimes timeout when a SAN is rebooted or goes through a failure and recovery.

Solution

You can adjust the disk timeout value in the Windows registry.

Discussion

Default timeouts on Windows servers may be too short for a SAN recovery. During the time your SAN is down and Windows is trying to write data, it is possible for data to be lost or corrupted if your timeout values are not high enough. You can change the timeouts on both Windows Server 2000 and 2003 by editing the system registry:

1. Click Start→Run, type **`regedit`**, and click OK.
2. In the left panel view, double-click the first `HKEY_LOCAL_MACHINE\SYSTEM\CurrentControlSet`, then click Services, and finally Disk.
3. Select the `TimeOutValue` and set the data value to `3c` (hexadecimal) or `60` (decimal).
4. Save the changes and exit the registry.

Once these changes have been made, Windows will wait 60 seconds before generating disk errors. If 60 seconds isn't long enough, you can adjust the value to suit your specific needs.

2.25 Renaming Datastores

Problem

You need to rename your datastores.

Solution

You can use vCenter to rename your datastores. Follow these simple steps.

Discussion

1. Log in to your vCenter server and select the ESXi host that has the datastore you wish to rename.
2. Click the Configuration Tab and then select Storage.
3. Finally, select the datastore and right-click and choose Rename (Figure 2-35).

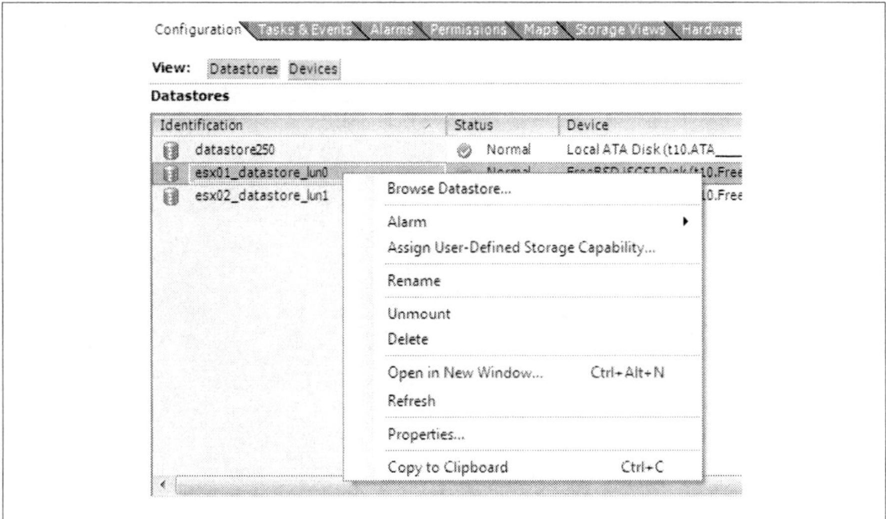

Figure 2-35. Renaming the datastore

4. Once the datastore is renamed, any ESXi host that has access to that datastore will see the new name, and it will be updated across all ESXi hosts.

CHAPTER 3

Networking

Networking is a crucial aspect of the ESXi virtual environment. It's important to understand the technology, including the different pieces that make it up and how they work together. In this chapter, we will look at different networking elements inside the ESXi platform and how to configure and build those different pieces.

3.1 Configuring ESXi Network Ports and the Firewall

Problem

You need to identify the ports used by ESXi services and ensure they are open for traffic to pass.

Solution

Review and discuss the ports and their functions within the environment.

Discussion

Connections to the ESXi host through the vCenter server, Secure Shell, or the Web must use specific ports. ESXi handles most communication through the following ports; they cannot currently be changed, so make sure they are open on your firewall if you have internal firewalls inside your network.

Port 902
: The vCenter server uses this port to send data to the ESXI servers it manages. The listening process (*vmware-authd*) on the ESXI server handles the flow of traffic.

Port 903
: Both the vCenter client and the web client use this port to provide mouse keyboard screen (MKS) service from the virtual machine to the end user over Transmission Control Protocol/Internet Protocol. This port also handles all interactions with the

virtual machine when it is accessed via the console in the vCenter client or via the Web.

Port 443

vCenter clients, web clients, and the Software Development Kit all use this port to send data to an ESXI server managed by the vCenter server. This port is also used if you connect to the ESXI server directly, bypassing the vCenter server. The clients will connect to the ESXI server via the Tomcat or SDK instance, and the running process on the ESXI server (*vmware-hostd*) will handle the traffic.

For a complete reference of all ports inside the vSphere product suite see: *http://kb.vmware.com/selfservice/microsites/search.do?language=en_US&cmd=displayKC&externalId=1012382*

When communications regarding VMware HA, migrations, cloning, or VMotion take place between multiple ESXI servers, it's important to have the following firewall ports open to ensure all the traffic gets from the source to the destination without any problems:

- Port 443 for virtual machine migrations, provisioning traffic and management
- Port 8182 for high availability traffic between ESXi hosts
- Port 8000 for vMotion requests

By default, to ensure you don't unintentionally leave open services that could be a security risk, ESXi is installed with no firewall ports open. You have to configure it to open the ports just mentioned, along with any that are needed for the actual services you run on your guests, such as web services, DNS, etc.

In Chapter 6, we will discuss how to manage the ESXi Firewall via the command line and how to enumerate the ports that are available using the `esxcli network firewall` command. Here, we'll take a look at some of the firewall features, using the vCenter client. It provides some useful additional features—notably, the ability to tie the starting and stopping of services to the opening and closing of ports. Any changes made via the command line will not take advantage of these settings.

Configure the firewall and services as follows:

1. Log in to the vCenter server and select the ESXi host from the inventory list.
2. Select the Configuration tab from the right window pane and navigate to Security Profile. A list of services and ports will appear in the right-hand window (Figure 3-1).

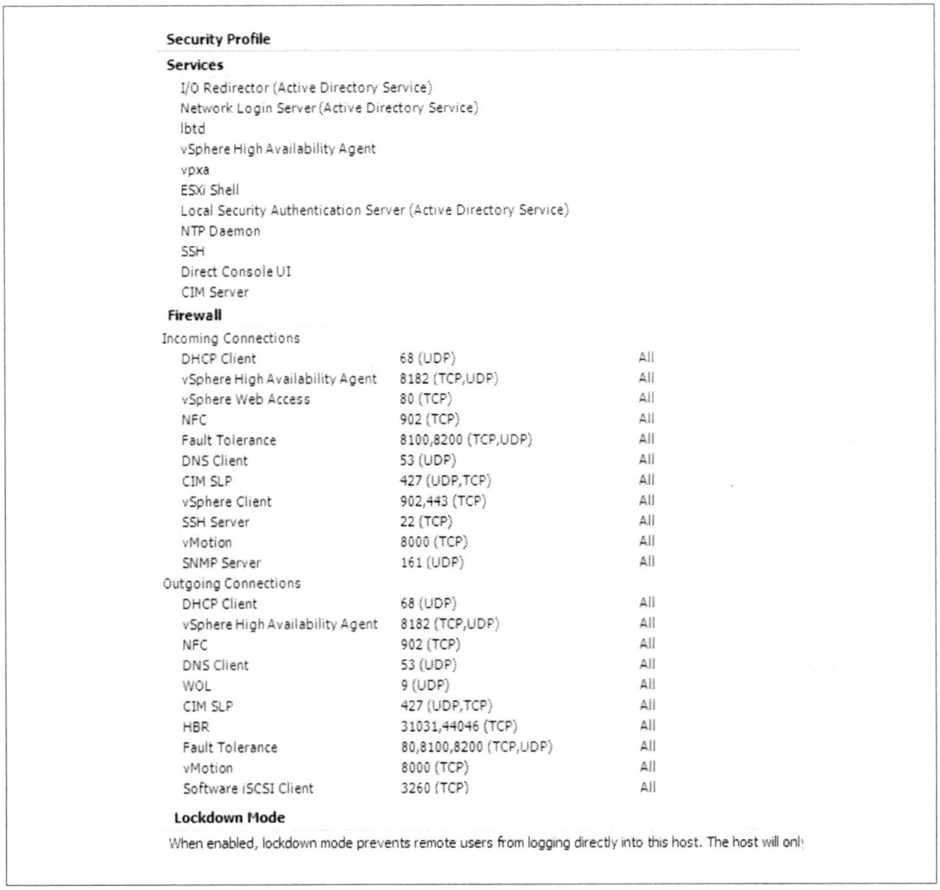

Security Profile

Services

I/O Redirector (Active Directory Service)
Network Login Server (Active Directory Service)
lbtd
vSphere High Availability Agent
vpxa
ESXi Shell
Local Security Authentication Server (Active Directory Service)
NTP Daemon
SSH
Direct Console UI
CIM Server

Firewall

Incoming Connections		
DHCP Client	68 (UDP)	All
vSphere High Availability Agent	8182 (TCP,UDP)	All
vSphere Web Access	80 (TCP)	All
NFC	902 (TCP)	All
Fault Tolerance	8100,8200 (TCP,UDP)	All
DNS Client	53 (UDP)	All
CIM SLP	427 (UDP,TCP)	All
vSphere Client	902,443 (TCP)	All
SSH Server	22 (TCP)	All
vMotion	8000 (TCP)	All
SNMP Server	161 (UDP)	All
Outgoing Connections		
DHCP Client	68 (UDP)	All
vSphere High Availability Agent	8182 (TCP,UDP)	All
NFC	902 (TCP)	All
DNS Client	53 (UDP)	All
WOL	9 (UDP)	All
CIM SLP	427 (UDP,TCP)	All
HBR	31031,44046 (TCP)	All
Fault Tolerance	80,8100,8200 (TCP,UDP)	All
vMotion	8000 (TCP)	All
Software iSCSI Client	3260 (TCP)	All

Lockdown Mode

When enabled, lockdown mode prevents remote users from logging directly into this host. The host will onl

Figure 3-1. Displaying firewall services and ports

3. Click the Properties link under the Firewall Options to open the Firewall Properties window. From here, you can open the port on the firewall by checking the box next to the service (Figure 3-2).

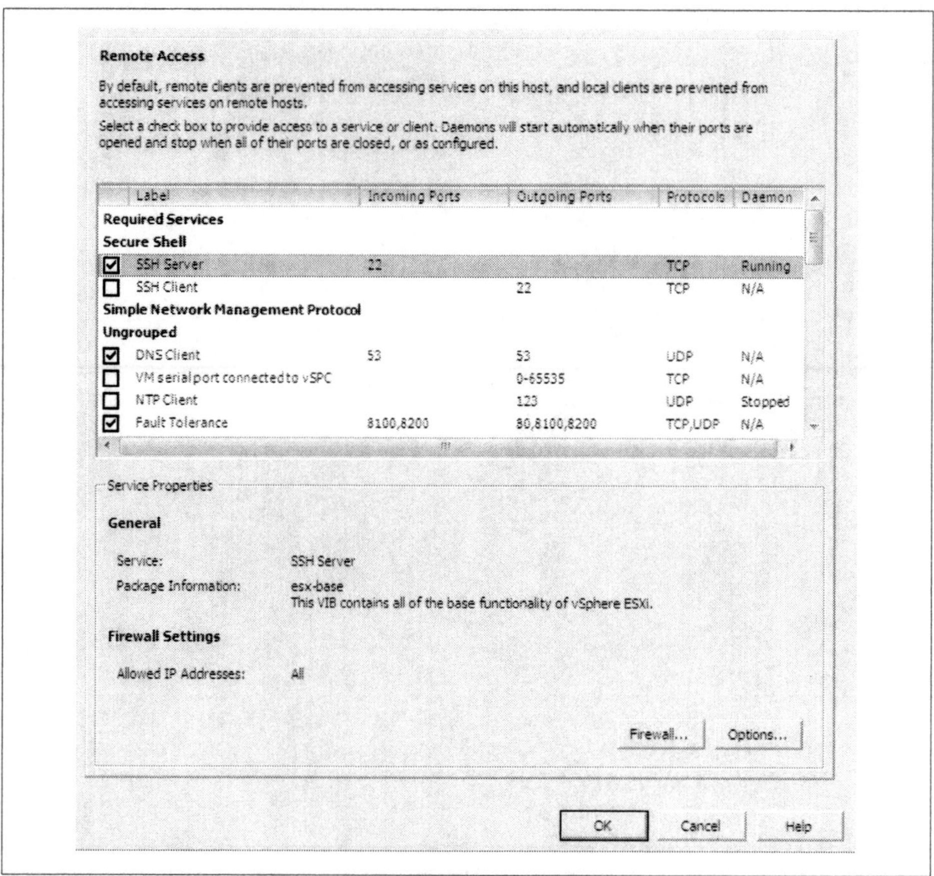

Figure 3-2. The services/firewall ports configuration screen

4. You can enable automatic starting and stopping by selecting a service and clicking the Properties link under the Services section. This new window will be displayed for certain services that support options such as SSH or NTP. Figure 3-3, for instance, shows the options available for SSH. Not all services offer these three options.

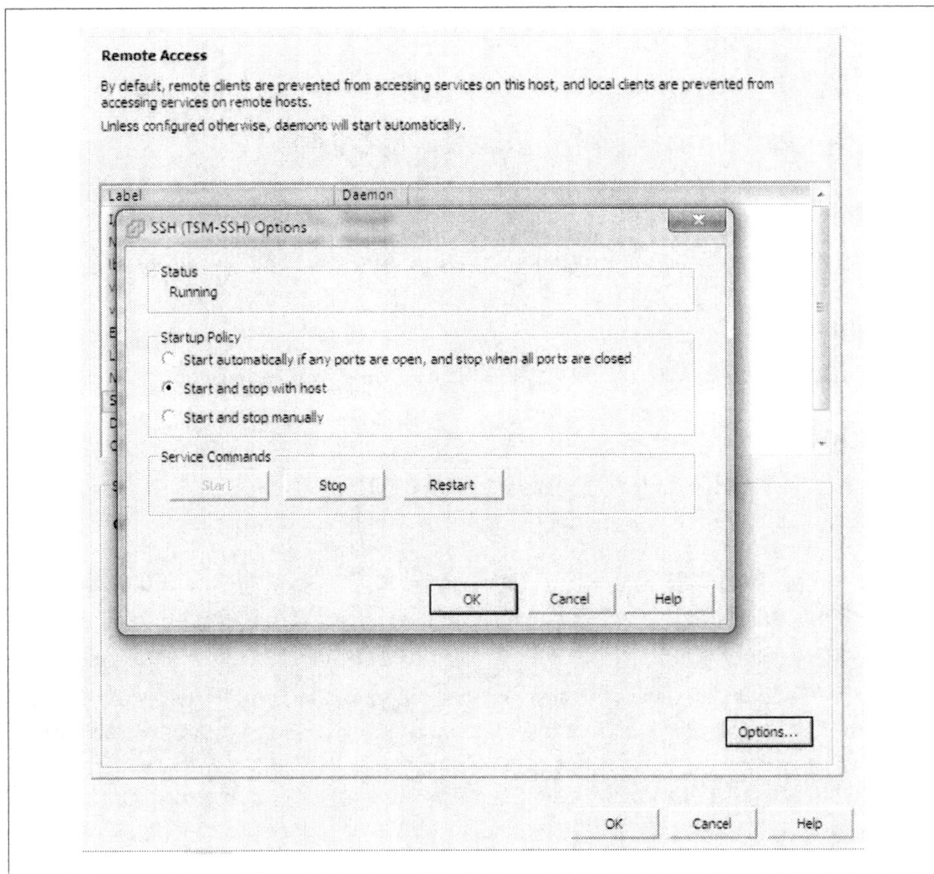

Figure 3-3. Service options for the SSH service

The configurable options for SSH running under ESXi are:

Start automatically if any ports are open, and stop when all ports are closed
: This is the default setting for many services, such as NTP and SSH. VMware recommends keeping this option checked.

Start and stop with host
: The service will start shortly after the host start-up scripts have been run and will stay up until the host shutdown scripts run, even if you close their ports on the firewall. Using this option might lead to a small delay in a service used for routine background traffic, such as NTP, if its port is opened after the host starts. However, once the port is opened, the connection will begin transmitting data.

Start and stop manually
: The ESXi Host will not attempt to start or stop services automatically. For example, NTP may not be started on a reboot, but if you start it manually and the necessary

firewall port is specified in the Remote Access area, the firewall will automatically open the port.

3.2 Creating a vSwitch for Virtual Machines

Problem

A vSwitch is needed for your virtual machines to interact with the physical network.

Solution

Use the vCenter server to build a complex or simple network for your virtual machines.

Discussion

A vSwitch, or virtual switch, behaves much like a physical switch. A vSwitch will automatically detect which virtual machines are connected and route the traffic either to other virtual machines using the VMkernel, or to the physical network using a physical Ethernet port (sometimes referred to as an uplink port). Each uplink or physical adapter will use a port on the vSwitch. By using vSwitches you can combine multiple network adapters, balance traffic, facilitate network port failover, and isolate network traffic.

A single ESXI server can have a mixture of Standard vSwitches and Distributed vSwitches. A single vSwitch has a default of 120 logical ports. However, a vSwitch can be configured with up to 1,016 active ports. A single virtual machine will use one port on the vSwitch. A logical port on the vSwitch is also a member of a port group, which we'll discuss later in this chapter. If you choose the standard defaults during the installation of ESXi, your initial vSwitch and *vswif* interfaces will already have been created for you.

Create a vSwitch and assign key configuration properties as follows:

1. Log in to the vCenter server and select the ESXi Host from the inventory list.
2. Select the Configuration tab from the right window pane and navigate to Networking. Any current network configurations will be displayed. Click the Add Networking link to create a new virtual switch.
3. Three options will be presented. Choose the default option, Virtual Machine, which allows you to add a labeled network for virtual machine traffic (Figure 3-4). Click Next to continue.

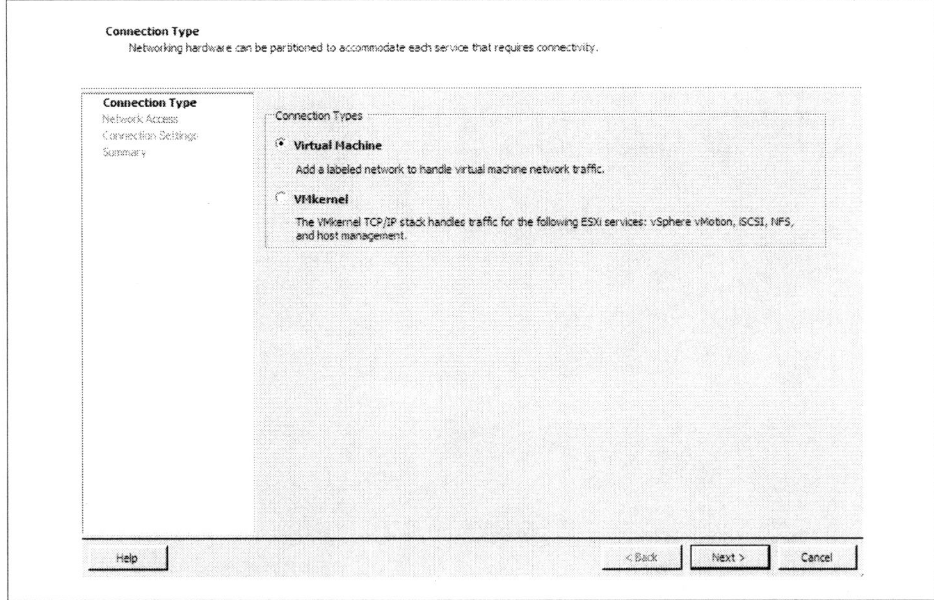

Figure 3-4. Selecting the network type

4. Select "Create a virtual switch" (Figure 3-5). A new vSwitch can be created with or without Ethernet adapters assigned to it.

   If the vSwitch is configured without network adapters, all traffic will be confined to that vSwitch itself. Traffic on each of the virtual machines on the same switch will be isolated from other virtual machines and vSwitches.

   A vSwitch that is configured with an Ethernet adapter will communicate with other physical hosts or virtual machines on its network. However, it can be isolated from other networks by using VLAN tagging.

   Click Next to continue.

5. The Port Group Properties section allows you to configure the network label (Figure 3-6). This is used to identify the network and will be used by the virtual machine to associate itself with that specific network. Optionally, if you are using VLANs in the physical network, you can specify a VLAN ID between 1 and 4094. This can generally be left blank, but check with your network administrator.

   Click Next to continue.

6. Once you're done configuring the vSwitch, click Finish to create it. The new vSwitch will now be available for use.

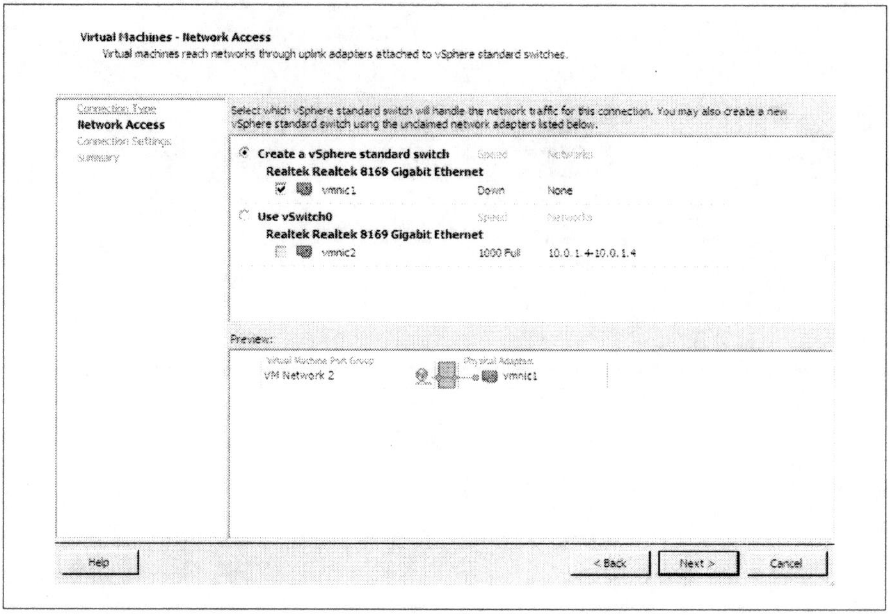

Figure 3-5. Creating a new vSwitch for vmnic1

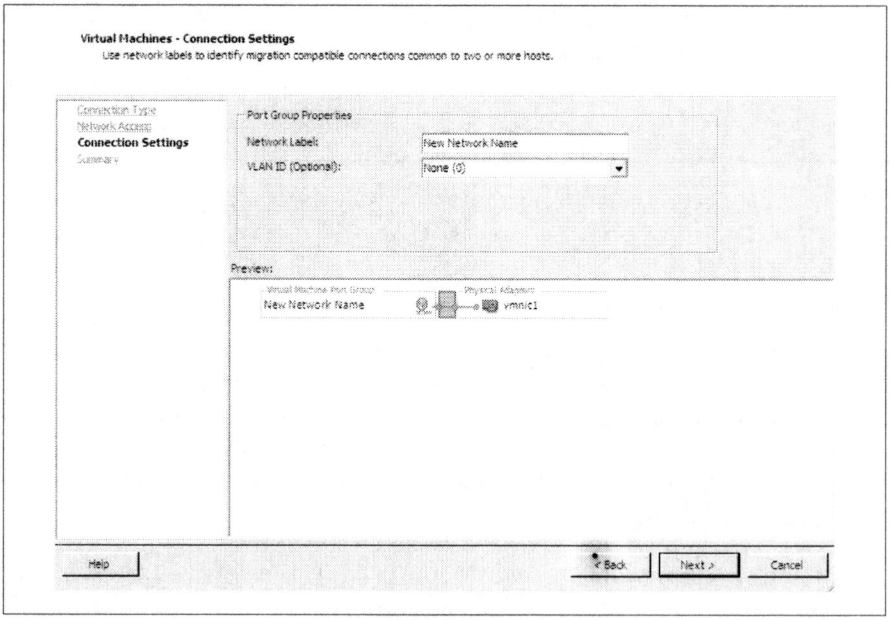

Figure 3-6. Entering property information for the new vSwitch

3.3 Removing a Virtual Switch

Problem

You need to remove a previously configured vSwitch.

Solution

Use the vCenter to remove the vSwitch.

Discussion

Removing a vSwitch is simple with vCenter. However, it may disrupt your network; therefore, you should take precautions before removing a vSwitch that has virtual machines attached to it. Those virtual machines will need to be moved to another vSwitch in order to maintain their connectivity on the physical network.

Follow these steps to remove a vSwitch using vCenter:

1. Log in to the vCenter server and select the ESXi host from the inventory list.
2. Select the Configuration tab from the right window pane and navigate to Networking.
3. All configured virtual switches will be displayed in the Network window. Identify the vSwitch to be removed and click the Remove link above it (Figure 3-7).

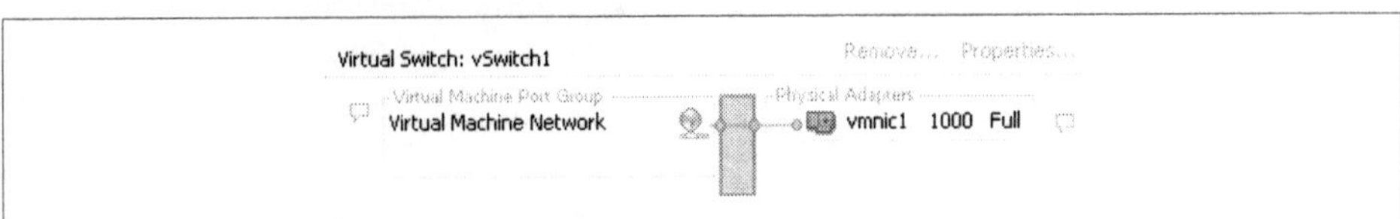

Figure 3-7. A vSwitch with the Remove link

4. A confirmation dialog box will appear asking if you want to remove the vSwitch. Select Yes. As mentioned earlier, be aware that any virtual machines connected to this vSwitch might lose their connections to the physical LAN.

3.4 Adding VMotion to Enable Virtual Machine Migration

Problem

You want to enable VMotion so virtual machines can be migrated to another ESXI server.

Solution

Use the vCenter client to create a vSwitch attached to a VMkernel port and to enable VMotion.

Discussion

VMotion allows you to migrate virtual machines between ESXi hosts without taking down the virtual machines or ESXi hosts. This is called migrating. The migration uses a VMkernel port.

We looked briefly at VMkernel ports in Chapter 2, during our discussion of the configuration and setup of such ports for iSCSI and NFS traffic. ESXi3 uses a VMkernel port to handle all network based traffic for software iSCSI, VMotion, and NFS, because these technologies are network-based and can use the same VMkernel.

However, you can also configure a VMkernel port with support for VMotion. Some architectural restrictions should be observed to make VMotion work, though:

- VMotion is designed to allow migration between similarly configured ESXi hosts. For example, CPU types must be compatible, and migration doesn't work between AMD and Intel processors.
- Typically, the VMkernel port that has VMotion configured will be on an isolated network away from all other traffic. This ensures that the complete network is available to transfer the necessary data while the migration is taking place.

VMkernel ports can be configured in the vCenter or via the command line. We will show you only how to use the vCenter client. If you read the recipes in Chapter 2 on configuring NFS and iSCSI, you will notice that the following steps are similar, but add the use of VMotion:

1. Log in to the vCenter server and select the ESXi host from the inventory list.
2. Select the Configuration tab from the right window pane and navigate to Networking. Any current network configurations will be displayed. Click the Add Networking link to create a new virtual switch.
3. Three options will be presented. Choose the VMkernel option, which allows you to add a VMkernel port to handle TCP/IP traffic for VMotion, NFS, or iSCSI (Figure 3-8). Click Next to continue.

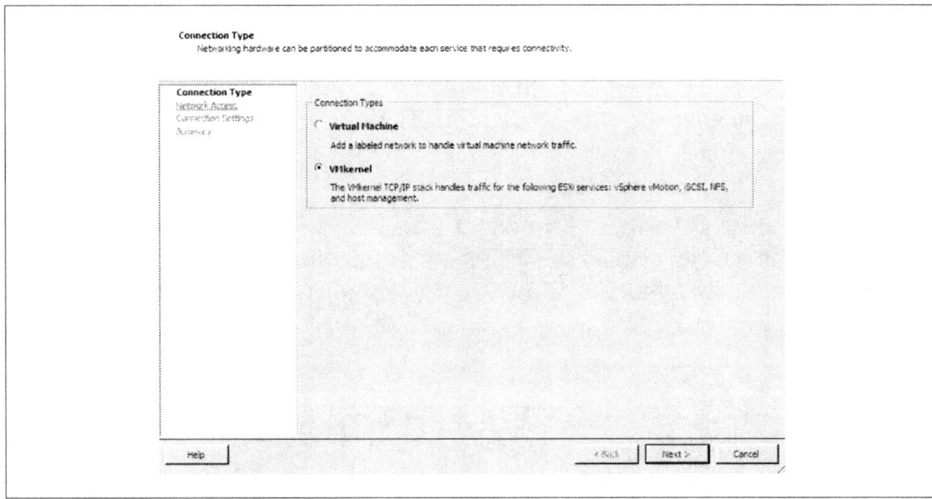
Connection Type
Networking hardware can be partitioned to accommodate each service that requires connectivity.
Connection Type
Connection Types
Virtual Machine
Add a labeled network to handle virtual machine network traffic.
VMkernel
The VMkernel TCP/IP stack handles traffic for the following ESXi services: vSphere vMotion, iSCSI, NFS, and host management.
Help
< Back
Next >
Cancel

Figure 3-8. Creating a new VMkernel port

4. Select "Create a vSphere standard switch" and select the *vmnic* that will be used to handle the VMotion traffic. Details about the configuration will be presented in the Preview window (Figure 3-9). Click Next to continue.

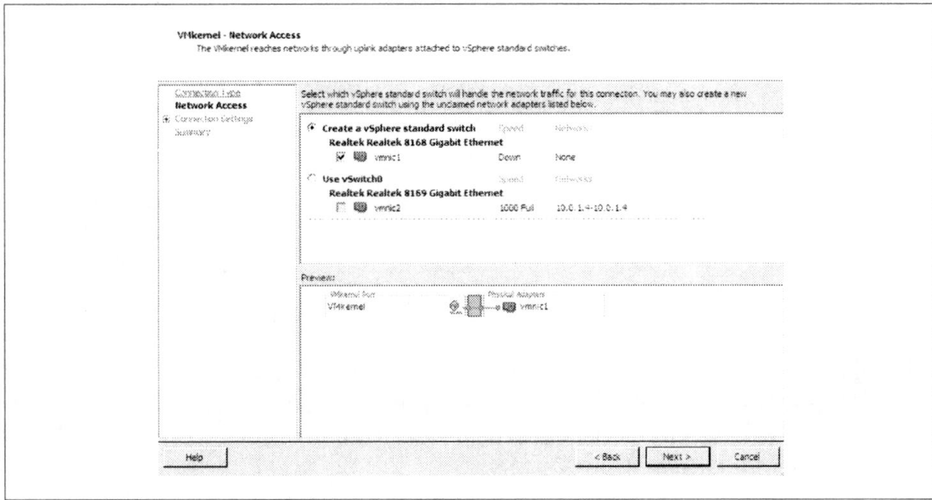
VMkernel - Network Access
The VMkernel reaches networks through uplink adapters attached to vSphere standard switches.
Network Access
Select which vSphere standard switch will handle the network traffic for this connection. You may also create a new vSphere standard switch using the unclaimed network adapters listed below.
Create a vSphere standard switch
Realtek Realtek 8168 Gigabit Ethernet
vmnic1
Down
None
Use vSwitch0
Realtek Realtek 8169 Gigabit Ethernet
vmnic2
1000 Full
10.0.1.4-10.0.1.4
Preview:
VMkernel
vmnic1
Help
< Back
Next >
Cancel

Figure 3-9. Creating a new VMkernel vSwitch for vmnic1

5. The Port Group Properties section allows you to configure the network label, which is used to identify the network. It's extremely important to use the exact same naming scheme on all your ESXi Servers to ensure that VMotion will initiate smoothly, remembering that network labels are case sensitive. If you are using Enterprise or higher licenses you can take advantage of Host Profiles to create a standardized network profile.

   If VLANs are used on your network, enter the relevant information in the VLAN ID field. The step that configures a VMkernel for VMotion is also done here: "Use this port group for VMotion" must be checked and enabled. This allows the port group to advertise that it is going to handle VMotion traffic (Figure 3-10).

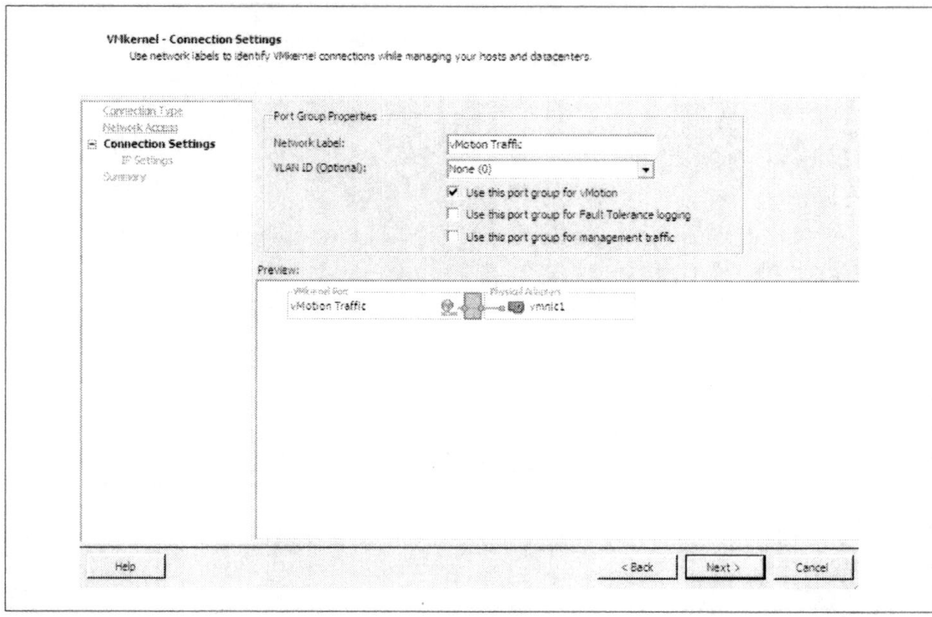

Figure 3-10. Adding new VMkernel properties information

6. Fill in the IP Address and Subnet Mask fields. If there are more detailed network settings that need to be configured, such as gateways, routing, and DNS servers, click the Edit button to configure them. Save your changes by clicking OK, and click Next to continue (Figure 3-11).

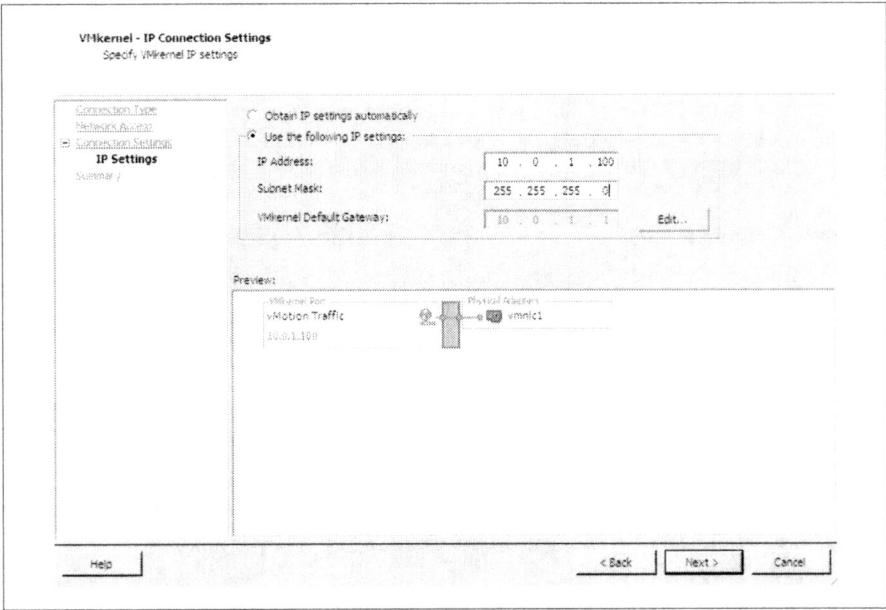

Figure 3-11. Setting vMotion IP address

7. View the summary on the Read to Complete screen and click Finish to finalize the configuration.

See Also

Recipe 2.12

3.5 Modifying the Speed of a Network Adapter

Problem

You need to make changes to the network speed on a physical network adapter.

Solution

Modify the network adapter's properties in the vCenter.

Discussion

The vCenter offers control over a much smaller set of features on the physical adapter than you can control using command-line tools. However, vCenter does let you change the port speed of specific network adapters.

To configure your network adapter's speed:

1. Log in to the vCenter server and select the ESXi host from the inventory list.
2. Select the Configuration tab from the right window pane and navigate to Networking. The current network configurations will be displayed.
3. Click the Properties link of the vSwitch that you wish to modify (Figure 3-12).

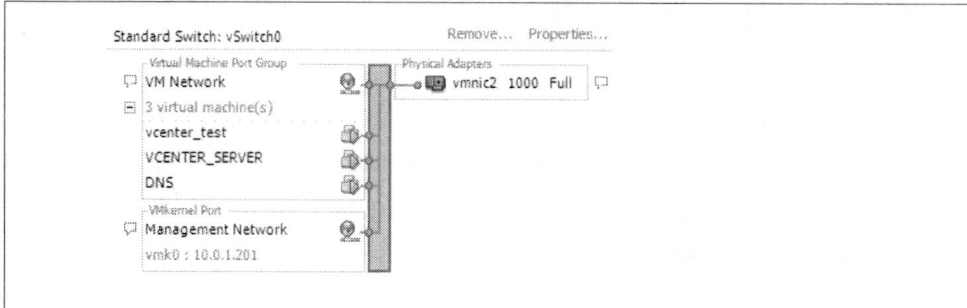

Figure 3-12. vSwitch Properties link

4. A new window will appear. Click the Network Adapters tab. From here, select the network adapter you wish to modify and click the Edit button.
5. A dialog box pops up allowing you to change the speed (Figure 3-13). Make your choice and click OK.

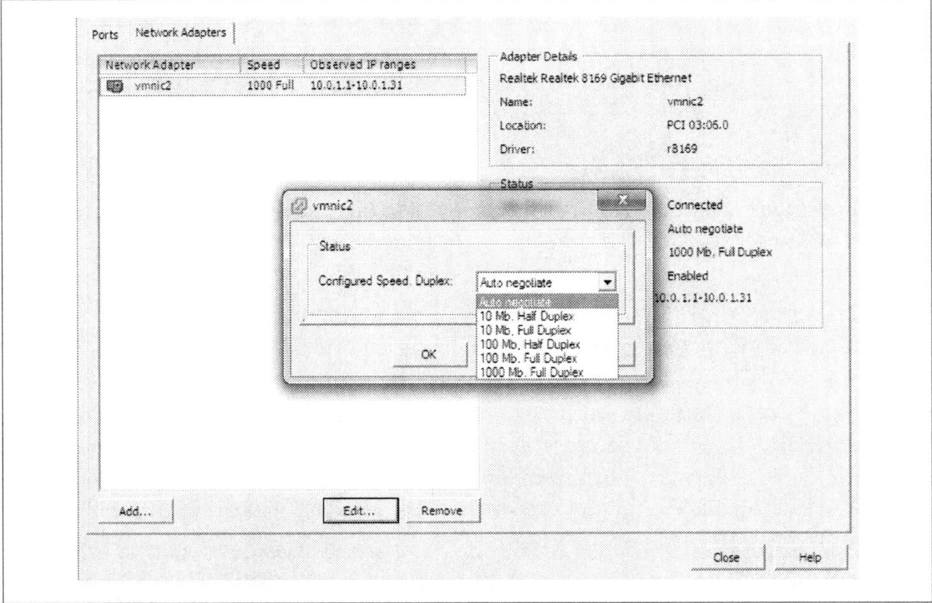

Figure 3-13. Network adapter properties

3.6 Choosing Network Elements that Protect Security

Problem

You want to make sure that the network tying your ESXi and virtual servers reflects your site's needs and matches up with the security on your physical networks.

Solution

Examine the different security measures available in the ESXi network and create the appropriate architecture or firewalls.

Discussion

Securing your virtual network is just as important as securing the physical network to which your ESXI servers are connected. A virtual network may be subjected to the same attacks as a physical network. Virtual machines that are isolated from a physical network could even be targets of attacks from other virtual machines within the same ESXi network, so it's important to take these things into consideration when planning your ESXi network configuration. In general, the security measures you use on your physical network should be replicated on your virtual network.

Within the ESXi network, virtual machines that are connected on separate network segments are isolated from each other, so they cannot read from, write to, or communicate with virtual machines on a separate network unless the ESXi network specifically enables such communication through vSwitches.

Some ways to add additional security are:

- Keep virtual machines isolated by using separate physical network adapters for each internal ESXi network. This setup is the most secure one, because you are not sharing virtual machine traffic over the same physical network adapter.

  For example, your physical network might have an external DMZ and an internal network. By connecting those separate physical networks to separate network adapters in ESXi, you physically separate the traffic. In contrast, putting those networks on a single network adapter would lead to the routing of internal and external traffic over the same network adapter inside ESXi, which could make the entire internal network just as vulnerable as your DMZ. Minimizing the potential attack locations will help you more easily defend your entire infrastructure.
- Use software-based firewalls inside the ESXI server's virtual network. Software-based firewalls can use Windows, Linux, or a virtual server appliance provided by a third-party vendor (*http://www.vmware.com/appliances/*) that sits between virtual machines.
- Create virtual LANs (VLANs). ESXi fully supports VLAN tagging to isolate your network segments. Using VLANs allows you to route traffic from multiple networks on the same network, while keeping traffic separated by the VLAN ID.

3.7 Setting the Basic Level 2 Security Policy

Problem

You need to establish security at the link level on your network interfaces.

Solution

Use the vCenter client to select the layer 2 security model that fits your environment.

Discussion

Port groups and vSwitches in ESXi have a layer 2 security policy with three different parameters you can control:

Promiscuous mode
: This option gives you access to the standard operating system feature of the same name. Promiscuous mode allows the virtual machine to receive all traffic that passes by on the network.

Although this mode can be beneficial for an administrator tracking network activities, it's a very insecure operation mode because users can see packets on the network that are designated for other systems. In other words, if enabled, it would be possible for virtual machines to see other virtual machines' traffic on the same network.

Therefore, by default, this option is set to Reject. Each virtual machine on the ESXI server receives only traffic directed to it.

Forged transmits
: This option is set to Accept by default, meaning that the ESXI server does not compare source IP addresses and MAC addresses. However, setting this to Reject causes the ESXI server to compare the source MAC address being transmitted by the operating system with the effective MAC address for its adapter.

MAC address changes
: This option is set to Accept by default, meaning that the ESXI server accepts irequests to change the MAC address associated with the sender. This affects traffic that the virtual machine receives.

If you are worried about MAC address impersonations, this can be set to Reject. However, ESXi will not honor requests to change the effective MAC address to anything other than the original MAC address. More information on this setting can be found in the ESXi documentation.

You can change these three settings using the vCenter as follows:

1. Log in to the vCenter server and select the ESXi host from the inventory list.
2. Select the Configuration tab from the right window pane and navigate to Networking. Any current network configurations will be displayed.
3. Click the properties link of the vSwitch that you wish to modify (Figure 3-14).

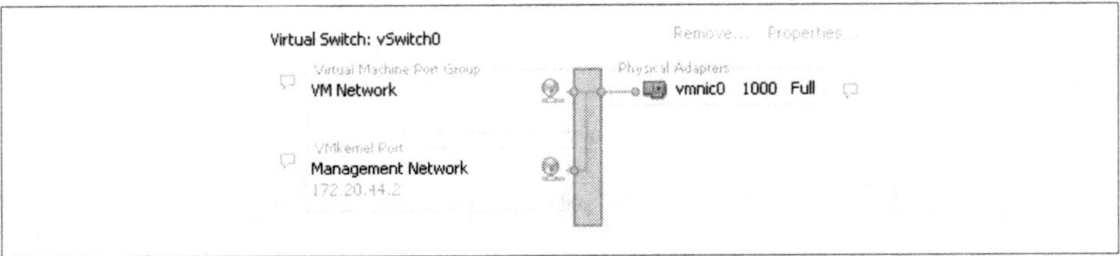

Figure 3-14. vSwitch Properties link

4. Select the vSwitch or port group that you wish to modify and click the Edit button (Figure 3-15).

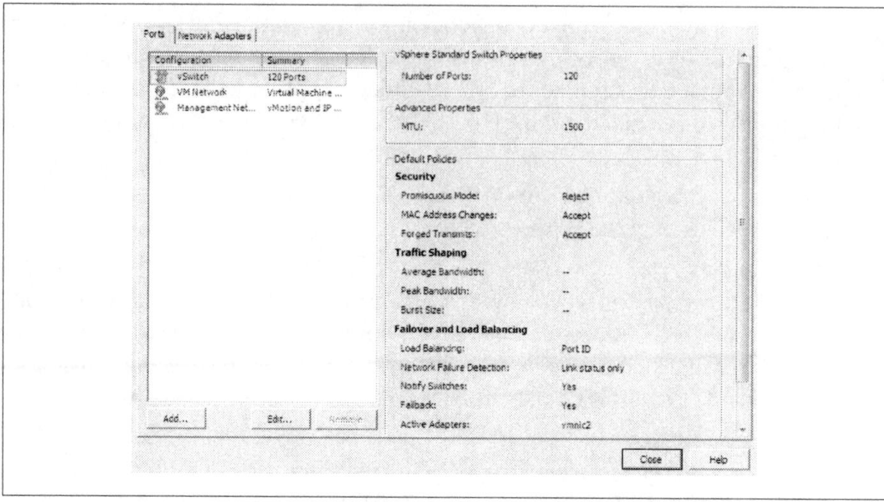

Figure 3-15. Viewing vSwitch properties

5. A new pop-up window will appear. Click the Security tab to change the security policy settings (Figure 3-16).

   From here, you can change the options to fit your needs.

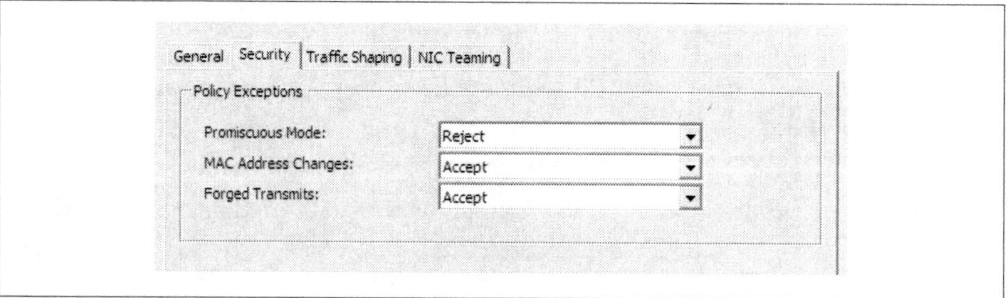

Figure 3-16. Changing security policy exceptions

3.8 Ethernet Traffic Shaping on Standard vSwitches

Problem

You want to make sure that a server does not overload or hog your network.

Solution

The ESXI server offers traffic shaping under the administrator's control.

Discussion

The ESXI server can throttle and shape network traffic by adjusting three outbound characteristics:

Average bandwidth
: The number of bits per second to allow across the vSwitch, averaged over time.

Peak bandwidth
: The maximum amount of bandwidth in kilobits per second (Kbps) the vSwitch or port group can handle. If the traffic exceeds the peak bandwidth specified, the packets will be queued for later transmission. If the queue is full, the packets will be discarded and dropped.

Burst size
: The maximum number of bytes that the port is allowed to burst. If the packet exceeds the burst size parameter, the remaining packets will be queued for later transmission. If the queue is full, the packets will be discarded and dropped. If you set the average and the peak, this is a multiplicative factor that helps to determine how long the bandwidth can exceed the average at any rate before it must come back down to the average. The higher the bandwidth goes, the less time it can stay there with any particular burst size.

These values can be configured using the vCenter client on a specific port group within the vSwitch. Bandwidth shaping in ESXi is currently supported only on outbound traffic; these characteristics are ignored for inbound traffic.

To make changes to the traffic shaping policy:

1. Log in to the vCenter server and select the ESXi host from the inventory list.
2. Select the Configuration tab from the right window pane and navigate to Networking. Any current network configurations will be displayed.
3. Click the properties link of the vSwitch you wish to modify (Figure 3-17).

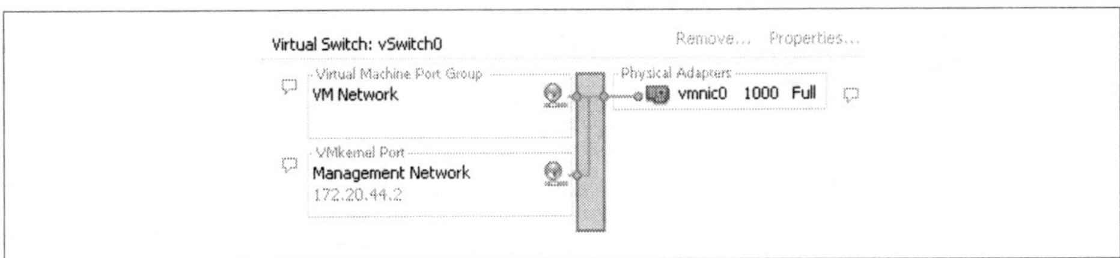

Figure 3-17. vSwitch Properties link

4. Select the vSwitch or port group you wish to modify and click the Edit button (Figure 3-18).

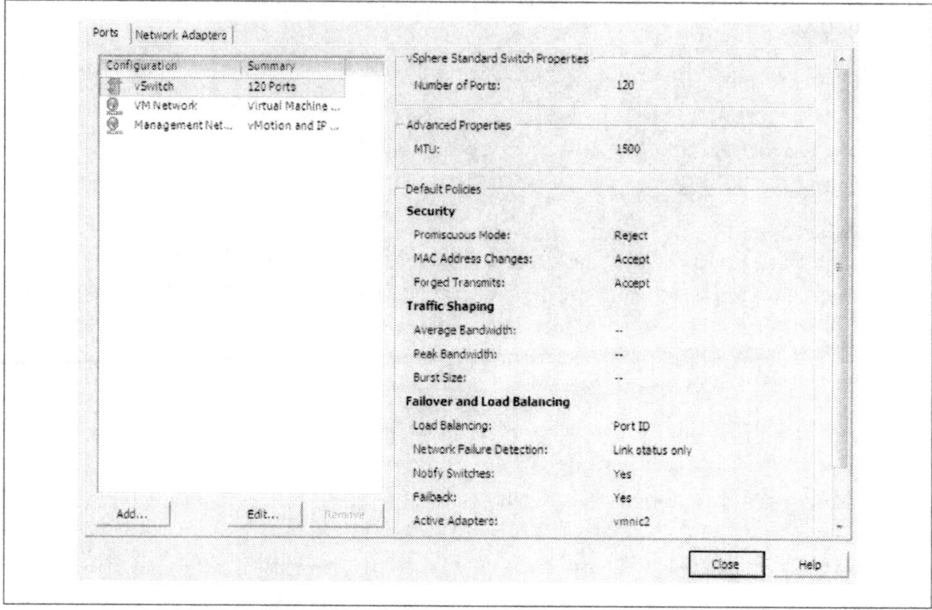

Figure 3-18. Viewing vSwitch properties

5. A new pop-up window will appear. Click the Traffic Shaping tab to change the policy exceptions (Figure 3-19).

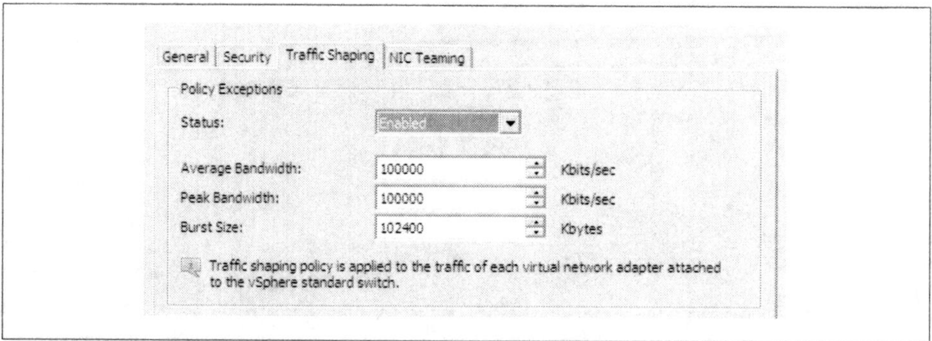

Figure 3-19. Traffic shaping enabled

6. Notice that the traffic shaping status is disabled by default. When this is disabled, you will not be able to make any changes to the various settings. To enable it, select Enabled from the status drop-down box, and the three configurable options will become available for you to modify to suit your needs.

   The traffic shaping policy is then applied to each individual virtual adapter that is attached to the port group (not to the entire vSwitch).

3.9 Load Balancing and Failover

Problem

You want to set up multiple network adapters on a vSwitch to perform load balancing and support failover.

Solution

Set up load balancing and failure detection policies within your ESXi network.

Discussion

Load balancing helps you distribute traffic evenly among network adapters, whereas failover protects you in case adapters or upstream network elements stop working. This can be particularly useful when setting up a service console network to appease ESXi's redundancy requirements for the service console.

When determining the policies that will be applied to your vSwitch, you need to consider three things:

Load-balancing policy
: Determines how outbound traffic will be distributed between the network adapters assigned to the vSwitch. It's important to understand that inbound traffic is not affected by this setting.

Network failover detection policy
: Determines how aggressively the server monitors links for failures.

Network adapter order
: Indicates which adapters are active and which are on standby.

The vCenter allows you to configure these options and a few related ones. By doing so, you can set up a load-balanced and failover-ready network within your ESXi environment:

1. Log in to the vCenter server and select the ESXi host from the inventory list.
2. Select the Configuration tab from the right window pane and navigate to Networking. Any current network configurations will be displayed.
3. Click the Properties link of the vSwitch you wish to modify (Figure 3-20).

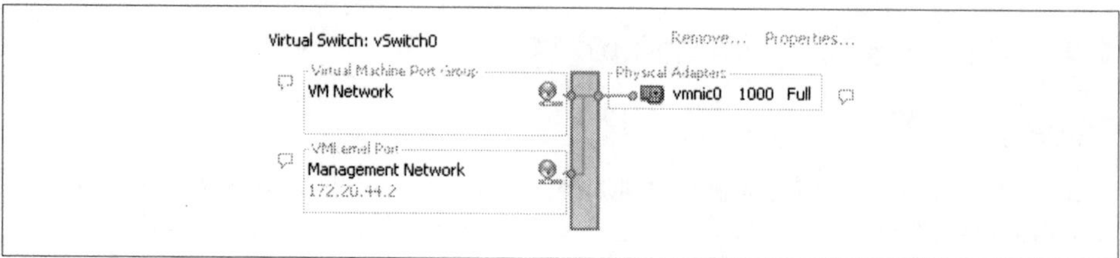

Figure 3-20. vSwitch Properties link

4. Select the vSwitch or port group you wish to modify and click the Edit button (Figure 3-21).

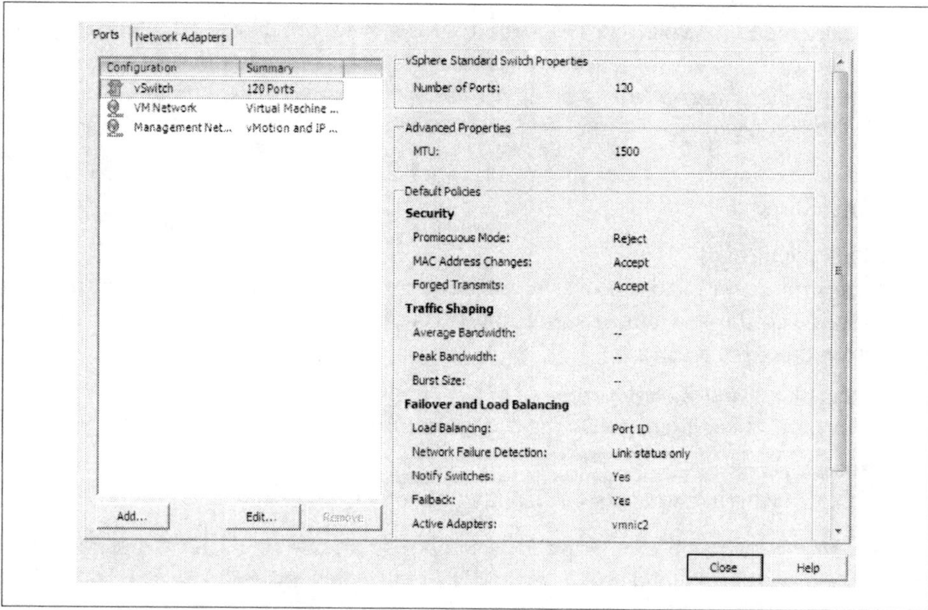

Figure 3-21. Viewing vSwitch properties

5. A new pop-up window will appear. Click the NIC Teaming tab to change the policy exceptions (Figure 3-22).

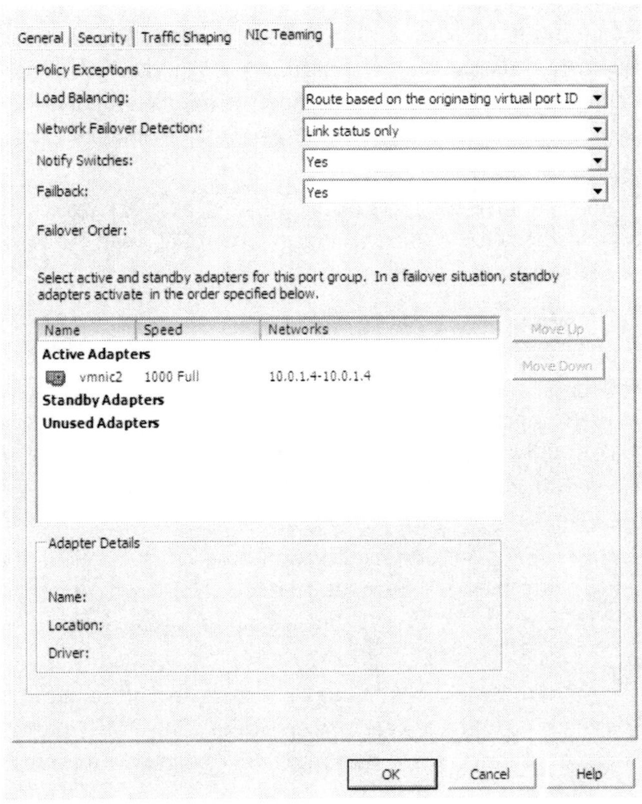

Figure 3-22. Showing the NIC teaming options

From here, the configurable options include:

Load balancing
: Allows you to choose one of four load-balancing methods:

  Route based on the originating virtual port ID
  : Choose an uplink based on where the virtual port's traffic entered the switch. This is useful because each virtual machine has a vSwitch port ID assigned to it and the load is balanced based on that port ID. It also encompasses all protocols, including TCP and UDP.

  Route based on IP hash
  : Choose an uplink based on the hash of the IP address from the source and the destination, assuming the physical uplink switches have been configured to use 802.3ad/LACP. This method will have some additional overhead as the packets are handled not on the virtual machine layer, but instead on the physical network.

Route based on source MAC hash

Choose an uplink based on a hash of the source MAC address. This option uses the virtual machine's MAC address for the basis of its load balancing. This can cause problems if you change your virtual machine's MAC address often or during a time when active network traffic is present.

Use explicit failover order

Always use the first available uplink chosen in order from the list of active adapters. Using this option will not give you any load balancing, but it will give you failover capabilities.

Network failover detection

Allows you to choose the method to be used for failover detection:

Link status only

This method relies solely on the link status from the network adapter. It will detect an external networking error such as a bad cable or upstream switch failure, but not physical switch configuration errors.

Beacon probing

This method sends out and listens for a beacon probe on all the NICs in the team. It will then use that information to determine whether there is a network failure. This option offers more end-to-end error checking.

Notify switches

If this is set to Yes, in the event of a failure, the server will send out a notice to the upstream switches to update their lookup tables. This is desirable, but it should not be used in conjunction with Microsoft Load Balancing in unicast mode.

Failback

Allows the originating physical adapter to fail back and take over the workload after a failure.

Failover order

Here you can specify which physical adapters will handle the load and in which order they will do it. There are three different modes:

Active adapters

These are used as the primary network connections, so long as the adapters are working.

Standby adapters

These are not used until an active adapter fails, whereupon one of these takes its place.

Unused adapters

These adapters will not be used under any circumstances.

3.10 Enabling Jumbo Frames on a VMkernel for iSCSI

Problem

You want to improve performance through the use of Jumbo Frames on your software iSCSI network.

Solution

Using the console on the physical ESXI server, you can enable Jumbo Frames support.

Discussion

The Jumbo Frames feature increases the maximum frame size beyond the traditional 1,500 bytes, thus potentially reducing overhead and speeding up traffic on the link. Before enabling this feature, please check with your hardware vendor to ensure it is supported.

As of ESXi 5.0, the following operating systems support Jumbo Frames and have the enhanced *vmxnet* driver that supports the feature:

- Microsoft Windows 2003 Server with Service Pack 2
- Red Hat Enterprise Linux 5
- SuSE Enterprise Linux 10

To enable jumbo frames you have to configure the VMkernel, the vSwitch, and each virtual machine on your server. This recipe and the next two cover these tasks.

Enable Jumbo Frames on a VMkernel port as follows:

1. Log in to the vCenter and select the ESXi host from the list.
2. Click the Configuration tab and click Networking.
3. Select the vSwitch that has the VMkernel Port on which you wish to enable Jumbo Frames on, Click the properties link on the right-hand side.
4. The vSwitch properties window will appear. Select the VMkernel Port under the Configuration section and click Edit.
5. A new window will appear. Under the General tab, look for the NIC Settings section which will allow you to set the MTU. This should be set to 9000 to enable Jumbo Frames. Once you make the selection, click OK and then OK again to return to the Networking section for the Host will appear as shown in Figure 3-23.

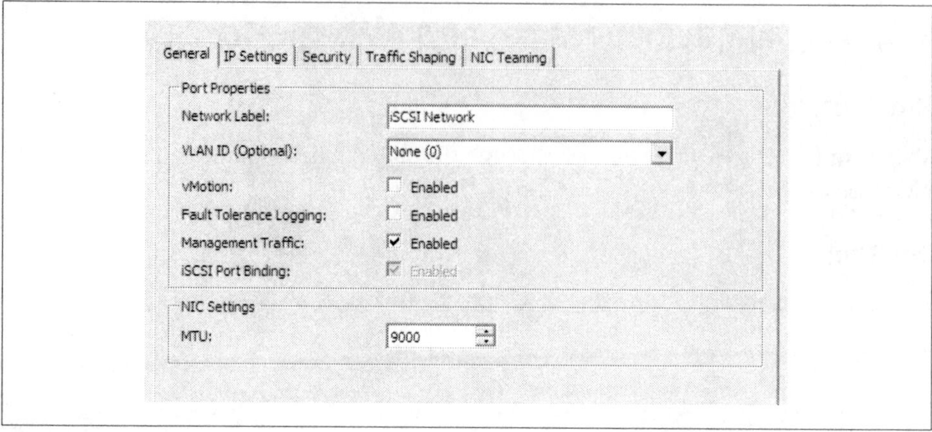

Figure 3-23. Changing MTU to support Jumbo Frames

See Also

Recipes 3.11 and 3.12

3.11 Enabling Jumbo Frames on a Standard vSwitch

Problem

You want to continue the task of enabling the use of Jumbo Frames by setting them up on your vSwitch.

Solution

Use the vCenter client and the vCenter to enable Jumbo Frames on a vSwitch.

Discussion

Enabling Jumbo Frames on a vSwitch is very similar to enabling the feature on a VMkernel port:

1. Log in to the vCenter and select the ESXi host from the list.
2. Click the Configuration tab and click Networking.
3. Select the vSwitch on which you wish to enable Jumbo Frames. Click the Properties link on the right-hand side.
4. Next, the vSwitch Properties window will appear. Select the vSwitch under the Configuration section and click Edit.
5. Next, a new window will appear. Under the General tab as shown in Figure 3-24, look for the NIC Settings section, which will allow you to set the MTU. This should

be set to 9000 to enable Jumbo Frames. Once you make the selection, click OK and then OK again to return to the Networking section for the Host.

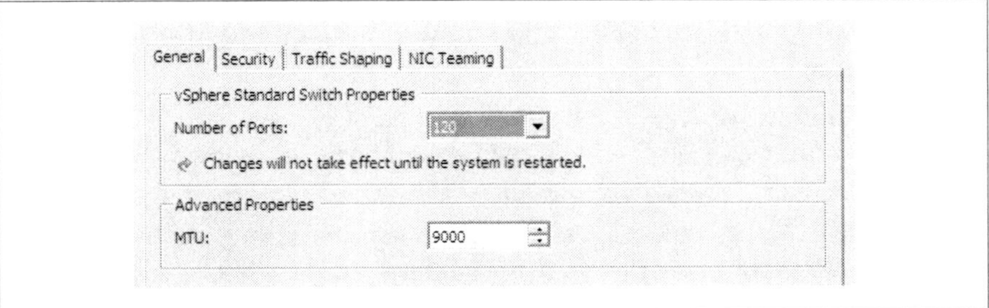

Figure 3-24. Enable Jumbo Frames on vSwitch

See Also

Recipes 3.10 and 3.12

3.12 Enabling Jumbo Frames on a Virtual Machine

Problem

You wish to enable Jumbo Frames on your virtual machines.

Solution

Using vCenter, you can enable Jumbo Frames on one or more virtual machines.

Discussion

To complete the configuration of Jumbo Frames, log in to the vCenter server and perform the following steps for each virtual machine on which you wish them to be supported:

There is an issue with vSphere 5.x with Jumbo Frames and the *vmxnet3* driver. If you are upgrading from ESXi/ESX 4.x you should keep the older version of the VMware tools. For more information, see the VMware KB entry (*http://kb.vmware.com/selfservice/microsites/search.do?language=en_US&cmd=displayKC&externalId=2006277*).

1. Select the virtual machine from the list presented to you and shut it down. Select the Summary tab, then select Edit Settings. You can also right-click on the virtual machine and select Edit Settings.
2. Select the network adapter from the hardware list and copy the MAC address that is displayed.
3. Now you must recreate the network adapter. Click the Add button and select Ethernet Adapter. Click Next. In the Adapter Type drop-down menu, select "Enhanced vmxnet." Click Next and then Finish.
4. Now that the network adapter has been recreated using the enhanced *vmxnet* driver, you need to add the old MAC address. The new NIC is still highlighted at this point. Select the network adapter from the hardware list, change the MAC address radio button to Manual, and enter the old MAC address (if you used Ctrl-C to copy it previously, you can use Ctrl-V to paste it). Click OK to continue.
5. It's important also to enable Jumbo Frames on the operating system running on the virtual machine. Power on the operating system and configure Jumbo Frames per instructions for that OS.

See Also

Recipes 3.10 and 3.11

3.13 Changing the ESXi Host IP Address

Problem

You need to change the IP address on your ESXi host.

Solution

In this recipe, we will outline the steps required to change the IP address of your ESXi host.

Discussion

In some situations you may be required to change the IP address of your ESXi host. For example, the network segment is being changed or you are doing a network restructure. Regardless, there are a few ways to reset and change the IP address. In this recipe, we'll look at using the direct console user interface (DCUI), which is the main screen on the ESXi host system.

1. If the ESXi Host is attached to the vCenter server, you will need to remove that server via the vCenter client. If your ESXi Host is not connected to a vCenter server, then skip to step 2. Log in using the vCenter client and put your ESXi Host in maintenance mode. This will move the virtual machines to other ESXI servers within the cluster. If you are not using a cluster, you may have to manually vMotion all the virtual machines before putting the ESXi host in maintenance mode. Once the ESXi host is in maintenance mode, you can right-click and select Remove.
2. Connect directly to the DCUI of the ESXi host. Press F2 to log in to the system.
3. Select the Restore Network Settings option and press enter. A confirmation window will appear letting you know all settings will be restored to defaults. Press F11 to reset the ESXi host as shown in Figure 3-25.

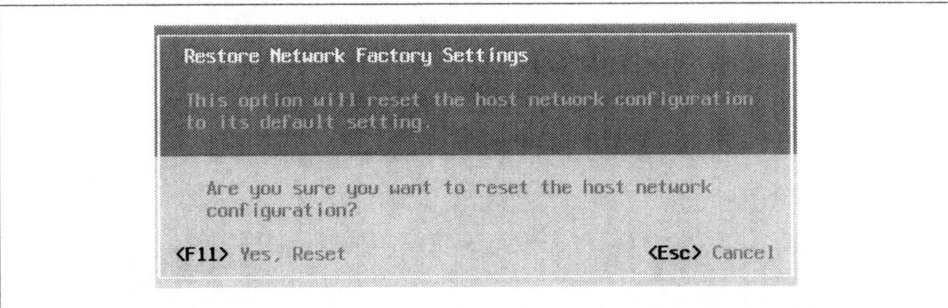

Figure 3-25. Restore ESXi to defaults

4. Once completed, you can use the Configure Management Network to reconfigure the ESXi host with the new IP address, the DNS, and the hostname.

3.14 Using the Remote Command Line to Locate Physical Ethernet Adapters

Problem

You have to map the physical Ethernet adapters to the appropriate *vmnic* without using vCenter.

Solution

Use command-line commands to identify the physical Ethernet adapters.

Discussion

There may be a time when you need to identify the physical Ethernet adapters that exist in your ESXi host. This can also be accomplished in the vCenter by clicking on the ESXi host, clicking the Configuration tab, and then clicking Networking.

To do so, log in to the physical console of the ESXI server and gain *root* privileges. Then run the `esxcli network nic list` command, which displays all the physical Ethernet adapters along with their speeds, drivers, MTUs, PCI devices, *vmnic*s, link status, and descriptions.

The following is an example of output on a server with 12 physical Ethernet adapters:

```
~ # esxcli network nic list

Name    PCI Device      Driver  Link  Speed  Duplex  MAC Address        MTU
------  -------------   ------  ----  -----  ------  -----------------  ----
vmnic1  0000:001:00.0   r8168   Down      0  Half    54:04:a6:48:7a:fd  1500

vmnic2  0000:003:05.0   r8169   Up     1000  Full    00:14:d1:1e:fe:f6  1500

~ #
```

(The description field is cut off in this example in order to fit the output on the page.) You can then use the `esxcli network vswitch standard list` command to see which vSwitches the Ethernet adapters (uplinks) are assigned to:

```
~ # esxcli network vswitch standard list
vSwitch0
   Name: vSwitch0
   Class: etherswitch
   Num Ports: 128
   Used Ports: 3
   Configured Ports: 128
   MTU: 1500
   CDP Status: listen
   Beacon Enabled: false
   Beacon Interval: 1
   Beacon Threshold: 3
   Beacon Required By:
   Uplinks: vmnic2
   Portgroups: VM Network, Management Network
~ #
```

See Also

Recipe 3.15

3.15 Changing the Ethernet Port Speed via the Command Line

Problem

You want to change the speed on an Ethernet port using the command line.

Solution

Use the `ESXicfg-nics` command on the desired physical adapter.

Discussion

Although the port speed on a physical adapter is easily changed within the vCenter, it's almost as important to understand how to change it using the command line in the event that the vCenter isn't available. Here's how:

1. Log in to the physical console of the ESXi host and gain *root* privileges.
2. List the available adapters by following the steps in the previous recipe, and make a note of the names of the adapters you wish to change.
3. Run the `esxcli network nic` command on each desired adapter to change the speed. For instance, the following command changes the *vmnic1* port speed to 100MBps with the duplex set to full (you can instead set the duplex to half by specifying the `-D half` option):

   ```
   esxcli network nic set -S 1000 -D full vmnic1
   ```

4. To verify the changes, you can run the `esxcli network nic list` command as outlined in the previous recipe:

   ```
   esxcli network nic list
   ```

See Also

Recipe 3.14

3.16 Enabling TCP Segmentation Offload Support on a Virtual Machine

Problem

You wish to enable TCP segmentation offload (TSO) support on a specific virtual machine.

Solution

Follow these steps to enable TSO support; in addition, we will enable the enhanced *vmxnet3* driver.

Discussion

By default VMware enables TSO (TCP Segmentation Offload) support on the VMkernel interface. However, it must be enabled on the virtual machine on which you wish to use this feature. The following operating systems that support the enhanced *vmxnet* network adapters.

- Microsoft Windows 2003 Enterprise Edition with Service Pack 2 (32 bit and 64 bit)
- Red Hat Enterprise Linux 4 (64 bit)

- Red Hat Enterprise Linux 5 (32 bit and 64 bit)
- SUSE Linux Enterprise Server 10 (32 bit and 64 bit)

The following steps are required to enable TSO support on a virtual machine. This can be replicated for each virtual machine. It's also important to make sure the virtual machine is powered off when making these changes.

1. Log in to the vCenter server using the vCenter client and select the virtual machine you wish to modify.
2. Click the Summary tab and click Edit Settings.
3. Select the network adapter from the list and write down the MAC address.
4. Click Remove to remove the network adapter from the virtual machine.
5. Click Add and select Ethernet Adapter and click Next. In the Adapter Type group, select the enhanced *vmxnet* option.
6. Select the network setting and the MAC address the older network adapter was using and click Next.
7. Click Finish and then click OK.

Your virtual machine will require VMtools Version 8 or newer for TSO to work with the enhanced network driver.

3.17 Enabling Jumbo Frames on a Distributed Switch

Problem

You need to enable Jumbo Frames on a vSphere distributed switch for iSCSI or NFS.

Solution

Inside the vCenter server, you can modify the switch to support Jumbo Frames. Changing this setting is a must for iSCSI-based connectivity to ensure maximum performance of the iSCSI traffic.

Discussion

The following steps will enable Jumbo Frames on the distributed switch by modifying the MTU settings.

1. Log in to the vCenter server and select the Networking view.
2. Right-click the Distributed Switch you wish to modify and select Edit Settings.
3. Click the Properties tab, and select the Advanced option.

4. Finally, set the Maximum MTU to the largest size among all the virtual network adapters that are connected to the distributed switch.
5. When completed, click the OK button. Jumbo Frames will now be enabled for that distributed switch and its adapters.

3.18 Changing DNS Entries on the ESXi Host

Problem

You need to change your ESXi host's DNS servers.

Solution

Follow these quick steps to change the DNS servers your ESXI servers use.

Discussion

1. Log in to the vCenter and select the ESXi host from the list.
2. Click the Configuration tab and then select the DNS and Routing link on the left-hand side.
3. On the right side of the window, click the Properties link.
4. In the DNS configuration tab, enter the name and domain you wish to use.
5. Choose to use a static DNS entry or have one obtained automatically from the network.
6. Enter the domain on which the ESXi host will search for domains.
7. Once completed, select the OK button.

3.19 Creating a vSphere Distributed Switch

Problem

You wish to create a vSphere Distributed Switch instead of using Standard vSwitches.

Solution

By following these steps you can create a vSphere Distributed Switch across your ESXi hosts, giving a unified network configuration.

Discussion

VMware introduced the Distributed Switch in ESX 4.x and has continued to improve this advanced switch with ESXi 5.0. By using Distributed Switches, you will create a unified switch configuration across all the hosts that are connected to that switch. This is very important when your virtual machines vMotion from server to server inside your cluster. In a traditional vSwitch configuration, you had to worry about the naming conventions of your vSwitches to ensure compatibility when doing vMotion. This is resolved when moving to a Distributed Switch, because it provides a common naming scheme across the ESXi hosts attached to the distributed switch.

Like traditional vSwitches, the Distributed Switches act like a hub, providing ports for the virtual machines to use. In addition, port groups are supported and, like a vSwitch, multiple network adapters are used as uplinks to the core network. In ESX 4.x, VMware started to support third-party switches, such as the Cisco 1000v, which uses the Distributed Switch API to provide additional features.

The following steps create a basic Distributed Switch. You will need to be running vCenter Server in order to create a Distributed Switch. In addition, once the Distributed Switch is created, you can add ESXi hosts to the switch.

1. Log in to vCenter and navigate to the Network view.
2. Right-click the Datacenter on which you wish to deploy the Distributed Switch and select New vSphere Distributed Switch. A new window will appear, allowing you to select from three different types of switches (Figure 3-26).

   vSphere Distributed Switch Version: 4.0
   : Supports ESX 4.0 and later

   vSphere Distributed Switch Version: 4.1.0
   : Supports ESX 4.1 and later

   vSphere Distributed Switch Version: 5.0
   : Supports ESX 5.0 and later (the default option)

   It's important to select the Distributed Switch that will be most compatible with the versions of ESXi that you are running.
3. Once you have selected the switch version, click Next.
4. In the Name area, enter the name for the Distributed Switch (Figure 3-27). Next, select the number of uplinks you plan to use with your Distributed Switch. The uplink ports should be available vmnic uplinks on each ESXi host. Once completed, click Next.

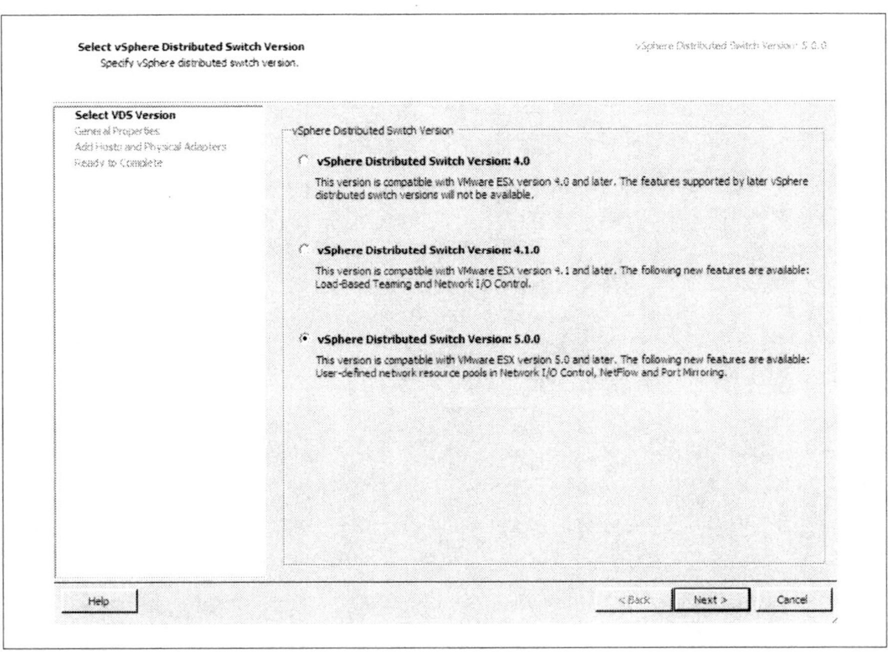

Figure 3-26. Select the Distributed Switch version

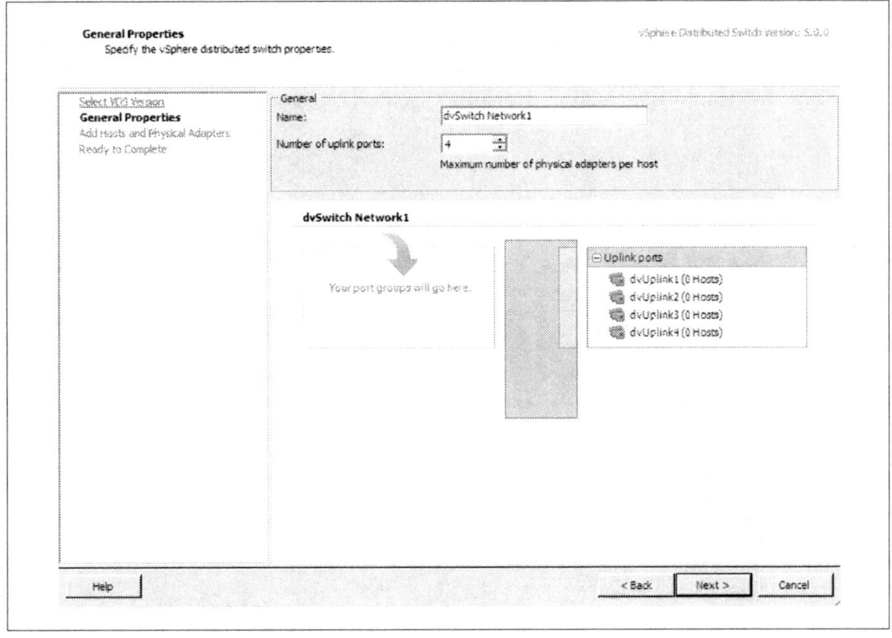

Figure 3-27. Set the name for the Distributed Switch

5. Next, assign the new Distributed Switch to the ESXi hosts and select the available network adapters. In our example we've assigned this switch to multiple ESXi hosts and assigned *vmnic1* as one of the uplinks (Figure 3-28).

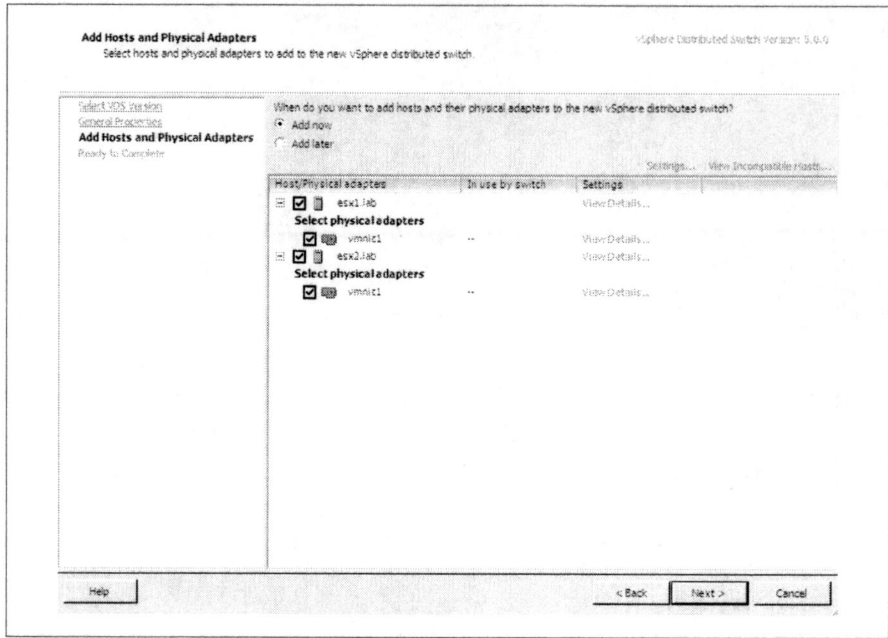

Figure 3-28. Select hosts and adapters for the Distributed Switch

6. Click Next, and finally click Finish to create the new distributed switch.

CHAPTER 4

Resource and vCenter Management

Resource management is key in any virtualized environment. In the context of VMware ESXi and vSphere, resource management includes clustering, HA, and the DRS. This chapter takes a look at the available technologies and how they work together to help you manage your environment effectively. We'll explore:

vSphere clusters
: Clusters within the ESXi environment allow you to pool multiple physical ESXi hosts to create a virtual pool of resources from the combined resources of all of the ESXi hosts. The three main elements of VMware clustering are the DRS, fault tolerance, and HA.

vSphere HA
: This provides you with a cost-effective and intelligent engine that can provide high availability within your ESXi cluster. For example, if you have a four-node cluster and one node in the cluster goes down, you can configure HA to automatically start up the virtual machines from the failed node on any remaining node that has available resources.

vSphere DRS
: The DRS actively monitors all virtual machines in a cluster and manages their resources. DRS can be configured to provide you, the administrator, with guidelines on which virtual machines can benefit from being moved to another host. You can also configure DRS to automatically take care of the migration through vMotion.

In this chapter we will discuss various aspects of these technologies and how to configure, set up, and maintain resources in vCenter.

4.1 Monitoring Virtual Machines Inside the vSphere Cluster

Problem

You wish to monitor a virtual machine inside the vSphere 5.0 cluster.

Solution

Enable virtual machine monitoring inside the vSphere cluster.

Discussion

vSphere 5 has the ability to monitor and watch virtual machines inside the cluster for a heartbeat. This allows virtual machines that time out or crash with the famous blue screen of death (in Windows) to be rebooted automatically. There are a few settings that can be configured and we'll take a look at those now.

VM monitoring
: This setting allows you to disable all monitoring, to monitor virtual machines only, or enable VM and application monitoring. Application monitoring is available via third-party scripts that interact with VMware Tools inside the guest to check and validate specific applications.

Monitoring sensitivity
: By default, there are three options that can be selected:

  Low
  : Checks are made at 2-minute intervals. A virtual machine will be rebooted after each failure for the first three failures every 7 days.

  Medium
  : Checks are made at 1-minute intervals. A virtual machine will be rebooted after each failure for the first three failures every 24 hours.

  High
  : Check are made at 30-second intervals. A virtual machine will be rebooted after each failure for the first three failures every hour.

Additionally, there is an option to create a custom monitoring policy. Do so as follows:

1. Load the vCenter client and log in to your vCenter server.
2. Right-click on the cluster on which you wish to enable VM monitoring and click Edit Settings.
3. Under vSphere HA on the left menu, click the VM Monitoring option (Figure 4-1).

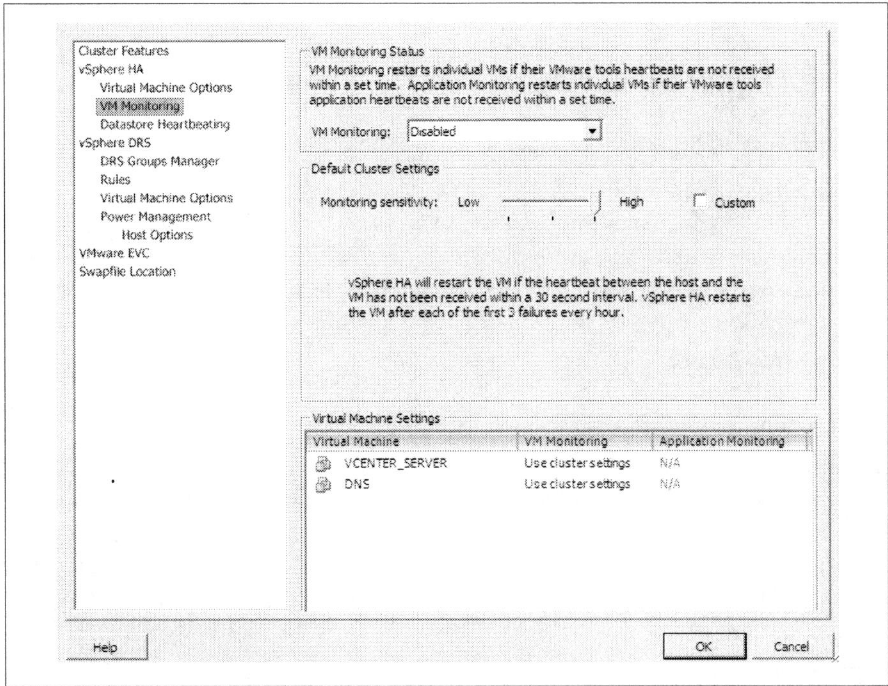

Figure 4-1. VM Monitoring

4. In the right-hand pane, select the configuration that is suitable for your environment. Once completed, click the OK button to save these changes to the cluster.

4.2 Understanding Virtual Machine Memory Use Through Reservations, Shares, and Limits

Problem

You want to apportion memory among your virtual machines to meet specific application needs.

Solution

Specify the minimum and maximum amounts of RAM that should be available to your virtual machines.

Discussion

Much like CPU resource management, which we'll discuss later in this chapter, memory management involves configuring reservations, shares, and limits. In this recipe, we will look at each resource setting and discuss their differences:

Available memory
: Allocates a particular amount of RAM on the ESXI server to the virtual machine when it is created. This amount reflects the initial amount of memory available for the virtual machine, but the value can grow or shrink as the virtual machine takes on work and contends with other virtual machines for memory.

Memory reservations
: Set a minimum amount of memory, measured in megabytes, that will always be available for a virtual machine.

Memory shares
: These work the same as CPU shares (described in Recipe 4.4) and are specified in increments of Low (500 shares), Normal (1,000 shares), High (2,000 shares), or Custom, which allows you to enter a custom value. Shares allow you to establish a priority when memory contention is taking place and memory is becoming overcommitted.

Memory limits
: Allow you to set a limit on the maximum amount of RAM that the virtual machine can consume. Memory limits are measured in megabytes. The memory limit on the virtual machine should be enough to satisfy the requirements of the OS inside the virtual machine. The initial available memory limit is specified when creating the virtual machine, but it can rise in accordance with the options discussed in this chapter.

  You'll start to see the benefits of using limits when you build your first virtualization cluster with a small number of virtual machines. This will allow you to manage user expectations and monitor your servers for actual usage so you can make adjustments later. However, you may notice performance degrade as you add more virtual machines to the cluster.

VMware also controls memory through the *vmmemctl* driver, which runs on a virtual machine and works with the server to reclaim unused memory and reassign it back to the resource pool for other virtual machines to use. This is called *ballooning* and kicks in when memory resources may be low or running out on the cluster.

Reservations not only help virtual machines to meet response time and workload requirements, but they can also lead to wasted idle resources. For example, if you give your virtual machine 1GB of memory but it's only using 256MB, the remaining memory will not be available to the other virtual machines to use.

A server can allocate more memory than the amount specified in a reservation, but it will never allocate more than the limit. When you use reservations and limits together, you should set the reservation for each machine to 50% of its limit and make sure it's set high enough for the operating system and applications to avoid surrender requests from the memory ballooning driver.

We recommend that you use limits only to satisfy specific needs. For other purposes, use shares instead. As with CPU shares, you can also leave the memory shares set to Normal as a base to start. However, if you have a mission-critical application that might have higher resource requirements, you can give it a High or Custom share value to ensure that the virtual machine will win the resources it needs when contention occurs.

You can set any of these memory measurements for a virtual machine as follows:

1. Load the vCenter client and log in to your vCenter server.
2. Right-click on the virtual machine and select Edit Settings from the menu. This will bring up another window where you can configure the virtual machine's memory resources (see Figure 4-2).
3. Click on the Resources tab. Here you can set specific memory, CPU, advanced CPU, and disk variables. We will specifically look at the memory options, so click Memory in the left-hand menu.
4. In the right-hand pane, you can specify Shares, Reservation, and Limit values for memory resources, as seen in Figure 4-2. When you've completed your configurations, click the OK button to save the changes and have them applied to the virtual machine.

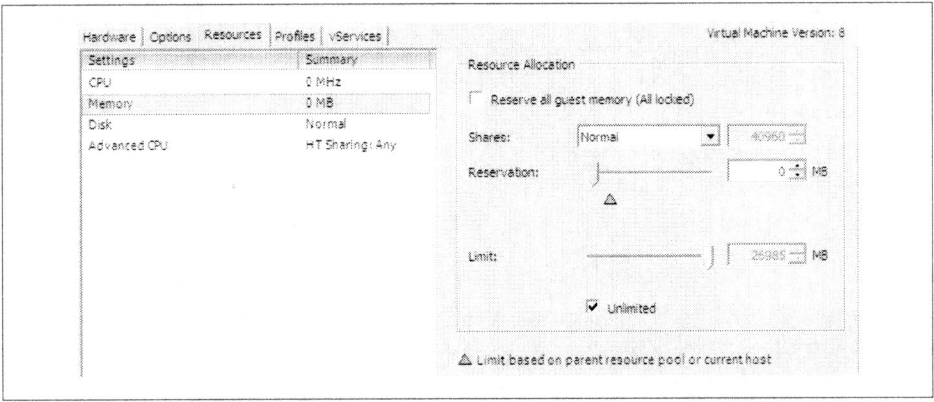

Figure 4-2. Memory resource configuration

4.3 Configuring Virtual Machine CPU Limits

Problem

You need to understand CPU limits and how to use them effectively.

Solution

Apply CPU limits using the vCenter.

Discussion

CPU limiting within the ESXi environment is a way to restrict the CPU consumption, measured in megahertz, for specific virtual machines. Setting a limit on a virtual machine's CPU consumption allows for better management of contention issues within your environment. It also allows you to know what the CPU on that virtual machine is capable of achieving when operating at full strength.

Setting the CPU limit too high or too low can cause performance issues on the virtual machine. The limit should be balanced such that there is enough CPU power at the machine's disposal to handle load spikes and high application usage, but not so high that CPU cycles are being wasted.

It's important to observe your virtual machines and adjust their CPU limits accordingly. For example, if you set a virtual machine's CPU limit at 1,000MHz but notice that its usage never exceeds 700MHz, you might consider adjusting the CPU limit on that virtual machine to 800MHz. By doing this, you are effectively freeing up 200MHz for other virtual machines and not wasting the cycles. That said, virtual machines' CPU usage is generally low, and the DRS will do a good job of managing those resources; if you set your virtual machine's limit to 1,000MHz, the unused cycles will be put back into the pool of resources.

Adding a CPU limit to a virtual machine is simple using the vCenter client:

1. Load the vCenter client and log in to your vCenter server.
2. Right-click on the virtual machine on which you wish to adjust the CPU limit and select Edit Settings from the menu. This will bring up another window in which you can configure the virtual machine's CPU limit.
3. Click on the Resources tab. From here you can set specific values for memory, CPU, advanced CPU, and disk variables. We will specifically look at the CPU limit variable in this recipe. Click the CPU option in the left window pane to configure this setting (Figure 4-3).

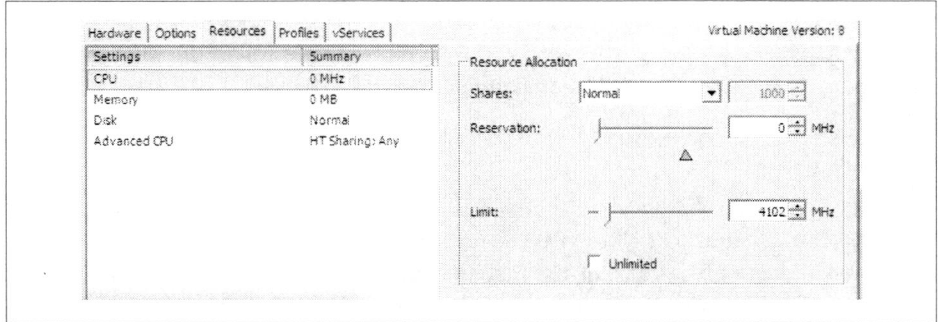

Figure 4-3. Setting a CPU limit

4. A slider bar next to the Limit label allows you to configure a CPU limit by dragging the bar; alternatively, you can enter an amount in the box or click the up and down arrows. As you can see in this example, we have given the virtual machine a CPU limit of 4,102MHz, a small amount of the CPU resources available in the DRS cluster. We could achieve the same effect by checking the Unlimited box.

   Once you are satisfied, click the OK button to make the change.

See Also

Recipes 4.4 and 4.5

4.4 Configuring Virtual Machine CPU Shares

Problem

You want to apportion CPU, memory, or disk resources among machines unequally, while remaining flexible in case resources change.

Solution

Configure CPU shares using the vCenter client.

Discussion

CPU shares allow you to regulate how many competitions a virtual machine will "win" when trying to access resources within the pool. For example, when contention occurs within the ESXi Host or cluster, a virtual machine with 2,000 shares will receive more CPU resources than a virtual machine with, say, 1,000 shares. Shares are configured relative to the other shares; thus, only the proportion of shares matters, not the values of the shares. Three virtual machines with share values of 1,000, 2,000, and 3,000 will act exactly the same as three virtual machines with share values of 1, 2, and 3. You may choose to use any number scheme you prefer, although we suggest leaving ample space between the numbers to make future additions to your resource pool easier to configure within your existing scheme (this way, you won't have to renumber the share values of all or many of your existing virtual machines).

When there is no contention for resources, shares mean very little to the operations of the virtual machines.

One benefit of using shares rather than limits or reservations is that when you upgrade the ESXi Host's memory or CPU, you will not have to adjust the resources used by each virtual machine; because each virtual machine keeps the same number of shares, new resources will automatically be apportioned in the same ratios as the old ones.

Using shares really comes in handy when planning your environment to ensure your resource pool is balanced. Of course, you can change a virtual machine's settings at any time if you specifically have to allocate *X* amount of resources, and at that point, shares may not be useful.

Typically, VMware recommends that you use shares instead of setting reservations, although we will discuss setting fixed reservations in the next recipe just in case you find yourself in a situation that requires it.

Let's take a look at configuring shares on a virtual machine using the vCenter client:

1. Load the vCenter client and log in to your vCenter server.
2. Right-click on the virtual machine to which you wish to assign the shares and select Edit Settings from the menu. This will bring up another window in which you can configure the virtual machine's CPU share values.
3. Click on the Resources tab. From here, you can set specific values for memory, CPU, advanced CPU, and disk variables. We will look at the CPU shares variable in this recipe. To configure it, click the CPU option in the left window pane (Figure 4-4).

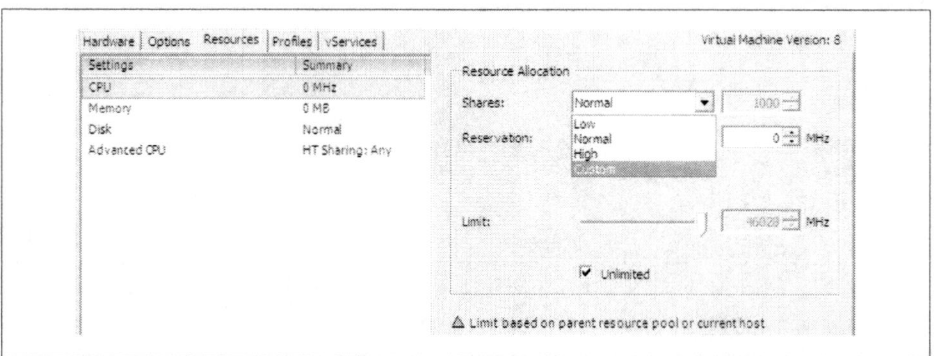

Figure 4-4. Setting CPU shares

4. In the drop-down box next to the Shares label you can choose between Low (500 shares), Normal (1,000 shares), High (2,000 shares), and Custom. Giving a virtual

machine more shares increases its chances of "winning" when virtual machines compete for more CPU cycles.

Generally, you can start with the Normal share selection until you reach a point of contention, at which point you can go back and adjust your virtual machines based on their usage and requirements.

Once you have selected the appropriate level for your virtual machine, click the OK button to save this change.

See Also

Recipes 4.3 and 4.5

4.5 Configuring Virtual Machine CPU Reservations

Problem

You want to reserve some percentage of the CPU on the ESXI server for specific virtual machines.

Solution

Configure CPU reservations on the virtual machines using the vCenter client.

Discussion

In addition to shares and limits, you can also set *reservations* on your virtual machines. A reservation is a set number in megahertz that you allocate to a particular virtual machine. Typically, this is between 5% and 10% of the processor's capacity, but it will vary based on your environment.

Setting a reservation guarantees that a certain minimum amount of resources will be available to the virtual machine, so that it can power on (if these resources do not exist or are not available, the virtual machine will not power on). Once the virtual machine is started, the reservation amount is taken away from the pool of resources over which other virtual machines compete. In other words, each of the virtual machines will take its individual reservation first, and then compete with the other virtual machines for the remainder of the (unreserved) resources.

You can add a reservation to a virtual machine through the vCenter client:

1. Load the vCenter client and log in to your vCenter server.
2. Right-click the virtual machine you wish to modify and select Edit Settings from the menu. This will bring up another window, which you will use to configure the virtual machine's CPU reservation.

3. Click on the Resources tab. From here you can set specific values for memory, CPU, advanced CPU, and disk variables. We will look at the CPU Reservation variable in this recipe; to configure it, click the CPU option in the left window pane (Figure 4-5).
4. CPU reservations are the second available option. Notice there is a slider bar as well as a box in which you can specify how much CPU to allocate to the virtual machine: you can drag the bar to the desired amount, type a value in the box, or click the up and down arrows (also shown in Figure 4-5).

   Once you have selected the appropriate level for your virtual machine, click the OK button to save this change.

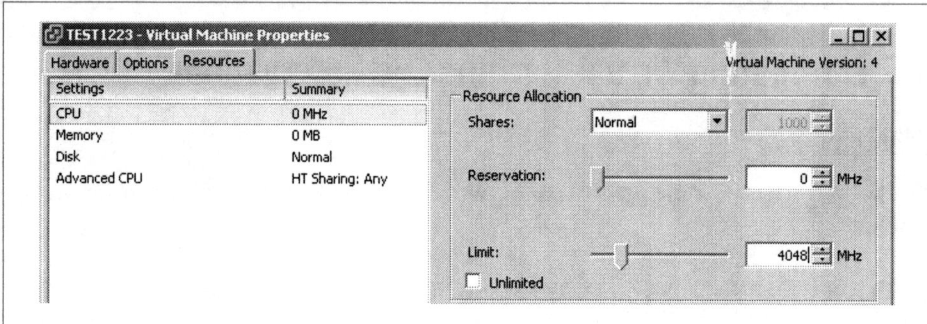

Figure 4-5. Setting CPU reservations

See Also

Recipes 4.3 and 4.4

4.6 Setting Up Resource Pools

Problem

You want to group virtual machines and manage the allocation of resources to various groups.

Solution

Create resource pools and assign resources to them.

Discussion

Resource pools are a great way to manage and divide resources among groups or departments within your organization.

Before resource pools can be enabled on a cluster, you will need to ensure DRS is enabled (see Recipe 4.12).

To enable a resource pool on a cluster, log in to your vCenter server and follow these steps:

1. Right-click on the cluster in which you wish to create the resource pool and choose New Resource Pool (Figure 4-6).

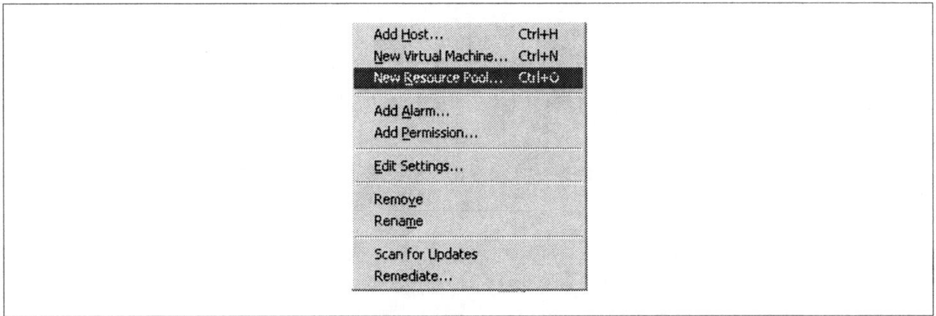

Figure 4-6. Creating a new resource pool

2. You will now be presented with a new window from which you can configure the resource pool (Figure 4-7).

   The CPU and memory resource allocations for the resource pool work similarly to the way they work for virtual machines. For example, we have given this resource pool a reservation of 12,066MB of memory and 12,066MHz of CPU. Because we left the Expandable option checked, the pool can burst above the 12,066MHz reservation if required and if the resources are available in the cluster. Refer to Recipes 4.7 and 4.8 for more detailed information.

   You can adjust these values to suit your needs and divide your resource pools between production, development, etc.

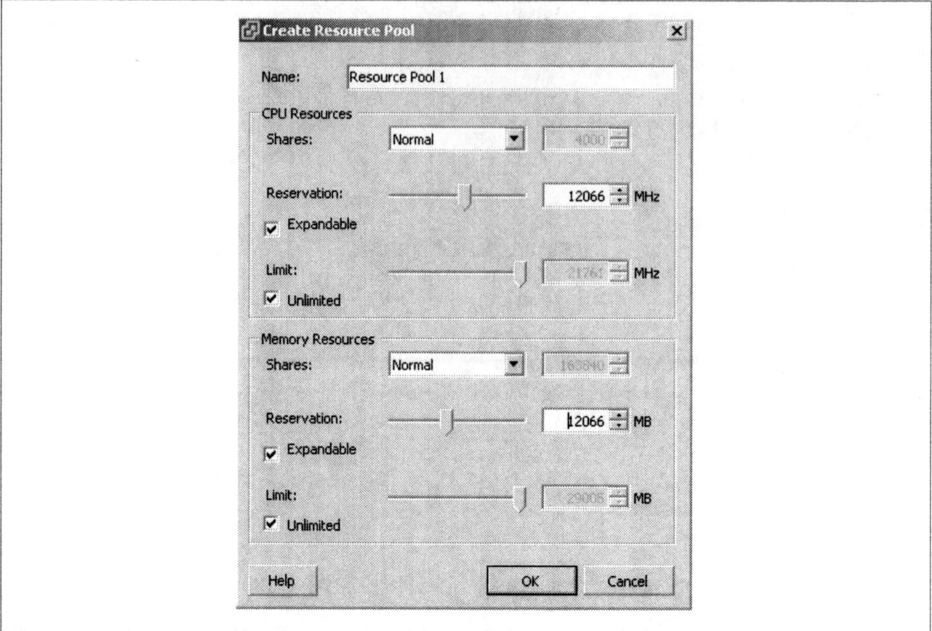

Figure 4-7. Setting values on the new resource pool

3. When you're finished, click the OK button and the resource pool will be added.

Adding new virtual machines to the resource pool can be done in two ways:

- By dragging the virtual machine into the resource pool in the vCenter client
- By placing a new virtual machine into an existing resource pool when you create the virtual machine

See Also

Recipe 4.7

4.7 Understanding Resource Pools

Problem

You want to understand how resource pools work and what capabilities they offer.

Solution

Investigate the various resource pool options and how to use them.

Discussion

Resource pools can be used to create partitions of available CPU and memory. Resource pools help you better manage and use resources across different departments or within a group of servers.

For example, perhaps you want to give your production team 20GHz of CPU and 20GB of memory, and your development team 10GHz of CPU and 10GB of memory. You can accomplish this by creating resource pools and assigning the virtual machines for the given departments to their respective pools (Figure 4-8).

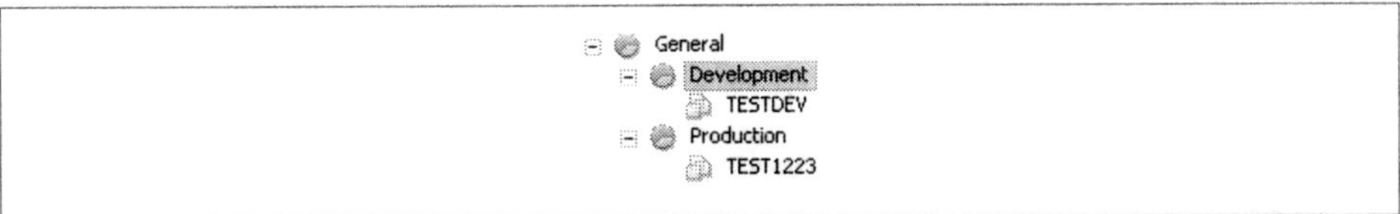

Figure 4-8. Example resource pool layout

Notice that in Figure 4-8 we have a master resource pool called General and two sub-resource pools called Development and Production. In this configuration, the subresource pools are assigned resources from the master (General) resource pool. In this example, the Development and Production subresource pools have been assigned the amounts shown in Figure 4-9.

CPU Reservation:	**0 MHz**	Memory Reservation:	**0 MB**
CPU Reservation Used:	**17667 MHz**	Memory Reservation Used:	**20964 MB**
CPU Unreserved:	**4094 MHz**	Memory Unreserved:	**8041 MB**
CPU Reservation Type:	**Expandable**	Memory Reservation Type:	**Expandable**

View: CPU Memory

Name	Reservation - MHz	Limit - MHz	Shares	Shares Value	% Shares	Type	App Owner
Development	12496	Unlimited	Normal	4000	50	Expandable	
Production	5171	Unlimited	Normal	4000	50	Expandable	

Figure 4-9. Example resource pool reservations

Let's take a closer look at the reservations we've given each resource pool:

General resource pool
: The General resource pool has 4,094MHz and 8,041MB of unreserved resources available for the development and production subpools to use. It is not handed out all at once at the start, but rather is made available as needed (see the next recipe for details).

Development subresource pool
: We have given the Development resource pool a total of 12,496MHz of reserved CPU.

Production subresource pool
: The Production resource pool has only 5,171MHz of reserved CPU.

In this example, if the resources required by the Production pool exceed 5,171MHz of CPU, it will borrow resources from the master resource pool, which has 4,094MHz available.

See Also

Recipes 4.6, 4.8, and 4.12

4.8 Expandable Reservations in Resource Pools

Problem

You want to understand expandable reservations.

Solution

Investigate expandable reservations and when and how they should be used.

Discussion

Expandable reservations give extra flexibility when you allocate resources to a specific resource pool. You can assign a minimum set of resources to each subresource pool and allow it, by defining the reservation as Expandable, to get more resources from the ESXI server as needed. Thus, on a day when the development team is racing to do a lot of bug fixing to meet a deadline, its subresource pool may expand beyond the normal limits. On another day, the production subresource pool may get more resources.

However, be aware that once a reservation has been exceeded/expanded, those additional resources will not be freed up again until the virtual machine is shut down and you explicitly reduce its reservation. You should also be careful when using expandable resource pools to ensure that your virtual machines do not become dependent on extra resources being available. If a subresource pool routinely expands far beyond its original allocation, you should increase the original allocation and add more hardware resources if necessary.

Notice that in Figure 4-10 we have two resource pools, Development and Production, which are each set to Expandable. Examining this figure further, you'll see that we have 4,094MHz of CPU and 8041MB of memory unreserved at the top level of our resource pool. Because both of our subresource pools are set to Expandable, when they use the reservations we have set for them, they can borrow from the unreserved values available in the top-level resource pool.

CPU Reservation:	0 MHz	Memory Reservation:	0 MB
CPU Reservation Used:	17667 MHz	Memory Reservation Used:	20964 MB
CPU Unreserved:	4094 MHz	Memory Unreserved:	8041 MB
CPU Reservation Type:	Expandable	Memory Reservation Type:	Expandable

View: CPU Memory

Name	Reservation - MHz	Limit - MHz	Shares	Shares Value	% Shares	Type	App Owner
Development	12496	Unlimited	Normal	4000	50	Expandable	
Production	5171	Unlimited	Normal	4000	50	Expandable	

Figure 4-10. Expandable resource pools

Expandable reservations also come in handy when a resource pool has used all of its resources and a virtual machine needs to be powered on; if the resource pool has no available resources left, it can borrow resources from the top-level pool to ensure that the virtual machine can be powered on.

Let's look at how to configure expandable reservations on a resource pool:

1. Load the vCenter client and log in to your vCenter server.
2. Right-click on the resource pool you wish to edit and select Edit Settings (Figure 4-11).

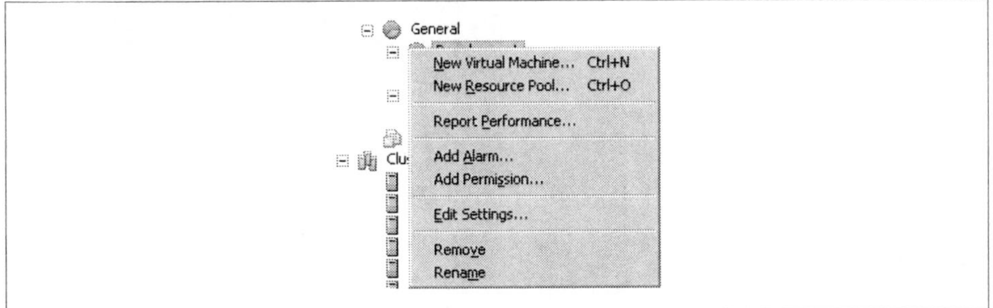

Figure 4-11. Editing a resource pool

3. The Edit Settings screen (Figure 4-12) lets you adjust the memory and CPU resources reserved for the selected resource pool. Notice that you can set expandable reservations on both CPU and memory resources, independently. To enable expandable resources, put a check in the Expandable box.

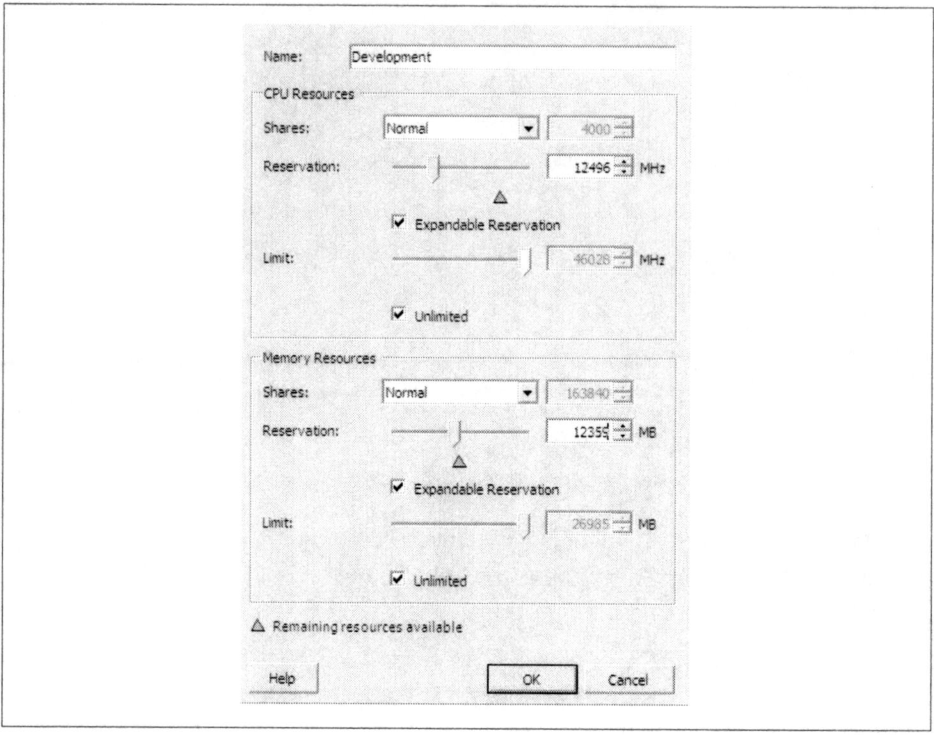

Figure 4-12. Editing expandable reservations

Once you're finished, click OK to have the changes applied.

See Also

Recipe 4.6

4.9 Creating a Cluster

Problem

You want to create a cluster to manage the resources offered by multiple ESXI servers together.

Solution

Use the vCenter client to create a VMware Cluster.

Discussion

Creating a cluster inside the vCenter allows you to combine multiple ESXi hosts in a centralized group by placing all of their CPU and memory resources into a general pool for use by virtual machines. When you add an ESXi Host to a cluster, the resources will automatically become available for use by the virtual machines.

For example, Figure 4-13 shows two ESXi hosts, each of which has 16GB of memory and two quad-core CPUs (i.e., 8 CPUs per ESXi host, for a total of 16). Because clustering pools the resources, you effectively have an enormous unified pool of CPUs and memory for the virtual machines to run. Combining a cluster with HA and DRS will further enhance your environment.

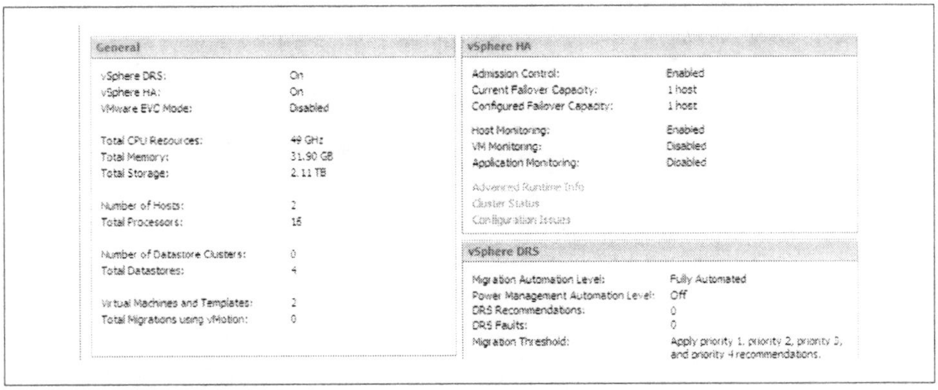

Figure 4-13. VMware cluster overview

There are a few requirements that should be completed prior to creating a cluster.

Storage
: All ESXi hosts should have access to the same shared storage. This can be a SAN via iSCSI, Fibre Channel, FCoE, or NFS.

VMFS volumes
: Virtual machines need to access all the VMFS datastores that are presented to the ESXI servers in the cluster. This is important to facilitate HA in case of a physical hardware failure.

Processor support
: The physical ESXI servers that make up the cluster should have the same family of processor, such as Intel or AMD. You cannot mix Intel and AMD processors inside the same cluster. The second most important thing is to ensure the processor models inside the family are compatible with each other. VMware includes an EVC mode that allows the combination of different processor generations to work by taking the highest (newest) grade processor and downgrading it to the slow older model. If you are mixing processor generations, you should enable this feature.

Networking
: The ESXi hosts must be configured to use a common vMotion network. This network must be accessible between all ESXI servers inside the cluster.

> You do not need a license to create ESXi clusters. However, to take advantage of HA and DRS, you will need to obtain a license key from VMware.

VMware has done a really nice job of making it simple to add a new cluster in the vCenter:

1. Load the vCenter client and log in to your vCenter server.
2. Right-click on the datacenter name and select New Cluster (Figure 4-14).

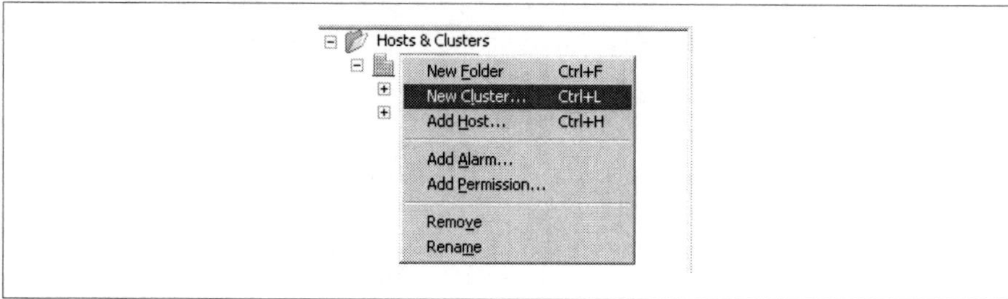

Figure 4-14. Adding a new cluster to a datacenter

The New Cluster Wizard will launch to guide you through the process of creating the new cluster. The first screen in the wizard will ask you to enter a name for the cluster and indicate whether or not to enable two features:

Turn on vSphere HA
: This feature is available only to users who have a license for the HA product extension. When you enable VMware HA, it will detect and provide rapid recovery of virtual machines if an ESXi Host fails. This is an optional feature and doesn't need to be enabled to create a basic cluster.

Turn on VSphere DRS
: This feature also requires a license. DRS allows the vCenter server to manage hosts as an aggregate pool of resources. Clusters can be broken down into smaller groups by using resource pools. VMware DRS also allows the vCenter to manage resources on virtual machines, even placing them on different hosts if used in conjunction with VMotion. This is an optional feature that is not required to create a cluster.

When you've made your selections, press the Next button to continue. Additional cluster features (including DRS and HA) can be enabled or disabled at a later time using processes described elsewhere in this chapter.

3. VMware EVC will allow you to enable enhanced vMotion between different CPU types. You can select different ESXi hosts, and this feature is limited to both AMD and Intel. You cannot mix Intel and AMD servers in the same cluster at this time. This feature is useful if you have hosts with older CPUs and are adding in new hosts and wish to enable compatibility. Once finished, select Next.
4. Next, you will be asked where to store the swapfiles for the virtual machines. VMware gives you two options here:
   - Store the swapfile in the same directory as the virtual machine. (Recommended.)
   - Store the swapfile in the datastore specified by the host. (This option is not recommended because you could experience degraded performance.)

   Make your selection, then press the Next button to continue.
5. Finally, review the summary and click Finish to initiate building the cluster.

You can now add ESXi hosts to the cluster (see Recipe 4.10).

See Also

Recipes 4.10 and 4.12

4.10 Adding Hosts to a Cluster

Problem

You wish to add more hosts to your ESXi cluster.

Solution

Use the vCenter client to add new hosts to an existing ESXi cluster.

Discussion

Adding additional ESXI servers to an already established cluster is easy in vCenter:

1. Load the vCenter client and log in to your vCenter server.
2. Right-click on the datacenter name and select Add Host. This launches the Add Host Wizard in a new window (Figure 4-15).

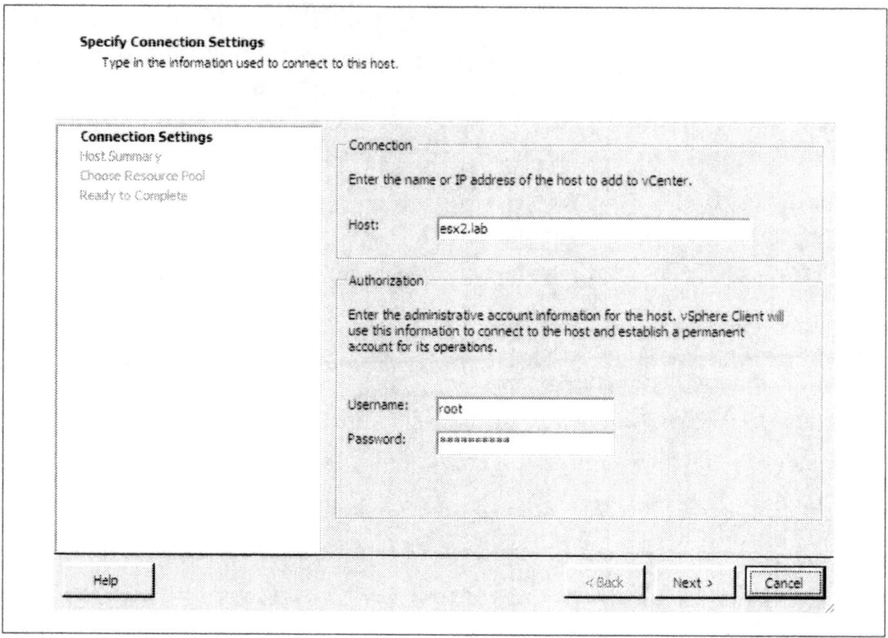

Figure 4-15. Adding your IP address and login information in the Add Host Wizard

The first screen in the Add Host Wizard will ask you for some basic information:

Hostname
: Enter the hostname of the server, such as *ESXi01.yourdomain.com*. Although ESXi allows you to use an IP address, you should *always* use a fully qualified domain name as the hostname to ensure maximum compatibility, because ESXi relies heavily on DNS.

Username
: Enter the username of the user who has administrative privileges. Typically, this is the *root* user, although this can be changed if required.

Password
: Enter the password for the username just entered.

When you are satisfied with your entries, click the Next button.

3. Next, you will be presented with an informational summary showing you the name, model, version, and vendor of the host that is being added and a list of any virtual machines on that host. Click Next to continue.
4. Next, select the licenses that will be applied to this ESXi Host. If you are using evaluation licenses, you can select that option as well. Click Next.
5. Next, Lockdown mode, when enabled, prevents remote users from logging into the ESXi Host using administrative accounts such as root or admin (Figure 4-16). If this mode is enabled and no other accounts exist, the ESXi Host can be managed

only from the vCenter. However, the administrative accounts will be able to log in to the console on the ESXi Host. This feature can be changed at a later time; if you are unsure you can leave it unchecked and enable lockdown mode later if security becomes a concern. Click Next to continue the installation.

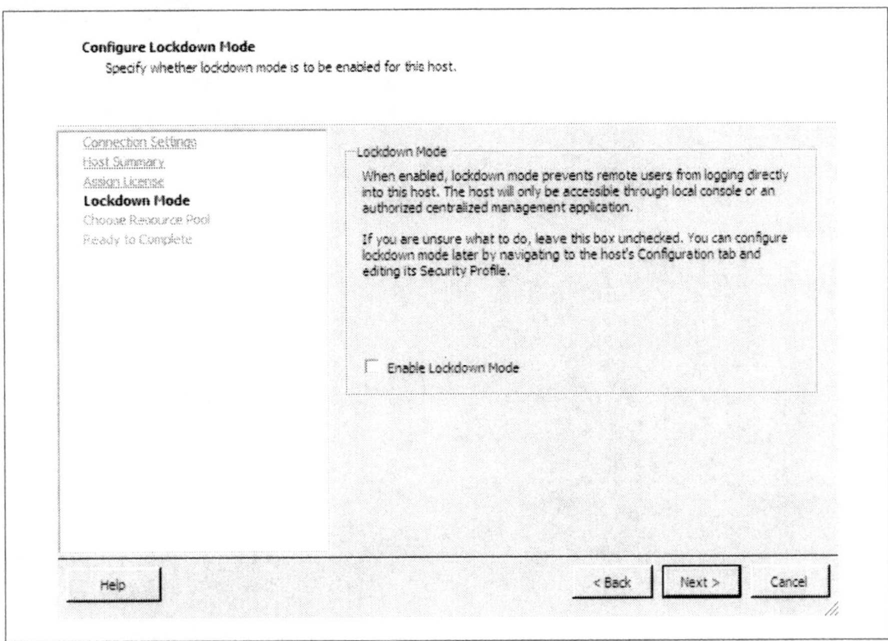

Figure 4-16. Enable lockdown mode

6. The next screen in the wizard is the resource pool configuration screen. You will be presented with two options, as shown in Figure 4-17. These options are pretty self-explanatory, but we'll take a quick look at them anyway:

   Put all of this host's virtual machines into the cluster's root resource pool. Resource pools currently present on the host will be deleted.
   : Assuming you have a resource pool set up in your cluster, this option will take all the virtual machines from the single ESXi resource pool and move them into the cluster's pool. Once that operation is completed, it will remove the resource pools from the single ESXI server. Be careful here—remember that the virtual machines currently in the pool are getting their resources based on their pool's settings, and adding virtual machines to the pool could take resources away from the existing virtual machines.

   Create a new resource pool for this host's virtual machines and resource pools. This preserves the host's current resource pool hierarchy.
   : This option allows you to keep the resource pools you have already set up on your single ESXi Host. It will create new resource pools within the cluster that match those currently available on the ESXi Host.

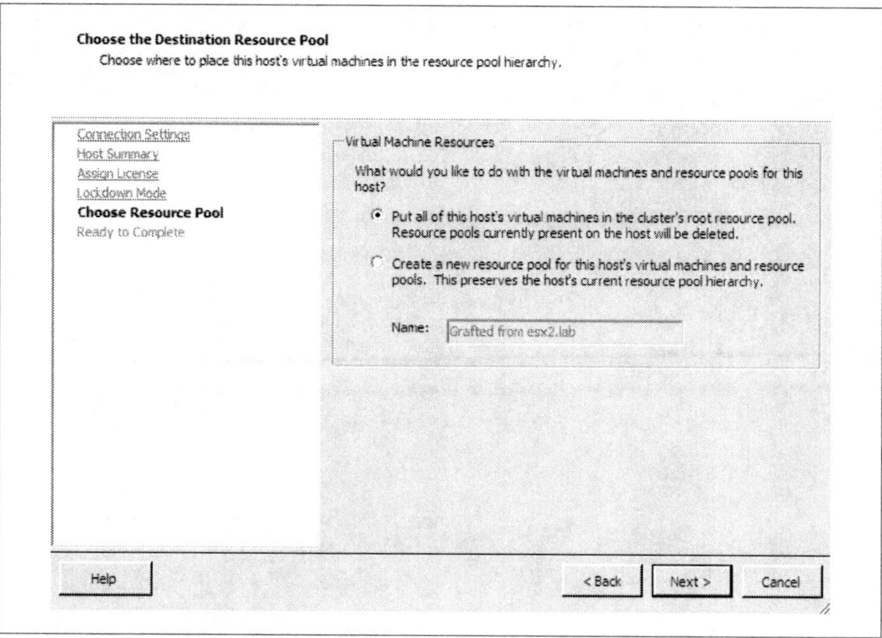

Figure 4-17. Resource pool settings

Once you have selected which resource pool option you want to use, click the Next button to continue.

7. You will now be presented with a summary. Use the Back button if you need to make any changes, and when you're satisfied click the Finish button to add the ESXi Host to the cluster.

   If HA is enabled on the cluster in which the host is being added, the host will automatically be configured for HA. If you are not adding the host to an HA cluster, the host will run standalone.

See Also

Recipe 4.9

4.11 Enabling Hyperthreading on a Virtual Machine

Problem

You wish to enable hyperthreading on a virtual machine, after it is enabled on your physical server.

Solution

Follow the steps to enable hyperthreading on a specific virtual machine.

Discussion

Some CPU's come with hyperthreading support, which is not to be confused with multi-core processors. Hyperthreading allows multiple threads to be spawned off the primary CPU to help balance processing. However, in a virtualized environment, this might not always be the best solution. Hyperthreading doesn't double the CPU speed, it just allows the server to split the logical CPU into multiple logical CPUs, creating a virtualized CPU. Hyperthreading can, in some situations, provide a benefit with virtual machines. However, it can also decrease performance, because it contains the potential to place additional workloads on the primary logical CPU.

To enable hyperthreading on a virtual machine, follow these steps (Figure 4-18). We assume that hyperthreading has already been enabled in the physical ESXI server's BIOS.

1. Load the vCenter client and log in to your vCenter server.
2. Select the virtual machine from the inventory list, then right-click on the virtual machine and select Edit Settings.
3. Click the Resources Tab and select Advanced CPU.
4. Here you will see three options that control hyperthreading. None of the options affect the way the virtual machine is allocated CPU time.

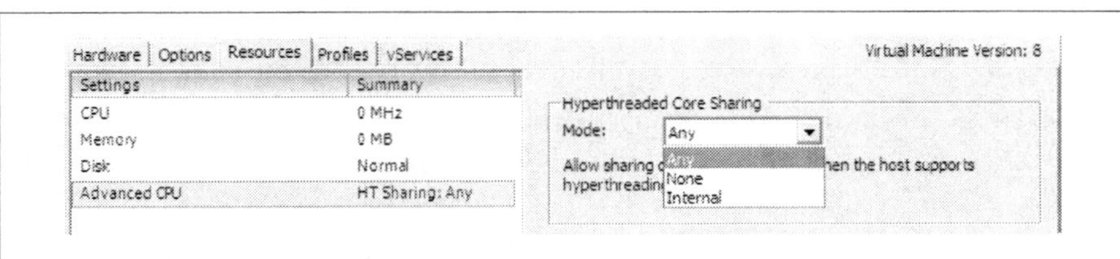

Figure 4-18. Enable hyperthread core sharing

Any
: This is the default setting when turning on hyperthreading for a virtual machine. This will allow the virtual machine to share virtual CPU time across multiple virtual machines.

None
: This setting will prevent the virtual machine from sharing its CPU and from borrowing CPU time from other virtual machines. The processor acts as a dedicated core.

Internal
: This setting may be useful if you have an SMP-enabled virtual machine. The setting allows the virtual machine to borrow CPU time from multiple processors, but does not allow sharing with other virtual machines.

5. Once you have selected the settings that best reflect your environment, click OK.

4.12 Enabling DRS in a Cluster

Problem

You wish to enable DRS in your current cluster.

Solution

Use the vCenter Client tool to enable DRS.

Discussion

Enabling DRS inside an already created cluster is easy using the vCenter client. If you have VMware vSphere Enterprise, DRS is integrated already. With the standard version of vSphere, DRS is an optional add-on. Regardless of which version you have, we'll walk you through the steps of enabling DRS and explain the different settings along the way:

1. Load the vCenter client and log in to your vCenter server.
2. Right-click on your cluster and select Edit Settings from the menu. This will bring up another window with configuration options for the cluster. We are going to be looking at the General area as well as the VMware DRS area and its subsections.
3. Click the General label in the left-hand window. You will now be able to rename your cluster and enable or disable vSphere HA and vSphere DRS on the cluster (Figure 4-19). Put a check next to Enable vSphere DRS.
4. Click on the vSphere DRS item in the menu tree on the left and you will be presented with a choice between three different automation levels (Figure 4-20).

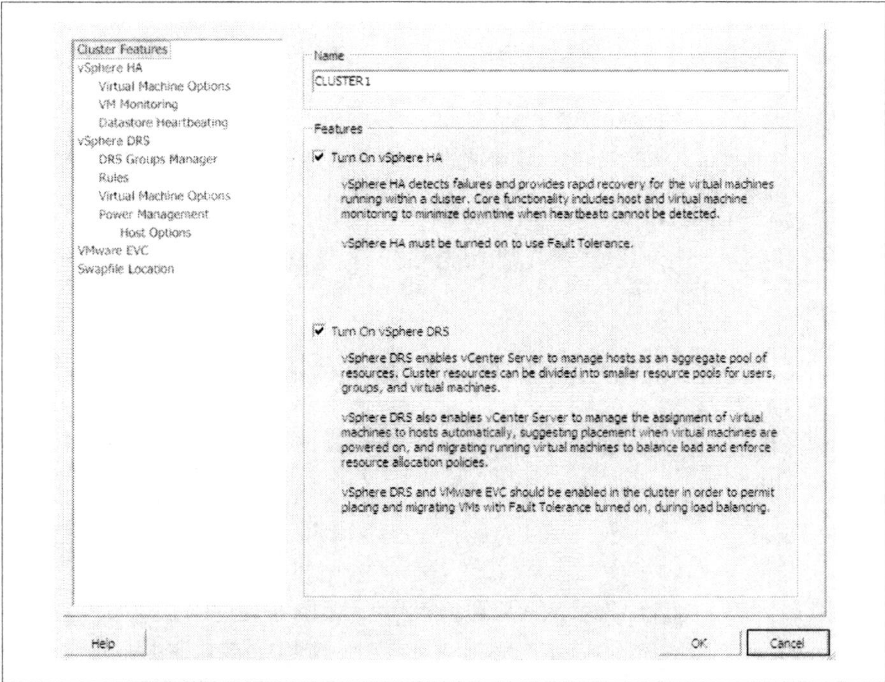

Figure 4-19. Enabling DRS on a cluster

The choices are:

Manual
: When you power on a virtual machine, DRS will display a list of suggested hosts for placement. Also, if it determines that there is a better host for a virtual machine, DRS will suggest a manual migration.

Partially automated
: When you power on a virtual machine, DRS will automatically put it on the host it feels is the best. As with the manual level of automation, when a cluster node becomes unbalanced, DRS will give you a list of suggested hosts for placement of the virtual machine(s).

Fully automated
: When you power on a virtual machine, DRS will automatically place it on the most suitable host. When a cluster becomes unbalanced, DRS will automatically start the VMotion process and automatically move the virtual machine(s) without involving the system administrator.

The migration threshold, shown below the automation options, is based on a star system of 1 through 5, where 1 is the most conservative and 5 is the most aggressive:

Level 1
: This is the most conservative level of automation and applies only to 5-star recommendations.

Level 2
: This level of automation applies to recommendations with 4 or more stars and aims to improve the cluster's load balance.

Level 3
: This is the default level of automation and applies to recommendations with 3 or more stars.

Level 4
: This level of automation applies to 2 or more stars.

Level 5
: This is the most aggressive method of automation and applies to recommendations with any number of stars.

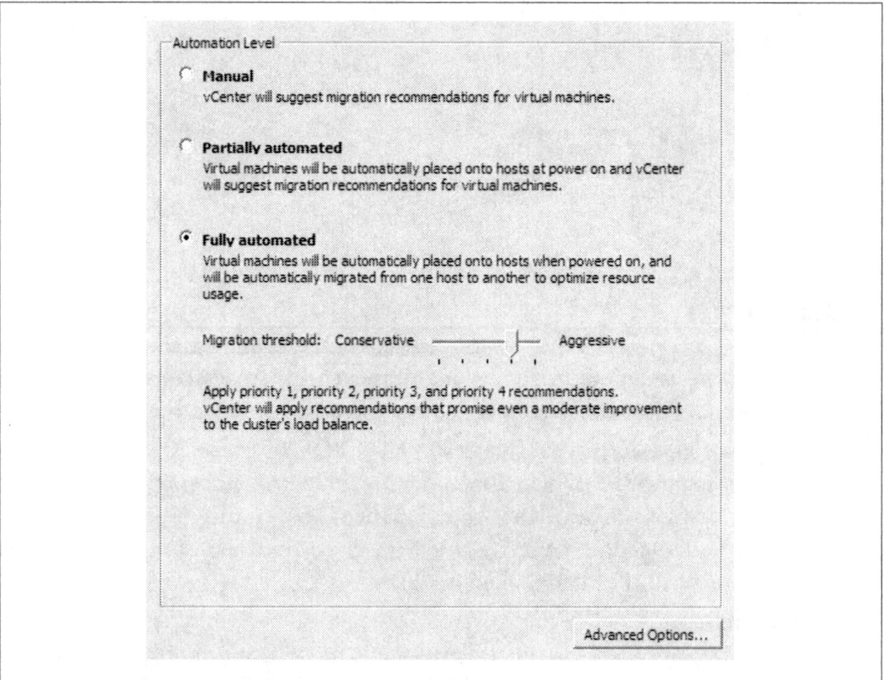

Figure 4-20. DRS automation levels

Essentially, the higher the automation level you use, the more minor and frequent migrations you will see if DRS deems improvements can be made. A less aggressive selection will result in changes only when DRS deems that they will make a large improvement to the cluster's load balance.

Within the DRS environment you can also set a *per-virtual-machine automation level*, which will override the automation level set on the entire cluster. By setting the automation levels on this more granular basis, you can fine-tune your cluster for your specific needs (Figure 4-21).

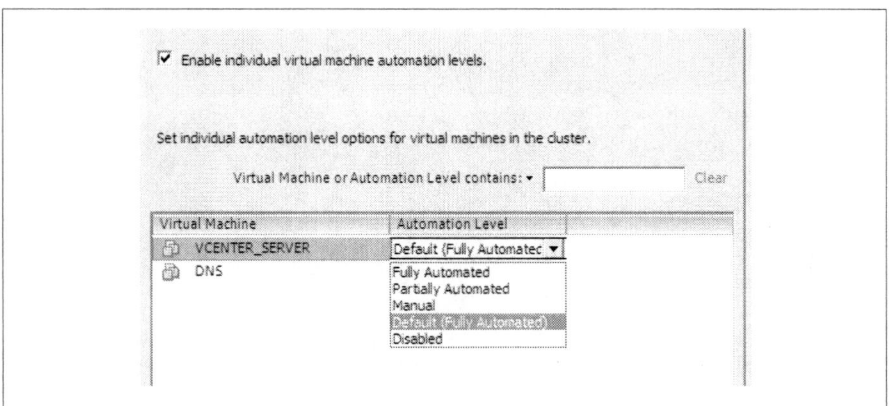

Figure 4-21. Virtual machine automation levels

Another important feature of DRS is the ability to set rules and guidelines for virtual machines within the cluster. Along with the star system, these affect the choices made by DRS. You can specify two kinds of rules for your virtual machines:

- *Affinity rules* allow you to specify certain virtual machines that should be run on the same host and in multi–virtual-machine environments when better performance can be achieved by such a configuration. For example, machines that communicate frequently may perform better when run on the same host.
- *Antiaffinity rules* allow you to force virtual machines to run on separate hosts. This can be important when you have two servers that are in a failover or load-balancing environment and you want them to *always* run on separate ESXi nodes in the cluster.

In Figure 4-22, we have set an antiaffinity rule telling DRS that we want the virtual machines *TESTDEV* and *TEST1223* to run on separate physical ESXi nodes. DRS will always ensure that those virtual machines are separate from one another.

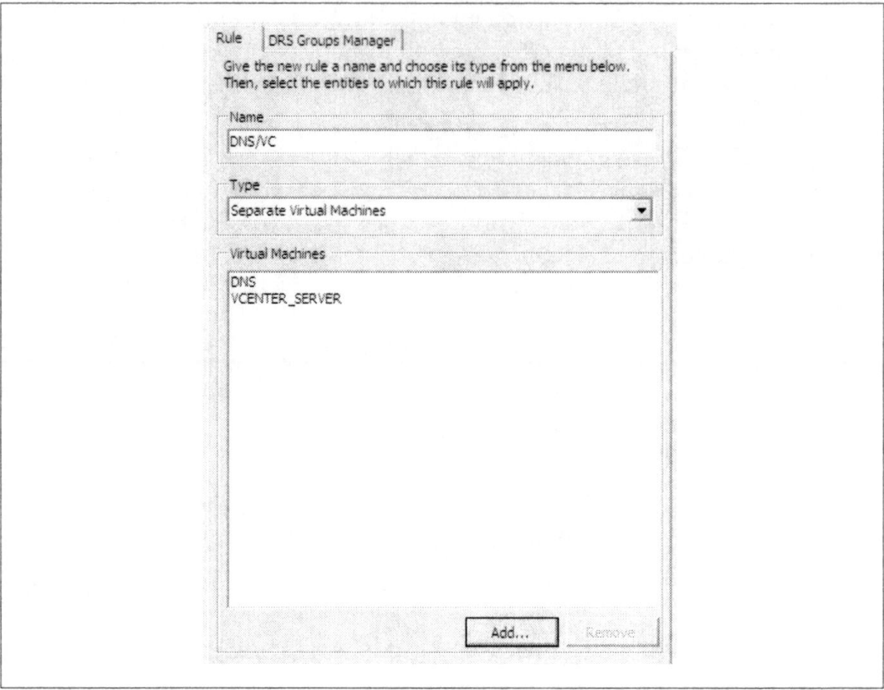

Figure 4-22. Virtual machine DRS rules

Some tips about using DRS:

- When removing a host from a cluster, always put that host in maintenance mode.
- When you have your automation level set to Manual and DRS makes strong recommendations (typically, level 4 or 5), follow them. Otherwise, balance and fairness within the cluster will deteriorate.
- Let DRS automatically handle most virtual machines, and set the override on virtual machines that you do not want DRS to automatically handle.

4.13 Understanding Cluster States and Warnings

Problem

You need to know the different states and warnings that are possible within a cluster.

Solution

Familiarize yourself with the various states in the vCenter and what they mean.

Discussion

VMware has three separate warnings that give the administrator basic information about the state of the cluster, virtual machine, or ESXi Host.

For example, if there is no network redundancy on the service console port, you will see a yellow triangle on your cluster. The detailed configuration issues will then be listed on the Summary tab of the cluster, telling you what configuration warnings exist.

Let's take a look at the three different statuses that VMware provides for clusters:

Green (valid)
: Clusters are considered valid as long as they have no configuration issues, resource overcommitments, or failed ESXi Hosts. A valid cluster will have a working configuration and all resources will be available for use by the virtual machines. In addition to all the resources being available, a valid cluster will also have one host available for standby in case an ESXi Host fails.

Yellow (overcommitted)
: This warning shows a potential risk of resources. For example, removing a host from the cluster might cause the reserve of available resources to fall below the level needed by the virtual machines. Minor configuration issues, such as no network redundancy on the service port network group, may also trigger this status.

Red (invalid)
: A cluster can become invalid when there are not enough resources available to handle all the virtual machines in the cluster. Clusters can also become invalid because of configuration issues such as HA becoming disabled on an ESXi Host or one of the ESXi Hosts in the cluster going down without being properly taken offline in the vCenter (and thereby taking away necessary resources).

  A cluster can become invalid or overcommitted if one or more hosts fail. A cluster can also become invalid if the vCenter is unable to power on a virtual machine, if an HA cluster's capacity is lower than the configured failover, or if the primary hosts in the cluster do not respond in a timely fashion to HA heartbeat checks.

  Depending on the type of failure that causes the cluster to become invalid, you may attempt to resolve the issue by adding more resources, reconfiguring HA on the ESXi Host, or powering off unneeded virtual machines so that the resource requirements of the other virtual machines can be satisfied.

  It's very important to remedy an invalid cluster as soon as possible to avoid the cluster becoming imbalanced.

4.14 Using ESXi CPU/RAM Hot Add/Hotplug Support

Problem

You want to add more CPUs or memory to a virtual machine.

Solution

Using technology within VMware ESXi 5.x, you can add CPUs, memory, and devices to a virtual machine while it is running.

Discussion

vSphere 5.x Enterprise, Enterprise Plus, and Advanced customers have the ability to hotplug or hot add CPUs, memory, and devices to their virtual machines without powering them off. These new technologies illustrate the improvements VMware is making in its products in an effort to reduce downtime on mission-critical applications and servers.

Hot add support in ESXi 5.x is limited to a specific set of guest operating systems. Please refer to the HCL located at: *http://www.vmware.com/resources/compatibility/search.php?deviceCategory=software*

To enable hot add support on a virtual machine:

1. Log in to your vCenter server, right-click on the virtual machine on which you wish to enable support, and select Edit Settings.
2. Click Advanced and select Memory/CPU Hotplug.
3. Select "Enable memory hot add" for the virtual machine, and then select "Hot add CPU support" for the virtual machine.
4. Click OK when you're finished to finalize the changes.

VMware Tools must be installed on the guest OS for this procedure to work correctly.

4.15 Surviving a vCenter Server Failure or Outage

Problem

Your vCenter server has gone down or refuses to start, and you want to continue operations until the problem can be fixed.

Solution

This recipe discusses what pieces of ESXi will continue to run when your vCenter server is down or offline.

Discussion

When your vCenter server needs an upgrade or maintenance, or when it suffers a crash, it's important to know what pieces of the environment can and will function without the benefit of a vCenter server orchestrating and managing the various resources within the environment.

When the vCenter server is offline, your virtual machines will continue to function, along with HA. However, other key pieces will be unavailable or will work in a degraded mode. Tables 4-1 through 4-8 list the impacts that a vCenter server outage can have on an environment.

Table 4-1. vCenter Server outage effects on VMware HA

VMware Infrastructure Function	Available	Comment
Restart virtual machine	Yes	No impact
Admission control	No	vCenter Server is required as the source of the load information
Add new host to cluster	No	vCenter Server is required to resolve IP addresses of cluster members
Allow hosts to rejoin the cluster	Yes	Resolved host information is stored on the ESXi Host itself in */etc/FT_HOST*

Table 4-2. vCenter Server outage effects on VMware DRS

VI Function	Available	Comment
Manual	No	Requires vCenter Server to manage
Automatic	No	Requires vCenter Server to manage
Affinity rules	No	Requires vCenter Server to manage

Table 4-3. vCenter Server outage effects on resource pools

VI Function	Available	Comment
Create	No	Requires vCenter Server to manage
Add virtual machine	No	Requires vCenter Server to manage
Remove VM	No	Requires vCenter Server to manage

Table 4-4. vCenter Server outage effects on vMotion

VI Function	Available	Comment
vMotion	No	Requires vCenter Server to manage

Table 4-5. vCenter Server outage effects on ESXi Host

VI Function	Available	Comment
Shutdown	Degraded	Through a direct connection to the ESXi Host Server only
Start-up	Yes	Expires within 14 days
Maintenance mode	Degraded	Requires vCenter Server to manage
Deregister	No	Requires vCenter Server to manage
Register	No	Requires vCenter Server to manage

Table 4-6. vCenter Server outage effects on virtual machines

VI Function	Available	Comment
Power on	Degraded	Expires in 14 days; direct connection to ESXi Host Server only
Power off	Degraded	Direct connection to ESXi Host Server only
Register	No	Requires vCenter Server to manage
Deregister	No	Requires vCenter Server to manage
Hot migration	No	Requires vCenter Server (vMotion)
Cold migration	Degraded	Within the same ESXi Host only

Table 4-7. vCenter Server outage effects on templates

VI Function	Available	Comment
Convert from virtual machine	Degraded	Direct connection to host only; requires vCenter Server to manage
Convert to virtual machine	Degraded	Direct connection to host only; requires vCenter Server to manage
Deploy virtual machine	No	Requires vCenter Server to manage

Table 4-8. vCenter Server outage effects on virtual machines (guests)

VI Function	Available	Comment
Guest OS (virtual machine)	Yes	No impact, will run without vCenter server

CHAPTER 5

Useful Tools and References

VMware has traditionally been configured and managed through the vCenter client. However, there are many tools that can manage and provide useful information via the Command Line Interface provided on the ESXI server. In this chapter, we'll examine some important command-line utilities that will aid you in monitoring and configuring your ESXI server, and we'll take a look at general best practices for setting up services that will be crucial for your ESXI server.

5.1 Entering Maintenance Mode via the Command Line

Problem

You are unable to access your vCenter server to initiate the maintenance mode command inside the vCenter. This can occur if there is a network outage, database corruption, or failed hardware. The method shown here will allow you to put the ESXi Host in maintenance mode and will allow for a safe shutdown if needed.

Solution

This command is not supported as of ESXi 5.0 in the *esxshell* and will require an additional installation on a Windows Server to access the vCLI Toolkit. Putting ESXi hosts in maintenance mode should be completed inside the vCenter if possible.

Discussion

To enter the maintenance mode, use this command:

```
vicfg-hostops.pl --server <ip> --username root --password <pass> --operation enter
```

To exit the maintenance mode, enter:

```
vicfg-hostops.pl --server <ip> --username root --password <pass> --operation exit
```

5.2 Displaying Server Information

Problem

You want to display current information about your ESX Server.

Solution

Run the `esxcfg-info` command on the ESXI server.

Discussion

This command-line tool is a powerful yet simple way to find out about your ESXI server and its environment. By using the `esxcfg-info` command, you can get detailed information about your configuration and server hardware:

```
~ # esxcfg-info -h
Usage: esxcfg-info mode
   -a, --all           Print all information
   -w, --hardware      Print hardware information
   -r, --resource      Print resource information
   -s, --storage       Print storage information
   -n, --network       Print network information
   -y, --system        Print system information
   -o, --advopt        Print advanced options
   -u, --hwuuid        Print hardware uuid
   -b, --bootuuid      Print boot partition uuid
   -e, --boottype      Print boot type (VMVisor Only)
   -c, --cmdline       Print vmkernel command line
   -F, --format        Print the information in the given format
                       Valid values are "xml" and "perl"
   -h, --help          Print this message.
```

The options can be entered in any combination to display the specified information. If you run the `esxcfg-info` command alone or with the `-a` switch, it will dump all values. The following example displays the first few lines of output on one of our systems:

```
$ esxcfg-info | more
+Host :
   \==+Hardware Info :
      |----BIOS UUID............................................0x44 0x45 0x4c
0x4c 0x34 0x0 0x10 0x38 0x80 0x56 0xb6 0xc0 0x4f 0x4b 0x46 0x31
      |----Product Name.........................................PowerEdge R900
      |----Vendor Name..........................................Dell Inc.
      |----Serial Number........................................XXXXXXXX
      |----Hardware Uptime......................................1762529093951
...............
```

The information you can gather about your system from this command is so comprehensive that you may wish to export it to a text file, like this:

```
esxcfg-info > esxcfginfo12102008.txt
```

The -F option will also let you export the data in XML or Perl formatting. This can be useful if you wish to parse the output and store it in a proprietary or third-party application.

An example of exporting the network and storage information in Perl format as follows (we've truncated the output in this example to save space):

```
~ # esxcfg-info -s -n -F perl > test1.log
$host = {
{ #network_info
   current_max_virtual_switches => 256,
   next_reboot_max_virtual_switches => 256,
   { #console_nic_info
      console_nics => [
      ],
   },
   { #routing_info
      kernel_gateway => "0.0.0.0",
      kernel_ipv6_gateway => "::",
      console_gateway => "0.0.0.0",
      console_gateway_device => ",
      console_ipv4_gateway_interface => ",
      console_ipv6_gateway_interface => ",
      vmkernel_ipv4_gateway_interface => ",
      vmkernel_ipv6_gateway_interface => ",
      vmkernel_routes => [
         route => {
            network => "172.16.102.0/24",
            gateway => "0.0.0.0",
            interface => "vmk0",
         },
```

An example of exporting network and storage information in XML format is as follows (we've truncated the output in this example to save space):

```
~ # esxcfg-info -s -n -F xml | more

<network-info>
   <value name="current-max-virtual-switches" type="uint32" format="dec">256</value>
   <value name="next-reboot-max-virtual-switches" type="uint32" format="dec">256</value>
   <console-nic-info>
      <console-nics>
      </console-nics>
   </console-nic-info>
   <routing-info>
      <value name="kernel-gateway" type="string">10.0.1.1</value>
      <value name="kernel-ipv6-gateway" type="string">::</value>
      <value name="console-gateway" type="string">0.0.0.0</value>
      <value name="console-gateway-device" type="string"></value>
      <value name="console-ipv4-gateway-interface" type="string"></value>
      <value name="console-ipv6-gateway-interface" type="string"></value>
      <value name="vmkernel-ipv4-gateway-interface" type="string"></value>
      <value name="vmkernel-ipv6-gateway-interface" type="string"></value>
      <vmkernel-routes>
         <route>
```

```
            <value name="network" type="string">0.0.0.0/0</value>
            <value name="gateway" type="string">10.0.1.1</value>
            <value name="interface" type="string">vmk0</value>
        </route>
        <route>
            <value name="network" type="string">10.0.1.0/24</value>
            <value name="gateway" type="string">0.0.0.0</value>
            <value name="interface" type="string">vmk0</value>
        </route>
    </vmkernel-routes>
</routing-info>
```

5.3 Viewing the ESXi Version

Problem

You want to find the version of ESXi you are running. This may be needed for a variety of reasons, such as for upgrading or support issues.

Solution

There are multiple ways to find the version of ESXi you are running. Two easy ways we'll cover are:

- Displaying it within the vCenter
- Creating a report

Discussion

To find the version of ESXi that you are running within the vCenter, click on your ESXi Host. The version will be displayed to the right of the hostname. For instance, Figure 5-1 shows we are running ESXi 5.0.0 build 469512.

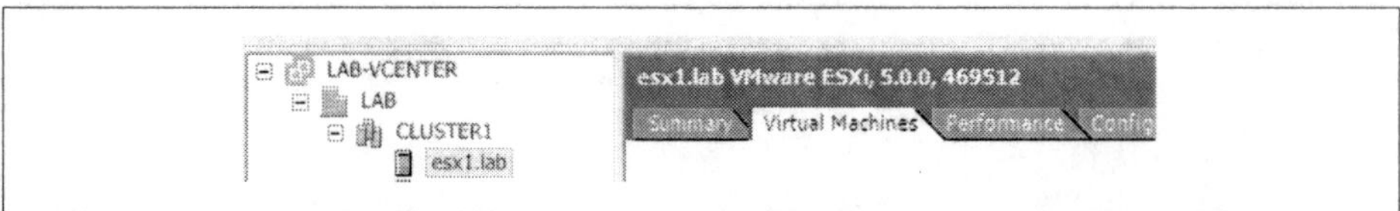

Figure 5-1. Displaying the ESXi version in the vCenter

If you need to store the version, you can generate a report within the vCenter. Choose File→Report→Host Summary and save the file. The results include the version information.

5.4 Changing the Virtual Disk from BusLogic to LSI Logic

Problem

You need to change the virtual disk SCSI driver after a physical-to-virtual conversion.

Solution

Use the vCenter to make the change.

Discussion

After using VMware's Converter application, you may notice that your virtual machine's SCSI controller has switched from LSI Logic to BusLogic. This is because on some OSs—notably, Windows 2003—the VMware Converter automatically uses the BusLogic driver, unlike when you create a new virtual machine using the vCenter client, which uses an LSI Logic driver. The LSI Logic driver offers better performance, so it's a good idea to switch back:

1. Log in to your vCenter server, navigate to the virtual machine whose bus/controller you wish to change, and power it off.
2. Once the virtual machine is powered off, click the tab labeled Summary, then click Edit Settings.
3. A new window will appear (Figure 5-2). Click on the SCSI Controller 0 option listed under the Hardware tab.

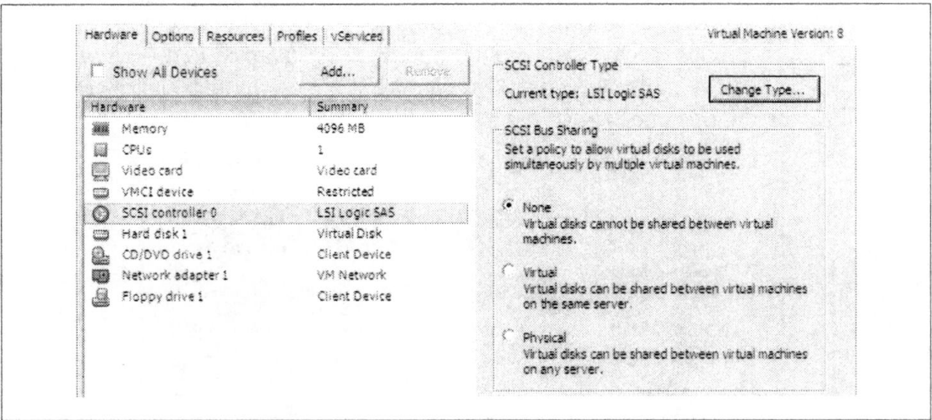

Figure 5-2. Configuring your hardware in the vCenter

4. Click the Change Type button on the right side of the screen. A new window will appear in which you can change your SCSI controller type (Figure 5-3). Choose the type you wish to switch to (in this case, LSI Logic). A warning will pop up

saying that changing the controller may have unexpected results when the virtual machine boots.

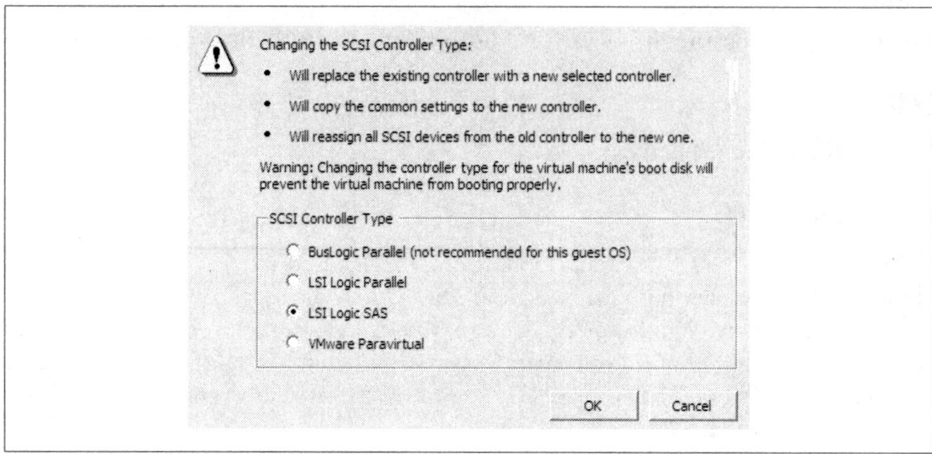

Figure 5-3. Changing the SCSI controller type

5. To complete the process, press the OK button. Then, on the Settings screen, press the OK button again. VMware will make the changes needed and convert the virtual machine to the new SCSI controller type.
6. Power on the virtual machine to finalize the changes.
7. A Virtual Machine Question screen will pop up, warning you that you should be cautious when changing the controller type. Select Yes, and then click OK (Figure 5-4). If your virtual machine has problems booting with the new driver, switch back to the old one and reboot again.

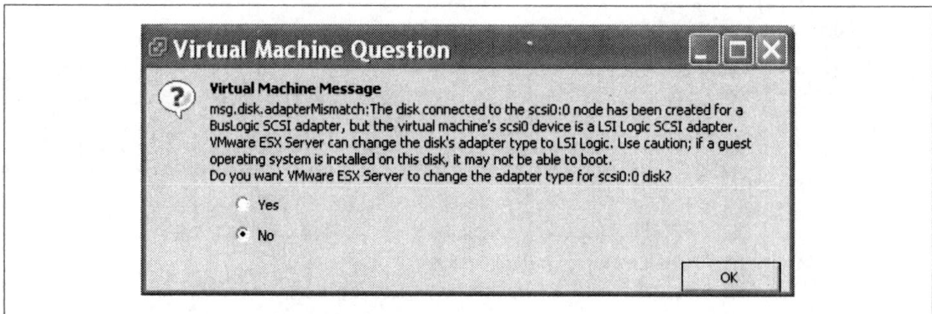

Figure 5-4. Warning when virtual machine boots

5.5 Hiding the VMware Tools Icon

Problem

Many VMware users would like to hide or remove the VMware Tools icon, and are frustrated because the VMware Tools configuration offers no way to do it.

Solution

You can hide the Tools icon by editing the Windows registry.

Discussion

Open the registry and navigate to the following key:

```
HKEY_CURRENT_USER\Software\VMware, Inc.\VMware Tools\ShowTray
```

Do this with caution and back up your registry first!

Set the `ShowTray` variable to `0` (zero) and save it. Reboot your virtual machine, and the settings will be reflected; the Tools icon will now be hidden.

5.6 Viewing Disk Partitions via the Console

Problem

You want to view information on the current mounts and disks attached to your ESXI server.

Solution

Use the `vdf -h` command to view this information.

Discussion

Using the ESXi Shell, you can run the following command to see a list of datastores, their status, size, etc. Typical output looks like this:

```
~ # esxcli storage filesystem list
Mount Point             Volume Name           UUID                Mounted  Type
----------------------- -------------------- ------------------ -------  ------
/vmfs/volumes/4f535fea-  datastore250 (1)     4f535fea-a7b3e465-  true     VMFS-5
a7b3e465-7829-                                7829-5404a6487afd
5404a6487afd

/vmfs/volumes/4f546274-  esx02_datastore_lun1 4f546274-32257e8a-  true     VMFS-5
32257e8a-132c-                                132c-5404a64c91b1
5404a64c91b1

/vmfs/volumes/4f54625f-  esx01_datastore_lun0 4f54625f-e702187c-  true     VMFS-5
e702187c-a9aa-                                a9aa-5404a64c91b1
5404a64c91b1

/vmfs/volumes/2a35d7e3-                       2a35d7e3-f089ea92-  true     vfat
f089ea92-3611-                                3611-fd54134d921f
fd54134d921f

/vmfs/volumes/cc7ca9e2-                       cc7ca9e2-579492ac-  true     vfat
579492ac-832f-                                832f-d7eabf6ec3f9
d7eabf6ec3f9

/vmfs/volumes/4f3669f1-                       4f3669f1-dd9e8a3e-     true  vfat
dd9e8a3e-e9ba-                                e9ba-000c290e79de
000c290e79de
```

This example shows our local OS-level disks and partitions (here, `datastore1`) along with the VMFS filesystems that are recognized only by the ESXI server.

5.7 Monitoring CPU Usage

Problem

You want to monitor your ESXI server's CPU usage.

Solution

Use the *esxtop* utility.

Discussion

From the command line on your ESXI server, run the following:

```
esxtop
```

If you are familiar with the Unix *top* utility, *esxtop* will feel similar. Once *esxtop* is running, press **c** to switch to CPU mode. This will display your server's current CPU usage statistics (Figure 5-5).

```
 5:29:03am up  3:22, 299 worlds, 3 VMs, 3 vCPUs; CPU load average: 0.01, 0.01, 0.01
PCPU USED(%): 3.3 3.0 1.2 2.8 2.9 0.5 0.5 1.0 AVG: 1.9
PCPU UTIL(%): 3.5 3.3 1.4 2.9 3.2 0.7 0.6 1.2 AVG: 2.1

   ID      GID NAME             NWLD   %USED    %RUN    %SYS   %WAIT %VMWAIT    %RDY   %IDLE  %OVRLP   %CS
    1        1 idle                8  784.34  800.00    0.01    0.00       -  800.00    0.00    1.70    0.
 1479     1479 VMware vCloud D     5    4.80    4.59    0.23  495.20    0.24    0.20   95.14    0.00    0.
  820      820 hostd.2877         16    1.71    1.70    0.01 1598.16       -    0.11    0.00    0.00    0.
 1476     1476 vShield Manager     5    1.12    1.01    0.11  498.87    0.23    0.12   98.82    0.01    0.
 8315     8315 esxtop.11850        1    0.95    0.96    0.00   99.04       -    0.00    0.00    0.00    0.
  998      998 vpxa.3077          18    0.47    0.45    0.01 1799.48       -    0.09    0.00    0.00    0.
 6508     6508 TEST                5    0.30    0.24    0.06  499.68    0.48    0.09   99.35    0.00    0.
 1285     1285 fdm.3377           18    0.21    0.21    0.00 1799.70       -    0.08    0.00    0.00    0.
    8        8 helper             77    0.14    0.14    0.00 7699.67       -    0.04    0.00    0.00    0.
 1050     1050 sh.3140             1    0.12    0.12    0.00   99.87       -    0.01    0.00    0.00    0.
  605      605 vmsyslogd.2642      3    0.04    0.04    0.00  299.94       -    0.02    0.00    0.00    0.
 1038     1038 vmware-usbarbit     2    0.03    0.03    0.00  199.96       -    0.00    0.00    0.00    0.
    2        2 system              9    0.03    0.03    0.00  899.94       -    0.04    0.00    0.00    0.
  642      642 vmkiscsid.2686      2    0.01    0.01    0.00  199.97       -    0.01    0.00    0.00    0.
 8199     8199 sshd.11676          1    0.01    0.01    0.00   99.99       -    0.00    0.00    0.00    0.
    9        9 drivers            11    0.01    0.01    0.00 1099.95       -    0.01    0.00    0.00    0.
 1091     1091 openwsmand.3181     3    0.01    0.01    0.00  299.97       -    0.01    0.00    0.00    0.
  863      863 dcbd.2923           1    0.01    0.00    0.00   99.99       -    0.00    0.00    0.00    0.
  705      705 storageRM.2761      2    0.00    0.00    0.00  199.99       -    0.00    0.00    0.00    0.
 1403     1403 sfcb-ProviderMa    10    0.00    0.00    0.00 1000.00       -    0.00    0.00    0.00    0.
  743      743 vprobed.2800        3    0.00    0.00    0.00  300.00       -    0.00    0.00    0.00    0.
```

Figure 5-5. Default CPU display for esxtop

The first line displayed tells you:

- The current time (5:29:03 a.m., in our example)
- The time elapsed since the last reboot
- The number of currently running virtual machines and virtual CPUs
- CPU averages over 1, 5, and 15 minutes

The `PCPU(%)` line displays the percentage of CPU use per physical CPU and the total average across all the physical CPUs.

The `CCPU(%)` line shows the CPU time as reported by the ESXI server or console. This is a user time variable, as opposed to the PCPU, which measures time from the CPU's point of view.

Below the PCPU and CCPU lines, the following attributes are available:

`ID`
: The number of the processor.

`GID`
: The ID of the running world's resource pool.

`NAME`
: The name of the currently running process.

`NWLD`
: The number of worlds in the group.

`%USED`
: The percentage of physical CPU used by the resource pool, virtual machine, or world.

`%RUN`
: The percentage of total time scheduled (not taking into account hyperthreading and system time).

`%SYS`
: System time: the time that elapses while kernel code is running.

`%WAIT`
: The total percentage of time the resource pool or world has spent in a wait state.

`%RDY`
: The percentage of time the resource pool, virtual machine, or world has spent ready to run but waiting to get a CPU.

`%IDLE`
: The percentage of time the VCPU world has spent in an idle loop (this applies only to the VCPU world; for other worlds, this field will be zero).

`%OVRLP`
: The percentage of time spent by system services working on behalf of other worlds.

`%CSTP`
: The percentage of time the world has spent in a ready, co-descheduled state (this state applies only to SMP VMs).

`%MLMTD`
: The percentage of time the world spent ready to run but deliberately wasn't scheduled to avoid violating the CPU limit settings.

`LWID`
: Leader World ID (World Group ID).

`%STATE TIMES`
: Set of CPU statistics made up of the following percentages. For a world, the percentages are a percentage of one physical CPU core.

`EVENT COUNTS/s`
: Set of CPU statistics made up of per second event rates.

`CPU ALLOC`
: Set of CPU statistics made up of the following CPU allocation configuration parameters.

`SUMMARY STATS`
: Set of CPU statistics made up of the following CPU configuration parameters and statistics. These statistics apply only to worlds and not to virtual machines or resource pools.

`POWER STATS`
: Current CPU power consumption for a resource pool (in Watts).

You can find additional information regarding performance monitoring at *http://pubs.vmware.com/vsphere-50/index.jsp?topic=/com.vmware.vsphere.monitoring.doc_50/GUID-AC5FAD2D-96DE-41C4-B5C6-A06FE65F34C6.html*.

See Also

Recipes 5.8, 5.9, and 5.10

5.8 Monitoring Memory

Problem

You want to monitor your ESXI server's memory using the command line.

Solution

Use the *esxtop* utility.

Discussion

From the command line on your ESXI server, run the following command:

```
esxtop
```

Once *esxtop* is running, press the `m` key to switch to memory mode. This will display your server's current memory usage statistics. Your output will be similar to that in Figure 5-6. Note that here we have two virtual machines running, *TEST01* and *TEST02*.

```
 5:35:22am up  3:29, 294 worlds, 3 VMs, 3 vCPUs; MEM overcommit avg: 0.00, 0.00, 0.00
PMEM  /MB: 16330   total:   968     vmk,  2675 other,  12686 free
VMKMEM/MB: 16251 managed:   652 minfree,  5962 rsvd,  10289 ursvd,  high state
PSHARE/MB:    34  shared,    19  common:    15 saving
SWAP  /MB:     0    curr,     0 rclmtgt:                 0.00 r/s,   0.00 w/s
ZIP   /MB:     0  zipped,     0   saved
MEMCTL/MB:     0    curr,     0  target,  1633 max

  GID NAME               MEMSZ    GRANT    SZTGT     TCHD   TCHD_W    SWCUR    SWTGT   SWR/s   SWW/s  LLSW
 6508 TEST             4096.00     6.00    27.32     0.00     0.00     0.00     0.00    0.00    0.00     0
 1476 vShield Manager  3072.00  1061.31  1193.22    30.72     0.00     0.00     0.00    0.00    0.00     0
 1479 VMware vCloud D  2560.00  1426.78  1583.55   204.80   179.20     0.00     0.00    0.00    0.00     0
  820 hostd.2877         57.98    47.18     0.00    47.18    47.18     0.00     0.00    0.00    0.00     0
  998 vpxa.3077          22.39    14.66     0.00    14.66    14.66     0.00     0.00    0.00    0.00     0
 1285 fdm.3377           17.98    12.40     0.00    12.40    12.40     0.00     0.00    0.00    0.00     0
  642 vmkiscsid.2686     16.75     2.54     0.00     2.54     2.54     0.00     0.00    0.00    0.00     0
 1401 sfcb-ProviderMa    16.07    13.64     0.00    13.64    13.64     0.00     0.00    0.00    0.00     0
  972 vobd.3037           9.05     1.25     0.00     1.25     1.25     0.00     0.00    0.00    0.00     0
 1403 sfcb-ProviderMa     8.34     5.03     0.00     5.03     5.03     0.00     0.00    0.00    0.00     0
  605 vmsyslogd.2642      6.57     4.46     0.00     4.46     4.46     0.00     0.00    0.00    0.00     0
  604 vmsyslogd.2641      4.62     3.71     0.00     3.71     3.71     0.00     0.00    0.00    0.00     0
 1508 sfcb-ProviderMa     3.74     1.50     0.00     1.50     1.50     0.00     0.00    0.00    0.00     0
 1253 sfcb-ProviderMa     3.69     1.71     0.00     1.71     1.71     0.00     0.00    0.00    0.00     0
 1304 dcui.3402           3.48     1.07     0.00     1.07     1.07     0.00     0.00    0.00    0.00     0
  613 vmkeventd.2662      3.01     1.18     0.00     1.18     1.18     0.00     0.00    0.00    0.00     0
 1038 vmware-usbarbit     2.82     0.34     0.00     0.34     0.34     0.00     0.00    0.00    0.00     0
```

Figure 5-6. Default memory view for esxtop

If you are familiar with the Unix *top* utility, *esxtop* has a similar feel, but it provides added information specific to your ESXI server. The first line displayed tells you:

- The current time (5:35:22 a.m., in our example)
- The time since the last reboot

- The number of currently running worlds, virtual machines, and virtual CPUs
- Memory overcommitment averages over 1, 5, and 15 minutes

The next line, `PMEM`, break downs the total physical memory. In this example, the ESXI server has 16GB (1,6330MB) of memory. Let's take a look at the variables:

`total`
: The total amount of memory in the ESXI server

`cos`
: How much memory is allocated to the ESXI server console

`vmk`
: The amount of memory being used by the ESXI server VMkernel

`other`
: The amount of memory being used by everything but the VMkernel and the console

`free`
: The amount of memory that is free on the server

The `VMKMEM` line displays the memory statistics for the VMkernel, including these variables:

`managed`
: The total amount of machine memory being managed by the ESX Server's VMkernel

`minfree`
: The minimum amount of virtual memory that the ESXi tries to keep free

`rsvd`
: The amount of memory reserved by resource pools

`ursvd`
: The total amount of unreserved machine memory

`state`
: The current state of machine memory; this will have one of the four values outlined in this excerpt from the official VMware document (DOC-9279)[1]

> The memory "state" is "high," if the free memory is greater than or equal to 6% of "total" – "cos." [It] is "soft" at 4%, "hard" at 2%, and "low" at 1%. So, high implies that the machine memory is not under any pressure and low implies that the machine memory is under pressure.
>
> While the host's memory state is not used to determine whether memory should be reclaimed from VMs (that decision is made at the resource pool level), it can affect what mechanisms are used to reclaim memory if necessary. In the high and soft states, ballooning is favored over swapping. In the hard and low states, swapping is favored over ballooning.

1. *http://communities.vmware.com/docs/DOC-9279*

Please note that "minfree" is part of "free" memory; while "rsvd" and "ursvd" memory may or may not be part of "free" memory. "reservation" is different from memory allocation.

`COSMEM` displays memory statistics that are being reported by the ESXI server console. All values are specified in megabytes. The values present here are:

`free`
: The amount of idle memory your ESXI server has

`swap_t`
: The total swap space configured on your ESXI server

`swap_f`
: The amount of free swap space your ESXI server has

`r/s`
: The rate at which memory is being swapped from the disk

`w/s`
: The rate at which memory is being swapped to the disk

`PSHARE` tells you the current page-sharing status in the following categories. All values are specified in megabytes:

`shared`
: The amount of physical memory being shared

`common`
: The amount of physical memory that is being shared among worlds

`saving`
: The amount of physical memory that is saved because of page sharing

`SWAP` tells you about the swap usage on the ESXI server. Again, all values are in megabytes:

`curr`
: The current amount of swap memory being used by the ESX Server.

`target`
: The disk location where the ESXI server expects the swap memory file to be

`r/s`
: The rate at which the ESXI server is swapping memory in from the disk

`w/s`
: The rate at which the ESXI server is swapping memory out to the disk

`MEMCTL` displays the memory ballooning statistics. All stats are measured in megabytes:

`curr`
: The amount of memory that has been reclaimed using the `vmmemctl` module

`target`
: The total amount of memory the ESXI server hopes to reclaim using the `vmmemctl` module

`max`
: The maximum physical memory that the ESXI server can reclaim using the `vmmemctl` module

After the general status lines, the output shows the memory usage of each virtual machine. The line with a white background contains a header.

Additional variables can be configured by pressing the **F** key while in *esxtop* memory mode.

The variables reported for each virtual machine are:

`%ACTV`
: The percentage of guest physical memory that is being referenced by the guest.

`MEMSZ`
: The amount of physical memory allocated to a resource pool or virtual machine.

`MCTLSZ`
: The amount of memory that has been reclaimed from the resource pool by ballooning.

`SWCUR`
: The current amount of swap memory, in megabytes, being used by the virtual machine or resource pool.

`SWR/s`
: The rate at which the ESXI server is swapping memory from the disk for the virtual machine or resource pool.

`SWW/s`
: The rate at which the ESXI server is swapping memory to the disk for the virtual machine or resource pool.

`OVHD`
: The current overhead for the resource pool in megabytes.

`AMIN`
: The memory reservation for this resource pool or virtual machine.

`AMAX`
: The memory limit for this resource pool or virtual machine. A value of –1 means unlimited.

`ASHRS`
: The memory shares for this resource pool or virtual machine.

`NHN`
: The current home node for the resource pool or virtual machine. This statistic is applicable only on NUMA systems. If the virtual machine has no home node, a dash (-) appears.

`NRMEM`
: The current amount of remote memory allocated to the virtual machine or resource pool. This statistic is applicable only on NUMA systems.

`N% L`
: The current percentage of memory allocated to the virtual machine or resource pool that is local.

`MEMSZ (MB)`
: The amount of physical memory allocated to a resource pool or virtual machine.

`GRANT (MB)`
: The amount of guest physical memory mapped to a resource pool or virtual machine.

`SZTGT (MB)`
: The amount of machine memory the ESXi VMkernel wants to allocate to a resource pool or virtual machine.

`TCHD (MB)`
: A working set estimate for the resource pool or virtual machine.

`MCTLSZ (MB)`
: The amount of physical memory reclaimed from the resource pool by way of ballooning.

`MCTLTGT (MB)`
: The amount of physical memory the ESXi system attempts to reclaim from the resource pool or virtual machine by way of ballooning.

`MCTLMAX (MB)`
: The maximum amount of physical memory the ESXi system can reclaim from the resource pool or virtual machine by way of ballooning. This maximum depends on the guest operating system type.

`SWCUR (MB)`
: Current swap usage by this resource pool or virtual machine.

`SWTGT (MB)`
: The target where the ESXi Host expects the swap usage by the resource pool or virtual machine to be.

`SWR/s (MB)`
: Rate at which the ESXi Host swaps in memory from disk for the resource pool or virtual machine.

For additional details, please refer to the VMware documentation located at *http://pubs.vmware.com/vsphere-50/index.jsp?topic=/com.vmware.vsphere.monitoring.doc_50/GUID-AC5FAD2D-96DE-41C4-B5C6-A06FE65F34C6.html*.

See Also

Recipes 5.7, 5.9, and 5.10

5.9 Monitoring Storage Performance

Problem

You want to find out how well your storage system is working with the ESXI server.

Solution

Using *esxtop*, you can also monitor your disk statistics and troubleshoot your storage infrastructure.

Discussion

From the command line on your ESXI server, run the following:

```
esxtop
```

If you are familiar with the Unix *top* command, *esxtop* will feel similar. Once *esxtop* is running, press the **d** key to switch to storage mode. This will display statistics for your server's SCSI adapters, including HBAs attached through iSCSI and the Fibre NAS. Figure 5-7 shows multiple adapters, including local SCSI, Fibre, and iSCSI HBAs, but there is no indication on this screen as to which adapter belongs to which storage type.

```
5:38:54am up  3:32, 296 worlds, 3 VMs, 3 vCPUs; CPU load average: 0.01, 0.01, 0.01

ADAPTR PATH                NPTH   CMDS/s  READS/s WRITES/s MBREAD/s MBWRTN/s DAVG/cmd KAVG/cmd GAVG/cmd QAV
 vmhba2 -                     0     0.00     0.00     0.00     0.00     0.00     0.00     0.00     0.00
vmhba32 -                     1     0.00     0.00     0.00     0.00     0.00     0.00     0.00     0.00
vmhba33 -                     1     0.20     0.00     0.20     0.00     0.00     0.16     0.03     0.19
vmhba34 -                     0     0.00     0.00     0.00     0.00     0.00     0.00     0.00     0.00
vmhba35 -                     0     0.00     0.00     0.00     0.00     0.00     0.00     0.00     0.00
vmhba36 -                     0     0.00     0.00     0.00     0.00     0.00     0.00     0.00     0.00
vmhba37 -                     0     0.00     0.00     0.00     0.00     0.00     0.00     0.00     0.00
vmhba38 -                     2     0.99     0.00     0.99     0.00     0.01     0.62     0.01     0.63
```

Figure 5-7. Default storage view (truncated) for esxtop

The first line displayed tells you the following information:

- The current time (5:38:54 a.m., in our example)
- The time since the last reboot
- The number of currently running worlds, virtual machines, and vCPUs
- The CPU load averages for the system

The header that follows lists columns that will describe each disk. To view additional variables while in *esxtop*, you can press the **f** key to toggle them:

`ADAPTR`
: The adapter for which statistics are being shown.

`NPATH`
: The number of paths available to the adapter.

`AQLEN`
: The storage adapter queue depth. This is the maximum number of ESXI server VMkernel active commands that the adapter driver is configured to support.

`LQLEN`
: The number of active commands the LUN is allowed to have.

`QUED`
: The commands that the system is currently queuing. This applies to worlds/LUNs only.

`READS/s`
: The number of commands being read per second. Multiple paths will be shown separately.

`WRITES/s`
: The number of writes issued per second. Multiple paths will be shown separately.

`MBREAD/s`
: The number of megabytes read per second. Multiple paths will be shown separately.

`MBWRTN/s`
: The number of megabytes written per second. Multiple paths will be shown separately.

`DAVG/cmd`
: The device latency per command between the storage and the adapter.

`KAVG/cmd`
: The VMkernel latency per command.

`GAVG/cmd`
: The average guest OS latency per command.

Other useful tools to monitor disk usage, such as *perfmon* and *iostat*, can also be launched from the ESXI server's command line. These are useful tools that are native to Linux and that can help you troubleshoot alongside *esxtop*.

See Also

Recipes 5.7, 5.8, and 5.10

5.10 Monitoring Network Usage

Problem

You want to monitor your network adapters via the command line.

Solution

Use the *esxtop* utility to monitor network usage.

Discussion

From the command line on your ESXI server, run the following:

```
esxtop
```

Once *esxtop* is running, press the `n` key to switch to network mode. This will display your server's current network statistics (Figure 5-8).

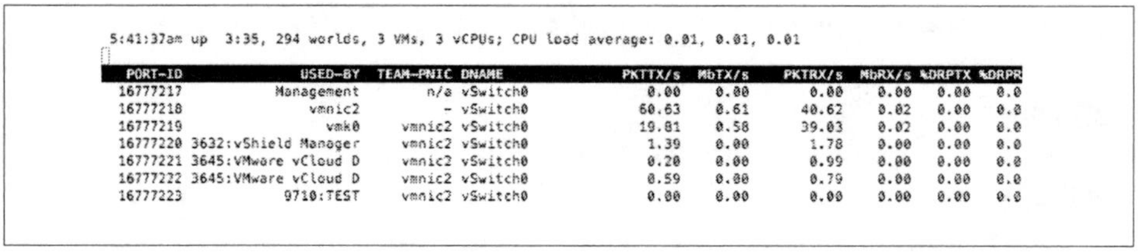

```
5:41:37am up  3:35, 294 worlds, 3 VMs, 3 vCPUs; CPU load average: 0.01, 0.01, 0.01

  PORT-ID              USED-BY  TEAM-PNIC DNAME              PKTTX/s  MbTX/s    PKTRX/s  MbRX/s %DRPTX %DRPR
 16777217           Management        n/a vSwitch0              0.00    0.00       0.00    0.00   0.00   0.0
 16777218               vmnic2          - vSwitch0             60.63    0.61      40.62    0.02   0.00   0.0
 16777219                 vmk0     vmnic2 vSwitch0             19.81    0.58      39.03    0.02   0.00   0.0
 16777220 3632:vShield Manager     vmnic2 vSwitch0              1.39    0.00       1.78    0.00   0.00   0.0
 16777221 3645:VMware vCloud D     vmnic2 vSwitch0              0.20    0.00       0.99    0.00   0.00   0.0
 16777222 3645:VMware vCloud D     vmnic2 vSwitch0              0.59    0.00       0.79    0.00   0.00   0.0
 16777223            9710:TEST     vmnic2 vSwitch0              0.00    0.00       0.00    0.00   0.00   0.0
```

Figure 5-8. Default network view for esxtop

If you are familiar with the Unix *top* command, *esxtop* will feel similar. Let's take a look at some of the values displayed in Figure 5-8:

`PORT ID`
: The virtual network device port ID

`UPLINK`
: Whether or not the network port is an uplink (`Y` = yes, `N` = no)

`USED BY`
: The virtual network device user

`DTYP`
: The virtual network device type (`H` = hub, `S` = switch)

`DNAME`
: The virtual network device name

`PKTTX/s`
: The number of packets transmitted per second

`MbTX/s`
: The number of megabits transmitted per second

`PKTRX/s`
: The number of packets received per second

`MbRX/s`
: The number of megabits received per second

`%DRPTX`
: The percentage of transmitted packets that were dropped

`%DRPRX`
: The percentage of received packets that were dropped

See Also

Recipes 5.7, 5.8, and 5.9

5.11 Managing Virtual Switches

Problem

You want to manage internal virtual switch (vSwitch) entities within your ESXi environment.

Solution

Run the `esxcli network vswitch standard` command on the ESXI server.

Discussion

You'll find this one of the most useful commands to use from your ESXi shell. It allows you to list, add, modify, or delete virtual Ethernet switches on your server using standard vSwitches. The second command here is specific to the distributed vSwitches which at this time, you can only view.

```
~ # esxcli network vswitch standard -h

Available Namespaces:
  policy                  Commands to manipulate network policy settings governing the
                          given virtual switch.
  portgroup               Commands to list and manipulate Port Groups on an ESXi host.
  uplink                  Commands to add and remove uplink on given virtual switch.

Available Commands:
  add                     Add a new virtual switch to the ESXi networking system.
  list                    List the virtual switches current on the ESXi host.
  remove                  Remove a virtual switch from the ESXi networking system.
  set                     This command sets the MTU size and CDP status of a given
                          virtual switch.


~ # esxcli network vswitch dvs -h
```

```
Usage: esxcli network vswitch dvs {cmd} [cmd options]

Available Namespaces:
  vmware                Commands to retrieve VMware vSphere Distributed Switch
                        information
```

The -l option lists the virtual switches and port groups that are configured on your ESXI server. Its output will look something like this:

```
~ # esxcli network vswitch standard list
vSwitch0
   Name: vSwitch0
   Class: etherswitch
   Num Ports: 128
   Used Ports: 3
   Configured Ports: 128
   MTU: 1500
   CDP Status: listen
   Beacon Enabled: false
   Beacon Interval: 1
   Beacon Threshold: 3
   Beacon Required By:
   Uplinks: vmnic0
   Portgroups: VM Network, Management Network

vSwitch1
   Name: vSwitch1
   Class: etherswitch
   Num Ports: 128
   Used Ports: 1
   Configured Ports: 128
   MTU: 1500
   CDP Status: listen
   Beacon Enabled: false
   Beacon Interval: 1
   Beacon Threshold: 3
   Beacon Required By:
   Uplinks:
   Portgroups: vMotion
```

As you can see in this example, we have two vSwitch: *vSwitch0* contains our VM and Management Network portgroup, and *vSwitch1* contains our vMotion portgroup.

Using the add option, you can add more virtual switches to your ESXI server:

```
esxcli network vswitch standard add -v vSwitch1 -P 128
```

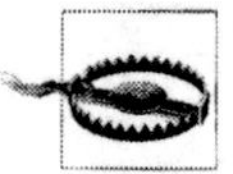

Check your options carefully before entering each of these commands. If you enter incorrect options, you risk being disconnected from your ESXI server.

Using the -l option again will show you that the new virtual switch has been added but doesn't have a portgroup or an uplink:

```
~ # esxcli network vswitch standard list
...
vSwitch1
   Name: vSwitch1
   Class: etherswitch
   Num Ports: 128
   Used Ports: 1
   Configured Ports: 128
   MTU: 1500
   CDP Status: listen
   Beacon Enabled: false
   Beacon Interval: 1
   Beacon Threshold: 3
   Beacon Required By:
   Uplinks:
   Portgroups:
```

To configure a portgroup on your new virtual switch, use the `-v` (lowercase) option along with the `-p` (lowercase) option to designate the new portgroup being added to the vSwitch.

```
~ # esxcli network vswitch standard portgroup add -v vSwitch1 -p vMotion
```

Again using the `-l` option to verify the changes, you will notice that the backup network portgroup has been added under *vSwitch1* but that it has not yet been assigned to an uplink:

```
~ # esxcli network vswitch standard list
vSwitch1
   Name: vSwitch1
   Class: etherswitch
   Num Ports: 128
   Used Ports: 1
   Configured Ports: 128
   MTU: 1500
   CDP Status: listen
   Beacon Enabled: false
   Beacon Interval: 1
   Beacon Threshold: 3
   Beacon Required By:
   Uplinks:
   Portgroups: vMotion
```

The `-u` option (uppercase) allows us to assign the PNIC (physical NIC) to the virtual switch. In this example, we are configuring physical Ethernet port 1 to vSwitch1.

```
~ # esxcli network vswitch standard uplink add -u vmnic1 -v vSwitch1
```

Verify your configuration change again and notice this time that the uplinks on the vSwitch and the portgroup have been assigned to *vmnic1*:

```
~ # esxcli network vswitch standard list
...
vSwitch1
   Name: vSwitch1
   Class: etherswitch
```

```
Num Ports: 128
Used Ports: 2
Configured Ports: 128
MTU: 1500
CDP Status: listen
Beacon Enabled: false
Beacon Interval: 1
Beacon Threshold: 3
Beacon Required By:
Uplinks: vmnic1
Portgroups: vMotion
```

And finally, to remove a *vmnic* from a vSwitch and portgroup, use the following command. The -u represents the uplink and -v the vSwitch in which the uplink will be removed.

```
esxcli network vswitch standard uplink remove -u vmnic1 -v vSwitch1
```

5.12 Generating a Logfile for VMware Support

Problem

VMware support may require you to send in a configuration dump of your ESXI server for troubleshooting specific issues.

Solution

Use `vm-support` to gather the data needed for troubleshooting.

Discussion

If you open a ticket with VMware support, VMware might request you to send a *support bundle*. This is an archive package filled with logs and other information about your ESXI server. Luckily, there is a very simple and powerful command that will generate a tar file that includes everything necessary. The `vm-support` command is also useful for your own troubleshooting:

```
~ # vm-support -h
Usage: vm-support [options]

Options:
  -h, --help            show this help message and exit
  -g GROUPS, --groups=GROUPS
                        Gather data from listed groups
  -a MANIFESTS, --manifests=MANIFESTS
                        Gather from listed manifests
  -e EXCLUDEMANIFESTS, --excludemanifests=EXCLUDEMANIFESTS
                        Exclude the listed manifests
  --listmanifests       List available manifests
  -G, --listgroups      List available manifest groups
  -t, --listtags        List available manifest tags
  -p, --performance     Gather performance data
```

```
  -d DURATION, --duration=DURATION
                        Duration of performance monitoring (in seconds)
  -i INTERVAL, --interval=INTERVAL
                        Interval between performance snapshots
  -v VM, --vm=VM        Gather detailed information about this specific VM (ie
                        --vm <path to .vmx file>)
  -V, --listvms         List currently registered VMs
  -w WORKINGDIR, --workingdir=WORKINGDIR
                        Directory to create .tgz in
  -D, --dryrun          Prints out the data that would have been gathered
  -s, --stream          stream data to stdout
  -q, --quiet           Output only the location of the bundle
  -E ERRORFILE, --errorfile=ERRORFILE
                        Prints (non-fatal) errors to specified file (overrides
                        --quiet and --stream)
  --loglevel=LOGLEVEL   Set logging to specified level: 0-50 (0=most verbose)
  --version             Display the vm-support version
  -l, --listfiles       List all files gathered by vm-support
~ #
```

The -v option displays all the running virtual machines on the ESXI server:

```
~ # vm-support -V

Available worlds to debug:

vmid=1104       TEST01
vmid=1116       TEST02
vmid=1124       TEST03
```

To bundle up all your logs on the ESXI server, just run vm-support without arguments. This process will take about 5 to 15 minutes and will produce a *.tgz* file in the same directory where the command is run. You will see something similar to this while the tarball is being generated:

```
~ # vm-support
19:03:41: Creating /var/tmp/esx-test01-2011-10-10--19.03.tgz
```

When the command completes, it will give you detailed information on the location of the file and how to submit it to VMware support:

```
19:07:17: Done.
Please attach this file when submitting an incident report.
To file a support incident, go to http://www.vmware.com/support/sr/sr_login.jsp
To see the files collected, run: tar -tzf '/var/tmp/esx-test01-2011-10-10--19.05.tgz'
```

You can do a lot of other things with this command, such as collect performance data or run an SCSI trace on a virtual machine. Use the -h option to see the available options.

5.13 Checking ESXi Patches

Problem

You want to see what patches are applied to your ESX Server.

Solution

Run the *esxupdate* utility.

Discussion

A typical run of this command produces output like:

```
~ # esxcli software vib list
Name                  Version                             Vendor  Acceptance Level
--------------------  ----------------------------------  ------  ----------------
ata-pata-amd          0.3.10-3vmw.500.0.0.469512          VMware  VMwareCertified
ata-pata-atiixp       0.4.6-3vmw.500.0.0.469512           VMware  VMwareCertified
ata-pata-cmd64x       0.2.5-3vmw.500.0.0.469512           VMware  VMwareCertified
ata-pata-hpt3x2n      0.3.4-3vmw.500.0.0.469512           VMware  VMwareCertified
ata-pata-pdc2027x     1.0-3vmw.500.0.0.469512             VMware  VMwareCertified
ata-pata-serverworks  0.4.3-3vmw.500.0.0.469512           VMware  VMwareCertified
ata-pata-sil680       0.4.8-3vmw.500.0.0.469512           VMware  VMwareCertified
ata-pata-via          0.3.3-2vmw.500.0.0.469512           VMware  VMwareCertified
block-cciss           3.6.14-10vmw.500.0.0.469512         VMware  VMwareCertified
ehci-ehci-hcd         1.0-3vmw.500.0.0.469512             VMware  VMwareCertified
esx-base              5.0.0-0.0.469512                    VMware  VMwareCertified
esx-tboot             5.0.0-0.0.469512                    VMware  VMwareCertified
ima-qla4xxx           2.01.07-1vmw.500.0.0.469512         VMware  VMwareCertified
ipmi-ipmi-devintf     39.1-4vmw.500.0.0.469512            VMware  VMwareCertified
ipmi-ipmi-msghandler  39.1-4vmw.500.0.0.469512            VMware  VMwareCertified
ipmi-ipmi-si-drv      39.1-4vmw.500.0.0.469512            VMware  VMwareCertified
misc-cnic-register    1.1-1vmw.500.0.0.469512             VMware  VMwareCertified
misc-drivers          5.0.0-0.0.469512                    VMware  VMwareCertified
net-be2net            4.0.88.0-1vmw.500.0.0.469512        VMware  VMwareCertified
net-bnx2              2.0.15g.v50.11-5vmw.500.0.0.469512  VMware  VMwareCertified
net-bnx2x             1.61.15.v50.1-1vmw.500.0.0.469512   VMware  VMwareCertified
net-cnic              1.10.2j.v50.7-2vmw.500.0.0.469512   VMware  VMwareCertified
net-e1000             8.0.3.1-2vmw.500.0.0.469512         VMware  VMwareCertified
net-e1000e            1.1.2-3vmw.500.0.0.469512           VMware  VMwareCertified
net-enic              1.4.2.15a-1vmw.500.0.0.469512       VMware  VMwareCertified
net-forcedeth         0.61-2vmw.500.0.0.469512            VMware  VMwareCertified
net-igb               2.1.11.1-3vmw.500.0.0.469512        VMware  VMwareCertified
net-ixgbe             2.0.84.8.2-10vmw.500.0.0.469512     VMware  VMwareCertified
net-nx-nic            4.0.557-3vmw.500.0.0.469512         VMware  VMwareCertified
net-r8168             8.013.00-3vmw.500.0.0.469512        VMware  VMwareCertified
net-r8169             6.011.00-2vmw.500.0.0.469512        VMware  VMwareCertified
net-s2io              2.1.4.13427-3vmw.500.0.0.469512     VMware  VMwareCertified
net-sky2              1.20-2vmw.500.0.0.469512            VMware  VMwareCertified
net-tg3               3.110h.v50.4-4vmw.500.0.0.469512    VMware  VMwareCertified
ohci-usb-ohci         1.0-3vmw.500.0.0.469512             VMware  VMwareCertified
sata-ahci             3.0-6vmw.500.0.0.469512             VMware  VMwareCertified
sata-ata-piix         2.12-4vmw.500.0.0.469512            VMware  VMwareCertified
sata-sata-nv          3.5-3vmw.500.0.0.469512             VMware  VMwareCertified
sata-sata-promise     2.12-3vmw.500.0.0.469512            VMware  VMwareCertified
sata-sata-sil         2.3-3vmw.500.0.0.469512             VMware  VMwareCertified
sata-sata-svw         2.3-3vmw.500.0.0.469512             VMware  VMwareCertified
scsi-aacraid          1.1.5.1-9vmw.500.0.0.469512         VMware  VMwareCertified
scsi-adp94xx          1.0.8.12-6vmw.500.0.0.469512        VMware  VMwareCertified
scsi-aic79xx          3.1-5vmw.500.0.0.469512             VMware  VMwareCertified
```

```
scsi-bnx2i              1.9.1d.v50.1-3vmw.500.0.0.469512   VMware  VMwareCertified
scsi-fnic               1.5.0.3-1vmw.500.0.0.469512        VMware  VMwareCertified
scsi-hpsa               5.0.0-17vmw.500.0.0.469512         VMware  VMwareCertified
scsi-ips                7.12.05-4vmw.500.0.0.469512        VMware  VMwareCertified
scsi-lpfc820            8.2.2.1-18vmw.500.0.0.469512       VMware  VMwareCertified
scsi-megaraid-mbox      2.20.5.1-6vmw.500.0.0.469512       VMware  VMwareCertified
scsi-megaraid-sas       4.32-1vmw.500.0.0.469512           VMware  VMwareCertified
scsi-megaraid2          2.00.4-9vmw.500.0.0.469512         VMware  VMwareCertified
scsi-mpt2sas            06.00.00.00-5vmw.500.0.0.469512    VMware  VMwareCertified
scsi-mptsas             4.23.01.00-5vmw.500.0.0.469512     VMware  VMwareCertified
scsi-mptspi             4.23.01.00-5vmw.500.0.0.469512     VMware  VMwareCertified
scsi-qla2xxx            901.k1.1-14vmw.500.0.0.469512      VMware  VMwareCertified
scsi-qla4xxx            5.01.03.2-3vmw.500.0.0.469512      VMware  VMwareCertified
uhci-usb-uhci           1.0-3vmw.500.0.0.469512            VMware  VMwareCertified
tools-light             5.0.0-0.0.469512                   VMware  VMwareCertified
```

As you can see, we have an extensive history of patches that have been applied to our server. This command is useful for confirming that specific patches have been applied, or learning about the history of a machine that has been running for a while but for which you have just been given responsibility.

5.14 Enabling NTP in the vCenter

Problem

You want to enable NTP on your ESXi host.

Solution

By using the vCenter, you can easily configure NTP on your ESX host.

Discussion

Keeping your ESXI servers and virtual machines in sync is crucial to your virtual environment. Using NTP to manage time on your ESXi Server and the virtual machines ensures that your virtual machines are not losing CPU cycles due to mismatched time synchronization.

This example shows you how to configure time via the vCenter, the preferred method of for your ESXI server. However, if you are feeling brave, you can refer to Recipe 5.15 to configure NTP via the command line.

To get started, log in to the vCenter with your administrator account. Then follow these steps:

1. Click on the ESXI server on which you want to configure NTP. Under Configuration, select Time Configuration. You will then see a brief overview of your NTP configuration and NTP client stats (Figure 5-9).

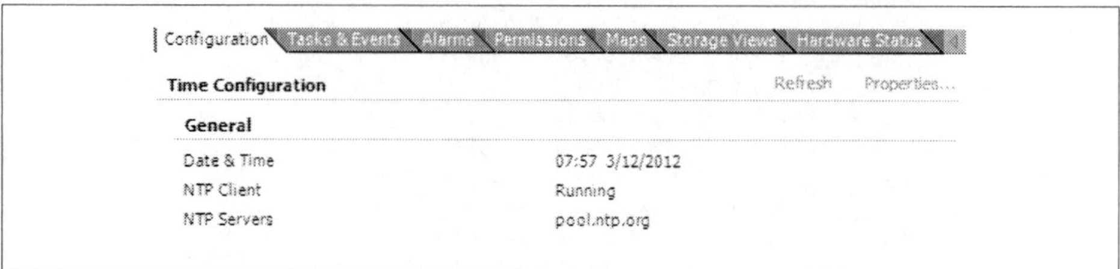

Figure 5-9. The default timeserver configuration page

2. Continue by clicking the Properties link in the upper right corner of the Time Configuration overview screen. You will be presented with a new window with options to configure NTP (Figure 5-10).

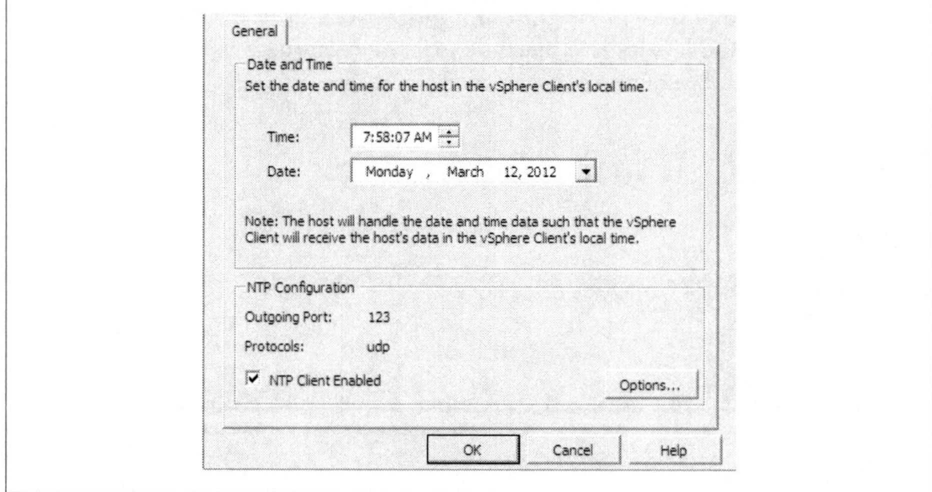

Figure 5-10. The Time Configuration page showing various information

3. Click the Options button near the bottom right corner. You will be presented with a new window where you can select the appropriate startup policy. In our example, we chose "Start automatically if any ports are open, and stop when all ports are closed" (Figure 5-11). Note: If you are running ESXi, your first choice will read "Start automatically."

   When you press OK, the vCenter will change the firewall rules for you automatically and will allow traffic through this port.

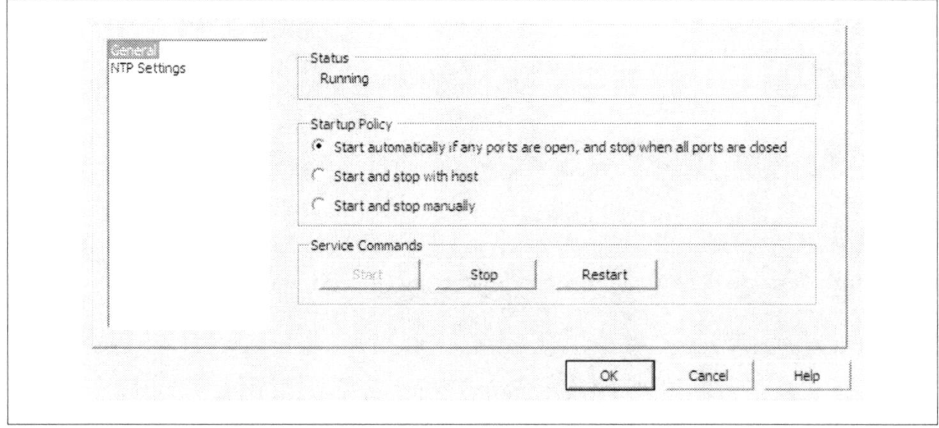

Figure 5-11. Selecting a startup NTP policy

4. Click on the NTP Settings link, and you will be shown the list of active NTP servers (Figure 5-12). If you are setting up NTP for the first time, there will be nothing listed here.

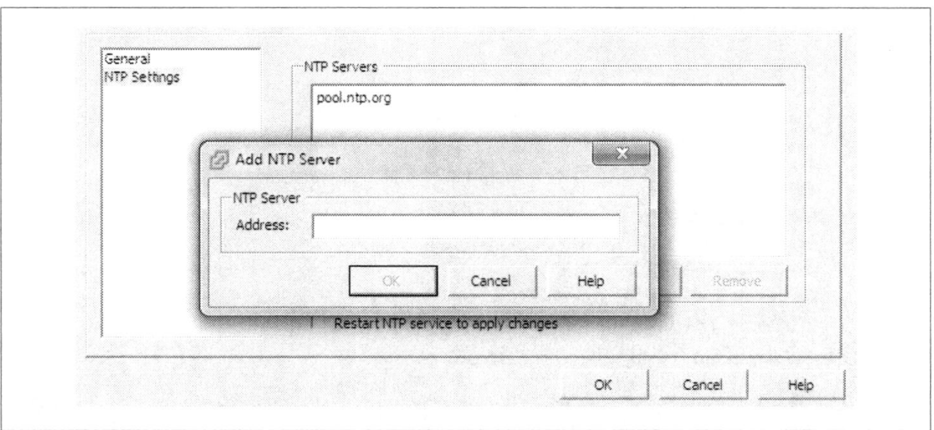

Figure 5-12. Displaying the current time servers

5. Click the Add button to add your NTP servers. If you have a default of 127.0.0.1, you can safely remove that entry by clicking it and then clicking the Remove button. Press OK to apply the changes and start the NTP service.

   ESXi will automatically provision the correct firewall rules, allowing connections on port 123. You will notice that the system time is synchronized shortly after the NTP service is started.

See Also

Recipe 5.15

5.15 Changing the ESXI Server's Time

Problem

You want to enable NTP on your ESXi host using the command line.

Solution

Using the service console, you can configure NTP services on your ESXi host.

Discussion

Although Recipe 5.14 showed you how to enable NTP interactively, you may want to do it in a script. All the steps shown in Recipe 5.14 can also be performed through shell commands:

1. To get started, log in to the ESXi Shell and run the following command:

   ```
   ~ # esxcli system time set --help
   Usage: esxcli system time set [cmd options]

   Description:
     set          Set the system clock time. Any missing parameters will
                  default to the current time

   Cmd options:
     -d|--day=<long>       Day
     -H|--hour=<long>      Hour
     -m|--min=<long>       Minute
     -M|--month=<long>     Month
     -s|--sec=<long>       Second
     -y|--year=<long>      Year
   ```

2. Next, set the time to match your current time.

   ```
   esxcli system time set -d 29 -H 20 -m 50 -M 11 -s 30 -y 2011
   ```

3. The following command opens the firewall port to ensure all NTP-related traffic is allowed through:

   ```
   esxcli network firewall ruleset set -e true -r ntpClient
   ```

The NTP client will now be enabled and the time will set on the ESXI server correctly.

See Also

Recipe 5.14 on page 174

5.16 Restarting the vCenter Agent

Problem

You want to restart the vCenter agent on your ESXI server via the ESXi shell.

Solution

You can restart the agent from the command line.

Discussion

From time to time, you may have to restart the virtual center agent on your ESXI server. For example, the vCenter may not see changes made with command-line utilities until you restart the agent. You can do this with the following command:

```
/sbin/services.sh restart
```

While the agent is restarting, you may see your ESXI server become disconnected from the vCenter. Don't worry, your virtual machines will continue to run, and the ESXI server will reconnect once the agent and the vCenter server reestablish a connection.

5.17 Finding Virtual Machine Snapshots

Problem

You need to find snapshots for your virtual machines.

Solution

You can list all the snapshots via the command line.

Discussion

This command will list all the snapshots in your virtual machine's directories:

```
~ # ls -Ral /vmfs/volumes/* |grep .vmsn
-rw-------    1 root     root         4304896432 Mar 12 12:01 DNS-Snapshot1.vmsn
```

This is helpful if you need to track down which virtual machines currently have snapshots associated with them.

Snapshots will consume a lot of disk space if left unattended and should be reverted when possible.

5.18 Renaming a Virtual Machine via the vCenter

Problem

You need to rename a virtual machine.

Solution

You can rename virtual machines in the vCenter.

Discussion

Log in to your vCenter server and follow these quick steps:

1. Power off the virtual machine you want to rename.
2. Rename the virtual machine by right-clicking and choosing Rename.
3. Migrate the virtual machine to another datastore.

This method requires you to have more than one datastore available to your ESXI servers. However, it is the quickest method available to rename a virtual machine, because it will actually copy the virtual machine's files to the new datastore and rename them accordingly.

5.19 Setting ESXi Options Using the Command Line

Problem

You want to set advanced configuration variables on your ESXI server, but you can't use the vCenter (or you want to automate the process by using command-line tools).

Solution

Run the `esxcli system settings advanced` command on the ESXI server.

Discussion

This command allows you to adjust the advanced configuration values from the command line. These values can also be changed inside the vCenter, which is much easier; however, if the vCenter isn't available, this command will allow you to make the needed adjustments. Options you can change are:

```
~ # esxcli system settings advanced
Usage: esxcli system settings advanced {cmd} [cmd options]

Available Commands:
  list                  List the advanced options available from the VMkernel.
  set                   Set the value of an advanced option.
```

To get an idea of what is configurable via the command line, run the `list` command. This will give you a very large output of options that can be tweaked:

```
~ # esxcli system settings advanced list
   Path: /Irq/BestVcpuRouting
   Type: integer
   Int Value: 0
   Default Int Value: 0
   Min Value: 0
   Max Value: 1
   String Value:
   Default String Value:
   Valid Characters:
   Description: 1: try to route the virtual interrupt to the best vcpu; 0 to disable

   Path: /Irq/IRQRebalancePeriod
   Type: integer
   Int Value: 50
   Default Int Value: 50
   Min Value: 10
   Max Value: 20000
   String Value:
   Default String Value:
   Valid Characters:
   Description: time in ms between attempts to rebalance interrupts
...
```

Inside these directories are text files that contain configurable values. For example, the *Misc* subdirectory has a file named *HostName* that contains a value like the following:

```
~ # esxcli system settings advanced list -o /Misc/HostName
   Path: /Misc/HostName
   Type: string
   Int Value: 0
   Default Int Value: 0
   Min Value: 0
   Max Value: 0
   String Value: localhost.test.com
   Default String Value: localhost
   Valid Characters: **
   Description: Host name
```

The `-s` switch lets you set a specific parameter. For instance, the following command changes the hostname of the ESXI server:

```
esxcli system settings advanced set -s servername.test.com -o /Misc/hostName
```

5.20 Configuring Authentication Choices Using the Command Line

Problem

ESXi 3.5/4.x ONLY - You want to use the command line to set authentication parameters such as the type of authentication, the authentication server, and password aging.

Solution

Run the `esxcfg-auth` command on the ESXI server.

Discussion

The `esxcfg-auth` command allows you to configure different authentication methods on your ESXI server. We won't go into detail on the configurable options here, because we discuss setting up an Active Directory in Chapter 6. However, here's a list of those options:

```
$ esxcfg-auth -h
usage: esxcfg-auth [options]

options:
  --enablemd5               Enable MD5 password storage
  --disablemd5              Disable MD5 password storage
  --enableshadow            Enable Shadow password storage
  --disableshadow           Disable Shadow password storage
  --enablenis               Enable NIS Authentication
  --disablenis              Disable NIS Authentication
  --nisdomain=domain        Set the NIS domain
  --nisserver=server        Set the NIS server
  --enableldap              Enable LDAP User Management
  --disableldap             Disable LDAP User Management
  --enableldapauth          Enable LDAP Authentication
  --disableldapauth         Disable LDAP Authentication
  --ldapserver=server       Set the LDAP Server
  --ldapbasedn=basedn       Set the base DN for the LDAP server
  --enableldaptls           Enable TLS connections for LDAP
  --disableldaptls          Disable TLS connections for LDAP
  --enablekrb5              Enable Kererbos Authentication
  --disablekrb5             Disable Kererbos Authentication
  --krb5realm=domain        Set the Kerberos Realm
  --krb5kdc=server          Set the Kebreros Key Distribution Center
  --krb5adminserver=server Set the Kerberos Admin Server
  --enablead                Enable Active Directory Authentication
  --disablead               Disable Active Directory Authentication
  --addomain=domain         Set the Active Directory Domain
  --addc=server             Set the Active Directory Domain Controller
  --usepamqc=values         Enable the pam_passwdqc module
  --usecrack=values         Enable the pam_cracklib module
```

```
--enablecache             Enables caching of login credentials
--disablecache            Disables caching of login credentials
--passmaxdays=days        Set the maximum number of days a password remains valid
--passmindays=days        Set the minimum number of days a password remains valid
--passwarnage=days        Set the number of days a warning is given before a
                          password expires
--maxfailedlogins=count   Sets the maximum number of login failures before the
                          account is locked out, setting to 0 will disable this
-p, --probe               Print the settings to the console
-v, --verbose             Enable verbose logging
-h, --help                show this help message and exit
```

5.21 Manipulating the Crash Dump Partition

Problem

You wish to manage the VMkernel crash dump partition. Normally, this is set up during the installation of your ESXI server and will not require any further maintenance. However, a tool is available if you need to look at or manipulate it.

Solution

Run the `esxcli system coredump` command on the ESXI server.

Discussion

A dump partition is a section of your hard drive that is set aside as a place for information from crashes to be automatically stored for later retrieval and use in troubleshooting. There are a few options available here, `network` and `partition`, which will gather statistics and data to include in the core dump file.

```
~ # esxcli system coredump
Usage: esxcli system coredump {cmd} [cmd options]

Available Namespaces:
  network               Operations pertaining to the VMkernel Core dump configuration
                        on network dump servers.
  partition             Operations pertaining to the VMkernel Core dump configuration
                        on VMkernel Diagnostic partitions.
```

Running the command with the `list` option lists the ESXI server's crash dump partition, which is normally set up when ESXi is installed. A typical output will look similar to this:

```
~ # esxcli system coredump partition list
Name                  Path                                        Active  Configured
--------------------  ------------------------------------------  ------  ----------
mpx.vmhba1:C0:T0:L0:7 /vmfs/devices/disks/mpx.vmhba1:C0:T0:L0:7     true        true
```

You will probably never need to make changes to this partition.

5.22 Configuring a Firewall on the Command Line

Problem

You want to configure the firewall on your ESXI server using the command line.

Solution

Run the `esxcli network firewall` command on the ESXI server.

Discussion

VMware makes it easy to configure the firewall on your ESXi Hosts with the following command. Generally, the firewall is configured via the vCenter client. However, it is important to understand how to do this via the command line as well. The configuration options are listed here:

```
~ # esxcli network firewall
Usage: esxcli network firewall {cmd} [cmd options]

Available Namespaces:
  ruleset               Commands to list and update firewall ruleset configuration

Available Commands:
  get                   Get the firewall status
  load                  Load firewall module and rulesets configuration
  refresh               Load ruleset configuration for firewall
  set                   Set firewall enabled status and default action
  unload                Allow unload firewall module
                                     Show this message
```

We won't go into detail on the configuration options here because we discuss configuring your firewall in Chapter 6.

See Also

Recipe 6.11

5.23 Managing ESXi Driver Modules

Problem

You wish to manage modules that are loaded in the VMkernel on a system boot.

Solution

Run the `esxcli system module` command on the ESXI server.

Discussion

The `esxcli system module` command provides you with a way to adjust the driver modules that are loaded during the ESXI server's startup sequence. Here's a list of the configurable options:

```
~ # esxcli system module
Usage: esxcli system module {cmd} [cmd options]

Available Namespaces:
  parameters            Operations that allow manipulation of parameters of VMkernel
                        loadable modules and device drivers. Operations include list
                        and set options.

Available Commands:
  get                   Show the ELF header information for the given VMkernel module.
  list                  List the VMkernel modules that the system knows about.
  load                  Load a VMkernel module with the given name if it is enabled.
                        If the module is disabled then the use of --force is required
                        to load the module.
  set                   Allow enabling and disabling of a VMkernel module.
```

Use the `list` option to find out which modules are loaded on boot and whether any modules are disabled. In our example, we have no modules disabled (modules that are disabled will display as `false`):

```
~ # esxcli system module list
Name                 Is Loaded  Is Enabled
-------------------  ---------  ----------
vmkernel                  true        true
procfs                    true        true
vmkplexer                 true        true
vmklinux_9                true        true
vmklinux_9_2_0_0          true        true
random                    true        true
usb                       true        true
ehci-hcd                  true        true
usb-uhci                  true        true
hid                       true        true
dm                        true        true
nmp                       true        true
vmw_satp_local            true        true
vmw_satp_default_aa       true        true
vmw_psp_lib               true        true
vmw_psp_fixed             true        true
vmw_psp_rr                true        true
vmw_psp_mru               true        true
libata                    true        true
usb-storage               true        true
vfat                      true        true
vprobe                    true        true
vmci                      true        true
iscsi_trans               true        true
etherswitch               true        true
netsched                  true        true
```

```
cnic_register                 true          true
e1000                         true          true
iscsi_linux                   true          true
libfc                         true          true
libfcoe                       true          true
ata_piix                      true          true
mptspi                        true          true
lvmdriver                     true          true
deltadisk                     true          true
multiextent                   true          true
heartbeat                     true          true
shaper                        true          true
cdp                           true          true
ipfix                         true          true
fence_overlay                 true          true
tcpip3                        true          true
dvsdev                        true          true
dvfilter                      true          true
esxfw                         true          true
vmkibft                       true          true
vmfs3                         true          true
nfsclient                     true          true
vmkstatelogger                true          true
migrate                       true          true
cbt                           true          true
svmmirror                     true          true
hbr_filter                    true          true
vmkapei                      false          true
```

The get option allows you to view information specific to a module. For example, here is the output of the vmfs3 module:

```
~ # esxcli system module get -m vmfs3
   Module: vmfs3
   Module File: /usr/lib/vmware/vmkmod/vmfs3
   License: VMware
   Version: Version 14.54, Built on: Aug 18 2011
   Signed Status: VMware Signed
   Signature Issuer: VMware, Inc.
   Signature Digest: cfae f194 c756 d2a1 b1ae eae1 8e59 3e93 29d5 4aac 55db ea10 46a7
                     5b3e 5008 e9e3
   Signature FingerPrint: cb44 247a 1614 cea1 2079 362d ec86 9d0e
   Provided Namespaces: esx@nover
   Required Namespaces: com.vmware.vmkapi@v2_0_0_0, scsiVMware@0, vmkernel@nover
```

5.24 Configuring Storage Multipathing

Problem

You want to manage the paths between the ESXI server and its storage devices via the command line instead of using the vCenter client.

Solution

By running the `esxcli storage core path` command on the ESXI server, you can configure the pathing information for your SAN storage.

Discussion

The easiest way to manage your storage's paths is using the vCenter. However, VMware also provides the `esxcli storage core path` command to enable you to manage them via the command line.

Let's take a look at the options available for configuring multipathing via the ESXi Shell:

```
~ # esxcli storage core path
Usage: esxcli storage core path {cmd} [cmd options]

Available Namespaces:
  stats                 Stats operations pertaining to the pluggable storage archite-
                        ctures' device paths on the system.

Available Commands:
  list                  List all the SCSI paths on the system.
  set                   Provide control to allow a user to modify a single path's
                        state. This effectively allows a user to enable or disable
                        SCSI paths. The user is not able to change the full range of
                        path states, but can toggle between 'active' and 'off'. Please
                        NOTE changing the Path state on any path that is the only path
                        to a given device is likely to fail. The VMkernel will not
                        change the path's state if changing the state would cause an
                        'All paths down' state or the device is currently in use.
```

Using the following command, you can get the output of your current paths, adapter information, target, LUN, etc. The following output on our development system shows our current paths to the local disk, Local VMware, Disk. In addition, we can also see the driver we are using, which is NMP, which is the native multipathing driver built into ESXi, and the drive type in this example its IDE.

```
~ # esxcli storage core path list
usb.vmhba32-usb.0:0-mpx.vmhba32:C0:T0:L0
   UID: usb.vmhba32-usb.0:0-mpx.vmhba32:C0:T0:L0
   Runtime Name: vmhba32:C0:T0:L0
   Device: mpx.vmhba32:C0:T0:L0
   Device Display Name: Local USB Direct-Access (mpx.vmhba32:C0:T0:L0)
   Adapter: vmhba32
   Channel: 0
   Target: 0
   LUN: 0
   Plugin: NMP
   State: active
   Transport: usb
   Adapter Identifier: usb.vmhba32
   Target Identifier: usb.0:0
   Adapter Transport Details: Unavailable or path is unclaimed
   Target Transport Details: Unavailable or path is unclaimed
```

```
iqn.1998-01.com.vmware:esx2-6d027a7c-00023d000002,iqn.esx,t,1-t10.
                       FreeBSD_iSCSI_Disk_____001d60f814da000________________
   UID: iqn.1998-01.com.vmware:esx2-6d027a7c-00023d000002,iqn.esx,t,1-t10.
        FreeBSD_iSCSI_Disk_____001d60f814da000________________
   Runtime Name: vmhba38:C1:T0:L0
   Device: t10.FreeBSD_iSCSI_Disk_____001d60f814da000________________
   Device Display Name: FreeBSD iSCSI Disk
                        (t10.FreeBSD_iSCSI_Disk_____001d60f814da000________________)
   Adapter: vmhba38
   Channel: 1
   Target: 0
   LUN: 0
   Plugin: NMP
   State: active
   Transport: iscsi
   Adapter Identifier: iqn.1998-01.com.vmware:esx2-6d027a7c
   Target Identifier: 00023d000002,iqn.esx,t,1
   Adapter Transport Details: iqn.1998-01.com.vmware:esx2-6d027a7c
   Target Transport Details: IQN=iqn.esx Alias= Session=00023d000002 PortalTag=1

iqn.1998-01.com.vmware:esx2-6d027a7c-00023d000002,iqn.esx,t,1-t10.
                       FreeBSD_iSCSI_Disk_____001d60f814da001________________
   UID: iqn.1998-01.com.vmware:esx2-6d027a7c-00023d000002,iqn.esx,t,1-t10.
        FreeBSD_iSCSI_Disk_____001d60f814da001________________
   Runtime Name: vmhba38:C1:T0:L1
   Device: t10.FreeBSD_iSCSI_Disk_____001d60f814da001________________
   Device Display Name: FreeBSD iSCSI Disk
                        (t10.FreeBSD_iSCSI_Disk_____001d60f814da001________________)
   Adapter: vmhba38
   Channel: 1
   Target: 0
   LUN: 1
   Plugin: NMP
   State: active
   Transport: iscsi
   Adapter Identifier: iqn.1998-01.com.vmware:esx2-6d027a7c
   Target Identifier: 00023d000002,iqn.esx,t,1
   Adapter Transport Details: iqn.1998-01.com.vmware:esx2-6d027a7c
   Target Transport Details: IQN=iqn.esx Alias= Session=00023d000002 PortalTag=1

iqn.1998-01.com.vmware:esx2-6d027a7c-00023d000002,iqn.esx,t,1-t10.
                       FreeBSD_iSCSI_Disk_____001d60f814da002________________
   UID: iqn.1998-01.com.vmware:esx2-6d027a7c-00023d000002,iqn.esx,t,1-t10.
        FreeBSD_iSCSI_Disk_____001d60f814da002________________
   Runtime Name: vmhba38:C1:T0:L2
   Device: t10.FreeBSD_iSCSI_Disk_____001d60f814da002________________
   Device Display Name: FreeBSD iSCSI Disk
                        (t10.FreeBSD_iSCSI_Disk_____001d60f814da002________________)
   Adapter: vmhba38
   Channel: 1
   Target: 0
   LUN: 2
   Plugin: NMP
   State: active
```

```
   Transport: iscsi
   Adapter Identifier: iqn.1998-01.com.vmware:esx2-6d027a7c
   Target Identifier: 00023d000002,iqn.esx,t,1
   Adapter Transport Details: iqn.1998-01.com.vmware:esx2-6d027a7c
   Target Transport Details: IQN=iqn.esx Alias= Session=00023d000002 PortalTag=1

iqn.1998-01.com.vmware:esx2-6d027a7c-00023d000001,iqn.esx,t,1-t10.
                        FreeBSD_iSCSI_Disk______001d60f814da000_________________
   UID: iqn.1998-01.com.vmware:esx2-6d027a7c-00023d000001,iqn.esx,t,1-t10.
        FreeBSD_iSCSI_Disk______001d60f814da000_________________
   Runtime Name: vmhba38:C0:T0:L0
   Device: t10.FreeBSD_iSCSI_Disk______001d60f814da000_________________
   Device Display Name: FreeBSD iSCSI Disk
                        (t10.FreeBSD_iSCSI_Disk______001d60f814da000_________________)
   Adapter: vmhba38
   Channel: 0
   Target: 0
   LUN: 0
   Plugin: NMP
   State: active
   Transport: iscsi
   Adapter Identifier: iqn.1998-01.com.vmware:esx2-6d027a7c
   Target Identifier: 00023d000001,iqn.esx,t,1
   Adapter Transport Details: iqn.1998-01.com.vmware:esx2-6d027a7c
   Target Transport Details: IQN=iqn.esx Alias= Session=00023d000001 PortalTag=1

iqn.1998-01.com.vmware:esx2-6d027a7c-00023d000001,iqn.esx,t,1-t10.
                        FreeBSD_iSCSI_Disk______001d60f814da001_________________
   UID: iqn.1998-01.com.vmware:esx2-6d027a7c-00023d000001,iqn.esx,t,1-t10.
        FreeBSD_iSCSI_Disk______001d60f814da001_________________
   Runtime Name: vmhba38:C0:T0:L1
   Device: t10.FreeBSD_iSCSI_Disk______001d60f814da001_________________
   Device Display Name: FreeBSD iSCSI Disk
                        (t10.FreeBSD_iSCSI_Disk______001d60f814da001_________________)
   Adapter: vmhba38
   Channel: 0
   Target: 0
   LUN: 1
   Plugin: NMP
   State: active
   Transport: iscsi
   Adapter Identifier: iqn.1998-01.com.vmware:esx2-6d027a7c
   Target Identifier: 00023d000001,iqn.esx,t,1
   Adapter Transport Details: iqn.1998-01.com.vmware:esx2-6d027a7c
   Target Transport Details: IQN=iqn.esx Alias= Session=00023d000001 PortalTag=1

iqn.1998-01.com.vmware:esx2-6d027a7c-00023d000001,iqn.esx,t,1-t10.
                        FreeBSD_iSCSI_Disk______001d60f814da002_________________
   UID: iqn.1998-01.com.vmware:esx2-6d027a7c-00023d000001,iqn.esx,t,1-t10.
        FreeBSD_iSCSI_Disk______001d60f814da002_________________
   Runtime Name: vmhba38:C0:T0:L2
   Device: t10.FreeBSD_iSCSI_Disk______001d60f814da002_________________
   Device Display Name: FreeBSD iSCSI Disk
                        (t10.FreeBSD_iSCSI_Disk______001d60f814da002_________________)
   Adapter: vmhba38
```

```
   Channel: 0
   Target: 0
   LUN: 2
   Plugin: NMP
   State: active
   Transport: iscsi
   Adapter Identifier: iqn.1998-01.com.vmware:esx2-6d027a7c
   Target Identifier: 00023d000001,iqn.esx,t,1
   Adapter Transport Details: iqn.1998-01.com.vmware:esx2-6d027a7c
   Target Transport Details: IQN=iqn.esx Alias= Session=00023d000001 PortalTag=1

sata.vmhba33-sata.0:0-t10.ATA____WDC_WD2500KS2D00MJB0
                         ________________________WD2DWCANK7551048
   UID: sata.vmhba33-sata.0:0-t10.ATA____WDC_WD2500KS2D00MJB0
       ________________________WD2DWCANK7551048
   Runtime Name: vmhba33:C0:T0:L0
   Device: t10.ATA____WDC_WD2500KS2D00MJB0________________________WD2DWCANK7551048
   Device Display Name: Local ATA Disk (t10.ATA____WDC_WD2500KS2D00MJB0
                     ________________________WD2DWCANK7551048)
   Adapter: vmhba33
   Channel: 0
   Target: 0
   LUN: 0
   Plugin: NMP
   State: active
   Transport: sata
   Adapter Identifier: sata.vmhba33
   Target Identifier: sata.0:0
   Adapter Transport Details: Unavailable or path is unclaimed
   Target Transport Details: Unavailable or path is unclaimed
```

5.25 Managing NFS Mounts

Problem

You want to manage the remote storage mounted over NFS.

Solution

Run the `esxcli storage nfs` command on the ESXI server.

Discussion

Using this tool, you can list, mount, and unmount NFS exports from the VMkernel.

Let's take a look at the options available for the `esxcli storage nfs` command:

```
~ # esxcli storage nfs
Usage: esxcli storage nfs {cmd} [cmd options]

Available Commands:
  add                    Add a new NAS volume to the ESXi Host and mount it with the
                         given volume name
```

```
  list                  List the NAS volumes currently known to the ESXi host
  remove                Remove an existing NAS volume from the ESXi host
```

The `list` option displays the current NFS mounts on your ESXI server:

```
~ # esxcli storage nfs list
NFSMOUNT01 is /NFS from 172.20.44.100 mounted
```

One of the most important requirements of NAS and software-based iSCSI is that you need to have a VMkernel port configured on the ESX Server's network. Assuming the VMkernel port is already configured, you can add a new mount as follows:

```
$ esxcli storage nfs add -H 172.20.44.101 -s /nfs02 -v NFSMOUNT02
Connecting to NAS volume: NFSMOUNT02
NFSMOUNT02 created and connected.
```

5.26 Managing Disk Volumes

Problem

You want to use the command line to manage snapshots or replica volumes.

Solution

Run the `esxcli storage filesystem` command on the ESXI server.

Discussion

VMware added a new command-line tool in ESXi to enable the management of disk snapshot/replica volumes. This new command allows you to:

- Find these resources and view information about them
- Mount or unmount a volume
- Change the signature on a volume (resignaturing)
- Make the mounting of a volume persistent across reboots

This command can come in handy if you need to mount a snapshot of your LUN because of corruption on the original LUN.

Let's take a look at the options available for the `esxcli storage filesystem` command:

```
~ # esxcli storage filesystem
Usage: esxcli storage filesystem {cmd} [cmd options]

Available Commands:
  automount             Request mounting of known datastores not explicitly unmounted.
  list                  List the volumes available to the host. This includes VMFS,
                        NAS, and VFAT partitions.
  mount                 Connect to and mount an unmounted volume on the ESXi host.
  rescan                Issue a rescan operation to the VMkernel to have is scan sto-
                        rage devices for new mountable filesystems.
  unmount               Disconnect and unmount and existing VMFS or NAS volume. This
```

```
will not delete the configuration for the volume, but will
remove the volume from the list of mounted volumes.
```

5.27 Configuring Ethernet Adapters

Problem

You want to manage and set specific variables on the physical Ethernet adapters in the ESXI server.

Solution

Run the `esxcli network nic` command on the ESXI server.

Discussion

Let's take a look at the options available for the `esxcli network nic` command:

```
~ # esxcli network nic
Usage: esxcli network nic {cmd} [cmd options]

Available Commands:
  down                  Bring down the specified network device.
  get                   Get the generic configuration of a network device.
  list                  This command will list the Physical NICs currently installed
                        and loaded on the system.
  set                   Set the general options for the specified ethernet device.
  up                    Bring up the specified network device.
```

To list all Ethernet ports in the server, use the `list` option. The output will give you a variety of information about the interface, including the driver, PCI, speed, duplex, and MTU, along with a description. Multiple interfaces will be displayed as *vmnic0*, *vmnic1*, and so on. For example:

```
~ # esxcli network nic list
Name    PCI Device     Driver  Link  Speed  Duplex  MAC Address   MTU   Description
------  -------------  ------  ----  -----  ------  -----------   ----  -----------------
vmnic0  0000:002:01.0  e1000   Up     1000  Full    00:0c:29:     1500  Intel Corporation
                                                    7f:3a:5d            Gigabit Ethernet
                                                                        Controller
vmnic1  0000:002:04.0  e1000   Up     1000  Full    00:0c:29:     1500  Intel Corporation
                                                    7f:3a:67            Gigabit Ethernet
                                                                        Controller
```

You can also set the speed of your interface using the options that follow. The following example sets the speed to 100MBps and the duplex mode to full duplex on the *vmnic0* interface (note that if you are changing the speed, you must also specify a duplex mode):

```
esxcli network nic set -S 100 -D full -n vmnic0
```

Changing the adapter to use the maximum speed can be accomplished using the `-S` option. Remember, you can use the `-l` option to verify your changes.

5.28 Rescanning Host Bus Adapters

Problem

You wish to rescan the HBAs in your ESXI server. This is useful if you add new LUNs or need to troubleshoot the HBAs.

Solution

Run the `esxcli storage core` command on the ESXI server.

Discussion

Use these commands to rescan a single adapter, or all the adapters on your ESXI server:

```
~ # esxcli storage core
Usage: esxcli storage core {cmd} [cmd options]

Available Namespaces:
  adapter               Operations on SCSI Host Bus Adapters on the system.
  device                Operations pertaining to the pluggable storage architectures'
                        logical devices on the system. The operation currently allowed
                        is to list the available devices on the system and the filters
                        attached to each
  path                  Operations pertaining to the pluggable storage architectures'
                        SCSI device paths on the system.
  plugin                Operations pertaining to the pluggable storage architectures'
                        plugins. The operation currently allowed is to list the available
                        plugins on the system with the type of those plugins.
  claiming              Operations pertaining to the pluggable storage direct path
                        claiming system. These operations will allow a user to directly
                        control the claiming and unclaiming process. These operations are
                        considered temporary and any claiming operations that need to
                        survive a reboot should use claimrules instead.
  claimrule             Operations pertaining to the pluggable storage architecture
                        claiming rule system. These operations operate on the rules used
                        to determine the PSA plugin used to claim storage paths.
```

The following example rescans the specified HBA card for new LUNs. A typical scan, without adding any new LUNs, will look like this:

```
esxcli storage core adapter rescan --all
```

5.29 Managing Add-ons from the Command Line

Problem

You wish to manage available add-ons via the command line using ESXi4.

Solution

Run the `esxcli software` command on the ESXI server.

Discussion

The following command allows you to enable, disable, and list all the available add-ons (perhaps better understood as modules):

```
~ # esxcli software
Usage: esxcli software {cmd} [cmd options]

Available Namespaces:
  sources               Query depot contents for VIBs and image profiles
  acceptance            Retrieve and set the host acceptance level setting
  profile               Display, install, update, or validates image profiles
  vib                   Install, update, remove, or display individual VIB packages
```

The command is easy to use and pretty self-explanatory. If you have already installed ESX4, you may have noticed during the installation a new option to load add-ons. By default, your ESX4 installation will get a preloaded list of add-ons. The ones loaded by default on our Dell 1950 are shown in the following list:

```
~ # esxcli software vib list
Name                  Version                             Vendor  Acceptance Level
--------------------  ----------------------------------  ------  ----------------
ata-pata-amd          0.3.10-3vmw.500.0.0.469512          VMware  VMwareCertified
ata-pata-atiixp       0.4.6-3vmw.500.0.0.469512           VMware  VMwareCertified
ata-pata-cmd64x       0.2.5-3vmw.500.0.0.469512           VMware  VMwareCertified
ata-pata-hpt3x2n      0.3.4-3vmw.500.0.0.469512           VMware  VMwareCertified
ata-pata-pdc2027x     1.0-3vmw.500.0.0.469512             VMware  VMwareCertified
ata-pata-serverworks  0.4.3-3vmw.500.0.0.469512           VMware  VMwareCertified
ata-pata-sil680       0.4.8-3vmw.500.0.0.469512           VMware  VMwareCertified
ata-pata-via          0.3.3-2vmw.500.0.0.469512           VMware  VMwareCertified
block-cciss           3.6.14-10vmw.500.0.0.469512         VMware  VMwareCertified
ehci-ehci-hcd         1.0-3vmw.500.0.0.469512             VMware  VMwareCertified
esx-base              5.0.0-0.0.469512                    VMware  VMwareCertified
esx-tboot             5.0.0-0.0.469512                    VMware  VMwareCertified
ima-qla4xxx           2.01.07-1vmw.500.0.0.469512         VMware  VMwareCertified
ipmi-ipmi-devintf     39.1-4vmw.500.0.0.469512            VMware  VMwareCertified
ipmi-ipmi-msghandler  39.1-4vmw.500.0.0.469512            VMware  VMwareCertified
ipmi-ipmi-si-drv      39.1-4vmw.500.0.0.469512            VMware  VMwareCertified
misc-cnic-register    1.1-1vmw.500.0.0.469512             VMware  VMwareCertified
misc-drivers          5.0.0-0.0.469512                    VMware  VMwareCertified
net-be2net            4.0.88.0-1vmw.500.0.0.469512        VMware  VMwareCertified
net-bnx2              2.0.15g.v50.11-5vmw.500.0.0.469512  VMware  VMwareCertified
net-bnx2x             1.61.15.v50.1-1vmw.500.0.0.469512   VMware  VMwareCertified
```

```
net-cnic              1.10.2j.v50.7-2vmw.500.0.0.469512   VMware  VMwareCertified
net-e1000             8.0.3.1-2vmw.500.0.0.469512         VMware  VMwareCertified
net-e1000e            1.1.2-3vmw.500.0.0.469512           VMware  VMwareCertified
net-enic              1.4.2.15a-1vmw.500.0.0.469512       VMware  VMwareCertified
net-forcedeth         0.61-2vmw.500.0.0.469512            VMware  VMwareCertified
net-igb               2.1.11.1-3vmw.500.0.0.469512        VMware  VMwareCertified
net-ixgbe             2.0.84.8.2-10vmw.500.0.0.469512     VMware  VMwareCertified
net-nx-nic            4.0.557-3vmw.500.0.0.469512         VMware  VMwareCertified
net-r8168             8.013.00-3vmw.500.0.0.469512        VMware  VMwareCertified
net-r8169             6.011.00-2vmw.500.0.0.469512        VMware  VMwareCertified
net-s2io              2.1.4.13427-3vmw.500.0.0.469512     VMware  VMwareCertified
net-sky2              1.20-2vmw.500.0.0.469512            VMware  VMwareCertified
net-tg3               3.110h.v50.4-4vmw.500.0.0.469512    VMware  VMwareCertified
ohci-usb-ohci         1.0-3vmw.500.0.0.469512             VMware  VMwareCertified
sata-ahci             3.0-6vmw.500.0.0.469512             VMware  VMwareCertified
sata-ata-piix         2.12-4vmw.500.0.0.469512            VMware  VMwareCertified
sata-sata-nv          3.5-3vmw.500.0.0.469512             VMware  VMwareCertified
sata-sata-promise     2.12-3vmw.500.0.0.469512            VMware  VMwareCertified
sata-sata-sil         2.3-3vmw.500.0.0.469512             VMware  VMwareCertified
sata-sata-svw         2.3-3vmw.500.0.0.469512             VMware  VMwareCertified
scsi-aacraid          1.1.5.1-9vmw.500.0.0.469512         VMware  VMwareCertified
scsi-adp94xx          1.0.8.12-6vmw.500.0.0.469512        VMware  VMwareCertified
scsi-aic79xx          3.1-5vmw.500.0.0.469512             VMware  VMwareCertified
scsi-bnx2i            1.9.1d.v50.1-3vmw.500.0.0.469512    VMware  VMwareCertified
scsi-fnic             1.5.0.3-1vmw.500.0.0.469512         VMware  VMwareCertified
scsi-hpsa             5.0.0-17vmw.500.0.0.469512          VMware  VMwareCertified
scsi-ips              7.12.05-4vmw.500.0.0.469512         VMware  VMwareCertified
scsi-lpfc820          8.2.2.1-18vmw.500.0.0.469512        VMware  VMwareCertified
scsi-megaraid-mbox    2.20.5.1-6vmw.500.0.0.469512        VMware  VMwareCertified
scsi-megaraid-sas     4.32-1vmw.500.0.0.469512            VMware  VMwareCertified
scsi-megaraid2        2.00.4-9vmw.500.0.0.469512          VMware  VMwareCertified
scsi-mpt2sas          06.00.00.00-5vmw.500.0.0.469512     VMware  VMwareCertified
scsi-mptsas           4.23.01.00-5vmw.500.0.0.469512      VMware  VMwareCertified
scsi-mptspi           4.23.01.00-5vmw.500.0.0.469512      VMware  VMwareCertified
scsi-qla2xxx          901.k1.1-14vmw.500.0.0.469512       VMware  VMwareCertified
scsi-qla4xxx          5.01.03.2-3vmw.500.0.0.469512       VMware  VMwareCertified
uhci-usb-uhci         1.0-3vmw.500.0.0.469512             VMware  VMwareCertified
tools-light           5.0.0-0.0.469512                    VMware  VMwareCertified
```

Disabling add-ons is simple:

```
esxcli software vib remove -n tools-light
```

Enabling add-ons is also very simple:

```
esxcli software vib install -n tools-light
```

Only one add-on can be enabled or disabled in each command.

In a listing, when the star preceding the add-on is red, the associated add-on is installed but disabled.

5.30 Managing VMkernel Network Routes

Problem

You want to set or change the routes the VMkernel uses to reach networks.

Solution

Run the `vicfg-route` command using the vCLI toolkit. This command is not supported as of ESXi 5.0 in the esxshell and will require an additional installation on a Windows Server to access the vCLI Toolkit.

Discussion

VMware gives you the ability to modify the network routes via the command line using `vicfg-route`. Alternatively, you can configure the routes using the vCenter client.

Let's take a look at the options available for the `vicfg-route` command:

```
Synopsis: vicfg-route.pl OPTIONS [<gateway>]


Command-specific options:
   --add
    -a
          Add route to the VMkernel (valid for vSphere 4.0 and later),
                   requires <network> (described below)
                   <network> can be specified in 3 ways:
                          * As a single argument in <IP>/<Mask> format
                          * Or as a <IP> <Netmask> pair
                          * Or as 'default'
   --del
    -d
          Delete route from the VMkernel (valid for vSphere 4.0 and later),
                   requires <network> (described below)
                   <network> can be specified in 3 ways:
                          * As a single argument in <IP>/<Mask> format
                          * Or as a <IP> <Netmask> pair
                          * Or as 'default'
   --family (default 'v4')
    -f Address family to work on ('v4' or 'v6').  Default to 'v4' (valid for vSphere
       4.0 and later)
   --list
    -l List configured routes for the VMkernel
   --vihost
    -h The host to use when connecting via a vCenter server
```

As you can see, VMware provides some nice usage examples for the `vicfg-route` command. Let's take a look at using the `-l` option to display the current routes on our ESXI server. Your display might be similar to the following:

```
vicfg-route -l
```

```
VMkernel Routes:
Network             Netmask             Gateway             Inter
default             0.0.0.0             10.0.1.1            vmk0
10.0.1.0            255.255.255.0       Local Subnet        vmk0
```

To add a route to the 172.20.44.0 network using the gateway of 172.20.44.254, we would do something like this:

```
vicfg-route -a 172.20.46.0/24 172.20.44.254
```

or this:

```
vicfg-route -a 172.20.44.0 255.255.255.0 172.20.44.254
```

To set the default gateway for the VMkernel, issue the following command:

```
vicfg-route -a default 172.20.44.254
```

And finally, to delete a route, use the `-d` option. For example:

```
vicfg-route -d 172.20.46.0/24 172.20.44.254
```

You can also use the vCenter to manage your ESXI server's routes, which is the preferred method.

5.31 Configuring Software iSCSI Options

Problem

You need to manage your software-based iSCSI connections on your ESXI server.

Solution

Run the `esxcli iscsi` command on the ESXI server.

Discussion

Although the vCenter provides access to all the options you can manipulate on iSCSI devices, you might want to manage them through command-line tools. Let's take a look at a few of the options available to the `esxcli iscsi` command:

```
~ # esxcli iscsi
Usage: esxcli iscsi {cmd} [cmd options]

Available Namespaces:
  adapter               Operations that can be performed on iSCSI adapters
  networkportal         Operations that can be performed on iSCSI Network
                        Portal (iSCSI vmknic)
  physicalnetworkportal Operations that can be performed on iSCSI Physical Network
                        Portal (vmnic)
  session               Operations that can be performed on iSCSI sessions
  ibftboot              Operations that can be performed on iSCSI IBFT boot table
  logicalnetworkportal  Operations that can be performed on iSCSI Logical Network
                        Portal (vmknic)
```

```
    plugin                  Operations that can be performed on iSCSI management plugins
    software                Operations that can be performed on software iSCSI
```

Running the `esxcli iscsi` command with the `get` switch will query the server to let you know whether software-based iSCSI is enabled. In our case, it is not enabled:

```
~ # esxcli iscsi software get
false
```

Using the `-e` option, we can enable software-based iSCSI and open the firewall ports it requires:

```
~ # esxcli iscsi software set -e yes
Software iSCSI Enabled
```

Finally, using the -e switch, we can disable software-based iSCSI on the ESXI server. Note that if you do this, you will need to manually restart the firewall to ensure the ports are closed for iSCSI:

```
~ # esxcli iscsi software set -e no
Software iSCSI Disabled. (Reboot Required)
```

If you choose to manage your software-based iSCSI via the command line, these changes might not be immediately reflected in the vCenter; you will need to reboot the ESXi Server.

See Also

Recipe 5.32

5.32 Configuring Hardware iSCSI Options

Problem

You want to configure and display basic information for the hardware iSCSI cards used by an ESXI server.

Solution

Run the `iscsi adapter` command on the ESXi Server.

Discussion

VMware provides a command-line utility you can use to list and configure a few options for hardware iSCSI. However, you may also find additional options that can be configured on your iSCSI HBA; check with the manufacturer to see if it offers a Linux command-line configuration tool.

Let's take a look at the options available with the `esxcli iscsi` command:

```
~ # esxcli iscsi adapter
Usage: esxcli iscsi adapter {cmd} [cmd options]
```

```
Available Namespaces:
  auth                Operations that can be performed on iSCSI adapter authentications
  discovery           Operations that can be performed on iSCSI adapter discovery
  target              Operations that can be performed on iSCSI targets
  capabilities        Operations that can be performed on iSCSI adapter capabilities
  firmware            Operations that can be performed on iSCSI adapter firmware
  param               Operations that can be performed on iSCSI adapter parameters

Available Commands:
  get                 List the iSCSI information for the iSCSI Host Bus Adapter.
  list                List all the iSCSI Host Bus Adapters on the system.
  set                 Set the iSCSI name and alias for the iSCSI Host Bus Adapter.
```

You can display a small set of configurable values for your hardware-based iSCSI adapters using this command. For instance, in the following example, we specified *vmhba19*, one of our iSCSI ports, in the `-A` option to learn about its configured values (keep in mind that your device ID will probably be different from ours):

```
~ # esxcli iscsi adapter get -A vmhba19

vmhba19
   Name: iqn.1998-01.com.vmware:test11-4f0fa379
   Alias:
   Serial Number:
   Hardware Version:
   Asic Version:
   Firmware Version:
   Option Rom Version:
   Driver Name: iscsi_vmk
   Driver Version:
   TCP Protocol Supported: false
   Bidirectional Transfers Supported: false
   Maximum Cdb Length: 64
   Can Be NIC: false
   Is NIC: false
   Is Initiator: true
   Is Target: false
   Using TCP Offload Engine: false
   Using ISCSI Offload Engine: false
```

See Also

Recipe 5.31

5.33 Upgrading Software VIBs

Problem

You want to upgrade a VIB using the command line.

Solution

Run the `esxcli software vib update` command on the ESXI server.

Discussion

The following command will update the VIB package to a newer version. However, this will not install new VIB packages. This is useful for third-party VIBs that add new features to the ESXI server.

```
esxcli software vib update -n <name of vib
```

5.34 Displaying Storage Path Information

Problem

You want to see which Linux device, service console partition, or VMFS volume is associated with each *vmhba*.

Solution

Run the `esxcli storage core path` command on the ESXI server.

Discussion

The `storage core path` command shows how *vmhba* adapters are mapped on the server to physical Linux devices. Let's take a look at the available options:

```
~ # esxcli storage core path
Usage: esxcli storage core path {cmd} [cmd options]

Available Namespaces:
  stats                 Stats operations pertaining to the pluggable storage
                        architectures' device paths on the system.

Available Commands:
  list                  List all the SCSI paths on the system.
  set                   Provide control to allow a user to modify a single path's state.
                        This effectively allows a user to enable or disable SCSI paths.
                        The user is not able to change the full range of path states, but
                        can toggle between 'active' and 'off'. Please NOTE changing the
                        Path state on any path that is the only path to a given device is
                        likely to fail. The VMkernel will not change the path's state if
                        changing the state would cause an 'All paths down' state or the
                        device is currently in use.
```

The `list` option displays all devices, regardless of whether a console device is connected. The *vmhba* adapter is displayed along with the associated mount point:

```
~ # esxcli storage core path list
usb.vmhba32-usb.0:0-mpx.vmhba32:C0:T0:L0
   UID: usb.vmhba32-usb.0:0-mpx.vmhba32:C0:T0:L0
```

```
   Runtime Name: vmhba32:C0:T0:L0
   Device: mpx.vmhba32:C0:T0:L0
   Device Display Name: Local USB Direct-Access (mpx.vmhba32:C0:T0:L0)
   Adapter: vmhba32
   Channel: 0
   Target: 0
   LUN: 0
   Plugin: NMP
   State: active
   Transport: usb
   Adapter Identifier: usb.vmhba32
   Target Identifier: usb.0:0
   Adapter Transport Details: Unavailable or path is unclaimed
   Target Transport Details: Unavailable or path is unclaimed

iqn.1998-01.com.vmware:esx2-6d027a7c-00023d000002,iqn.esx,t,1-t10.
                       FreeBSD_iSCSI_Disk______001d60f814da000_________________
   UID: iqn.1998-01.com.vmware:esx2-6d027a7c-00023d000002,iqn.esx,t,1-t10.
        FreeBSD_iSCSI_Disk______001d60f814da000_________________
   Runtime Name: vmhba38:C1:T0:L0
   Device: t10.FreeBSD_iSCSI_Disk______001d60f814da000_________________
   Device Display Name: FreeBSD iSCSI Disk
                        (t10.FreeBSD_iSCSI_Disk______001d60f814da000_________________)
   Adapter: vmhba38
   Channel: 1
   Target: 0
   LUN: 0
   Plugin: NMP
   State: active
   Transport: iscsi
   Adapter Identifier: iqn.1998-01.com.vmware:esx2-6d027a7c
   Target Identifier: 00023d000002,iqn.esx,t,1
   Adapter Transport Details: iqn.1998-01.com.vmware:esx2-6d027a7c
   Target Transport Details: IQN=iqn.esx Alias= Session=00023d000002 PortalTag=1

iqn.1998-01.com.vmware:esx2-6d027a7c-00023d000002,iqn.esx,t,1-t10.
                       FreeBSD_iSCSI_Disk______001d60f814da001_________________
   UID: iqn.1998-01.com.vmware:esx2-6d027a7c-00023d000002,iqn.esx,t,1-t10.
        FreeBSD_iSCSI_Disk______001d60f814da001_________________
   Runtime Name: vmhba38:C1:T0:L1
   Device: t10.FreeBSD_iSCSI_Disk______001d60f814da001_________________
   Device Display Name: FreeBSD iSCSI Disk
                        (t10.FreeBSD_iSCSI_Disk______001d60f814da001_________________)
   Adapter: vmhba38
   Channel: 1
   Target: 0
   LUN: 1
   Plugin: NMP
   State: active
   Transport: iscsi
   Adapter Identifier: iqn.1998-01.com.vmware:esx2-6d027a7c
   Target Identifier: 00023d000002,iqn.esx,t,1
   Adapter Transport Details: iqn.1998-01.com.vmware:esx2-6d027a7c
   Target Transport Details: IQN=iqn.esx Alias= Session=00023d000002 PortalTag=1
```

```
iqn.1998-01.com.vmware:esx2-6d027a7c-00023d000002,iqn.esx,t,1-t10.
                       FreeBSD_iSCSI_Disk______001d60f814da002_________________
   UID: iqn.1998-01.com.vmware:esx2-6d027a7c-00023d000002,iqn.esx,t,1-t10.
        FreeBSD_iSCSI_Disk______001d60f814da002_________________
   Runtime Name: vmhba38:C1:T0:L2
   Device: t10.FreeBSD_iSCSI_Disk______001d60f814da002_________________
   Device Display Name: FreeBSD iSCSI Disk
                        (t10.FreeBSD_iSCSI_Disk______001d60f814da002_________________)
   Adapter: vmhba38
   Channel: 1
   Target: 0
   LUN: 2
   Plugin: NMP
   State: active
   Transport: iscsi
   Adapter Identifier: iqn.1998-01.com.vmware:esx2-6d027a7c
   Target Identifier: 00023d000002,iqn.esx,t,1
   Adapter Transport Details: iqn.1998-01.com.vmware:esx2-6d027a7c
   Target Transport Details: IQN=iqn.esx Alias= Session=00023d000002 PortalTag=1

iqn.1998-01.com.vmware:esx2-6d027a7c-00023d000001,iqn.esx,t,1-t10.
                       FreeBSD_iSCSI_Disk______001d60f814da000_________________
   UID: iqn.1998-01.com.vmware:esx2-6d027a7c-00023d000001,iqn.esx,t,1-t10.
        FreeBSD_iSCSI_Disk______001d60f814da000_________________
   Runtime Name: vmhba38:C0:T0:L0
   Device: t10.FreeBSD_iSCSI_Disk______001d60f814da000_________________
   Device Display Name: FreeBSD iSCSI Disk
                        (t10.FreeBSD_iSCSI_Disk______001d60f814da000_________________)
   Adapter: vmhba38
   Channel: 0
   Target: 0
   LUN: 0
   Plugin: NMP
   State: active
   Transport: iscsi
   Adapter Identifier: iqn.1998-01.com.vmware:esx2-6d027a7c
   Target Identifier: 00023d000001,iqn.esx,t,1
   Adapter Transport Details: iqn.1998-01.com.vmware:esx2-6d027a7c
   Target Transport Details: IQN=iqn.esx Alias= Session=00023d000001 PortalTag=1

iqn.1998-01.com.vmware:esx2-6d027a7c-00023d000001,iqn.esx,t,1-t10.
                       FreeBSD_iSCSI_Disk______001d60f814da001_________________
   UID: iqn.1998-01.com.vmware:esx2-6d027a7c-00023d000001,iqn.esx,t,1-t10.
        FreeBSD_iSCSI_Disk______001d60f814da001_________________
   Runtime Name: vmhba38:C0:T0:L1
   Device: t10.FreeBSD_iSCSI_Disk______001d60f814da001_________________
   Device Display Name: FreeBSD iSCSI Disk
                        (t10.FreeBSD_iSCSI_Disk______001d60f814da001_________________)
   Adapter: vmhba38
   Channel: 0
   Target: 0
   LUN: 1
   Plugin: NMP
   State: active
   Transport: iscsi
```

```
   Adapter Identifier: iqn.1998-01.com.vmware:esx2-6d027a7c
   Target Identifier: 00023d000001,iqn.esx,t,1
   Adapter Transport Details: iqn.1998-01.com.vmware:esx2-6d027a7c
   Target Transport Details: IQN=iqn.esx Alias= Session=00023d000001 PortalTag=1

iqn.1998-01.com.vmware:esx2-6d027a7c-00023d000001,iqn.esx,t,1-t10.
                       FreeBSD_iSCSI_Disk______001d60f814da002________________
   UID: iqn.1998-01.com.vmware:esx2-6d027a7c-00023d000001,iqn.esx,t,1-t10.
        FreeBSD_iSCSI_Disk______001d60f814da002________________
   Runtime Name: vmhba38:C0:T0:L2
   Device: t10.FreeBSD_iSCSI_Disk______001d60f814da002________________
   Device Display Name: FreeBSD iSCSI Disk
                        (t10.FreeBSD_iSCSI_Disk______001d60f814da002________________)
   Adapter: vmhba38
   Channel: 0
   Target: 0
   LUN: 2
   Plugin: NMP
   State: active
   Transport: iscsi
   Adapter Identifier: iqn.1998-01.com.vmware:esx2-6d027a7c
   Target Identifier: 00023d000001,iqn.esx,t,1
   Adapter Transport Details: iqn.1998-01.com.vmware:esx2-6d027a7c
   Target Transport Details: IQN=iqn.esx Alias= Session=00023d000001 PortalTag=1

sata.vmhba33-sata.0:0-t10.ATA_____WDC_WD2500KS2D00MJB0
                    __________________________WD2DWCANK7551048
   UID: sata.vmhba33-sata.0:0-t10.ATA_____WDC_WD2500KS2D00MJB0
        __________________________WD2DWCANK7551048
   Runtime Name: vmhba33:C0:T0:L0
   Device: t10.ATA_____WDC_WD2500KS2D00MJB0__________________________WD2DWCANK7551048
   Device Display Name: Local ATA Disk (t10.ATA_____WDC_WD2500KS2D00MJB0
                        __________________________WD2DWCANK7551048)
   Adapter: vmhba33
   Channel: 0
   Target: 0
   LUN: 0
   Plugin: NMP
   State: active
   Transport: sata
   Adapter Identifier: sata.vmhba33
   Target Identifier: sata.0:0
   Adapter Transport Details: Unavailable or path is unclaimed
   Target Transport Details: Unavailable or path is unclaimed
```

The stats option adds the ability to take a deeper look into the path information.

```
~ # esxcli storage core path stats get
usb.vmhba32-usb.0:0-mpx.vmhba32:C0:T0:L0
   UID: usb.vmhba32-usb.0:0-mpx.vmhba32:C0:T0:L0
   Runtime Name: vmhba32:C0:T0:L0
   Successful Commands: 19410
   Blocks Read: 246676
   Blocks Written: 20172
   Read Operations: 16653
   Write Operations: 1809
```

```
      Reserve Operations: 0
      Reservation Conflicts: 0
      Failed Commands: 477
      Failed Blocks Read: 0
      Failed Blocks Written: 0
      Failed Read Operations: 0
      Failed Write Operations: 0
      Failed Reserve Operations: 0
      Total Splits: 18654
      PAE Commands: 18474

   iqn.1998-01.com.vmware:esx2-6d027a7c-00023d000002,iqn.esx,t,1-t10.
                           FreeBSD_iSCSI_Disk______001d60f814da000________________
      UID: iqn.1998-01.com.vmware:esx2-6d027a7c-00023d000002,iqn.esx,t,1-t10.
           FreeBSD_iSCSI_Disk______001d60f814da000________________
      Runtime Name: vmhba38:C1:T0:L0
      Successful Commands: 561
      Blocks Read: 0
      Blocks Written: 0
      Read Operations: 0
      Write Operations: 0
      Reserve Operations: 0
      Reservation Conflicts: 0
      Failed Commands: 24
      Failed Blocks Read: 0
      Failed Blocks Written: 0
      Failed Read Operations: 0
      Failed Write Operations: 0
      Failed Reserve Operations: 0
      Total Splits: 0
      PAE Commands: 0

   iqn.1998-01.com.vmware:esx2-6d027a7c-00023d000002,iqn.esx,t,1-t10.
                           FreeBSD_iSCSI_Disk______001d60f814da001________________
      UID: iqn.1998-01.com.vmware:esx2-6d027a7c-00023d000002,iqn.esx,t,1-t10.
           FreeBSD_iSCSI_Disk______001d60f814da001________________
      Runtime Name: vmhba38:C1:T0:L1
      Successful Commands: 288
      Blocks Read: 0
      Blocks Written: 0
      Read Operations: 0
      Write Operations: 0
      Reserve Operations: 0
      Reservation Conflicts: 0
      Failed Commands: 24
      Failed Blocks Read: 0
      Failed Blocks Written: 0
      Failed Read Operations: 0
      Failed Write Operations: 0
      Failed Reserve Operations: 0
      Total Splits: 0
      PAE Commands: 0

   iqn.1998-01.com.vmware:esx2-6d027a7c-00023d000002,iqn.esx,t,1-t10.
                           FreeBSD_iSCSI_Disk______001d60f814da002________________
```

```
   UID: iqn.1998-01.com.vmware:esx2-6d027a7c-00023d000002,iqn.esx,t,1-t10.
        FreeBSD_iSCSI_Disk______001d60f814da002_________________
   Runtime Name: vmhba38:C1:T0:L2
   Successful Commands: 1901
   Blocks Read: 1122
   Blocks Written: 0
   Read Operations: 1062
   Write Operations: 0
   Reserve Operations: 0
   Reservation Conflicts: 0
   Failed Commands: 0
   Failed Blocks Read: 0
   Failed Blocks Written: 0
   Failed Read Operations: 0
   Failed Write Operations: 0
   Failed Reserve Operations: 0
   Total Splits: 0
   PAE Commands: 0

iqn.1998-01.com.vmware:esx2-6d027a7c-00023d000001,iqn.esx,t,1-t10.
                        FreeBSD_iSCSI_Disk______001d60f814da000_________________
   UID: iqn.1998-01.com.vmware:esx2-6d027a7c-00023d000001,iqn.esx,t,1-t10.
        FreeBSD_iSCSI_Disk______001d60f814da000_________________
   Runtime Name: vmhba38:C0:T0:L0
   Successful Commands: 56284
   Blocks Read: 233318
   Blocks Written: 52797
   Read Operations: 1121
   Write Operations: 52722
   Reserve Operations: 1
   Reservation Conflicts: 0
   Failed Commands: 54
   Failed Blocks Read: 0
   Failed Blocks Written: 0
   Failed Read Operations: 0
   Failed Write Operations: 36
   Failed Reserve Operations: 0
   Total Splits: 189
   PAE Commands: 0

iqn.1998-01.com.vmware:esx2-6d027a7c-00023d000001,iqn.esx,t,1-t10.
                        FreeBSD_iSCSI_Disk______001d60f814da001_________________
   UID: iqn.1998-01.com.vmware:esx2-6d027a7c-00023d000001,iqn.esx,t,1-t10.
        FreeBSD_iSCSI_Disk______001d60f814da001_________________
   Runtime Name: vmhba38:C0:T0:L1
   Successful Commands: 68523
   Blocks Read: 261722
   Blocks Written: 52796
   Read Operations: 13689
   Write Operations: 52721
   Reserve Operations: 1
   Reservation Conflicts: 0
   Failed Commands: 54
   Failed Blocks Read: 0
   Failed Blocks Written: 0
```

```
    Failed Read Operations: 0
    Failed Write Operations: 36
    Failed Reserve Operations: 0
    Total Splits: 198
    PAE Commands: 0

 iqn.1998-01.com.vmware:esx2-6d027a7c-00023d000001,iqn.esx,t,1-t10.
                     FreeBSD_iSCSI_Disk______001d60f814da002_________________
    UID: iqn.1998-01.com.vmware:esx2-6d027a7c-00023d000001,iqn.esx,t,1-t10.
         FreeBSD_iSCSI_Disk______001d60f814da002_________________
    Runtime Name: vmhba38:C0:T0:L2
    Successful Commands: 278
    Blocks Read: 0
    Blocks Written: 0
    Read Operations: 0
    Write Operations: 0
    Reserve Operations: 0
    Reservation Conflicts: 0
    Failed Commands: 1
    Failed Blocks Read: 0
    Failed Blocks Written: 0
    Failed Read Operations: 0
    Failed Write Operations: 0
    Failed Reserve Operations: 0
    Total Splits: 0
    PAE Commands: 0

 sata.vmhba33-sata.0:0-t10.ATA_____WDC_WD2500KS2D00MJB0
                      __________________________WD2DWCANK7551048
    UID: sata.vmhba33-sata.0:0-t10.ATA_____WDC_WD2500KS2D00MJB0
         __________________________WD2DWCANK7551048
    Runtime Name: vmhba33:C0:T0:L0
    Successful Commands: 101610
    Blocks Read: 296388
    Blocks Written: 322170
    Read Operations: 2345
    Write Operations: 97847
    Reserve Operations: 74
    Reservation Conflicts: 0
    Failed Commands: 553
    Failed Blocks Read: 0
    Failed Blocks Written: 0
    Failed Read Operations: 0
    Failed Write Operations: 0
    Failed Reserve Operations: 0
    Total Splits: 90906
    PAE Commands: 0
```

See Also

Recipe 5.35

5.35 Managing SCSI Device Mappings with ESXi5 vSphere

Problem

You want to manage your SCSI device mappings via the command line with ESX4 vSphere.

Solution

Run the `esxcli storage core` command on the ESXI server.

Discussion

In ESXi 5, VMware replaced the `esxcli storage core` command with the storage core option within the esxcli command. Using this command will allow us to manage the storage mappings within the ESXi environment.

```
~ # esxcli storage core
Usage: esxcli storage core {cmd} [cmd options]

Available Namespaces:
  adapter              Operations on SCSI Host Bus Adapters on the system.
  device               Operations pertaining to the pluggable storage architectures'
                       logical devices on the system. The operation currently allowed
                       is to list the available devices on the system and the filters
                       attached to each
  path                 Operations pertaining to the pluggable storage architectures'
                       SCSI device paths on the system.
  plugin               Operations pertaining to the pluggable storage architectures'
                       plugins. The operation currently allowed is to list the available
                       plugins on the system with the type of those plugins
  claiming             Operations pertaining to the pluggable storage direct path
                       claiming system. These operations will allow a user to directly
                       control the claiming and unclaiming process. These operations
                       are considered temporary and any claiming operations that need
                       to survive a reboot should use claimrules instead.
  claimrule            Operations pertaining to the pluggable storage architecture
                       claiming rule system. These operations operate on the rules used
                       to determine the PSA plugin used to claim storage paths.

                Show this message.
```

See Also

Recipe 5.34

5.36 Managing VMkernel Ports

Problem

You want to create, update, or delete entries in the VMkernel configuration for VMotion, NAS, and software iSCSI.

Solution

Run the `esxcli network ip interface` command on the ESXI server.

Discussion

This command is used to configure the VMkernel ports on virtual switches. The VMkernel port is a special port that is used for vMotion, software-based iSCSI, and NFS access. Let's take a look at the available options:

```
~ # esxcli network ip interface
Usage: esxcli network ip interface {cmd} [cmd options]

Available Namespaces:
  ipv6                  Commands to get and set IPv6 settings for vmknic.
  ipv4                  Commands to get and set IPv4 settings for vmknic.

Available Commands:
  add                   Add a new VMkernel network interface.
  list                  This command will list the VMkernel network interfaces
                        currently known to the system.
  remove                Remove a new VMkernel network interface from the ESXi host.
  set                   This command sets the enabled status and MTU size of a
                        given IP interface.
```

The `list` option shows the ports that are already created on our vSwitches. In our case, we have a vMotion port on *vmk0* (the lines are wrapped here to fit on the page):

```
~ # esxcli network ip interface list
vmk0
   Name: vmk0
   MAC Address: 00:0c:29:7f:3a:5d
   Enabled: true
   Portset: vSwitch0
   Portgroup: Management Network
   VDS Name: N/A
   VDS Port: N/A
   VDS Connection: -1
   MTU: 1500
   TSO MSS: 65535
   Port ID: 16777219
```

The following example allows you to add a new VMkernel port on the ESXI server and assign it to a port group. In the following example, we have created a VMkernel called `vmk1` and have assigned it to the `vMotion` port group. However, you must have a port group present before adding a new NIC to the system. You can create a new port group using the `esxcli network` command, as discussed in Recipe 5.11.

```
esxcli network ip interface add -i vmk1 -p vMotion
esxcli network ip interface ipv4 set -i vmk1 -I 192.168.1.41 -N 255.255.255.0 -t static
```

The `remove -i` option allows you to remove the VMkernel NIC from the system:

```
esxcli network ip interface remove -i vmk1
```

Another important option is `-m`, which allows you to set an MTU speed for the VMkernel NIC port. This is important for NFS or iSCSI connections, where you might use something similar to the following:

```
esxcli network ip interface set -m 9000 -i vmk1
```

If you use the `-l` option to verify the results, you will notice that the MTU speed is now set to 9,000 instead of the default 1,500.

CHAPTER 6

General Security

In this chapter we will provide solutions to help you maintain a secure virtual environment, using technologies that are already available to you in your VMware implementation. This chapter will cover a lot of basic Linux-related material focused around ESX 3.x/4.x, because the ESX Server has Red Hat Linux as its base. We will also discuss increasing security with ESXi 5.x, and the newer updated commands.

This chapter will focus on using the command line for security and monitoring tasks. Most of the tasks we'll examine (aside from user-related tasks such as role management) can be performed using the vCenter client, and in fact that is VMware's suggested method. However, we feel that users should know how to use alternative ways to manage their ESX Servers, in case there are problems that prevent the use of the vCenter client. Thus, we have chosen to focus on the command line in this chapter. If you need details on performing any of these tasks via the vCenter, we recommend that you familiarize yourself with an excellent document VMware provides on security (*http://www.vmware.com/files/pdf/vi35_security_hardening_wp.pdf*).

6.1 Enabling SSH on ESX 3.5 / ESX 4.x

Problem

ESX 3.5/4.x ONLY - You need to enable remote SSH access.

Solution

Follow the steps in the recipe to enable SSH. However, note that leaving direct *root* SSH disabled is the suggested configuration.

Discussion

SSH is a valuable service to have on your service console because it provides a way for an administrator to go behind the VMware GUI and issue commands directly to the OS running on the server. By default, ESXi does not have SSH enabled; in fact, VMware does not directly support running SSH on an ESXI server. If you need to enable it, however, you can do so by following these steps:

1. On your ESXi console, press Alt-F1 to open a command prompt. Next, enter **`unsupported`** along with your system's *root* password.
2. At the command line, edit the *inetd.conf* file, which maintains information for various services running on your ESXi console. The file is located at */etc/inetd.conf*. Look for the line that starts with `#ssh` and remove the pound sign (#). Save the file to finalize your changes.
3. You now need to restart the *inetd* service, because making the change in the configuration file does not do this automatically. To do so, enter the following command at the command line:

   ```
   /sbin/services.sh restart
   ```

   If you are running ESX 3.5 Update 4, you will instead need to issue the following command to restart SSH:

   ```
   kill - HUP inetd
   ```

Your SSH service is now enabled, and you can access your console by using your favorite SSH terminal program.

6.2 Enabling Direct Root Logins on Your ESX Server

Problem

ESX 3.5/4.x ONLY - Though they are normally disallowed, you want to enable direct *root* logins on your ESX Server.

Solution

Edit the SSH configuration file to allow direct *root* logins.

Discussion

By default, ESX 3.x servers are set to deny remote *root* logins. Depending on your environment and personal preference, however, you may wish to enable such logins on your ESX Server consoles.

To maintain a more secure environment, the best practice would be to implement a system administrator–type account and use `sudo` to perform these tasks. The suggested configuration by VMware leaves direct *root* SSH disabled.

To enable SSH on your ESX console, follow these steps:

1. Press Alt-F1 to open a command prompt and enter your system's *root* password.
2. Once you've logged in, edit the *sshd_config* file. This file contains multiple configuration variables for the SSHD daemon. We will be making only one change, to allow direct logins. Open the following file:

   ```
   /etc/ssh/sshd_config
   ```

3. Look for the line that says `PermitRootLogin`, which is most likely located toward the top of the file. Change it to:

   ```
   PermitRootLogin yes
   ```

4. Then save the configuration file and restart the SSHD daemon by entering one of the following at the command line:

   ```
   /etc/init.d/sshd restart
   ```

   or:

   ```
   service sshd restart
   ```

Your SSHD daemon is now set to permit direct *root* logins. Bear in mind that you are doing this at your own risk; best practice suggests leaving direct *root* SSH capabilities turned off.

6.3 Adding Users and Groups

Problem

ESX 3.5/4.x ONLY - You need to be able to manage the accounts for each of your users.

Solution

You can set up users and groups using the console, according to your needs. ESXi users can use lockdown mode to help secure their user environments.

Although not discussed in this recipe, all aspects of user management can also be handled via the vCenter client, and this is VMware's preferred method.

Discussion

You'll make use of two commands in this recipe: `useradd` and `groupadd`. You'll use the `useradd` command to make modifications to the */etc/passwd* and */etc/shadow* files, which store user information such as the UID, GID, path, shell, and home directory. You'll also use the `groupadd` command to modify the */etc/group* file, which stores the users' group information. To begin, log in to the ESX Server as *root* via SSH or the console.

For this example, we are going to assume that you need to set up two groups, a junior system administrator group and a senior system administrator group. We'll use the groupadd command to create the two groups from the command line:

```
groupadd jradmin
groupadd sradmin
```

Once you've created the groups, you will notice that they are listed in the */etc/group* file. Now we'll add users to the groups by using the useradd command from the command line. The useradd command has many different options, but we will only use the -g option to set the group membership:

```
useradd -g jradmin rtroy
useradd -g sradmin mhelmke
```

We now have two users, one assigned to the *jradmin* group and one assigned to the *sradmin* group. By setting up groups, you allow yourself to limit the areas each user can access. For example, if you are using sudo, you can give the *jradmin* group a less complete set of options than the *sradmin* group.

Our example invokes a very simple useradd command to set group membership. Other options are available to further customize your users' accounts and groups. Here is some detailed information on the useradd command:

```
Usage: useradd [options] LOGIN

Options:
  -b, --base-dir BASE_DIR     Base directory for the new user account
                home directory
  -c, --comment COMMENT       Set the GECOS field for the new user account
  -d, --home-dir HOME_DIR     Home directory for the new user account
  -D, --defaults              Print or save modified default useradd
                configuration
  -e, --expiredate EXPIRE_DATE  Set account expiration date to EXPIRE_DATE
  -f, --inactive INACTIVE     Set password inactive after expiration
                to INACTIVE
  -g, --gid GROUP             Force use GROUP for the new user account
  -G, --groups GROUPS         List of supplementary groups for the new
                user account
  -h, --help                  Display this help message and exit
  -k, --skel SKEL_DIR         Specify an alternative skel directory
  -K, --key KEY=VALUE         Overrides /etc/login.defs defaults
  -m, --create-home           Create home directory for the new user
                account
  -o, --nonunique            Allow create user with duplicate
                (nonunique) UID
  -p, --password PASSWORD     Use encrypted password for the new user
                account
  -r, --system                Create a system account
  -s, --shell SHELL           The login shell for the new user account
  -u, --uid UID               Force use the UID for the new user account
```

Similarly, here is an overview of the groupadd command:

```
Usage: groupadd [options] GROUP

Options:
  -f, --forceforce       Exit with success status if the specified
                group already exists
  -g, --gid GID          Use GID for the new group
  -h, --help             Display this help message and exit
  -K, --key KEY=VALUE    Overrides /etc/login.defs defaults
  -o, --nonunique       Allow create group with duplicate
               (nonunique) GID
```

Another important command is `userdel`, which allows you to remove a user from the system. You have the option of leaving her home directory intact, which will preserve any personal settings, scripts, or applications stored there.

The `userdel` command will remove entries from both the */etc/passwd* and */etc/shadow* files. However, if you are using `sudo`, the `userdel` command will not remove any entries from the *sudoers* file, so be sure to remove those as necessary.

To remove a user and simultaneously delete that user's home directory, use the `-r` option, as shown here:

```
userdel -r rtroy
```

To remove the user, but leave his or her home directory intact, omit the `-r` option:

```
userdel rtroy
```

Removing a group can be accomplished by using the `groupdel` command:

```
groupdel jradmin
```

This command removes the *jradmin* group from the server, deleting its entries in the */etc/group* and */etc/gshadow* files.

These commands offer many advanced features that you can find out about through their `--help` options or manpages.

See Also

Recipe 6.6

6.4 Allowing or Denying Users the Use of SSH

Problem

ESX 3.5/4.x ONLY - You want to control which users can access your ESX Server via SSH.

Solution

Configure individual account permissions to allow or deny SSH access to specific users.

Discussion

For security, it is generally better to create an individual account for each user and to avoid allowing multiple users to have access to the *root* account. This allows actions to be connected to the people performing them and is especially important for tracking problems in case an administrator "goes rogue." However, this approach does mean that you have to figure out how to allow these individual accounts to access the server securely.

By using the configuration options built into your SSH server, you can allow specific users to access your ESX Server directly, via SSH. To accomplish this, edit the SSH configuration file, located at */etc/ssh/sshd_config*. Look for the line that says `AllowUsers`. If this line is commented out with a `#`, remove the `#` sign. If you do not see a line containing this information, make a new line like the example that follows, making sure to change the usernames according to your needs. In this example entry, we allow *tom*, *chris*, *bob*, and any user whose username starts with the word *sysadmin* to have SSH access:

```
AllowUsers   tom    chris   bob    sysadmin*
```

Once you are satisfied, save the configuration (by pressing the `:wq!` keys in *vi*). At the command line, restart the *sshd* daemon to make your configuration changes take effect. To do this, enter either this command:

```
/etc/init.d/sshd restart
```

or this one:

```
service sshd restart
```

You can also deny specific users permission to access your ESX Server directly with SSH. To do this, look for a line in the */etc/ssh/sshd_config* file that says `DenyUsers`. If it is commented out with a `#`, remove the `#` sign. If you do not see a line containing this information, make a new line similar to the one that follows, remembering to change the usernames according to your needs. In this example, we deny access to *george*, *todd*, *tim*, and any user whose username starts with *b*:

```
DenyUsers    george  todd   tim    b*
```

Keep in mind when using the `*` wildcard character that, in our example, a user named *bob* would be denied access even if he is listed in the `AllowUsers` line as follows (that is, the deny rules take precedence over the allow rules):

```
AllowUsers   tom    chris   bob    sysadmin*
```

Save the file and restart the daemon as before.

The users who have been denied will be barred from logging into the system via SSH, and any login attempts they make will show up in the */var/log/messages* file.

6.5 Turning On the Message of the Day for Console Users

Problem

ESX 3.5/4.x ONLY - You want to display a specific message to each of your users when they attempt to log in to the server.

Solution

Edit the *sshd_config* file from the command line to enable the message of the day (MOTD).

Discussion

The MOTD allows you to display a note to users when they try to access your server via the console or SSH.

By default, the ESX Server is not set up to display the MOTD when users log in via SSH, so you need to change the *sshd_config* file to display it.

The first thing to do is navigate to your */etc/ssh* directory and open the *sshd_config* file with your favorite editor, as we do here using *vi*:

```
vi /etc/ssh/sshd_config
```

Change the following variable to enable SSH to display the MOTD by removing the # from the beginning of the line:

```
#PrintMotd yes
```

Save the file and restart the *sshd* services by issuing the following command:

```
service sshd restart
```

Now that the changes to the SSH configuration are in place, you can edit your */etc/motd* file to include any information you wish to display to your users when they log in. This file comes standard with most Linux distributions and can be edited with your favorite editor. By default, the file is empty.

6.6 Changing the Root Password via the Console

Problem

ESX 3.5/4.x ONLY - You want to change the *root* password.

Solution

Use the `passwd` command.

Discussion

Changing the *root* user's password on the ESX Host requires to you be logged in either via SSH or via the console directly. You will need to be logged in as *root* or become the *root* user using `sudo`. You can then change the password by issuing the following command:

```
passwd
```

If you are changing the password as sudo use the following:

```
sudo -s

passwd
```

You will be asked to enter the current password, enter the new password, and then reenter the new password a second time to confirm that you have typed it correctly. The next time you log in, you will need to use the new password.

6.7 Recovering a Lost Root Password

Problem

ESX 3.5/4.x ONLY - You lost or forgot your *root* password and you need to change it.

Solution

Log in as *root* via `sudo` and change the password, or edit the GRUB menu to boot in single-user mode.

Discussion

Because VMware uses a modified version of Red Hat Linux, recovering the *root* password is easy. We'll look at two different ways to recover the *root* password.

The first (and perhaps the easiest) method is by using `sudo`. If you have an account with full `sudo` permissions, you can become the *root* user this way and change the *root* password.

For the second option, you will need to use the service console or be connected to a kernel-based virtual machine (KVM). To begin, use the GRUB menu, which is the menu you are first displayed when your ESX Server is booting, to boot into single-user mode.

You will notice three options in the GRUB menu (Figure 6-1): VMware ESX Server, which boots your ESX Server normally; VMware ESX Server (debug mode), which turns on debugging options; and Service Console only (troubleshooting mode), which will drop you to the command line and not initiate any of the key services. There is also some descriptive text under the menu, giving you more advanced options to use within the GRUB menu.

```
GRUB  version 0.93  (638K lower / 1071040K upper memory)

VMware ESX Server
VMware ESX Server (debug mode)
Service Console only (troubleshooting mode)

   Use the ↑ and ↓ keys to select which entry is highlighted.
   Press enter to boot the selected OS, 'e' to edit the
   commands before booting, 'a' to modify the kernel arguments
   before booting, or 'c' for a command-line.
```

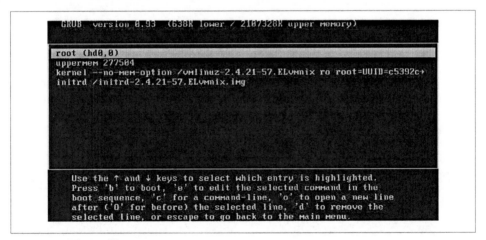

Figure 6-1. Boot menu for VMware ESX Server, showing boot selection

To begin the process of recovering your *root* password, you need to have the gray bar highlight the VMware ESX Server option on the menu. Press the letter **e** to bring up a more advanced menu, from which you will make a simple change to the kernel boot string. There are four menu options here, and you will use the line that starts with `kernel` (Figure 6-2). Highlight this line and press **e** again to enter edit mode.

```
GRUB  version 0.93  (638K lower / 2107328K upper memory)

root (hd0,0)
uppermem 277504
kernel --no-mem-option /vmlinuz-2.4.21-57.ELvmnix ro root=UUID=c5392c→
initrd /initrd-2.4.21-57.ELvmnix.img

   Use the ↑ and ↓ keys to select which entry is highlighted.
   Press 'b' to boot, 'e' to edit the selected command in the
   boot sequence, 'c' for a command-line, 'o' to open a new line
   after ('O' for before) the selected line, 'd' to remove the
   selected line, or escape to go back to the main menu.
```

Figure 6-2. Advanced boot options

Once in edit mode, go to the end of the line and add the word `single` (Figure 6-3). This tells the server to boot into single-user mode, allowing you to change the *root* password. Press Enter to return to the previous menu. Highlight the line starting with `kernel` and press the **b** key to initiate the single-user boot mode.

```
[ Minimal BASH-like line editing is supported.  For the first word, TAB
  lists possible command completions.  Anywhere else TAB lists the possible
  completions of a device/filename.  ESC at any time cancels.  ENTER
  at any time accepts your changes.]

=UUID=96cfae68-fd3d-4944-86c1-9ee3548021a9 mem=272M single_
```

Figure 6-3. Adding single-user mode to the boot line

The system will be booted into single-user mode, and you will be given a command prompt from which you can type the `passwd` command to change your *root* password.

When the password change is complete, issue the `reboot` command to reboot the server in its original mode. Once rebooted, you can log in with the new *root* password.

6.8 Disabling Direct Root Console Logins

Problem

ESX 3.5/4.x ONLY - Remote users can log in as *root* via the console, and you wish to prevent this for greater security.

Solution

Edit the configuration to prevent direct *root* login, even from the console.

Discussion

By default, remote users cannot log in to an ESX Server as *root*. However, they can log in as *root* on the console that is directly connected to the server. If you wish to lock down your ESX Servers even further, you can disable the ability to log in directly as *root* on that console. Users to whom you give *root* privileges can still become *root* through the `sudo` command, but you can use techniques discussed in Recipe 6.4 to restrict the commands they can execute. You cannot do this if they can log in directly as *root*.

In this example we will be modifying the */etc/securetty* file. When this file exists but is empty, direct *root* console logins are disabled. Follow these steps to implement this security measure:

1. Log in to your ESX Server and run the following commands to back up the */etc/securetty* file, in case you wish to revert your changes at a later time:

   ```
   mv /etc/securetty /etc/securetty_backup
   ```

2. Now create an empty *securetty* file, by running the following command:

   ```
   touch /etc/securetty
   ```

3. You'll also want to ensure that the *securetty* file is readable and writable only by the *root* user. To accomplish this, run the following commands:

```
chmod 400 securetty securetty_backup
chown root :root securetty securetty_backup
```

Once complete, verify that you can no longer log in to the console directly as the *root* user.

If you wish to revert your changes, simply copy the *securetty_backup* file to *securetty* using the following command:

```
cp /etc/securetty_backup securetty
```

If you try to log in from the console directly as the *root* user after restoring the *securetty* file, you should be able to do so.

For reference, your *securetty* file should contain lines such as the following, which list terminals and virtual terminals where *root* login is allowed:

```
console
vc/1
vc/2
vc/3
vc/4
vc/5
vc/6
vc/7
vc/8
vc/9
vc/10
vc/11
tty1
tty2
tty3
tty4
tty5
tty6
tty7
tty8
tty9
tty10
tty11
```

6.9 Securing the GRUB Bootloader Menu

Problem

ESX 3.5/4.x ONLY - The GRUB menu may be accessed during a reboot, and you wish to prevent knowledgeable users from changing the boot parameters and either damaging the server or accessing things they should not.

Solution

Require a password to access the GRUB boot menu.

Discussion

Setting a password for the ESX Server's GRUB boot menu ensures that your kernel boot parameters cannot be bypassed when the server is rebooting. For example, the parameters in the GRUB boot menu control to which hard drive and kernel your ESX Server boots. If these parameters are erroneously changed, your ESX Server may be unbootable.

To restrict access to this menu, you need to generate an encrypted password and put it in the */etc/grub.conf* configuration file.

Start by logging into your ESX Server with *root* permissions. From the command line, run the **`grub`** command. Next, at the grub prompt, enter **`md5crypt`**. You will be prompted for a password one time. Once your password has been validated, you will see an md5 hash text; copy this, because you will need to enter it in the */etc/grub.conf* file. When you have copied the md5 hash, exit the *grub* application by typing **`quit`**.

Now, edit this file with your favorite editor:

```
/etc/grub.conf
```

In order to set a password on your GRUB menu, you'll need to add a new variable to this file. Look for something similar to this:

```
...
default=1
timeout=10
```

Add the following line after the line that lists the `timeout` variable (keep in mind that, depending on your configuration, your timeout value may be slightly different). Substitute the hash string you saved for ***`hash_string`***:

```
password --md5 hash_string
```

Save the file and exit. When you reboot your ESX Server, you will not be able to edit any of the boot options at the GRUB menu without first entering a password. By adding a GRUB password, you are removing the last trick, practically speaking, by which someone with physical access to the system can gain unauthorized access to your server. About the only other things the attacker could do are boot from a CD or damage the system physically.

6.10 Disabling USB Drive Mounting

Problem

ESX 3.5/4.x ONLY - Allowing USB drives to be directly connected and mounted to your ESX Server may cause a security risk.

Solution

Disable the automatic mounting of USB devices on your ESX Server by editing the */etc/modules.conf* file.

Discussion

To get started, log in to your ESX Server as *root*. Then, edit the following file:

```
/etc/modules.conf
```

Search for the following entry and add a # sign at the beginning of the line:

```
alias usb-controller
```

After making the change, save the configuration file. You will need to reboot your server in order for the new settings to take effect.

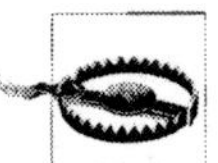

Disabling this might affect USB keyboards and mice in some configurations. It is suggested that you test thoroughly after making this change; if you are using a USB keyboard and/or mouse, you may not want to implement this solution.

6.11 Opening and Closing Firewall Ports via the Console

Problem

Although the vCenter has an option called *Security Profile* that can help you maintain a large number of preset firewalls, you may encounter situations where you will need to maintain a custom rule specific to an application you wish to run.

Solution

ESX has a great tool called `esxcli network firewall` that allows you to maintain your firewall from the command line.

Discussion

Before we get started, let's take a look at some of the configuration options the `esxcli network firewall` command offers:

```
~ # esxcli network firewall
Usage: esxcli network firewall {cmd} [cmd options]

Available Namespaces:
  ruleset               Commands to list and update firewall ruleset configuration

Available Commands:
  get                   Get the firewall status.
  load                  Load firewall module and rulesets configuration.
  refresh               Load ruleset configuration for firewall.
```

```
    set                 Set firewall enabled status and default action.
    unload              Allow unload firewall module.
```

ESXi 5.x includes a new client interface to manage the firewall. Table 6-1 summarizes the commands available:

Table 6-1. Firewall commands

Command	Comments
esxcli network firewall get	Returns the enabled or disabled status of the firewall and lists default actions.
esxcli network firewall set --defaultaction	Update default actions.
esxcli network firewall set --enabled	Set to true to enable the firewall, set to false to disable the firewall.
esxcli network firewall load	Load the firewall module and rule set configuration files.
esxcli network firewall refresh	Refresh the firewall configuration by reading the rule set files if the firewall module is loaded.
esxcli network firewall unload	Destroy filters and unload the firewall module.
esxcli network firewall ruleset list	List rule sets information.
esxcli network firewall ruleset set --allowedall	Set the allowedall flag.
esxcli network firewall ruleset set --enabled	Enable or disable the specified rule set.
esxcli network firewall ruleset allowedip list	List the allowed IP addresses of the specified rule set.
esxcli network firewall ruleset allowedip add	Allow access to the rule set from the specified IP address or range of IP addresses.
esxcli network firewall ruleset allowedip remove	Remove access to the rule set from the specified IP address or range of IP addresses.

To view the current firewall ruleset and see which services are enabled or disabled:

```
~ # esxcli network firewall ruleset list
Name                Enabled
------------------  -------
sshServer              true
sshClient             false
nfsClient             false
dhcp                   true
dns                    true
snmp                   true
ntpClient             false
CIMHttpServer          true
CIMHttpsServer         true
CIMSLP                 true
iSCSI                  true
vpxHeartbeats          true
updateManager         false
faultTolerance         true
webAccess              true
vMotion                true
vSphereClient          true
```

```
activeDirectoryAll    false
NFC                    true
HBR                    true
ftpClient             false
httpClient            false
gdbserver             false
DVFilter              false
DHCPv6                false
DVSSync               false
syslog                false
IKED                  false
WOL                    true
vSPC                  false
remoteSerialPort      false
fdm                    true
```

To enable a specific service in the firewall, replace SERVICENAMEHERE with a service name from the previous list.

```
esxcli network firewall ruleset set -r SERVICENAMEHERE -e true
```

To disable a specific service in the firewall, replace SERVICENAMEHERE with a service name from the previous list.

```
esxcli network firewall ruleset set -r SERVICENAMEHERE -e false
```

To see the state of the firewall:

```
~ # esxcli network firewall get
   Default Action: DROP
   Enabled: true
   Loaded: true
```

To enable the firewall:

```
esxcli network firewall set --default-action true
```

To disable the firewall:

```
esxcli network firewall set --default-action false
```

To reset the firewall after making changes:

```
~ # esxcli network firewall refresh
```

6.12 Checking Default ESX Ports

Problem

One of the most common issues people have is making sure that the correct firewall ports are opened for the tasks they are trying to accomplish.

Solution

Adding or customizing ports can be done through the Security Profile option in the vCenter or via the command line using the `esxcfg-firewall` command introduced in Recipe 6.11.

Discussion

Table 6-2 lists the essential ports you may have to adjust in your virtual environment when troubleshooting.

Table 6-2. Default ESXi ports

Port	Incoming	Outgoing	Description
22	TCP		SSH
53	UDP	UDP	DNS Client
68	UDP	UDP	DHCP Client
161	UDP		SNMP
80	TCP		vSphere FT, HTTP, nonencrypted web traffic, WS-Management
427	UDP	UDP	Service location (CIM client)
443	TCP		Secure HTTP access
902	TCP	UDP	Host access to other hosts, authentication for ESXi and remote consoles, status updates for heartbeats
903	TCP		Remote console traffic, vSphere Client Access
2049	TCP	TCP	NFS devices VMkernel Interface
2050–5000	TCP, UDP	UDP	HA and autostart
3260	TCP		iSCSI
5900–5906	TCP	TCP	RFB for management tools
5988	TCP	TCP	CIM Server over HTTPS
5989	TCP	TCP	CIM Server over HTTP
8000	TCP	TCP	vMotion traffic
8042–8045	TCP, UDP	TCP, UDP	HA and EMC autostart manager

See Also

Recipe 6.11

6.13 Turning on SNMP for Remote Administration

Problem

ESX 3.5/4.x ONLY - You wish to monitor and administer your servers remotely.

Solution

Use a third-party application such as Cacti, MRTG, or a commercial solution.

Discussion

Turning on SNMP to monitor your ESX Servers using open source products like Cacti or MRTG, or commercial productions such as WhatsUp Pro, can provide many benefits for the health of your environment. Here's how to enable SNMP:

1. Log in to your ESX Server as the *root* user. Navigate to the */etc/snmp* directory and edit the *snmpd.conf* file using your favorite editor (e.g., *vi*):

   ```
   vi snmpd.conf
   ```

2. Add the following lines to the configuration file. I normally add them toward the top:

   ```
   syscontact you@yourdomain.com
   syslocation location_of_server
   rocommunity public
   trapcommunity public
   trapsink *.*.*.*

   # VMware MIB modules. To enable/disable VMware MIB items,
   # add/remove the following entries.
   dlmod SNMPESX /usr/lib/vmware/snmp/libSNMPESX.so
   ```

3. Next, you will need to make a few more configuration adjustments to ensure that everything starts correctly if you need to reboot your server. Make sure the firewall ports are opened by running this command:

   ```
   esxcfg-firewall -q
   ```

   Look for the following information, which should be located toward the end of the output:

   ```
   Enabled services: CIMSLP ntpClient VCB swISCSIClient CIMHttpsServer snmpd
   vpxHeartbeats LicenseClient sshServer updateManager
   ```

   If *snmpd* is not listed, open its port by running:

   ```
   esxcfg-firewall -e snmpd
   ```

4. Enable the *snmpd* daemon to automatically start on system boot by running this command:

   ```
   chkconfig snmpd on
   ```

5. Restart the *snmpd* service and the firewall to ensure all services are refreshed by running the following commands:

```
service snmpd restart
service mgmt-vmware restart
```

You will want to verify everything you've done by using the `snmpwalk` command. This will query the *snmpd* process on your server and will return basic information about the system, including the kernel version, hostname, uptime, and specific information set in the */etc/snmp/snmpd.conf* file, such as the Name, Contact, and Location:

```
snmpwalk -v 1 -c public localhost system
```

Output will generally appear similar to the following:

```
SNMPv2-MIB::sysDescr.0 = STRING: Linux localhost.localdomain 2.4.21-57.ELvmnix #1
Wed Oct 15 19:00:05 PDT 2008 i686
SNMPv2-MIB::sysObjectID.0 = OID: NET-SNMP-MIB::netSnmpAgentOIDs.10
SNMPv2-MIB::sysUpTime.0 = Timeticks: (13700) 0:02:17.00
SNMPv2-MIB::sysContact.0 = STRING: root@localhost (edit snmpd.conf)
SNMPv2-MIB::sysName.0 = STRING: localhost.localdomain
SNMPv2-MIB::sysLocation.0 = STRING: room1 (edit snmpd.conf)
SNMPv2-MIB::sysORLastChange.0 = Timeticks: (0) 0:00:00.00
SNMPv2-MIB::sysORID.1 = OID: IF-MIB::ifMIB
SNMPv2-MIB::sysORID.2 = OID: SNMPv2-MIB::snmpMIB
SNMPv2-MIB::sysORID.3 = OID: TCP-MIB::tcpMIB
SNMPv2-MIB::sysORID.4 = OID: IP-MIB::ip
SNMPv2-MIB::sysORID.5 = OID: UDP-MIB::udpMIB
SNMPv2-MIB::sysORID.6 = OID: SNMP-VIEW-BASED-ACM-MIB::vacmBasicGroup
SNMPv2-MIB::sysORID.7 = OID: SNMP-FRAMEWORK-MIB::snmpFrameworkMIBCompliance
SNMPv2-MIB::sysORID.8 = OID: SNMP-MPD-MIB::snmpMPDCompliance
SNMPv2-MIB::sysORID.9 = OID: SNMP-USER-BASED-SM-MIB::usmMIBCompliance
SNMPv2-MIB::sysORDescr.1 = STRING: The MIB module to describe generic objects for
network interface sub-layers
SNMPv2-MIB::sysORDescr.2 = STRING: The MIB module for SNMPv2 entities
SNMPv2-MIB::sysORDescr.3 = STRING: The MIB module for managing TCP implementations
SNMPv2-MIB::sysORDescr.4 = STRING: The MIB module for managing IP and ICMP
implementations
SNMPv2-MIB::sysORDescr.5 = STRING: The MIB module for managing UDP implementations
SNMPv2-MIB::sysORDescr.6 = STRING: View-based Access Control Model for SNMP.
SNMPv2-MIB::sysORDescr.7 = STRING: The SNMP Management Architecture MIB.
SNMPv2-MIB::sysORDescr.8 = STRING: The MIB for Message Processing and Dispatching.
SNMPv2-MIB::sysORDescr.9 = STRING: The management information definitions for the
SNMP User-based Security Model.
SNMPv2-MIB::sysORUpTime.1 = Timeticks: (0) 0:00:00.00
SNMPv2-MIB::sysORUpTime.2 = Timeticks: (0) 0:00:00.00
SNMPv2-MIB::sysORUpTime.3 = Timeticks: (0) 0:00:00.00
SNMPv2-MIB::sysORUpTime.4 = Timeticks: (0) 0:00:00.00
SNMPv2-MIB::sysORUpTime.5 = Timeticks: (0) 0:00:00.00
SNMPv2-MIB::sysORUpTime.6 = Timeticks: (0) 0:00:00.00
SNMPv2-MIB::sysORUpTime.7 = Timeticks: (0) 0:00:00.00
SNMPv2-MIB::sysORUpTime.8 = Timeticks: (0) 0:00:00.00
SNMPv2-MIB::sysORUpTime.9 = Timeticks: (0) 0:00:00.00
```

If you run into problems, double-check your *snmpd.conf* file for typos, and ensure that the *snmpd* process is running and that your firewall ports are opened. You may also look in the */var/log/messages* logfile for any errors that may have occurred.

6.14 Using SNMP Version 3

Problem

ESX 3.5/4.x ONLY - SNMPv3 is preferred over versions 1 and 2 for security reasons. Version 3 allows for authentication between the agent and the management server, giving your SNMP traffic a more secure line of communication.

Solution

Enable SNMPv3 by editing the */etc/snmp/snmpd.conf* file.

Discussion

Follow these steps to enable version 3:

1. Log in to your ESX Server and stop the *snmpd* daemon:

   ```
   service snmpd stop
   ```

2. Edit the */etc/snmp/snmpd.conf* file. You can create a user by adding a line like the following, but replacing ***yourusername*** with the username you wish to add. This user will have read-only access; however, you can create a read/write user by using `rwuser` instead of the `rouser` variable:

   ```
   rouser yourusername auth system
   ```

3. Now you need to create a password for the user you just created by adding the following line to the */var/net-snmp/snmpd.conf* file. This will create an md5 password for the user:

   ```
   createUser yourusername MD5 secretpassword
   ```

4. After making the change, save your configuration and restart the *snmpd* service by issuing this command:

   ```
   service snmpd restart
   ```

5. Finally, verify that everything works correctly by issuing the following command:

   ```
   snmpwalk -v 3 -u yourusername -l authNoPriv -a MD5 -A secretpassword localhost
   ```

For detailed information on using SNMPv3, please refer to the *snmpd* website located at *http://net-snmp.sourceforge.net*.

6.15 Using Sudo

Problem

ESX 3.5/4.x ONLY - You have a lot of users working on your servers and you want to keep track of who does what.

Solution

Using sudo, you can safely and effectively give users the ability to run certain predefined root commands with complete audit tracking.

Discussion

The sudo command allows users to run commands specified in the */etc/sudoers* file. Using this mechanism, you can allow normal non-*root* users to execute necessary commands to manage your ESX Server, without having to give them direct or complete *root* access.

To run a restricted command, or any command that tries to perform an activity limited to *root*, authorized users must preface the command with the word sudo. The first time a user does this, before the command is executed, the user will be asked for his or her regular user password. By default, sudo will automatically ask for the user's password again if he or she attempts to execute another restricted command after a timeout period of 5 minutes. You can modify this setting by adding this variable to your */etc/sudoers* file (where *XX* represents the value in minutes):

```
timestamp_timeout XX
```

By default, the ESX Server will use *syslog* to maintain logging for sudo. You can track users by looking in this file. All successful and failed sudo command attempts are logged here. However, if you want this information to be stored somewhere else, you can specify a different logfile location within the sudo configuration file by editing the */etc/sudoers* file and adding a line like this:

```
Default logfile=/var/log/sudo.log
```

To get started with sudo, you will need to configure the */etc/sudoers* file with the users, groups, and commands you wish to allow on your ESX Server. Although you can edit the file using your favorite editor, Linux systems also provide the visudo command specifically for that purpose. The visudo command launches *vi* to manage the configuration file and is the option we suggest.

When editing the *sudoers* file, there are a few guidelines you should follow to ensure that you use the correct syntax. We've compiled a short list to help you:

- Groups within the *sudoers* file must correspond to groups that reside in your */etc/group* file. For example, an *admin* group would be represented by using *%admin*.
- If you have multiple users on the same line, separate them with commas.
- Commands can also be separated by commas, but remember spaces are considered part of the command.
- You can use the word `ALL` to indicate that a line applies to all groups, usernames, commands, or servers, depending on where you insert the word.
- By using the `NOPASSWD` value, you can allow your users to bypass entering their passwords (this is not recommended).
- By using a backslash (\) at the end of a line, you can wrap it to a new line without breaking the syntax.

See Also

Recipe 6.16

6.16 Configuring Sudo

Problem

ESX 3.5/4.x ONLY - Now that you have enabled `sudo`, you want to set it up according to your preferences.

Solution

Edit the */etc/sudoers* file.

Discussion

The nice thing about using `sudo` is that once you get a set of standards in place for your environment, adding new users, commands, or groups becomes a fairly quick process. However, setting it up initially may take some time and practice as you work out which command permissions to assign to your users.

Suppose we wanted to allow access to all *root* commands to a couple of users. We could do this with a line like the following:

```
ryan, matthew    ALL=(ALL) ALL
```

The real beauty of `sudo`, however, is its granular ability to allow users access to run only certain commands in specific locations on an ESX Server. For instance, if we wanted to grant *ryan* and *matthew* the ability to run only `esxcfg` commands and to restart the VMware management server, we could instead use a line like this:

```
ryan, matthew ALL= /usr/sbin/esxcfg-*, service mgmt-vmware restart
```

As mentioned in Recipe 6.15, you can also configure `sudo` to allow users to execute commands without having to enter their passwords. Here, we give *ryan* and *matthew* the ability to run all `esxcfg` commands and to restart the VMware management server, without having to enter a password by using the `NOPASSWD` variable:

```
ryan, matthew ALL= NOPASSWD: /usr/sbin/esxcfg-*, service mgmt-vmware restart
```

In this next example, we make *ryan*, *matthew*, and *bob* part of the *ADMINS* group and create a special *ESXCMD* group specifying which commands they can run. However, we disable the ability to use the `su` command:

```
Cmnd_Alias      ESXCMD = /usr/sbin/esxcfg-firewall,  /usr/bin/esxtop, \
                         /usr/sbin/esxcfginfo, /etc/init.d/mgmt-vmware


User_Alias      ADMINS = ryan, matthew, bob
ADMINS          ALL    = !/usr/bin/su, ESXCMD
```

This configuration is a reasonable attempt to ensure that these users cannot permanently become the *root* user by entering the `su` command. However, it doesn't prevent them from copying files to other locations. The goal is to create a policy that lets you track what your users are doing, while staying compliant with your company's security policies.

`Sudo` is a very powerful tool, and we've only begun to see what it can do. For more detailed information on complex setups, check out *http://www.gratisoft.us/sudo/man/sudoers.html*.

See Also

Recipe 6.15

6.17 Tracking Users via the CLI

Problem

ESX 3.5/4.x ONLY - There are times when you may want to monitor what a user is doing when accessing the ESX Server via SSH or directly from the console.

Solution

There are many different commands and logfiles you can use to obtain information on what users are doing, who is logging into the system, and so on.

Discussion

First we'll take a look at the logfiles, their locations, and what information they contain. There is one primary logfile that contains information about user logins: */var/log/*

messages. The *messages* logfile is a flat text file that can be searched using a command similar to the following:

```
grep sshd /var/log/messages
```

This command will search the logfile and display any lines containing the word *sshd*, thus telling you what your SSH users are up to. Depending on the size of your logfile, it might return a lot of information. Here is an example output from the preceding command:

```
Nov 10 08:25:32 esx6cluster2 sshd[30792]: Connection from 172.20.36.213 port 51085
Nov 10 08:25:35 esx6cluster2 sshd[30792]: Accepted password for root from
172.20.36.213 port 51085 ssh2
Nov 10 08:25:35 esx6cluster2 sshd(pam_unix)[30792]: session opened for user root by
(uid=0)
```

If you want to search for a specific user's login, you can do this by using the same command, but adapting it slightly:

```
grep sshd /var/log/messages | grep bob
```

You can also view the last 200 lines of the *messages* logfile by using the following command:

```
tail -200 /var/log/messages
```

and monitor the logfile for current activity by using the following command:

```
tail -f /var/log/messages
```

For more information on the `egrep` and `tail` commands, you can view their manpages by entering either `man egrep` or `man tail` at the command line.

Now let's take a look at some of the commands that are available to monitor users. Linux has inherited from Unix three useful commands for this purpose: `w`, `who`, and `last`. These commands allow you to monitor when and from where your users are connecting, what processes they are running, and other similar information.

Let's start with the `who` command. This tool allows an administrator to monitor who is connected to the system and to observe some of the characteristics relating to their connections. The `who` command has some useful options with which you should become familiar to help you identify users who are connected to your system.

To see a quick overview of how many users are connected to your ESX Server, run `who` with the `-q` option. If you want to see all the columns of information that the `who` command makes available, use the `-a` option (it is equivalent to specifying the options `-b -d --login -p -r -t -T -u`). By default, only files that are being accessed by at least one process are shown.

An example output when using the `-a` option might look like this:

```
[ryan@esx1test1 ryan]$ who -a
                        Nov 12 17:30                 616 id=si    term=0 exit=0
            system boot  Nov 12 17:30
            run-level 3  Nov 12 17:30                    last=S
                        Nov 12 17:30                 824 id=l3    term=0 exit=0
root      + tty1        Nov 12 20:53   .           1767
LOGIN       tty2        Nov 12 17:30               1768 id=2
LOGIN       tty3        Nov 12 17:30               1769 id=3
LOGIN       tty4        Nov 12 17:30               1770 id=4
                        Nov 12 17:30               1771 id=5
                        Nov 12 17:30               1772 id=6
ryan      + pts/0       Nov 13 13:55   .           9943 (10.0.1.200)
```

Looking at the output, you will see that the first four lines are related to system processes. The next line shows that the *root* user has logged in on the console using terminal *tty1*. The + character next to the username indicates that this user is able to use the `write` command. The following three lines, which begin with `LOGIN`, are login sessions that have yet to be established; they can be invoked by pressing Alt-F2, Alt-F3, and Alt-F4 at the ESX Server's terminal.

Running the `who` command without any options will allow you to see a general overview of your connected users, displaying for each only the username, IP address, terminal, and connection time and date. The last line in the following output shows that *root* is logged in via SSH, hence the *pts/0* terminal notation:

```
[root@esx1cluster1 root]# who
root      pts/0        Nov 13 10:44 (172.20.36.213)
```

Now let's turn to the `w` command, an extension of the `who` command that displays more detailed information about the users who are connected and their current running processes. This commonly used user-tracking tool is available not only on your ESX Server, but also on most Linux platforms.

The `w` command has a few options that provide valuable information. Here is the output if it is run without any options:

```
[root@esx1cluster1 root]# w
 11:07:11  up 1 day, 45 min,  1 user,  load average: 0.23, 0.23, 0.17
USER     TTY      FROM              LOGIN@   IDLE   JCPU   PCPU  WHAT
root     pts/0    172.20.36.213    10:44am  0.00s  0.04s  0.00s  w
```

Notice that the `w` command displays more detailed information than the `who` command:

The first row contains the current time, the system's uptime, how many users are connected, and the system load average for the last 1, 5, and 15 minutes. The second row contains the following information:

- `USER` represents the connected users.
- `TTY` is the terminal to which the user is connected.
- `FROM` displays the source IP address from which the user has connected.
- `LOGIN@` displays the time the user logged in to the system.

- `IDLE` displays the elapsed time since the user's last activity.
- `JCPU` displays the currently running processes attached to the *tty*.
- `PCPU` displays the time used by the current process (listed in the `WHAT` column).
- `WHAT` displays what the user is currently doing on the system.

As you can see, the `w` command supplies a good amount of information on the state of your system; it is useful not just for monitoring users, but also the load and system uptime.

Finally, we'll look at the `last` command. This command searches the */var/log/wtmp* file and lists all of the users who have logged in and out since the file was created.

From the manpage:

> Names of users and tty's can be given, in which case last will show only those entries matching the arguments. Names of ttys can be abbreviated, thus last 0 is the same as last tty0.
>
> When last catches a SIGINT signal (generated by the interrupt key, usually control-C) or a SIGQUIT signal (generated by the quit key, usually control-\), last will show how far it has searched through the file; in the case of the SIGINT signal last will then terminate.
>
> The pseudo user reboot logs in each time the system is rebooted. Thus last reboot will show a log of all reboots since the logfile was created.

As you can see, by using a combination of commands, you have complete access to data on who is logging into your system and what they are doing.

6.18 Configuring Active Directory Authentication

Problem

ESX 3.5/4.x ONLY - You want to enable Microsoft Active Directory on your system.

Solution

Edit the authentication configuration to use Microsoft Active Directory.

Description

By using Microsoft Active Directory to allow your users to connect to your ESX Server via SSH, you establish a point of accountability for the user and create less work for yourself when managing users. Not all environments have a Microsoft Active Directory server, so this is an optional configuration.

To get started, log in to the console on your ESX Server as the *root* user, or use the `su` command to become the *root* user. Then, you will need to prepare a few things in order to set up authentication.

First, make sure your ESX Server is synced to your NTP server. If you do not have an NTP server, we suggest setting one up, because it will make using ESX much easier. If you cannot set up an NTP server, use the `date` command on your ESX Server, and make sure the time and date match those on your Microsoft Active Directory server.

After you've verified that the time is correct on both servers, use the `esxcfg-auth` command to configure your ESX Server to authenticate from the Active Directory server, instead of using the native Linux */etc/passwd* file.

To get started, enter the following command, replacing ***yourdomain.com*** and ***dc.yourdomain.com*** with your respective Active Directory server names:

```
esxcfg-auth --enablead --addomain=yourdomain.com --addc=dc.yourdomain.com
```

As this command runs, it will automatically configure the necessary files and services to authenticate via your Active Directory server.

For your reference, the command will edit the */etc/krb5.conf* and */etcpam.d/system-auth* files and will open the necessary firewall rules. You should double-check each file by running the following commands, to ensure your variables were set correctly (if not, rerun `esxcfg-auth` to reconfigure):

```
more /etc/krb5.conf
```

Your output will look similar to this, but with your own domain:

```
[domain_realm]
.yourdomain.com = YOURDOMAIN.COM
yourdomain.com = YOURDOMAIN.COM

[libdefaults]
default_realm = YOURDOMAIN.COM

[realms]
YOURDOMAIN.COM = {
        admin_server = dc.yourdomain.com:464
        default_domain = yourdomain.com
        kdc = dc.yourdomain.com:88
}
```

```
more /etc/pam.d/system-auth
```

When you enable Active Directory, some extra variables will be added to your *system-auth* file. Here's what it looked like before:

```
account         required        /lib/security/$ISA/pam_unix.so

auth            required        /lib/security/$ISA/pam_env.so
auth            sufficient      /lib/security/$ISA/pam_unix.so  likeauth nullok
auth            required        /lib/security/$ISA/pam_deny.so

password        required        /lib/security/$ISA/pam_cracklib.so retry=3
password        sufficient      /lib/security/$ISA/pam_unix.so  nullok use_authtok
md5 shadow
password        required        /lib/security/$ISA/pam_deny.so
```

```
session         required        /lib/security/$ISA/pam_limits.so
session         required        /lib/security/$ISA/pam_unix.so
```

and what it looks like after enabling Active Directory:

```
account         sufficient      /lib/security/$ISA/pam_krb5.so
account         required        /lib/security/$ISA/pam_unix.so

auth            required        /lib/security/$ISA/pam_env.so
auth            sufficient      /lib/security/$ISA/pam_unix.so  likeauth nullok
auth            sufficient      /lib/security/$ISA/pam_krb5.so  use_first_pass
auth            required        /lib/security/$ISA/pam_deny.so

password        required        /lib/security/$ISA/pam_cracklib.so retry=3
password    sufficient  /lib/security/$ISA/pam_unix.so  nullok use_authtok md5 shadow
password        sufficient      /lib/security/$ISA/pam_krb5.so     use_authtok
password        required        /lib/security/$ISA/pam_deny.so

session         required        /lib/security/$ISA/pam_limits.so
session         required        /lib/security/$ISA/pam_unix.so
session         sufficient      /lib/security/$ISA/pam_krb5.so
```

Ensure that the firewall rules are in place by issuing this command:

```
esxcfg-firewall -q
```

Essentially, when you run the `esxcfg-auth` command, it will add the following rules to your firewall ruleset:

```
esxcfg-firewall -openport 88,tcp,out,KerberosClient
esxcfg-firewall -openPort 464,tcp,out,KerberosPasswordChange
esxcfg-firewall -openport 749,tcp,out,KerberosAdm
```

The final step, and the only minor drawback to running authentication through your Active Directory server, is that you must create an account on the Linux server for the user who is authenticating via the Active Directory. The username you add must match the username in the Active Directory:

```
useradd bsmith
```

You do not need to set a password on this account; the system will pull the password from the Active Directory. Essentially, the username on the Linux side assigns the UID and GID, which Linux requires.

To disable Active Directory authentication, use the following command:

```
esxcfg-auth  --disablead
```

6.19 Setting a Maximum Number of Failed Logins

Problem

By default, the ESX Server does not explicitly set a login failure count.

Solution

Using the `esxcfg-auth` command, you can lock a user out of the system after too many failed log-in attempts.

Discussion

To begin, connect to the ESX Server as *root* and issue the following command. For this example we will set the password maximum login value to `10`, but you may set this variable to any number that suits your specific environment:

```
esxcfg-auth --maxfailedlogins=10
```

Once the command has been run, you can verify it worked by running:

```
esxcfg-auth -p
```

You will see a line similar to the following in the output:

```
account         required    /lib/security/pam_tally.so   deny=10 no_magic_root
```

Notice that the `deny=10` and `no_magic_root` variables are now set. To revert to the default settings, run the same command but replace the `10` with a `0`. This will remove the entry from your */etc/pam.d/system-auth* file.

6.20 Limiting Access to the Su Command

Problem

ESX 3.5/4.x ONLY - You want to be certain that only certain user accounts have permission to acquire full *root* privileges using `su`.

Solution

Create a user group called *wheel* and configure it for access to `su`, adding to the group those users who need access.

Discussion

The *wheel* group is an operating system layer group that allows a limited number of specified users to use *root* commands, such as the `su` command. Using this method should be a second choice for implementing security on your ESX Server; the preferred method is implementing `sudo`, as discussed earlier in this chapter.

By default, only users who are part of the *wheel* group have the ability to run and execute the `su` command. By using a combination of pluggable authentication modules (PAM) and the *wheel* user group, you can limit access to `su` by requiring users to use `sudo` to access *root* commands.

Navigate to the */etc/pam.d/* directory and look for the *su* file. Open this file in your preferred editor and search for the line that begins with `#auth required`. Remove the # character so the line reads like this:

```
auth required /lib/security/$ISA/pam_wheel.so use_uid
```

You will also need to make sure that any user you want to be able to use the `su` command is in the *wheel* group. Open up the */etc/group* file with your favorite editor and look for the following line:

```
wheel:*:0:root
```

Assuming we want to give the users *bob* and *tim* access to the *wheel* group, we would change the line to look like this:

```
wheel:*:0:root,bob,tim
```

6.21 Setting User Password Aging

Problem

ESX 3.5/4.x ONLY - You want user passwords to expire after a certain time, forcing users to create new ones.

Solution

Create a password aging policy.

Discussion

Because ESX is running a modified version of Red Hat Linux, we can take advantage of some of its tools to help manage users. By default, a password aging policy is set with the following parameters:

```
Maximum Days = 90 (default)
Minimum Days = 0 (Allows password changes to occur anytime)
Warning Time = 7 days
```

As you begin to look at your password aging strategy, you will most likely notice that some accounts will have no aging policy; for example, the *vpxuser* and *root* users are exempt.

The `esxcfg-auth` command allows you to globally set the password policy by using the `--passmaxdays` attribute, as you'll see momentarily. This command offers a wide variety of options for tweaking and modifying authentication-related tasks on your ESX Server:

```
usage: esxcfg-auth [options]

options:
  --enablemd5            Enable MD5 password storage
  --disablemd5           Disable MD5 password storage
  --enableshadow         Enable Shadow password storage
```

```
--disableshadow        Disable Shadow password storage
--enablenis            Enable NIS Authentication
--disablenis           Disable NIS Authentication
--nisdomain=domain     Set the NIS domain
--nisserver=server     Set the NIS server
--enableldap           Enable LDAP User Management
--disableldap          Disable LDAP User Management
--enableldapauth       Enable LDAP Authentication
--disableldapauth      Disable LDAP Authentication
--ldapserver=server    Set the LDAP Server
--ldapbasedn=basedn    Set the base DN for the LDAP server
--enableldaptls        Enable TLS connections for LDAP
--disableldaptls       Disable TLS connections for LDAP
--enablekrb5           Enable Kererbos Authentication
--disablekrb5          Disable Kererbos Authentication
--krb5realm=domain     Set the Kerberos Realm
--krb5kdc=server       Set the Kebreros Key Distribution Center
--krb5adminserver=server
                       Set the Kerberos Admin Server
--enablead             Enable Active Directory Authentication
--disablead            Disable Active Directory Authentication
--addomain=domain      Set the Active Directory Domain
--addc=server          Set the Active Directory Domain Controller
--usepamqc=values      Enable the pam_passwdqc module
--usecrack=values      Enable the pam_cracklib module
--enablecache          Enables caching of login credentials
--disablecache         Disables caching of login credentials
--passmaxdays=days     Set the maximum number of days a password remains valid
--passmindays=days     Set the minimum number of days a password remains valid
--passwarnage=days     Set the number of days a warning is given before a
                       password expires
--maxfailedlogins=count
                       Sets the maximum number of login failures before the
                       account is locked out, setting to 0 will disable this
-p, --probe            Print the settings to the console
-v, --verbose          Enable verbose logging
-h, --help             Show this help message and exit
```

To change the password expiration policy, use the `--passmaxdays` option. This will globally change the value for all new users on your system. The best practice is to set this value to 90 days. Alternatively, you can use "0" to disable the `passmaxdays` variable on your system globally. However, doing so will not change any current user's password aging policy:

```
esxcfg-auth --passmaxdays=90   Sets the expiration to 90 days.
esxcfg-auth --passmaxdays=0    Disables system wide.
```

If you wish to change the password aging policy for existing users, you can do this using the `chage` command. For example:

```
chage -M -1 username    Disables aging.
chage -M 0 username     Enables aging.
chage -M 90 username    Sets to 90 days.
```

To view the current settings for `esxcfg-auth`, use the `-p` option. Doing so will display all the current authentication settings on your system that are managed by the `esxcfg-auth` command:

```
esxcfg-auth -p
```

Depending on the configuration you choose, one of seven files might be touched in the process of configuring `esxcfg-auth`. Let's take a look at the files that may be affected by the `esxcfg-auth` command and its function. First up is */etc/krb5.conf*, which contains information on your Kerberos setup:

```
/etc/krb5.conf


[domain_realm]
.yourdomain.com = YOURDOMAIN.COM
yourdomain.com = YOURDOMAIN.COM

[libdefaults]
default_realm = YOURDOMAIN.COM

[realms]
YOURDOMAIN.COM = {
        admin_server = dc.yourdomain.com:464
        default_domain = yourdomain.com
        kdc = dc.yourdomain.com:88
}
```

If you are connecting to an LDAP server, the */etc/openldap/ldap.conf* file contains information on the host, base, password model, SSL, and more:

```
/etc/openldap/ldap.conf


base dc=example,dc=com
host 127.0.0.1
pam_password md5
ssl no
```

Next up is the */etc/nscd.conf* file, which maintains the configuration for the name service cache daemon:

```
/etc/nscd.conf


    debug-level     0
    server-user     nscd

    auto-propagate group yes
    check-files     group yes
    enable-cache    group no
    negative-time-to-live    group       60
    positive-time-to-live    group       3600
    suggested-size group 211
```

```
check-files    hosts    yes
enable-cache   hosts    no
negative-time-to-live   hosts     20
positive-time-to-live   hosts     3600
suggested-size          hosts     211

auto-propagate passwd   yes
check-files    passwd   yes
enable-cache   passwd   no
negative-time-to-live   passwd    20
positive-time-to-live   passwd    600
suggested-size passwd   211
```

The */etc/yp.conf* file is called by *ypbind* when you are using NIS; most people won't need to use this so we won't list its contents here.

The */etc/login.defs* file handles default permissions, group and user IDs, password expiration, and other important variables that will be used when creating a new user on your system:

```
/etc/login.defs


CREATE_HOME    yes
GID_MAX   60000
GID_MIN   500
MAIL_DIR /var/spool/mail
PASS_MAX_DAYS 0
PASS_MIN_DAYS 0
PASS_MIN_LEN  5
PASS_WARN_AGE 7
UID_MAX   60000
UID_MIN   500
```

The */etc/nsswitch.conf* file contains the configuration information that NIS and LDAP use to determine information such as hostnames, password files, and group files:

```
/etc/nsswitch.conf


aliases:       files nisplus
automount:     files nisplus
bootparams:    nisplus [NOTFOUND=return] files
ethers:        files
group:         files
hosts:         files dns
netgroup:      nisplus
netmasks:      files
networks:      files
passwd:        files
protocols:     files
publickey:     nisplus
rpc:           files
services:      files
shadow:        files
```

The */etc/pam.d/system-auth* file contains a central location for system wide authentication settings:

```
/etc/pam.d/system-auth
#%PAM-1.0


account     required      /lib/security/$ISA/pam_unix.so

auth        required      /lib/security/$ISA/pam_env.so
auth        sufficient    /lib/security/$ISA/pam_unix.so           likeauth nullok
auth        required      /lib/security/$ISA/pam_deny.so

password    required      /lib/security/$ISA/pam_cracklib.so                retry=3
password    sufficient    /lib/security/$ISA/pam_unix.so                    nullok
use_authtok md5 shadow
password    required      /lib/security/$ISA/pam_deny.so

session     required      /lib/security/$ISA/pam_limits.so
session     required      /lib/security/$ISA/pam_unix.so
```

Notice that the `account`, `auth`, `password`, and `session` strings are used. The meanings of the fields in these lines depend on the module being configured.

The `passmaxday` value, along with other important information regarding your password aging policy, is located in the */etc/login.defs* file. You should always use the `esxcfg-auth` command when you need to change a variable in this file. Editing it directly will result in lost settings because VMware maintains the files discussed here via `esxcfg-auth` and does not expect them to be modified any other way.

6.22 Disabling Copy and Paste

Problem

By default, copy and paste functionality is enabled between the guest and the host where the remote console is running. The remote console can be used via the web interface or the vCenter client. You want to prevent any applications that may be running on the host from accessing secure information stored on the guest's clipboard.

Solution

Disable copy and paste.

Discussion

Log in to your vCenter client, which should be connected either directly to the ESX Server or to the vCenter server. Make sure the virtual machine on which you wish to change the settings is powered off.

Click the virtual machine, then click Edit Settings, followed by Options, and finally General, which is located under Advanced. From here, click Configuration Parameters, which will open a new dialog box containing advanced options.

Add the following parameters and set the values accordingly:

```
isolation.tools.copy.disable = true
isolation.tools.paste.disable = true
isolation.tools.setGUIOptions.enable = false
```

Once you've made these modifications, close the windows to save the configuration. Because these values get written to the virtual machine's *.vmx* file, they won't take effect until you restart the virtual machine.

6.23 Disabling Disk Shrinking on Virtual Machines

Problem

A default installation of the VMware tools will allow you to shrink a virtual machine's disk. The problem with leaving this option enabled is that any users, regardless of their permissions on the virtual machine, will be able to resize the virtual machine's disk.

Solution

By adding a few configuration parameters, you can ensure that your users cannot shrink the virtual machine's disk, thereby guaranteeing that it works at its maximum potential and limiting the possibility of the virtual machine becoming unavailable.

Discussion

To begin, log in to your vCenter client, which should be connected either directly to the ESX Server or to the vCenter server. Your virtual machine will need to be powered off.

Click the virtual machine, then click Edit Settings, followed by Options, and finally General, which is located under Advanced. From here, click Configuration Parameters, which will open a new dialog box containing advanced options.

Add the following parameters and set the values accordingly:

```
isolation.tools.diskWiper.disable = True
isolation.tools.diskShrink.disable = True
```

Once you've added the new variables, restart the virtual machine so that they will become active. If you want to resize your disks in the future using the VMware Tools, you can reset these values to `False` or remove them.

6.24 Disabling Unneeded Devices

Problem

When creating a new virtual machine, or doing a physical-to-virtual (p2v) conversion, you want to avoid adding unneeded devices that are not often used in a virtual environment, such as USB devices, floppy drives, parallel ports, and serial ports.

Solution

Edit the virtual machine settings as necessary.

Discussion

When you create a new virtual machine, you can choose whether or not to include these types of extra devices. However, when you do a p2v conversion, any hardware on the physical server will be replicated to the new virtual machine. Before powering on your new p2v-converted server, you may wish to use the vCenter to remove any unneeded devices.

Log in to your vCenter server and select the virtual machine you wish to modify, right-click on it, and choose Edit Settings. You will be prompted with the devices that are currently attached to your virtual machine; adjust them as needed.

6.25 Preventing Unwanted Device Additions and Removals

Problem

By default, users can use the VMware Tools to disconnect connected devices like CD-ROMs and Ethernet adapters. This can cause problems if the user has used the CD-ROM to install applications, or disconnects an Ethernet adapter and takes the virtual machine off the network.

Solution

To limit access to these features, set specific variables in the *.vmx* file. This can be accomplished using the vCenter.

Discussion

To begin, log in to your vCenter client, which should be connected either directly to the ESX Server or to the vCenter server. Make sure the virtual machine on which you wish to change the settings is powered off.

Click the virtual machine, then click Edit Settings, followed by Options, and finally General, which is located under Advanced. From here, click Configuration Parameters, which will open a new dialog box containing advanced options.

You will need to add the following parameters and set the values accordingly:

```
isolation.device.connectable.disable = TRUE
isolation.device.edit.disable = TRUE
Isolation.tools.connectable.disable = TRUE
```

Once the new variables have been added, you will need to restart the virtual machine for them to become active. You may disable these settings in the future by using the VMware Tools to either set the parameters to `False` or to remove them.

6.26 Disabling VMware Tools Settings Override

Problem

You wish to disable the option of allowing VMware Tools to make overriding modifications to variables that are managed on the ESX Server, ensuring that users cannot make configuration changes or bypass rules you have already established.

Solution

Adjust the settings in the configuration file.

Discussion

To begin, log in to your vCenter client, which should be connected either directly to the ESX Server or to the vCenter server. Make sure the virtual machine on which you wish to change the settings is powered off.

Click the virtual machine, then click Edit Settings, followed by Options, and finally General, which is located under Advanced. From here, click Configuration Parameters, which will open a new dialog box containing advanced options.

Look for the following value and set it to `false` if it's currently set to `true`. If it is not present, you can add it by clicking the Add Row option:

```
isolation.tools.setGUIOptions.enable = false
```

Restart the virtual machine so that your changes take effect.

CHAPTER 7

Automating ESXi Installations

Given the recent progress of ESX and ESXi, we can now automate the installation of the hypervisor using a few different methods, which we will discuss in this chapter. When deploying, upgrading, or configuring new ESXI servers, the last thing you'll want is to have to step through the complex startup process manually. It's slow and error-prone, and practically negates the value of virtualizing your servers in the first place. Nearly every site, therefore, automates the startup. VMware uses a customized version of Red Hat's Kickstart to allow the bulk installation and startup of ESXi.

7.1 Selecting a Different Boot Option with ESXi 5.x

Problem

You wish to upgrade or install ESXi.

Solution

We'll discuss the available methods that set the foundation for the remaining recipes in this chapter.

Discussion

Traditionally, system administrators installed ESXI servers from an ISO image using DVD/CD-ROM or USB key. Other ways are currently available as well. We discuss all the options here.

Download and create DVD/CD-ROM media
: This is the simplest option. Here you download the ISO image from *http://www.vmware.com* and burn it to media. Whether you are upgrading an existing installation or performing a fresh installation, the installer will interactively walk you through the upgrade process.

Creating a bootable USB key for installation or upgrades
: As the capacity of USB drives grows, it's more attractive to use them for installing ESXi. They are easier to manage than CDs or DVDs and can be used for multiple purposes. For additional information on creating bootable media using a USB key, see Recipe 7.10.

Using Kickstart for the upgrade or installation
: Automating installations using Kickstart and DHCP, and creating a PXE boot environment, is helpful from the standpoint of deployment and upgrading. It eliminates manual intervention and saves time and productivity. However, this option might take longer to build and install the required components. See Recipe 7.2.

Using the vSphere Auto Deploy appliance
: New in vSphere 5, VMware has built a Auto Deploy appliance that can be used to deploy your ESXI servers quickly and efficiently. Auto Deploy can provision hundreds of physical hosts with ESXi software. The image to deploy and the hosts to provision with the image can be specified by the administrator. Additionally, host profiles can be applied to the hosts and a vCenter instance can be assigned to the new ESXi hosts. For more information, please read Recipe 7.9.

vSphere Upgrade Manager
: Using VMware's Upgrade Manager Application, you can upgrade your ESXi host to the latest version of ESXi. This option is available via the vCenter and provides an easy upgrade path.

See Also

Recipe 7.2, Recipe 7.4, Recipe 7.5, Recipe 7.6

7.2 Building a Kickstart Configuration File for Automated Deployments

Problem

You wish to automate the installation of new ESXi installations or perform automated upgrades to existing ESX/ESXI servers over the network using PXE.

Solution

Use the VMware scripting option to easily deploy new ESXI servers.

Discussion

You can deploy new servers or upgrade existing ones using Kickstart scripts along with DHCP servers to create a PXE boot environment. This recipe will assume you already have the DHCP configurations done, and we will focus on the ESXi specific kickstart options.

The following is a basic Kickstart script that can be used to install ESXi and configure networking to have a base system.

```
# Accept the VMware End User License Agreement
vmaccepteula

# Set the root password for the DCUI and ESXi Shell
rootpw yourpasswordhere

# Install on the first local disk available on machine and overwrite the VMFS
datastore.
install --firstdisk --overwritevmfs

# Set the network to DHCP on the first network adapater, use the specified hostname
and do not create a portgroup for the VMs esxcli network --bootproto=dhcp
--device=vmnic0 --addvmportgroup=0


%firstboot --interpreter=busybox

# Add an extra nic to vSwitch0 (vmnic1)
esxcli network vswitch standard uplink add --uplink-name=vmnic1
--vswitch-name=vSwitch0

#Assign an IP-Address to the first VMkernel, this will be used for management
esxcli network ip interface ipv4 set --interface-name=vmk0 --ipv4=10.0.0.100
--netmask=255.255.255.0 --type=static

# Add vMotion Portgroup to vSwitch0, assign it VLAN ID 201 and create a VMkernel
interface
esxcli network vswitch standard portgroup add --portgroup-name=vMotion
--vswitch-name=vSwitch0
esxcli network vswitch standard portgroup set --portgroup-name=vMotion --vlan-id=201
esxcli network ip interface add --interface-name=vmk1 --portgroup-name=vMotion
esxcli network ip interface ipv4 set --interface-name=vmk1 --ipv4=10.0.0.101
--netmask=255.255.255.0 --type=static

# Enable vMotion on the newly created VMkernel vmk1
vim-cmd hostsvc/vmotion/vnic_set vmk1

# Add new vSwitch for VM traffic, assign uplinks, create a portgroup and assign a
VLAN ID
esxcli network vswitch standard add --vswitch-name=vSwitch1
esxcli network vswitch standard uplink add --uplink-name=vmnic1
--vswitch-name=vSwitch1
esxcli network vswitch standard uplink add --uplink-name=vmnic3
--vswitch-name=vSwitch1
esxcli network vswitch standard portgroup add --portgroup-name=Production
--vswitch-name=vSwitch1
esxcli network vswitch standard portgroup set --portgroup-name=Production
--vlan-id=101
```

```
# Set DNS and hostname
esxcli system hostname set --fqdn=esxi5.localdomain
esxcli network ip dns search add --domain=localdomain
esxcli network ip dns server add --server=10.1.1.10
esxcli network ip dns server add --server=10.2.2.10

# Enable SSH and the ESXi Shell
vim-cmd hostsvc/enable_ssh
vim-cmd hostsvc/start_ssh
vim-cmd hostsvc/enable_esx_shell
vim-cmd hostsvc/start_esx_shel


# reboots the host after the scripted installation is completed
sleep 30
reboot
```

The following list describes the variables and options most relevant to VMware that can be used in a Kickstart configuration script.

`accepteula` *or* `vmaccepteula` *(required)*
: Either of these commands will accept the default EULA. One must be included in the Kickstart file.

`clearpart` *(optional)*
: Causes the indicated partitions to be deleted before creating the partitions specified in the configuration (via the `partition` command). This is not required when using the `upgrade` command, because that simply reloads the existing partitions. Options include:

  `--drives=`
  : Removes all partitions from a specific drive.

  `--alldrives`
  : Ignores any `--drives` option and remove all partitions from the system. We strongly suggest that you physically disconnect any external SAN devices connected to the system before using this option.

  `--ignoreddrives=`
  : Specify drives that will be ignored during the install or upgrade process. These drives will not be touched.

  `--overwritevmfs`
  : Overwrite VMFS volumes. This option is not allowed by default.

  `--firstdisk=`
  : Allows you to specify which disk will be used first. The drives are selected in order of 1) local drives (local), 2) network (remote), and 3) USB drives (USB).

`dryrun` *(optional)*
: Will parse and validate the configuration scripts but not actually perform an installation. This can be used for testing your Kickstart configurations.

`install`
: This options specifies that you are doing a fresh and new installation.

`--disk=` *or* `--drive=`
: Selects which partition on the disk to use for the installation and will be used like `--disk=`***`diskname`***. The ***`diskname`*** can be one of the following:

Path
: The full path to the disk; for example: `--disk=/vmfs/devices/disks/mpx.vmhba2:C0:T0:L0`

MPX name
: The name of the disk, for example: `--disk=mpx.vmhba2:C0:T0:L0`

VML name
: The VML name of the disk; for example: `--disk=vml.0000000012345`

vmkLUN UID
: The LUN of the disk; for example: `--disk=vmkLUN_UID`

`--firstdisk=`
: Allows you to specify which disk will be used first. The drives are selected in order of 1) local drives (local), 2) network (remote), and 3) USB drives (USB).

`--overwritevmfs`
: This option will be required if you plan to overwrite an existing VMFS datastore.

`--preservevmfs`
: Preserves the VMFS datastore without impacting the data.

`--novmfsondisk`
: This option will prevent a VMFS datastore from being created on the disk during installation. This option can come in handy if you don't need a VMFS filesystem on local disk.

`installorupgrade`
: Specifies that we are doing a fresh and new installation or an upgrade.

`--disk=` *or* `--drive=`
: Selects which partition on the disk to use for the installation and will be used like `--disk=`***`diskname`***, the ***`diskname`*** can be one of the following:

Path
: The full path to the disk, for example: `--disk=/vmfs/devices/disks/mpx.vmhba2:C0:T0:L0`

MPX Name
: The name of the disk, for example: `--disk=mpx.vmhba2:C0:T0:L0`

VML name
: The VML name of the disk; for example: `--disk=vml.0000000012345`

vmkLUN UID

The LUN of the disk; for example: `--disk=vmkLUN_UID`

`--overwritevmfs`

Allows the installation of ESXi if a VMFS partition exists with an ESX or ESXi installation. Additionally, if this option is not specified, the installation will fail if a VMFS partition is not present.

`--forcemigrate`

If the installation of ESX or ESXi contains third-party MIBS, the installer will normally fail because it won't upgrade them. However, using this option forces installation of ESXi 5.0 without upgrading the MIBS.

`keyboard` *(optional)*

Sets the default keyboard type for the installation.

`keyboardtype`

The keyboard type used. It must contain one of the following languages:

> Belgian, Brazilian, Croatian, Czechoslovakian, Danish, Default, Estonian, Finnish, French, German, Greek, Icelandic, Italian, Japanese, Latin American, Norwegian, Polish, Portuguese, Russian, Slovenian, Spanish, Swedish, Swiss French, Swiss German, Turkish, US Dvorak, Ukranian, or United Kingdom.

`network`

Allow for network elements to be added to the system.

`--bootproto=[dhcp|static]`

Set whether the installation will obtain its IP address from DHCP or whether you will set the address manually.

`--device=`

This option denotes the uplink port you will be using for installation. This will be in the form of `vmnic0` or `vmnic`*`XX`* depending on your system's configuration.

`--ip=`

Sets the IP address of the system. This will be used in conjunction with the `--bootproto` option to set the local IP address manually.

`--gateway=`

The network gateway. This will be used in conjunction with the `--bootproto` option to set the gateway's IP address manually.

`--nameserver=`

Sets the nameservers for DNS resolution. Two IP addresses can be specified here in the format of `--nameserver="10.0.0.1,11.11.11.9"`. This will be used in conjunction with the `--bootproto` option to set the name server's IP address manually.

`--netmask=`

The network netmask. This will be used in conjunction with the `--bootproto` option to set the netmask manually.

`--hostname=`
: Sets the system hostname.

`--vlanid=`
: Assigns the network interface to a specific VLAN. This option can be used with `--bootproto` as either `static` or `dhcp`, depending on how you configure your network.

`--addvmportgroup=(0|1)`
: Create a VM Network Portgroup by default. Generally, this option is set to *1*.

`paranoid` *(optional)*
: If this option is specified, warning messages will cancel the installation. If this command is omitted during the installation, error messages will be logged and the installation will continue.

`part` *or* `partition` *(optional)*
: Creates an additional VMFS datastore during the installation. Only one datastore can exist per disk. This VMFS datastore cannot be created on the same disk as the installation.

`datastore` *name*
: Specifies where the partition will be mounted.

`--ondisk=` *or* `--ondrive=`
: The disk or drive in which the VMFS datastore will be created. Remember, this cannot be the drive used for the ESXi installation.

`--firstdisk`
: Allows you to specify which disk will be used first. The drives are selected in the order of 1) local drives (local), 2) network (remote), and 3) USB drives (USB).

`reboot` *(optional)*
: Reboots the ESXI server after the installation has completed.

`--noeject`
: The CD is not ejected after the installation.

`rootpw` *(required)*
: Sets the root password. Example:

```
rootpw VMwar3!#d4S
```

`--isencrypted`
: Specifies that the password is encrypted during installation. By default, the system has shadow password enabled, MD5-based passwords enabled for authentication purposes. The encrypted password would be in MD5 format here.

`password`
: The password that you wish to use during installation.

`upgrade`
: Specifies an upgrade to an existing ESXi installation.

  `--disk=` *or* `--drive=`
  : Selects which partition on the disk to use for the installation and will be used like `--disk=`***`diskname`***, the ***`diskname`*** can be one of the following:

    Path
    : The full path to the disk; for example: `--disk=/vmfs/devices/disks/mpx.vmhba2:C0:T0:L0`

    MPX Name
    : The name of the disk; for example: `--disk=mpx.vmhba2:C0:T0:L0`

    VML name
    : The VML name of the disk; for example: `--disk=vml.0000000012345`

    vmkLUN UID
    : The LUN of the disk; for example: `--disk=vmkLUN_UID`

  `--firstdisk=`
  : Allows you to specify which disk will be used first. The drives are selected in order of 1) local drives (local), 2) network (remote), and 3) USB drives (USB).

  `--deletecosvmdk`
  : If the system being upgraded is an older ESX installation, the old service console and associated vmdk files will be removed during installation. This will free up additional space.

  `--forcemigrate`
  : If the installation of ESX or ESXi contains third-party MIBS, the installer normally will fail because it won't upgrade them. However, using this option forces installation of ESXi 5.0 without upgrading the MIBS.

`%include` *or* `include`
: Specifies another installation that can be parsed during installation. There is only one argument to this command:

  `filename`
  : For example, `%include exampleconfig.cfg`

`%pre`
: Runs a predefined set of scripts or commands before the installation begins. For additional information, see Recipe 7.5.

  `--interpreter=[python|busybox]`
  : Specifies the interpreter to use during installation. The default is `busybox`.

`%post`
: Runs commands after the installation has completed. This can be useful when additional configuration options are needed.

`--interpreter=[python|busybox]`
: Specifies the interpreter to use during installation. The default is `busybox`.

`--timeout=` *`secs`*
: The timeout for the command. This is specified in seconds. If the scripts are not executed, the script will be forcibly terminated.

`--ignorefailure=[true|false]`
: If true, the installation will continue and complete even if there is a failure during the `%post`script process.

`%firstboot`
: Creates a set of init scripts to run during the first boot of the ESXi system. This will run only the first time and will not impact future boots. Multiple `%firstboot` options can be specified and will run in the order which they are specified in the Kickstart configuration file. For additional information, see Recipe 7.4.

`--intrepreter=[python|busybox]`
: Specifies the intrepreter to use during installation. The default is `busybox`.

7.3 Differences Between ESXi 4.x and ESXi 5.x Kickstart Commands

Problem

Older kickstart scripts from ESX 4 or ESX 3.5 don't work with ESXi 5.0.

Solution

In this recipe, we discuss the changes in the Kickstart command feature set.

Discussion

If you are currently deploying a new installation using a Kickstart script from ESXi 4.x, the following are the changes that will be required in order to successfully install ESXi 5.0 using Kickstart. We have noted for each command if it has been removed from Kickstart, if it is not supported by ESXi 5.0, or if specific options are not supported.

`accepteula` *or* `vmaccepteula`
: These options are available only with ESXi and are required.

`autopart`
: This command has been removed and replaced with `install`, `upgrade`, or `installorupgrade`.

`auth`
: This option is not supported in ESXi 5.0.

`authconfig`
: This option is not supported in ESXi 5.0.

`bootloader`
: This option is not supported in ESXi 5.0.

`esxlocation`
: This option is not supported in ESXi 5.0.

`firewall`
: This option is not supported in ESXi 5.0.

`firewallport`
: This option is not supported in ESXi 5.0.

`serialnum`
: This option is deprecated and removed in ESXi 5.0. Licenses can be applied to the ESXI server after installation is completed.

`vmserialnum`
: This option is deprecated and removed in ESXi 5.0. Licenses can be applied to the ESXI server after installation is completed.

`timezone`
: This option is not supported in ESXi 5.0.

`virtualdisk`
: This option is not supported in ESXi 5.0.

`zerombr`
: This option is not supported in ESXi 5.0.

`%firstboot`
: The **`--level`** option is not supported in ESXi 5.0.

`%packages`
: This option is not supported in ESXi 5.0.

7.4 Advanced Installation Scripting Using %firstboot

Problem

You wish to further enhance your ESXI server's configuration after the ESXi installation at the first reboot of the new ESXi installation.

Solution

Put Kickstart-specific commands and Bash shell commands in the `%firstboot` section of the Kickstart configuration.

Discussion

By including commands in the `%firstboot` section of the Kickstart configuration file, you can customize your ESXi configuration by creating virtual switches and network interfaces, making configuration file changes, and more. Recipe 7.2 discusses the advanced command-line options that are available. These can be combined in a flexible manner in the `%firstboot` section of your Kickstart configuration file. Let's look at a few common uses for that section:

The `%post` option can also be used to run commands after the installation.

Firewall configuration

This is one universal task that can be performed in the `%post` section.

The following lines, for instance, can be included in the `%post` section to open ports for syslog, sshclient, ntpclient, update manager, http, and iSCSI:

```
Method #1
esxcli network firewall ruleset set --ruleset-id syslog --enabled yes
esxcli network firewall ruleset set --ruleset-id sshClient --enabled yes
esxcli network firewall ruleset set --ruleset-id ntpClient --enabled yes
esxcli network firewall ruleset set --ruleset-id updateManager --enabled yes
esxcli network firewall ruleset set --ruleset-id httpClient --enabled yes
esxcli network firewall ruleset set --ruleset-id iSCSI --enabled yes
```

An alternative syntax that is more compact but uses more complex shell features is:

```
FIREWALL_ENABLE="syslog sshClient ntpClient updateManager httpClient iSCSI"
for SERVICES in ${FIREWALL_ENABLE}
do
 esxcli network firewall ruleset set --ruleset-id ${SERVICES} --enabled yes
done
```

Networking

Further customization might include a network setup using the built-in ESXi commands, which are not allowed in the general commands section because the commands in that section run before ESXi is installed. Let's take a look at how to create a simple network.

First, we'll assign the *vmnic2* Ethernet port to the *vSwitch0* switch. Then we'll create a portgroup named *vMotion* on *vSwitch0* and assign it to the network VLAN *201*:

```
esxcli network vswitch standard uplink add --uplink-name vmnic2
--vswitch-name vSwitch0
esxcli network vswitch standard portgroup add --portgroup-name vMotion
--vswitch-name vSwitch0
esxcli network vswitch standard portgroup set --portgroup-name vMotion
--vlan-id 201
```

See Also

Recipe 7.2

7.5 Advanced Installation Scripting Using %pre

Problem

You want to run additional scripts before the Kickstart configuration runs, or set up the environment in which it will run.

Solution

Put Kickstart-specific commands and Bash shell commands in the `%pre` section of the Kickstart configuration file.

Discussion

In the `%pre` section of Kickstart's configuration file, you can specify commands that you want to run just after the Kickstart configuration has been parsed. Using the `%pre` section, you can grab specific variables relating to your system, such as disk types, and create a partitioning schema based on the disks. For example, if you want to use the same Kickstart file on Dell servers and HP servers, you can check which type of disk is being used in the `%pre` section and partition the disk accordingly.

Let's take a look at a simple possibility. The following commands use some standard Unix text parsing to determine the ESXi server's network information from bootp for use when setting the network configuration:

```
%pre -interpreter=busybox
VMK_INT="vmk0"
VMK_LINE=$(localcli network ip interface ipv4 get | grep "${VMK_INT}")
IPADDR=$(echo "${VMK_LINE}" | awk '{print $2}')
NETMASK=$(echo "${VMK_LINE}" | awk '{print $3}')
GATEWAY=$(esxcfg-route | awk '{print $5}')
DNS="172.30.0.100,172.30.0.200"
HOSTNAME=$(nslookup "${IPADDR}" | grep Address | awk '{print $4}')

echo "network --bootproto=static --addvmportgroup=false --device=vmnic0 --ip=${IPADDR}
--netmask=${NETMASK} --gateway=${GATEWAY} --nameserver=${DNS} --hostname=${HOSTNAME}"
> /tmp/networkconfig
```

For more detailed information about using scripts in the `%pre` and `%firstboot` section, see *http://www.redhat.com/docs/manuals/enterprise/RHEL-3-Manual/sysadmin-guide/s1-kickstart2-preinstallconfig.html*.

See Also

Recipe Recipe 7.4 and Recipe 7.6

7.6 Advanced Installation Scripting Using %post

Problem

You wish to further enhance your ESXI servers' configuration after the ESXi installation has completed, or do other initial tasks before applications start.

Solution

Put Kickstart-specific commands and Bash shell commands in the `%post` section of the Kickstart configuration.

Discussion

By including commands in the `%post` section of the Kickstart configuration file, you can customize your ESXi configuration by creating virtual switches and network interfaces, making configuration file changes, and more. Recipe 7.2 discussed the advanced command-line options that are available to you. These can be combined in a rich manner in the `%post` section of your Kickstart configuration file. Let's look at a few common uses for that section:

The `%firstboot` option is a more efficient replacement for %post in some scenarios.

Modifying system configuration files

This is easy to automate using built-in Linux commands. The following example uses the standard Linux *echo* command to modify the */etc/resolv.conf* file to configure the nameservers for your ESXI server:

```
echo "search yourdomain.com" > /etc/resolv.conf
echo "nameserver 10.1.1.1" >> /etc/resolv.conf
echo "nameserver 10.2.2.2" >> /etc/resolv.conf
```

Time synchronization

You can use the `echo` command again, along with other Linux commands, to enable the *ntpd* service:

```
chkconfig ntpd on
echo "restrict 127.0.0.1" > /etc/ntp.conf
echo "restrict default kod nomodify notrap" >> /etc/ntp.conf
echo "server ntp1.domain.com" >> /etc/ntp.conf
echo "server ntp2.domain.com" >> /etc/ntp.conf
echo "driftfile /var/lib/ntp/drift" >> /etc/ntp.conf
```

See Also

Recipe 7.2

7.7 Methods of Upgrading ESX 4.0 Classic to ESXi 5.0

Problem

You wish to know the upgrade paths from ESX/ESXi 4.x to ESXi 5.0.

Solution

This recipe looks at the VMware-provided upgrade paths available for ESX upgrades.

Discussion

VMware has continued to develop the ESXi platform and we now have multiple ways to achieve an upgrade. In this recipe we will take a look at the upgrade paths available and the methods you can use to upgrade legacy ESX/ESXi 3.x/4.x servers to the latest version of ESXi 5.0 (Table 7-1).

Table 7-1. ESXi summary of upgrade paths

Upgrade methods	Upgrade from ESX/ESXi 4.x to ESXi 5.x
vSphere Upgrade Manager	Supported
Manually from CD/DVD or USB Key	Supported
Scripted upgrading using Kickstart	Supported
vSphere Auto Deploy	Not supported currently

The following are the latest upgrade path notes from VMware Knowledge-base Article 2004501. There are a total of eight scenarios that are available, allowing the administrator to select the best method for a specific environment (Table 7-2).

Table 7-2. ESXi supported upgrade paths

Upgrade scenario	vSphere 5.x supported
ESX/ESXi 3.x Hosts	Not supported for direct upgrade. You must upgrade version 3.x ESX and ESXi Hosts to ESX or ESXi Version 4.x before you can upgrade them to ESXi 5.0.
ESX 4.x Host that was upgraded from ESX 3.x with a partition layout incompatible with ESXi 5.0	Not supported. The VMFS partition cannot be preserved. Upgrading or migration is possible only if there is at most one VMFS partition on the disk that is being upgraded, and the VMFS partition must start after sector 1843200. Perform a fresh installation. To keep virtual machines, migrate them to a different system.

Upgrade scenario	vSphere 5.x supported
ESX/ESXi 4.x Host, migration or upgrade with vSphere Update Manager	Supported.
ESX/ESXi 4.x Host, interactive migration or upgrade	Supported.
ESX/ESXi 4.x Host, scripted upgrade	Supported.
4.x ESX Host on a SAN or SSD	Partially supported. You can upgrade the host as you would a normal ESX 4.x Host, but no provisions will be made to optimize the partitions on the disk. To optimize the partition scheme on the host, perform a fresh installation.
4.x ESX Host, missing Service Console .vmdk file, interactive migration from CD or DVD, scripted migration, or migration with vSphere Update Manager	Not supported.
ESX/ESXi 4.x Host, asynchronously released driver or other third-party customizations, interactive migration from CD or DVD, scripted migration, or migration with vSphere Update Manager	Supported with ESXi Image Builder CLI.

7.8 Upgrading ESXi 4.x to ESXi 5.0 via CD/DVD

Problem

You want to upgrade your ESX 4.x or ESXi 4.x to the latest version of ESXi 5.0 using the CD or DVD method.

Solution

By downloading the ISO image from *vmware.com*, you can create a bootable CD or DVD image to upgrade ESX to the latest version.

Discussion

Upgrading ESXi 4.x or ESX 4.0 to the latest version of ESXi 5.0 can be done manually via the CD/DVD method. This method will give you a few options for upgrades.

1. Download the latest ESXi 5.x image from *http://www.vmware.com* and either burn it to a CD/DVD or copy it to a USB key.
2. Insert the media into your physical ESXI server, and reboot.
3. From the ESXi 5.0 Boot Menu, select the ESXi Standard installer option (Figure 7-1). This will begin the installation/upgrade process. Press Enter.

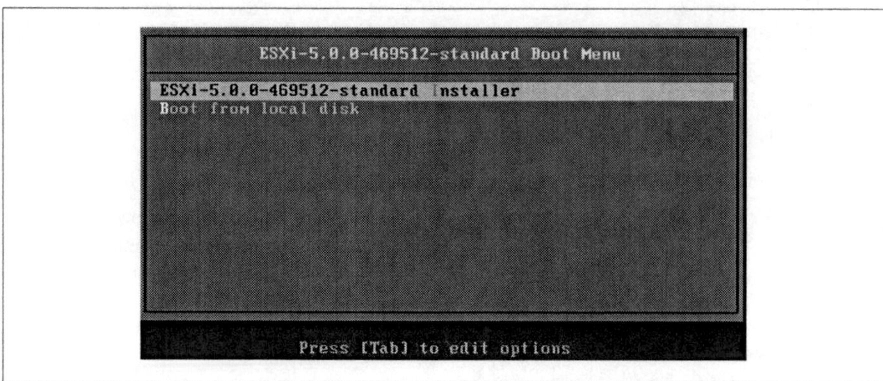

Figure 7-1. ESXi 5.x Installer boot menu

4. Next, select the disk on which you will either install or upgrade ESXi (Figure 7-2). If you have a SAN attached, the disk will be located under the remote section; otherwise it will be under local. Press Enter to continue. The installer will then prepare to use the disk (Figure 7-3).

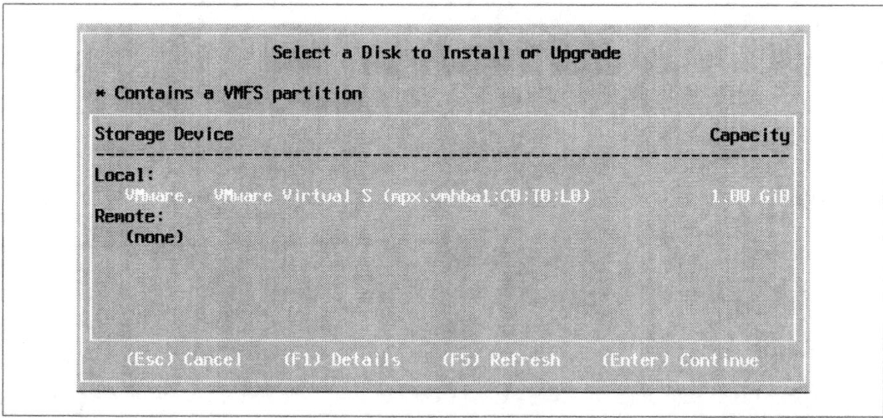

Figure 7-2. ESXi Installer: select disk to install or upgrade

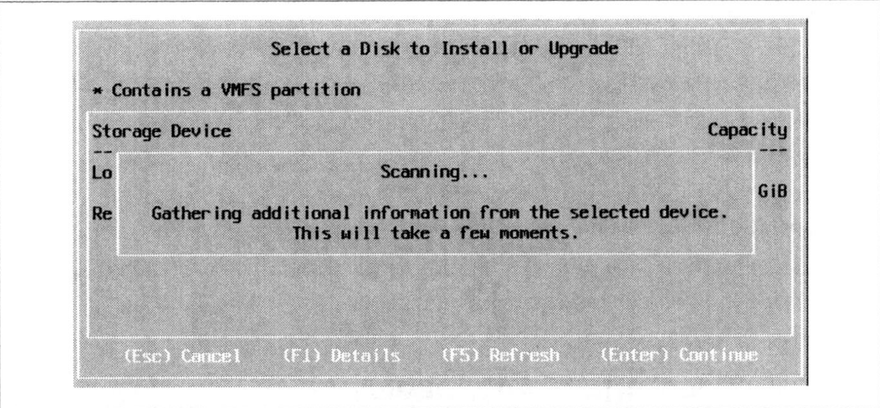

Figure 7-3. ESXi Installer: scanning drive for VMFS volume and installations

5. The installer will search for ESXi and ESX installations as well as VMFS filestores. Next, you will be presented with one of the following options (Figure 7-4):

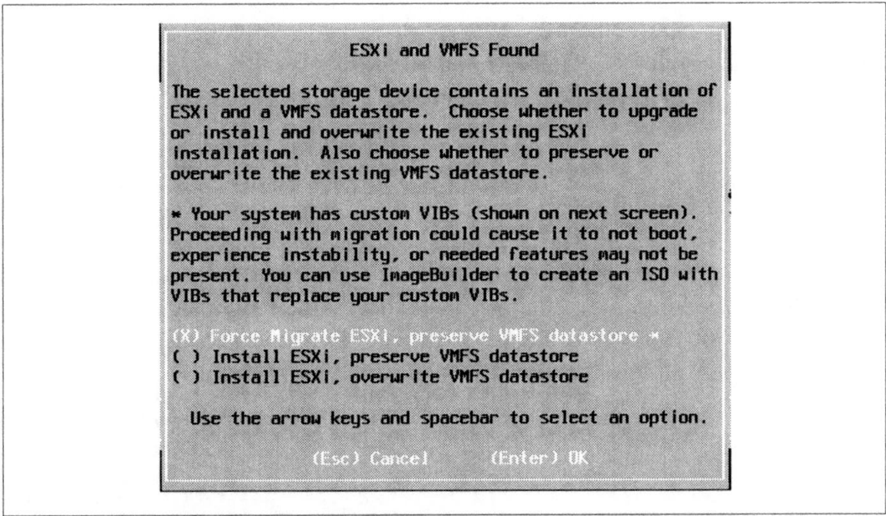

Figure 7-4. ESXi Installer: installation and upgrade options

Force migrate ESXi, preserve VMFS datastore
: This option will migrate your current version of ESX/ESXi 4 to ESXi 5 and keep the VMFS datastore intact.

Install ESXi, preserve VMFS datastore
: This option will install a fresh copy of ESXi 5.0 and will keep the VMFS datastore intact.

Install ESXi, preserve VMFS datastore
: This option will do a complete replacement of ESX/ESXi 4.x and the VMFS volume, creating a fresh installation.

6. Select the option that best fits your environment. Press Enter and the installation/upgrade will continue.
7. If you select the force migration option, you will need to press F11 to continue the installation.
8. Once completed, you will now have a fresh copy of ESXi installed and you can reboot by pressing the Enter key.

7.9 Installing vSphere Auto Deploy

Problem

You need to build a PXE boot environment to automatically deploy your ESXi 5.0 servers.

Solution

Using the Auto Deploy appliance provided by VMware, you can easily build a PXE boot environment to install ESXi over the network.

Discussion

vSphere Auto Deploy will allow the provisioning and reprovisioning of a small or larger number of ESXi hosts efficiently with the vCenter server. Using this new feature in vSphere 5.x, the vCenter server will load the ESXi image directly into the physical server's memory. This means that you no longer have to waste precious hard drive space for the installation of ESXi. Patching and updates are handled through image profiles and optionally through host profiles.

When a virtual machine boots for the first time, stateful information is saved inside the vCenter database.

Table 7-3. Auto deploy state information

Information type	Description	Source of state information
Image state	Executable software to run on an ESXi host	State of the image, possibly created with the Image Builder tool.
Configuration state	The configuration state of the ESXi Host: network information, boot parameters, IP address, etc.	The host profile that is stored on vCenter Server.
Dynamic state	Software-generated information, such as generated keys and runtime databases	State stored in the ESXi Host's memory and lost during the reboot process.

Information type	Description	Source of state information
Virtual machine state	Information about the virtual machines that are located on the ESXi host, such as where they are located, whether they are an HA cluster, etc.	If the virtual machine is in a vSphere HA cluster, deployment can succeed even if the vCenter server is unavailable because Auto Deploy retains the virtual machine information. If the virtual machine is not in a vSphere HA cluster, the vCenter server must be available to supply virtual machine information to Auto Deploy.
User input	Information that is manually entered by the administrator that cannot be stored in the profiles	Custom information is stored in an answer file. You can create a host profile that requires user input for certain values. When Auto Deploy applies a host profile that requires an answer to a newly provisioned host, the host comes up in maintenance mode. You can right-click the host and select Update Answer File to be prompted for the information. The answer file information is stored with the host. Each host has one answer file that can include multiple user input items.

A couple prerequisites that will not be discussed during the section on installation, but need to be present in your environment include:

- The DHCP/DNS Server
- The TFTP boot server

Now let's install the vSphere Auto Deploy. This can be found on the vCenter server installation DVD or ISO image.

1. Select the VMware Auto Deploy option and click Install (Figure 7-5).

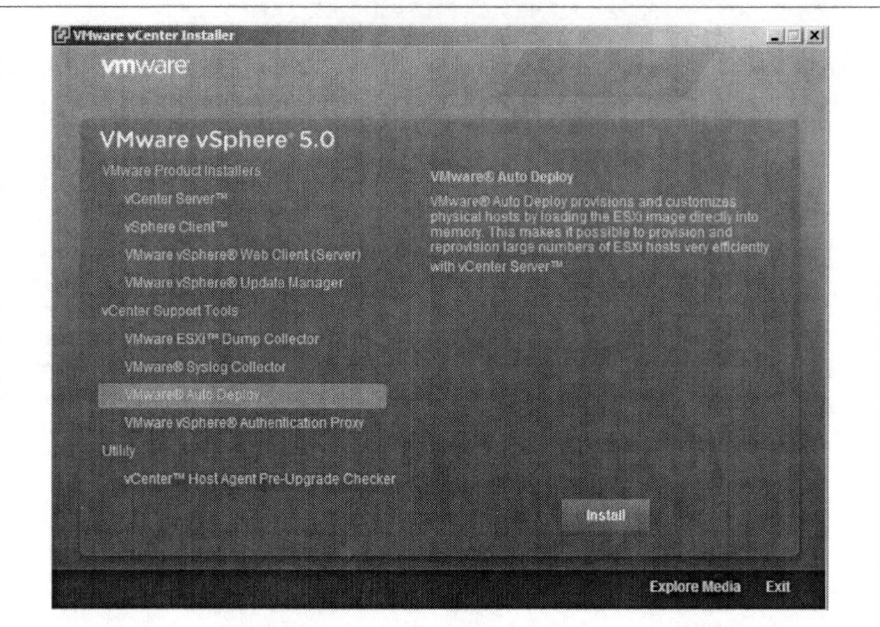

Figure 7-5. VMware Auto Deploy install screen

2. Click Next to start the installation process and accept the license agreements (Figure 7-6).
3. Select the installation destination and then select the maximum Auto Deploy repository (Figure 7-7). The default size is 2GB. If you have enough space, this can be increased to ensure there is enough space in the repository in the future. Generally, each image will be around 350MB. The default of 2GB will hold around four images, with a little extra space. Click Next.

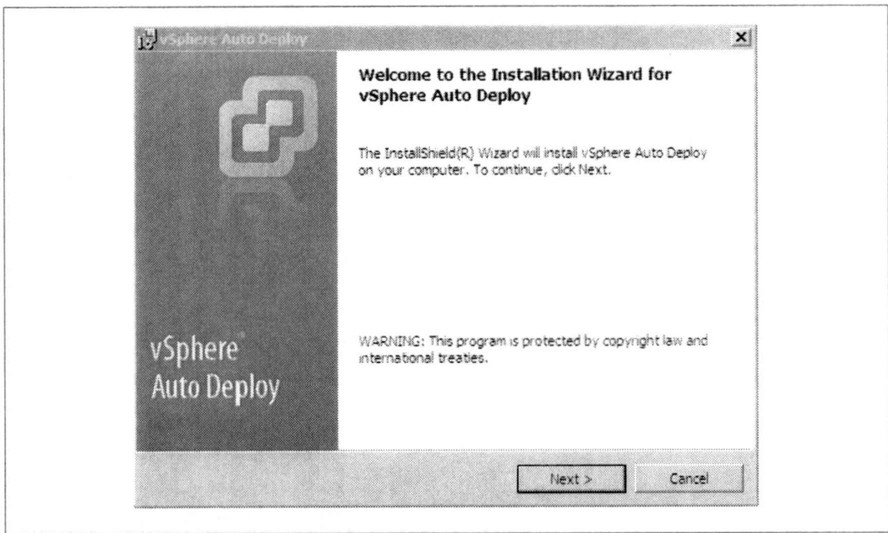

Figure 7-6. Auto Deploy Wizard

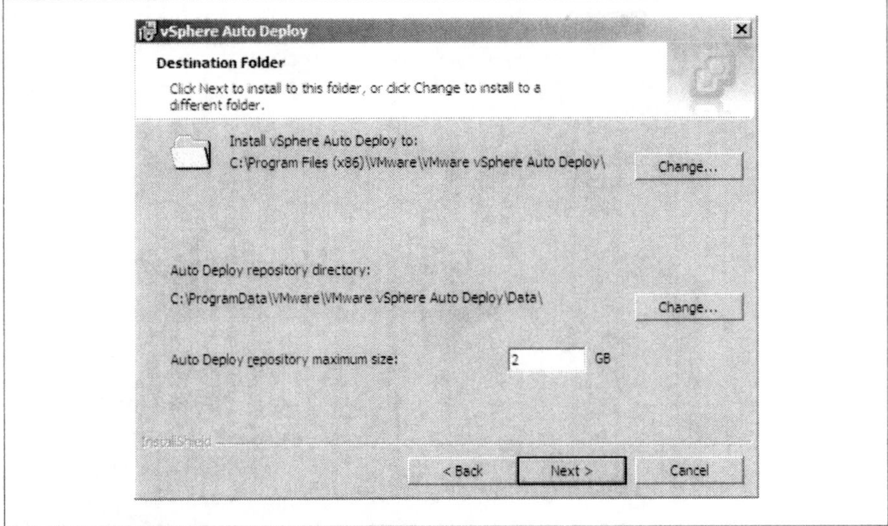

Figure 7-7. Auto Deploy: set repository size

4. Next, set the IP address or name of the server, the HTTP port you are running the vCenter server on, and the username and password of the vCenter Administrator account (Figure 7-8). Click Next. The installer will add an icon to the vCenter server home screen.

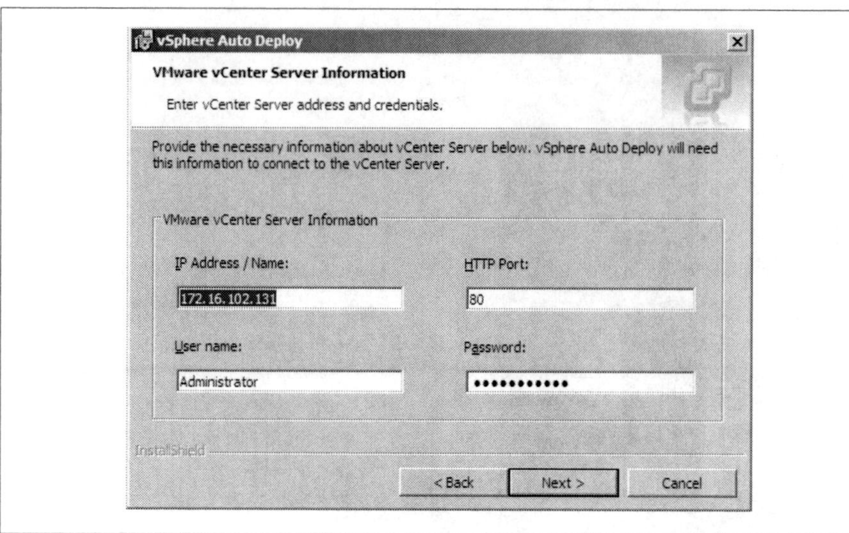

Figure 7-8. Auto Deploy: configure the vCenter server information

5. Next, set the port on which you wish the Auto Deploy server to run (Figure 7-9). The default port is 6501, and it's recommended you keep that default. Click Next. You will also want to make sure this port is open in your network firewall, if applicable.

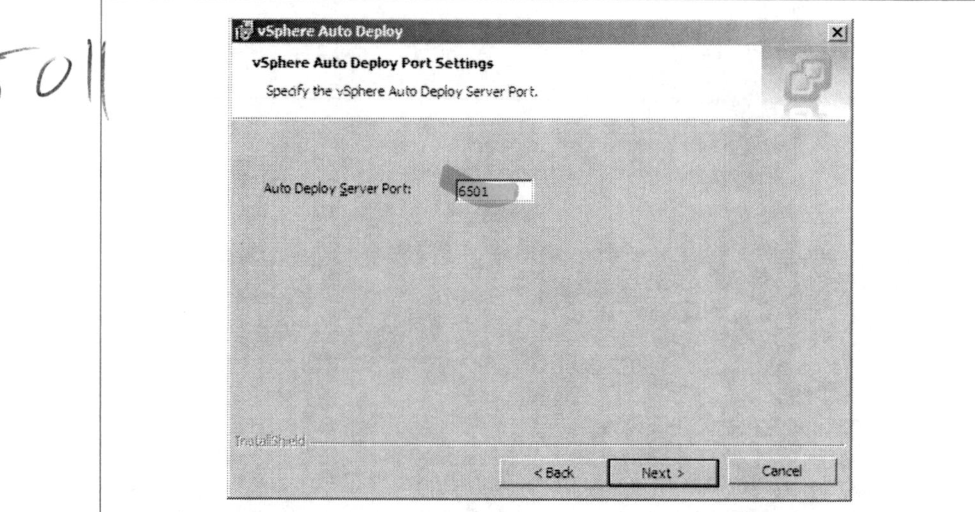

Figure 7-9. Auto Deploy: server port

6. Next, select how you wish Auto Deploy should be seen on the network (Figure 7-10). This will either be a FQDN or an IP address depending on how you connected to your vCenter server in step 4. Click Next to continue.

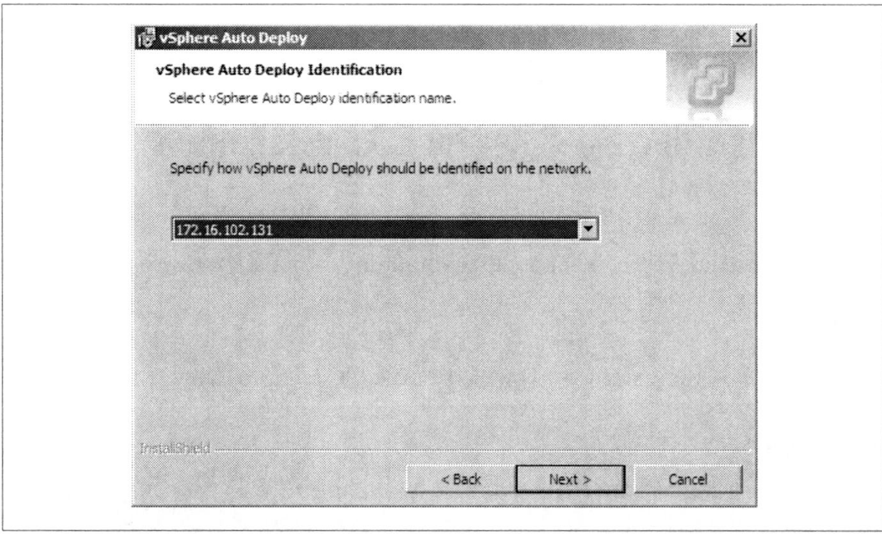

Figure 7-10. Auto Deploy: how it will be seen on the network

7. Finally, click Install to begin the installation process (Figure 7-11). Once completed, you can log in to vCenter using the vCenter client and manage a few available options.

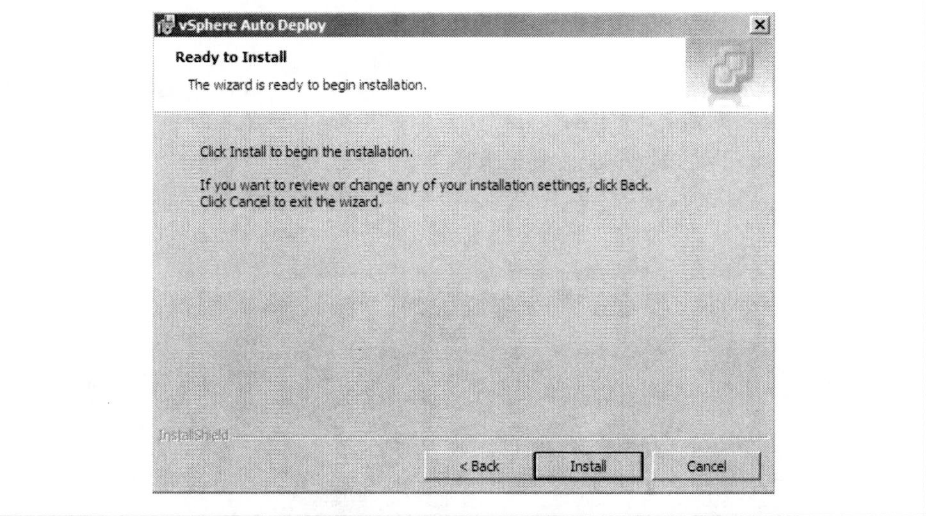

Figure 7-11. Auto Deploy: start of installation

This recipe has walked you through the installation process of the vSphere Auto Deploy components. As mentioned earlier, you will need an additional DHCP/DNS and TFTP server in the network segment to auto provision your new ESXi hosts with the vSphere

Auto Deploy capabilities. Please refer to the VMware Installation and Setup guide for additional information.

7.10 Formatting a USB Key for ESXi Installations

Problem

You wish to install ESXi 5.x manually without DVD media, but with a USB Key.

Solution

Format a USB key and copy the contents of the ESXi 5.x ISO image.

Discussion

We will take a look at the steps to create a bootable USB key for installing ESXi 5.x manually. Today, USB keys are becoming more popular then CD-ROMs/DVDs. We'll take a look and explore the process of copying the media to a USB key in this recipe.

First you will need to make sure you are on a Linux system as because this example will be performed via the Linux command line. You will also need to make sure the ESXi 5.x ISO image is downloaded from the VMware website.

1. First, insert the USB key into your Linux server and determine to which drive it is assigned. This will be something similar to /dev/sdb or /dev/sdc etc depending on how many drives you have.
2. Next, we will format the USB key using the following syntax: `/sbin/fdisk /dev/sdX`, replacing `X` with the drive letter your USB key was mounted as.
3. Next, type `d` to delete partitions until they are all deleted (Figure 7-12).
4. Next, type `n` to create primary partition 1 that extends over the entire disk.

```
Command (m for help): d
Selected partition 1

Command (m for help): n
Command action
   e   extended
   p   primary partition (1-4)
p
Partition number (1-4, default 1): 1
First sector (2048-1957887, default 2048):
Using default value 2048
Last sector, +sectors or +size{K,M,G} (2048-1957887, default 1957887):
Using default value 1957887

Command (m for help): t
```

Figure 7-12. Deleting/creating a partition

5. Next, type `t` to set the type to an appropriate setting for the FAT32 file system, such as `c` (Figure 7-13).

```
Command (m for help): t
Selected partition 1
Hex code (type L to list codes): l

 0  Empty           24  NEC DOS         81  Minix / old Lin bf  Solaris
 1  FAT12           27  Hidden NTFS Win 82  Linux swap / So c1  DRDOS/sec (FAT-
 2  XENIX root      39  Plan 9          83  Linux           c4  DRDOS/sec (FAT-
 3  XENIX usr       3c  PartitionMagic  84  OS/2 hidden C:  c6  DRDOS/sec (FAT-
 4  FAT16 <32M      40  Venix 80286     85  Linux extended  c7  Syrinx
 5  Extended        41  PPC PReP Boot   86  NTFS volume set da  Non-FS data
 6  FAT16           42  SFS             87  NTFS volume set db  CP/M / CTOS / .
 7  HPFS/NTFS/exFAT 4d  QNX4.x          88  Linux plaintext de  Dell Utility
 8  AIX             4e  QNX4.x 2nd part 8e  Linux LVM       df  BootIt
 9  AIX bootable    4f  QNX4.x 3rd part 93  Amoeba          e1  DOS access
 a  OS/2 Boot Manag 50  OnTrack DM      94  Amoeba BBT      e3  DOS R/O
 b  W95 FAT32       51  OnTrack DM6 Aux 9f  BSD/OS          e4  SpeedStor
 c  W95 FAT32 (LBA) 52  CP/M            a0  IBM Thinkpad hi eb  BeOS fs
 e  W95 FAT16 (LBA) 53  OnTrack DM6 Aux a5  FreeBSD         ee  GPT
 f  W95 Ext'd (LBA) 54  OnTrackDM6      a6  OpenBSD         ef  EFI (FAT-12/16/
10  OPUS            55  EZ-Drive        a7  NeXTSTEP        f0  Linux/PA-RISC b
11  Hidden FAT12    56  Golden Bow      a8  Darwin UFS      f1  SpeedStor
12  Compaq diagnost 5c  Priam Edisk     a9  NetBSD          f4  SpeedStor
14  Hidden FAT16 <3 61  SpeedStor       ab  Darwin boot     f2  DOS secondary
16  Hidden FAT16    63  GNU HURD or Sys af  HFS / HFS+      fb  VMware VMFS
17  Hidden HPFS/NTF 64  Novell Netware  b7  BSDI fs         fc  VMware VMKCORE
18  AST SmartSleep  65  Novell Netware  b8  BSDI swap       fd  Linux raid auto
1b  Hidden W95 FAT3 70  DiskSecure Mult bb  Boot Wizard hid fe  LANstep
1c  Hidden W95 FAT3 75  PC/IX           be  Solaris boot    ff  BBT
1e  Hidden W95 FAT1 80  Old Minix
Hex code (type L to list codes): c

Command (m for help): 
```

Figure 7-13. Selecting the filesystem type

6. Next, type `a` to set the active flag on partition 1 (Figure 7-14).

```
Command (m for help): a
Partition number (1-4): 1

Command (m for help): 
```

Figure 7-14. Setting the partition active

7. Next, type `w` to save the changes.
8. Now that the settings are changed and we have a partition table, let's format the partition: `/sbin/mkfs.vfat -F 32 -n USB /dev/sdX1`, replacing `X` with the drive letter your USB key was assigned.
9. Next, we need to mount the USB key to copy the ESXi installation to: `mount /dev/sdX1 /usbdisk`, replacing `X` with the drive letter your USB key was assigned.

10. Let's mount the ESXi ISO image to our Linux server so we can copy the contents to the USB key: `mount -o loop VMware-VMvisor-Installer-5.0.0-XXXXXX.x86_64.iso /esxi_cdrom`, replacing XXXXXX with the version of ESXi 5.x you downloaded.
11. Next, use the Linux `cp` command to copy the contents of the ISO image to the USB key: `cp -r /esxi_cdrom/* /usbdisk`
12. Next, move the isolinux.cfg file to syslinux.cfg, which allows you to boot the USB key: `mv /usbdisk/isolinux.cfg /usbdisk/syslinux.cfg`
13. Next, we need to edit the syslinux.cfg file using your favorite editor. This can be vi or nano or gedit if you have a desktop on your server. Open the file `/usbdisk/syslinux.cfg`, change the line `APPEND -c boot.cfg` to `APPEND -c boot.cfg -p 1`, and then save the file.
14. Finally, unmount the ISO image and USB key: `umount /usbdisk && umount /esxi_cdrom`

CHAPTER 8
vCloud Director Overview

This chapter provides an introduction to vCloud Director (vCD), a layer of vSphere that end users control over the consumption of virtual resources. The vCloud Director allows end users and small and large businesses to reduce or eliminate equipment maintenance and move into a cloud environment, either within an organization or with a service provider using a public or private cloud model. In this chapter, we will take a look at vCloud Director's requirements and the installation of the vCloud Director evaluation appliance.

8.1 What Is vCloud Director?

Problem

You are looking to offer a public or private cloud within your organization or externally to businesses.

Solution

In this recipe, we will discuss the vCloud Director and how it can impact your business.

Discussion

The vCloud Director works by taking pools of datacenter resources, including storage, networking, and compute resources, and creating virtual datacenters that operate independently of each other. This creates a highly secure and encapsulated environment, allowing multiple users or customers to create an infrastructure without having to invest or manage physical resources. The vCloud Director integrates with existing the vSphere 4 and 5 deployments and takes advantage of DRS, DVS, and HA.

The vCloud Director leverages an open standard, the vCloud API, to let developers outside of VMware build on the platform and automate processes that fit their business requirements. Additionally, vCloud Director uses open visualization format (OVF), which allows administrators and developers to create and package specific workloads across their cloud infrastructures.

Consuming resources via the vCloud Director is simple. End users have access to a web portal and API interface, allowing customers to use resources in multiple ways. This permits service providers to offer pay-as-you-go models, along with fixed resource consumption models, giving the end user additional flexibility. Resources can be monitored and charged back to the end user via the vCenter Chargeback application. This ensures accurate reporting of resources for billing purposes.

Some of the highlighted features of the vCloud Director include:

Virtual datacenters
: Virtual datacenters use the vSphere infrastructure to offer storage, memory, CPU and networking resources within a multitenant infrastructure driven by organizational units.

Highly secure
: Through vShield technologies at the network edge, each virtual datacenter created within the vCloud and the vSphere infrastructure is secure and independent.

Rapid provisioning
: By using catalogs and templates, this allows organizations to rapidly provision new virtual machines within the virtual datacenter.

Organizational units
: The ability to create multiple organizational units within the virtual datacenter allows custom business units for deployments.

Self-service portal
: A web-based portal manages the virtual datacenter for the organization.

The vCloud Director has multiple uses: it can be used in an organization for service providers, for developers, or within an organization to allow different business divisions to manage their own infrastructure. In this chapter we'll look at the requirements for the vCloud Director as well as requirements for deploying the vCloud Evaluation deployment appliance.

Figure 8-1 shows how the vCloud Director organizes the various vSphere resources and offers them to users. The following three resources are abstracted from the vSphere layer into the vCloud Director Cell, and then presented to the end user in the form of a virtual datacenter. Thus, end users can deploy new computing resources within their own secure environments.

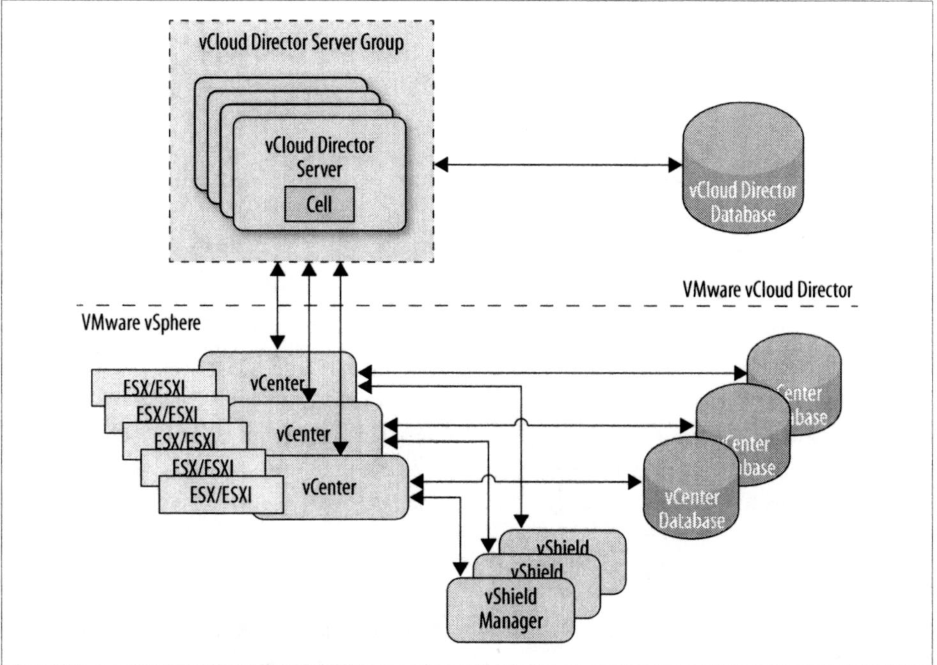

Figure 8-1. vCloud architecture (credit: vmware.com)

Storage
: VMFS datastores and NFS shares are allocated to virtual datacenters, allowing users to provision new virtual machines.

Networking
: Distributed virtual switches (dvSwitches) and portgroups are used to create the network components and fabric that make up the multitenant environment.

Compute
: The computing resources are pulled from vCenter Servers clusters and will be used within resource pools when provisioned in a vCloud Director virtual datacenter.

A virtual datacenter consists of two different types of organization units that represent how resources are allocated to the virtual datacenter.

Provider virtual datacenter
: A provider virtual datacenter combines the compute (CPU & Memory) and memory resources of a single vCenter server resource pool with the storage resources of one or more datastores available to that resource pool. Multiple provider virtual datacenters can be created for users in different geographic locations or business units, or for users with different performance requirements.

Organization virtual datacenter
: An organization virtual datacenter provides resources to an organization and is partitioned off from a provider virtual datacenter. Organization virtual datacenters provide an environment where virtual systems can be stored, deployed, and operated. They also provide storage for virtual media, such as floppy disks and CD-ROMs. A single organization can have a multiple organization virtual datacenter. An organization administrator specifies how resources from a provider virtual datacenter are distributed to the virtual datacenters in an organization.

Organizations use catalogs to store vApp templates and media files, such as ISO or OS images. Members of the organizations have access to the catalog and can use the resources inside that catalog to deploy new vApps that encompass the virtual machines.

vApps are encapsulated containers that represent all of the virtual machine and networking components of a specific application. vApps can be simple deployments such as a single server or as a complex multitier web appliance. Templates can be created from the vApps to be used for easily deploying additional resources within the organization.

Key benefits of deploying the vCloud Director include:

- Accelerating the deployment of new virtual machines through the OVF[1] and templates
- Accelerating the time it takes to deploy new virtual machines within the datacenter
- Enforcing network and end user isolation by using vShield within the vCloud Director
- Increasing flexibility by using standard ports, allowing easier integration with additional application stacks
- Decreasing costs by consolidating infrastructure and delivering resources within an easy-to-manage interface

8.2 What's New in vCloud Director 1.5

Problem

When upgrading or considering upgrading to the vCloud Director 1.5 what to expect.

Solution

This recipe highlights new features in the vCloud Director 1.5.

1. *http://www.dmtf.org/standards/ovf*

Discussion

As you look at upgrading from vCloud Director 1.0, consider some of the features and enhancements that will be available to you:

Fast provisioning
: Using linked clones allows users to quickly provision new virtual machines by using elements from other like virtual machines within the same vApp. This means the user won't have to wait for a new clone to be made, the vCloud Director will simply use the other virtual machine elements to create a full copy. This, additionally, reduces the storage space required because the virtual machines are linked via similar elements.

vApp custom properties
: Users can now pass custom data into the guest OS when deploying vApps within the vCloud Director. This allows developers and application developers the option to set specific variables such as SSH keys and other preconfigured options.

Blocking tasks and notifications
: The vCloud Director can now be configured to post notifications and messages to AMQP-based enterprise messaging brokers. This allows administrators to use existing messaging infrastructure for notifications on events within the vCloud Director.

Expanded vCloud API
: The vCloud Director now allows full access to all GUI-accessible actions via the vCloud API. This allows for more integration and growth when deploying a hybrid cloud model.

Microsoft SQL Server support
: The vCloud Director 1.5 now supports Microsoft SQL for the vCloud database. Previously, only Oracle was available.

vShield Edge VPN integration
: Users can now create site-to-site IPSec-VPN tunnels between multiple clouds. This allows for the secure transmission of data between multiple clouds, and is accessible via the vCloud API, allowing for easy deployment.

vCloud Director virtual appliance
: The vCloud Director appliance covered in Recipe 8-5 of this chapter is intended to allow for the evaluation of the vCloud Director environment without having a full deployment.

Firewall rules can be configured with CIDR blocks, IP ranges, and port ranges
: vCloud Director 1.5.1 allows you to enter CIDR blocks and IP ranges for the source and destination when creating firewall rules using the UI or REST API. In addition, you can enter port ranges for the source and destination ports using the UI (but not the REST API). If you create a firewall rule that includes port ranges using the UI, you will not be able to query the rule using the REST API.

Added system notification for a lost connection to the AMQP host
: If the vCloud Director loses its connection to the AMQP host, vCD sends an email to the recipients specified in the System Notification settings (Administration → System Settings → Email).

Enhanced cell management tool and log collection script
: This release includes a new version of the cell management tool. With this version, you are not required to enter an administrator username and password to access help and usage information. If a command requires a username and password, the cell management tool prompts you to enter the information.

Increased the retention maximum for vCenter Chargeback history
: In vCloud Director 1.5.1, the maximum possible setting for Chargeback Event History to Keep was increased from 365 days to 1,096 days.

8.3 vCloud Director Maximums

Problem

You need to find the maximum configurations for the vCloud Director.

Solution

Use this recipe to determine the maximum configurations for a vCloud Director deployment.

Discussion

The supported maximums inside a vCloud Director deployment are listed in Table 8-1. This is important information because the vCloud Director deployments are designed and put into production.

Table 8-1. vCloud Director maximums

Value/Item	vSphere 5.x maximum
Virtual machine count	20,000
Powered-on virtual machine count	10,000
Organizations	10,000
Virtual machines per vApp	64
vApps per organization	500
Number of networks	7,500
Hosts	2,000
vCenter servers	25
Virtual data centers	10,000

Value/Item	vSphere 5.x maximum
Datastores	1,024
Catalogs	1,000
Media	1,000
Users	10,000

8.4 vCloud Director Requirements

Problem

You wish to install vCloud Director in your environment.

Solution

Use this section as a reference for the installation requirements, to ensure your installation runs smoothly.

Discussion

Some specific requirements and guidelines must be followed to deploy the vCloud Director successfully. In this recipe we take a look at the basic requirements of, and some restrictions on the vSphere configuration. Additional detailed information can be found in the vCloud Director Install and Configure Guide available at the following location *http://www.vmware.com/pdf/vcd_15_install.pdf*

To deploy vCloud Director, you must create an environment inside of vSphere that adheres to the following restrictions:

- You must not enable Storage DRS on the clusters used by the vCloud Director.
- The clusters used by the vCloud Director must be configured with full DRS automation. This requires shared storage so each datastore is present on the hosts inside the cluster.
- Distributed Switches must be used for cross-host fencing and network pool allocations to the vCloud Director instances.
- There must be a trust between the vCloud Director application stack and the ESXI servers.
- All network segments must be available to all hosts within the cluster. This makes automation and deployment easy because all networks will be available.
- You must use Enterprise Plus licenses to gain full access to the features required for the vCloud Director.
- Refer to Table 8-2, 8-3, and 8-4 for additional hardware and software requirements for vCloud Director 1.5

Table 8-2. Supported operating systems

Operating system	Version
Red Hat Enterprise Linux	Version 5 (64 bit), Update 4
Red Hat Enterprise Linux	Version 5 (64 bit), Update 5
Red Hat Enterprise Linux	Version 5 (64 bit), Update 6

Table 8-3. Memory/disk requirements (installation of the vCloud Director)

Requirement	Comments
Minimum disk requirement	950MB (installation and log file), suggested 2TB to ensure enough space for growth
Minimum memory requirement	1GB Memory, 4GB suggested for optimal performance

Table 8-4. Supported databases

Database	Version
Oracle	10g & 11g standard and enterprise
Microsoft SQL	2005 & 2008 standard and enterprise

Please check the latest support matrix for all compatible versions of SQL. The link can be found at *http://partnerweb.vmware.com/comp_guide2/sim/interop_matrix.php*.

Table 8-5. vShield requirements

vShield requirements	Comments
1.0	No additional requirements
1.0 Update 1	No additional requirements
5.0	Required for static routing and VPN support

The vCloud Director can run on vCenter 4.0 Update 2, vCenter 4.0 Update 3, vCenter 4.1, vCenter 4.1 Update 1, and vCenter 5.0. vCenter 5.0 is required if you want Fast Provisioning, Hardware Version 8, or VPN support.

The vCloud Director supports the following versions of ESXi/ESX: ESXi/ESX 4.0 Update 1, ESXi/ESX 4.0 Update 2, ESXi/ESX 4.1, ESXi/ESX4.1 Update 1, and ESXi/ESX 5.0. ESXi/ESX 5.0 is required if you want Fast Provisioning, Hardware Version 8, or VPN support.

The vCloud Director has several impacts on your network because the environment will be shared among multiple users. Tables 8-6 and 8-7 summarize the network requirements needed by the vCloud Director.

Table 8-6. Incoming network ports

Port	Comments
111 - UDP/TCP	NFS Traffic
920 - TCP/UDP	NFS Traffic
61616 - TCP	ActiveMQ
61611 - TCP	ActiveMQ
80 - TCP	Incoming HTTP requests
443 - TCP	Incoming HTTPS requests

Outgoing network ports should *not* be connected to the public and the external facing networks. These ports are used for internal traffic between the vCloud Director and the ESX/ESXi hosts.

Table 8-7. Outgoing network ports

Port	Comments
25 - TCP/UDP	SMTP Services
53 - TCP/UDP	DNS
111 - TCP/UDP	NFS
123 - TCP/UDP	NTP
389 - TCP/UDP	LDAP
443 - TCP	vCenter and ESXi connections
514 - UDP	Syslog (this is optional)
902 - TCP	vCenter and ESXi connections
903 - TCP	vCenter and ESXi connections
920 - TCP/UDP	NFS
1433 - TCP	Microsoft SQL Database (default port)
1521 - TCP	Oracle SQL Database (default port)
5672 - TCP/UDP	AMQP messages for task extensions
61611 - TCP	ActiveMQ
61616 - TCP	ActiveMQ

For additional requirements outside the scope of this recipe, please refer to the vCloud Director Install and Configuration Guide (*www.vmware.com/pdf/vcd_15_install.pdf*).

8.5 vCloud Director (Evaluation Appliance)

Problem

You wish to evaluate the vCloud infrastructure without deploying an actual live environment.

Solution

Follow the steps in this recipe to deploy the evaluation appliance.

Discussion

VMware has made it easy for organizations to test the vCloud without making a large commitment of time and infrastructure. Customers looking to rapidly test and evaluate a vCloud environment can use the appliance released for that purpose in an Open Virtualization Appliance (*.ova*) format. Although the appliance includes a preconfigured Oracle XE database along with CentOS, please keep in mind that CentOS is not supported in a production environment.

In this recipe, we will take a look at deploying the vCloud Director Evaluation Appliance.

1. Log in to the vCenter, pull down the File menu, and then select Deploy OVF Template (Figure 8-2).

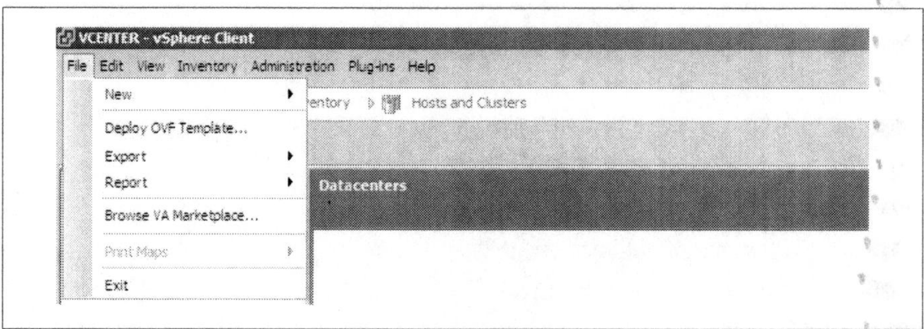

Figure 8-2. Deploy the OVF Template

2. Navigate to the OVF file you have downloaded from VMware's website. Once it is selected, click Next to begin the import process (Figure 8-3).

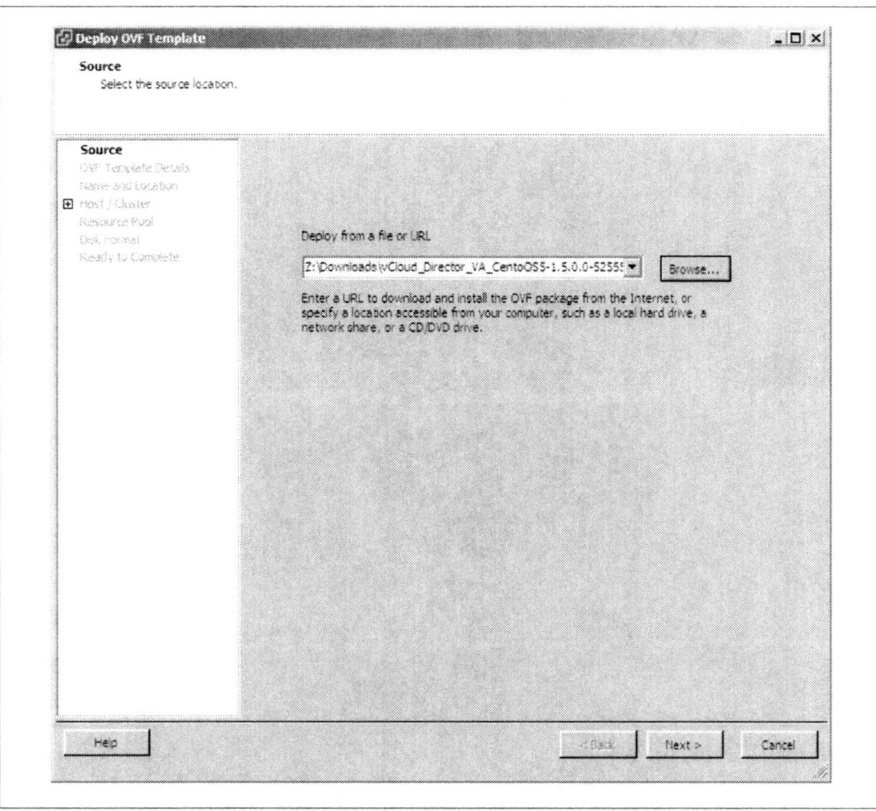

Figure 8-3. Deploy the OVF Template (source: OVF)

3. The wizard will display some general information about the OVF Appliance and will validate the publisher (Figure 8-4). Click Next to continue.

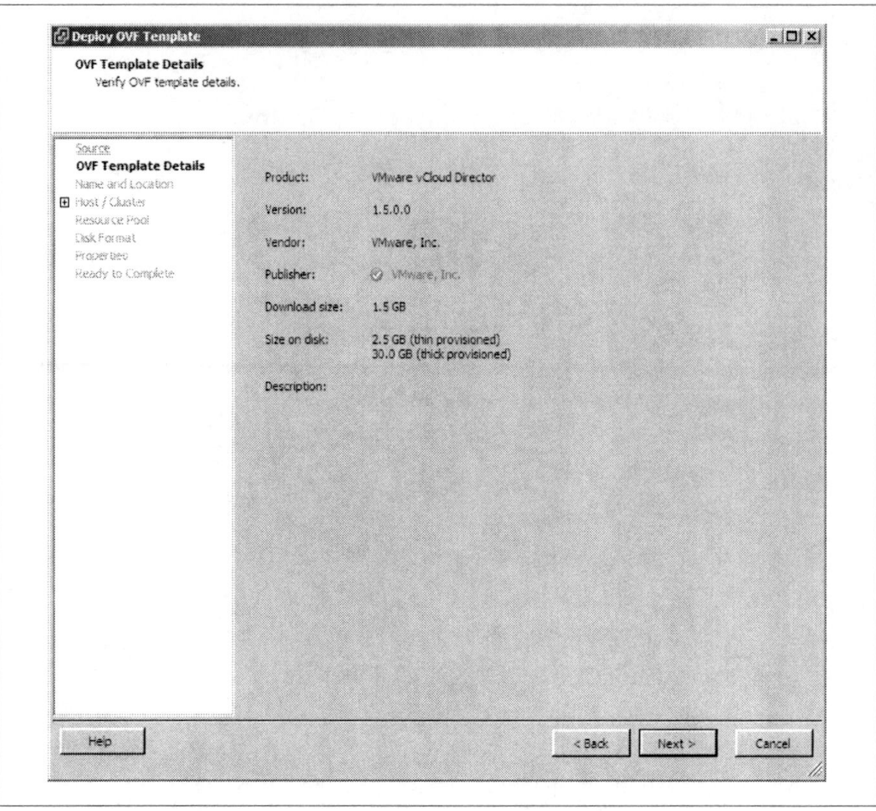

Figure 8-4. Deploy the OVF template: template detcils

4. Next, you will need to enter the name of the virtual machine that will be the vCloud Director Appliance (Figure 8-5). Click Next to continue.

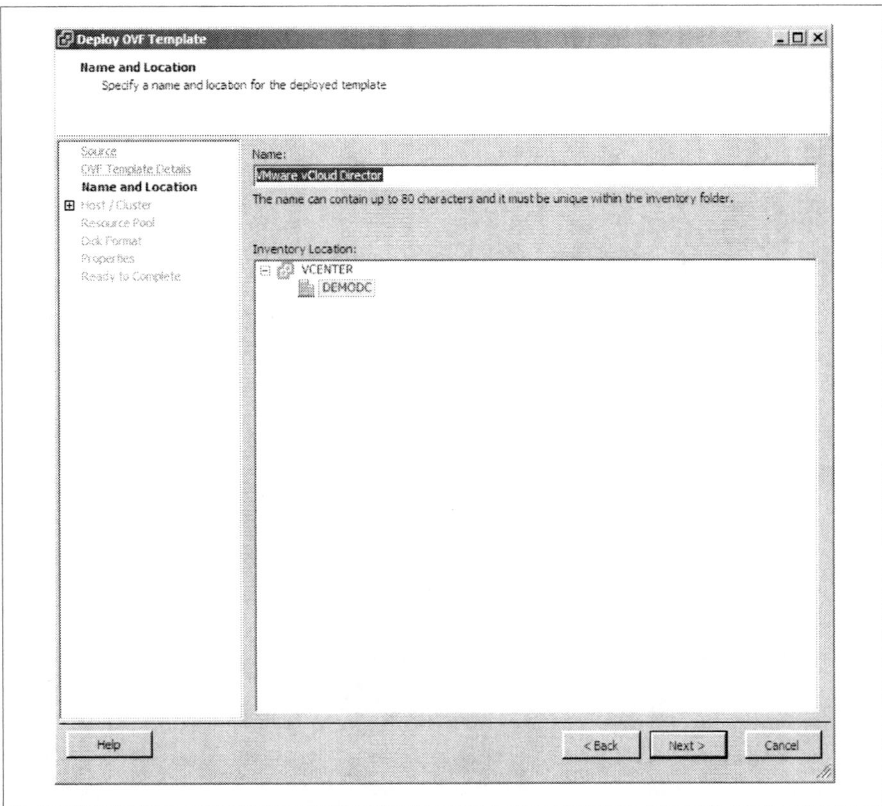

Figure 8-5. Deploy the OVF template: name and location

5. Select the host or cluster where you wish to deploy the appliance (Figure 8-6). Once selected, click Next to continue.

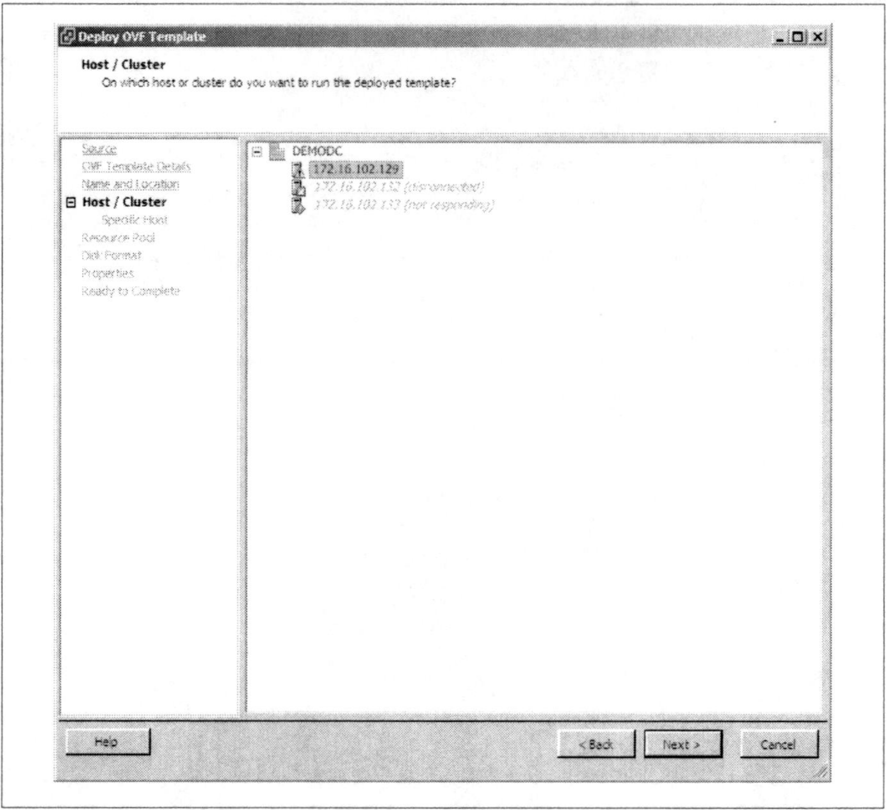

Figure 8-6. Deploy the OVF template: host and cluster

6. Select the disk format you would like to use for the virtual machine (Figure 8-7). Click Next to continue.

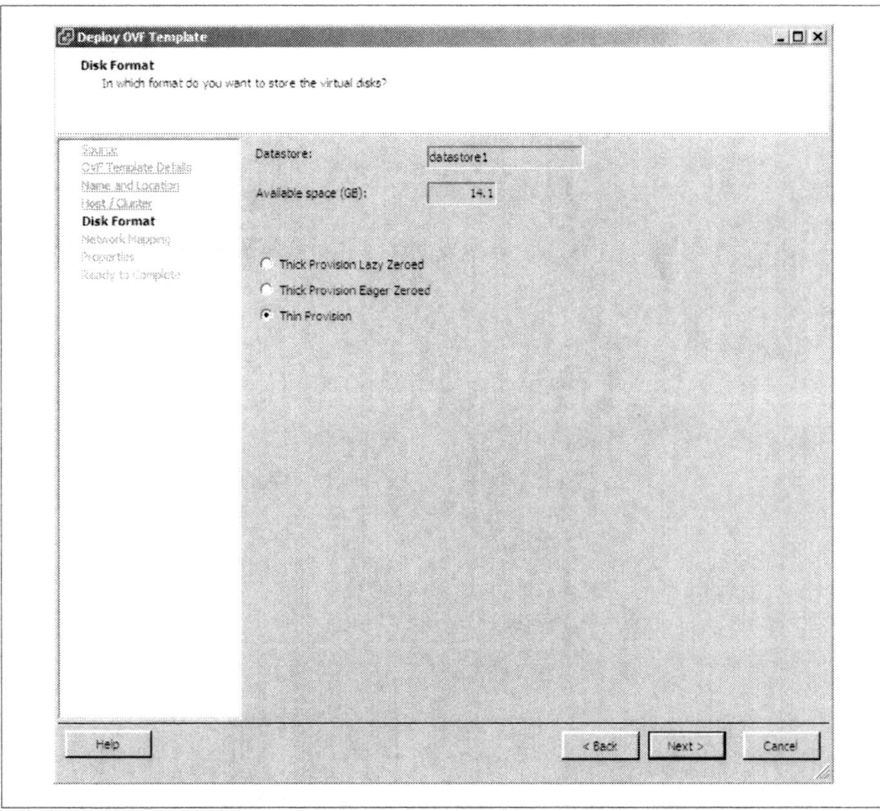

Figure 8-7. Deploy the OVF template: disk format

7. Select the network segments for your deployment. The vCloud Director will require two networks that are isolated from each other. Once the networks are selected, click Next to continue (Figure 8-8).

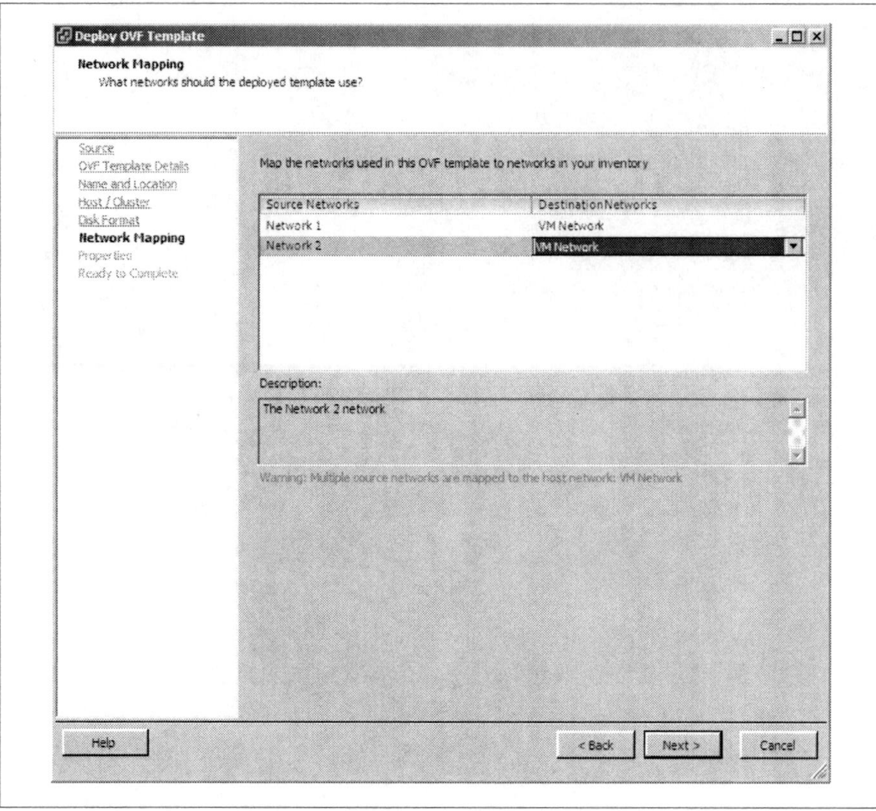

Figure 8-8. Deploy the OVF template: network mapping

8. Finally, you need to configure IP addresses and networking components for the vCloud Director Appliance. After entering these, click Next to continue (Figure 8-9).

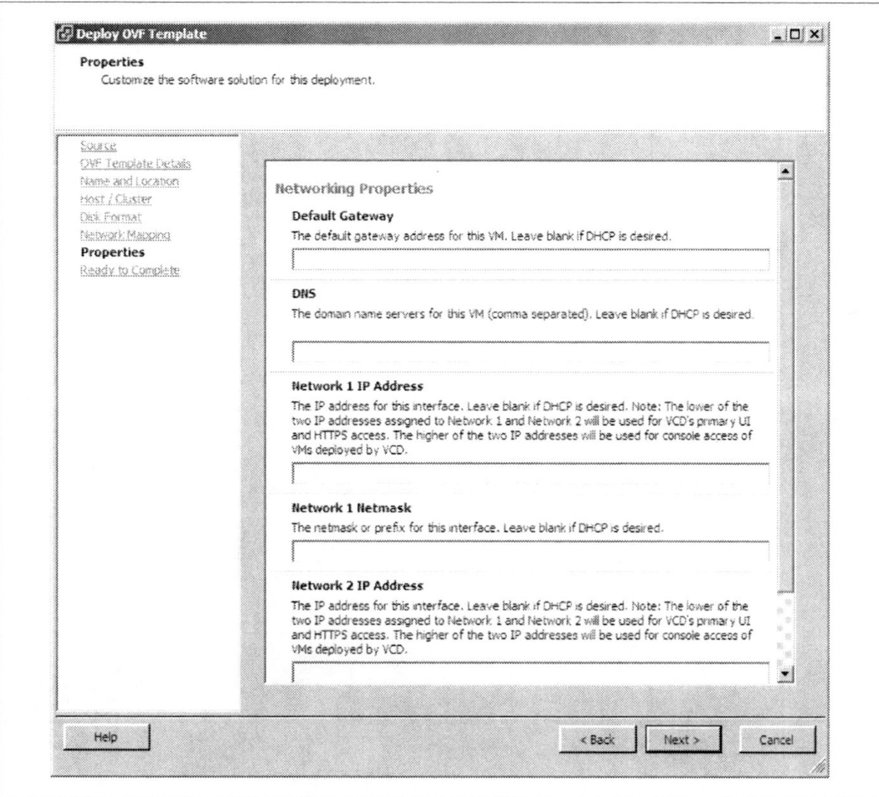

Figure 8-9. Deploy the OVF template: networking

9. Finally, click Finish to begin the process of deploying and configuring the appliance (Figure 8-10).
10. Once the vCloud virtual machine has deployed, you can access it via your browser at the URL: ***https://ip_address*** used during the configuration process.

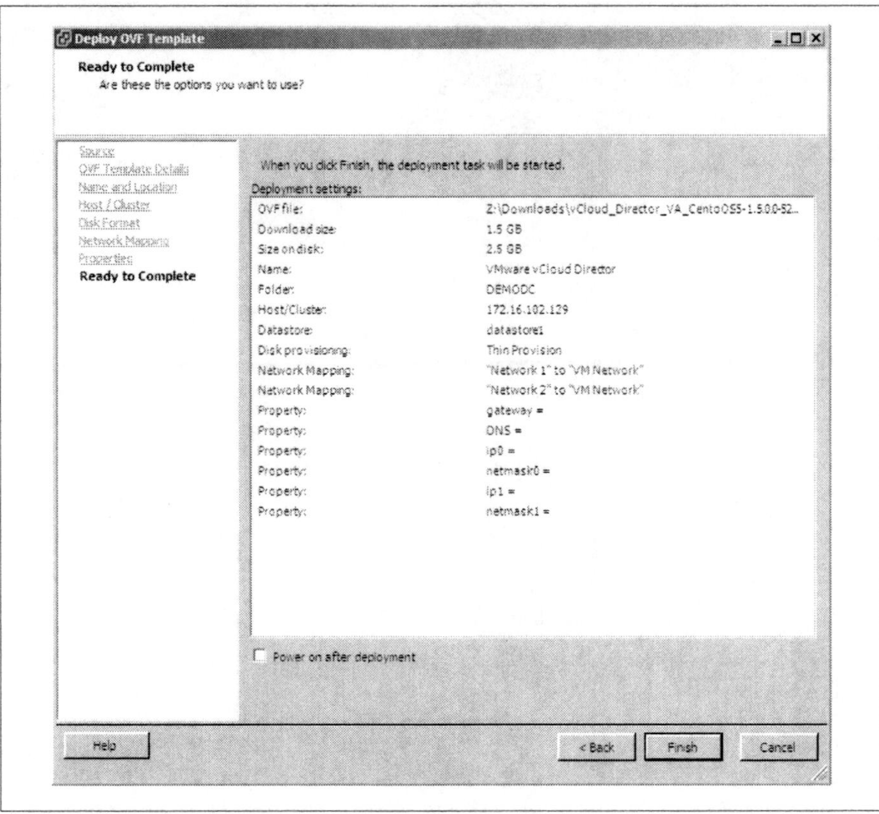

Figure 8-10. Deploy the OVF template: summary

11. Accept the EULA, click Next, enter your vCloud Director Key, and click Next to continue the setup wizard.
12. Enter the administrator credentials as shown in Figure 8-11. This will be the account used to log in to the vCloud Director interface to manage the system settings and organizations. Click Next to continue.

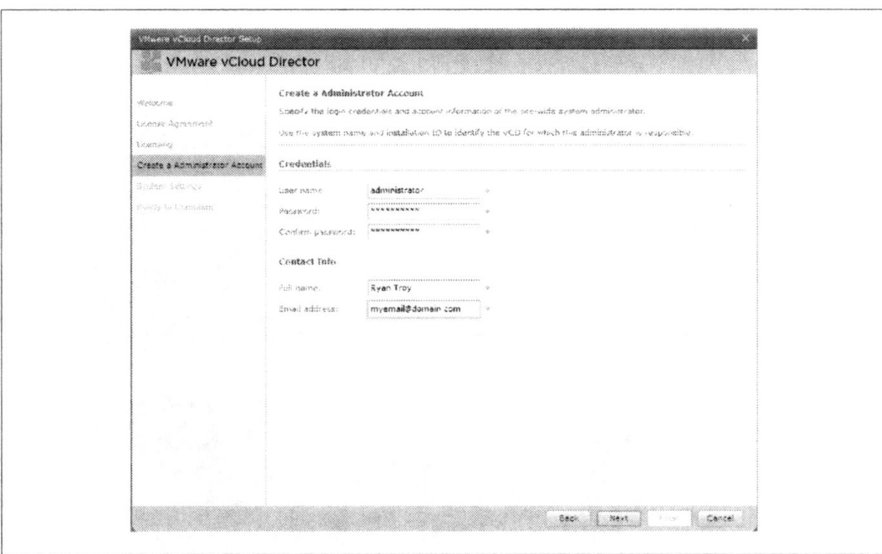

Figure 8-11. vCloud Director administrator account

13. Enter a system name for the vCloud Director installation and select a unique installation ID. Click Next, review the settings selected (Figure 8-12), and then click Finish to complete the wizard.

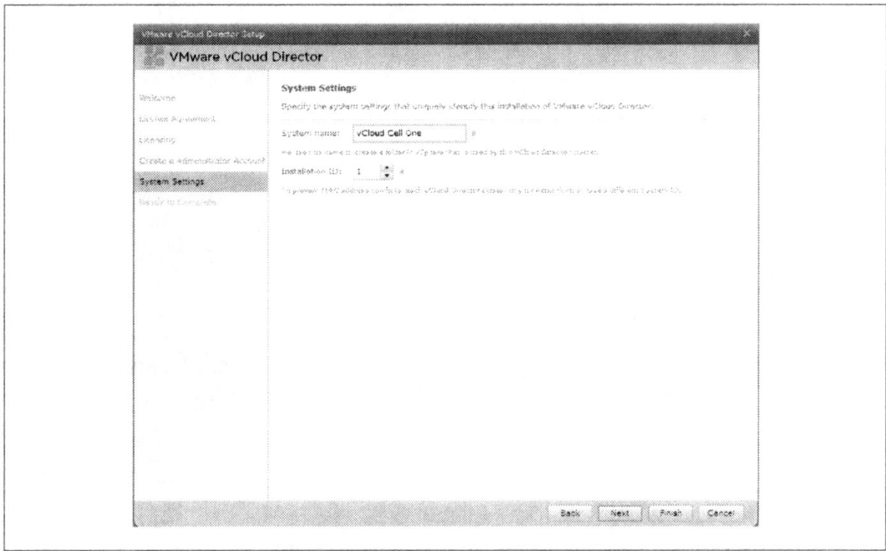

Figure 8-12. vCloud Director system settings

14. Now that vCloud is configured with some basic settings, you can log in (Figure 8-13) and start to manage the system.

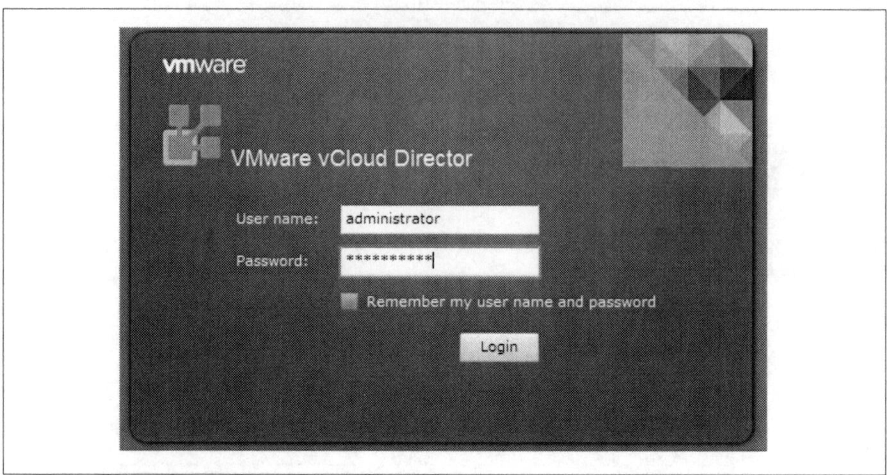

Figure 8-13. vCloud Director login

8.6 Deploying vShield Manager

Problem

You need to deploy the vShield Manager in order to configure the vCloud Director and provision organizations.

Solution

Deploy the OVA appliance provided by VMware for the vShield Manager.

Discussion

VMware vShield provides firewall, VPN, routing, and NAT services for the organizations that are deployed within the vCloud Director. Additionally, it creates secure network isolation internally and externally for organizations within the vCloud Director installation.

In this recipe, we will take a look at deploying the vShield Appliance to vCenter Server.

1. Log in to the vCenter, pull down the File menu, select Deploy OVF Template (Figure 8-14), and then click Next to continue to the installation.
2. Accept the EULA. Click Accept again, and then click Next to continue.

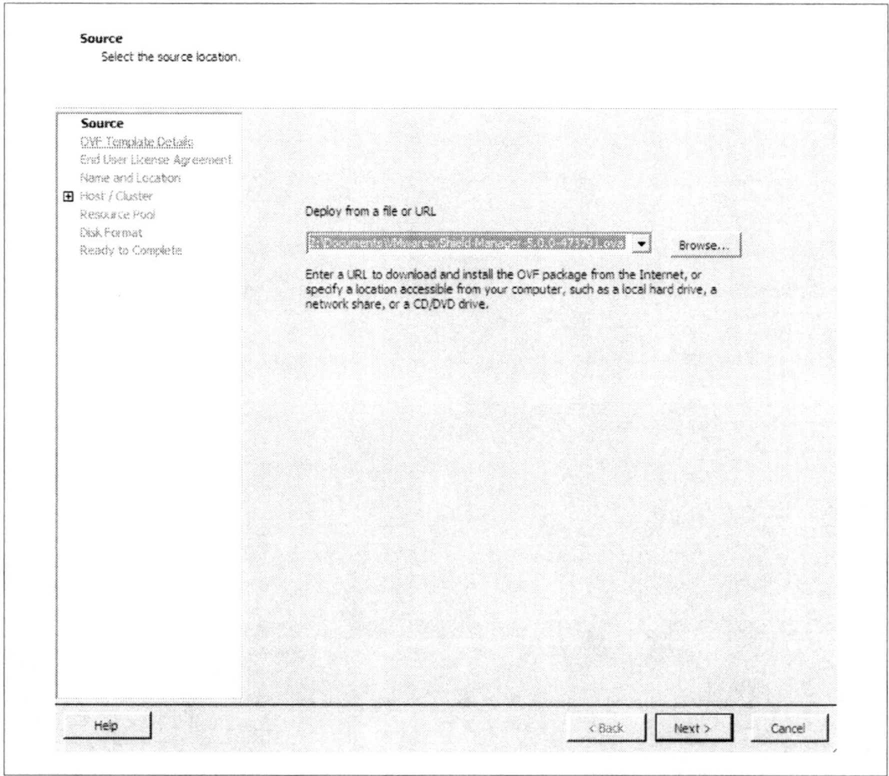

Figure 8-14. Select the vShield OVA file

3. Enter the name for the vShield Manager and the location in which it should be deployed (Figure 8-15).

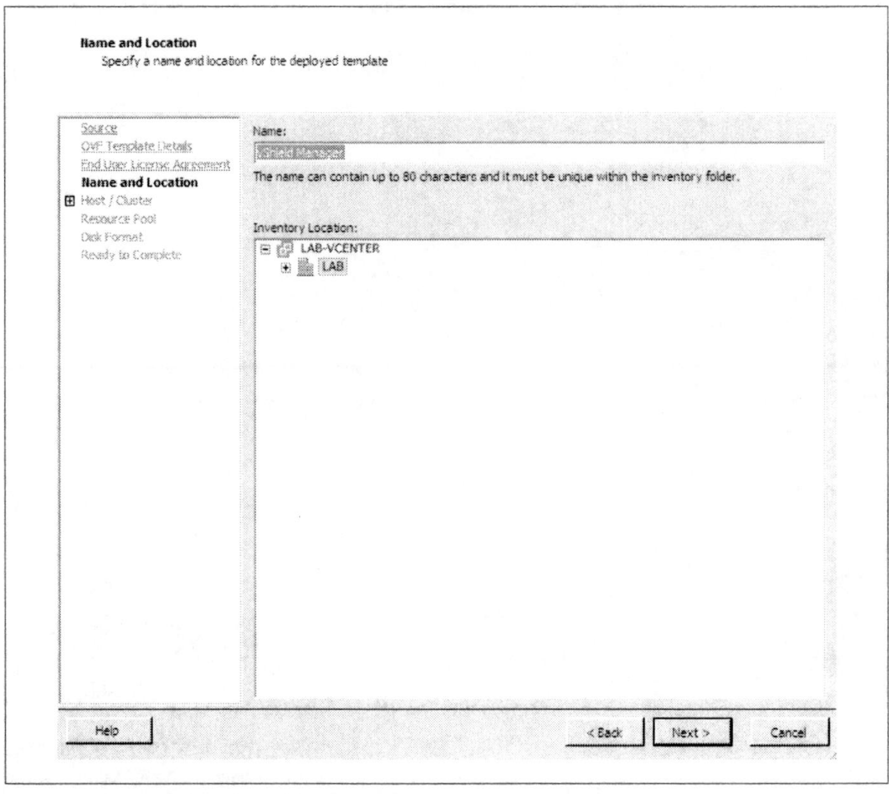

Figure 8-15. vShield name and location

4. Select the cluster to which you will deploy the new vShield Manager virtual machine as shown in Figure 8-16.

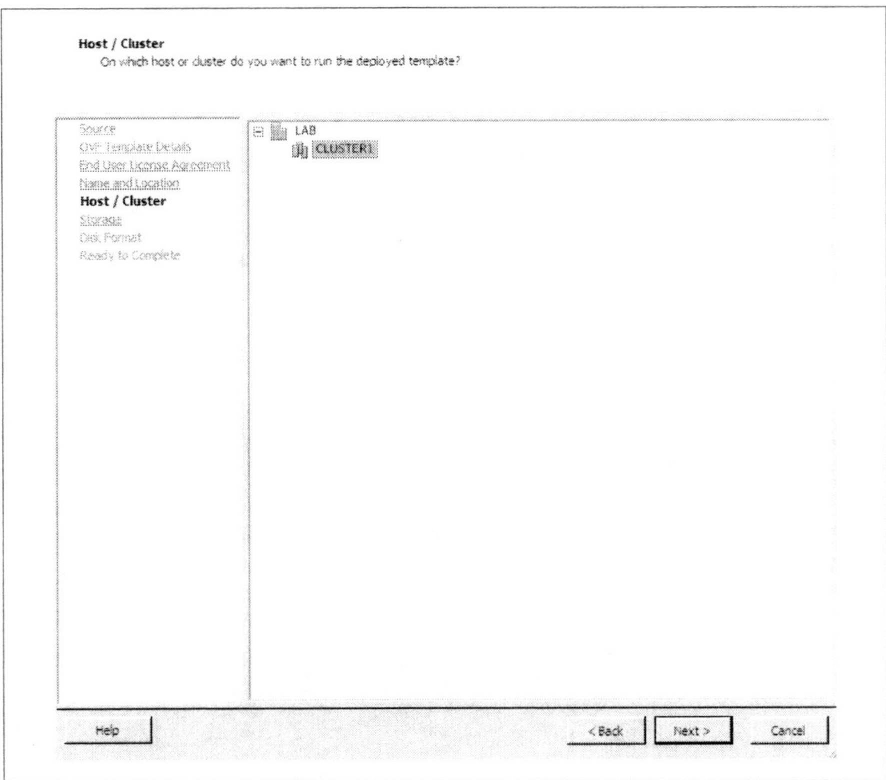

Figure 8-16. vShield selecting cluster

5. Select the Datastore in which the vShield Manager virtual machine should be deployed (Figure 8-17).

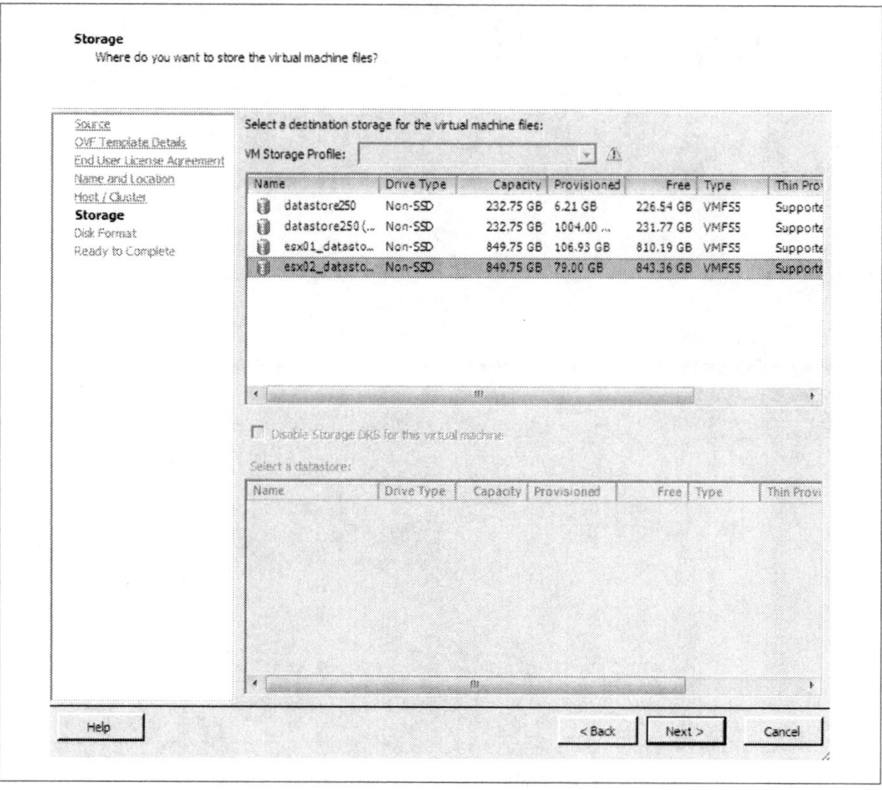

Figure 8-17. Select the datastore for the vShield virtual machine

6. Select the type of provisioning that fits your environment. You have three options here:

   Thick provision lazy zeroed
   : This option creates a virtual disk in the normal thick format.

   Thick provision eager zeroed
   : This option is compatible with fault tolerance and clustering.

   Thin provision
   : This option will save you disk space by not allocating all the space upfront when creating the virtual disk.

   Once you have selected the option that best fits your environment (Figure 8-18), click Next to continue the installation.

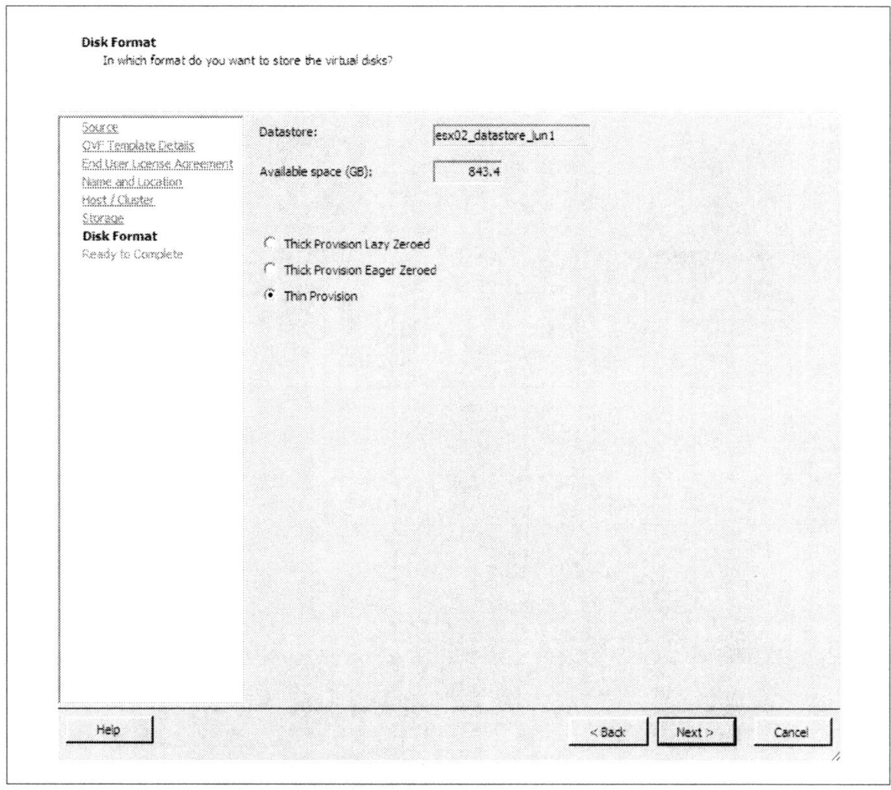

Figure 8-18. Select disk format for vShield

7. Review the settings (Figure 8-19). When you're satisfied, click the Finish button to begin deployment of the vShield Manager.

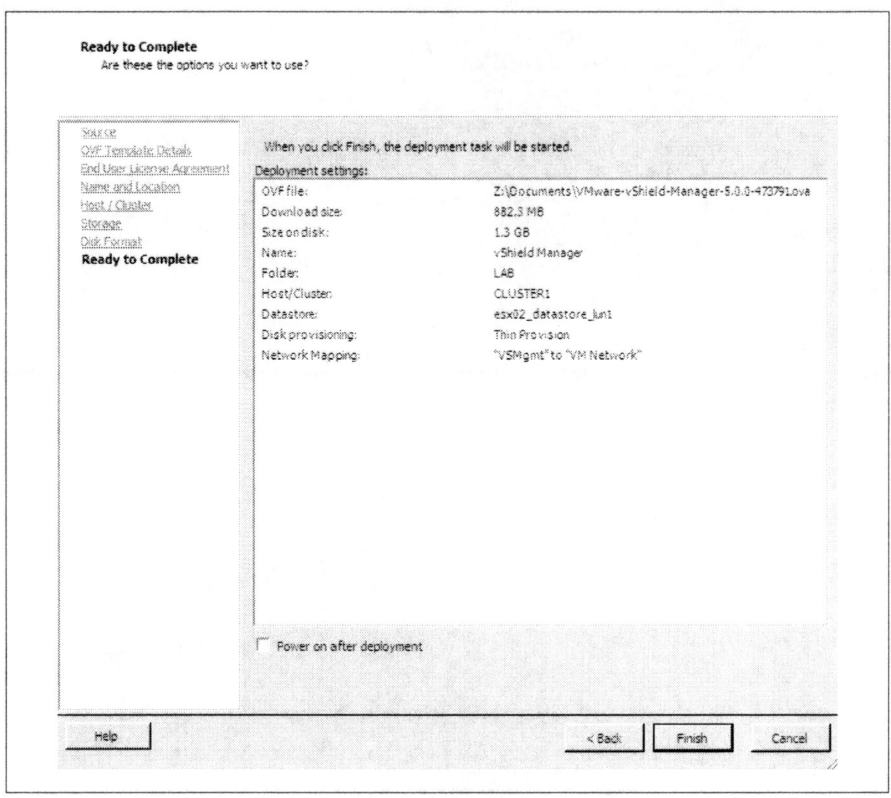

Figure 8-19. vShield Install summary

8. Once the vShield Manager virtual machine is done deploying, the IP address and network information will need to be configured. Log in to the vCenter server, select the vShield Manager virtual machine, and open the console as shown in Figure 8-20. The default login is *Admin* and the password is *Default*.

```
File View VM
INIT: Entering runlevel: 3
kjournald starting.  Commit interval 5 seconds
EXT3 FS on sda1, internal journal
EXT3-fs: mounted filesystem with ordered data mode.
kjournald starting.  Commit interval 5 seconds
EXT3 FS on sda3, internal journal
EXT3-fs: mounted filesystem with ordered data mode.
NET: Registered protocol family 10
kjournald starting.  Commit interval 5 seconds
EXT3 FS on sda1, internal journal
EXT3-fs: mounted filesystem with ordered data mode.
kjournald starting.  Commit interval 5 seconds
EXT3 FS on sda3, internal journal
EXT3-fs: mounted filesystem with ordered data mode.
kjournald starting.  Commit interval 5 seconds
EXT3 FS on sda1, internal journal
EXT3-fs: mounted filesystem with ordered data mode.
kjournald starting.  Commit interval 5 seconds
EXT3 FS on sda3, internal journal
EXT3-fs: mounted filesystem with ordered data mode.

manager login:
manager login: admin
Password:
manager> _
```

Figure 8-20. vShield Manager setup

9. Once logged in, type `enable`. When prompted for it, enter the password. Then type `setup` to configure the networking for the vShield Manager.
10. Enter the IP network information for the vShield Manager virtual machine. When completed, select **y** to save the configuration as (Figure 8-21).

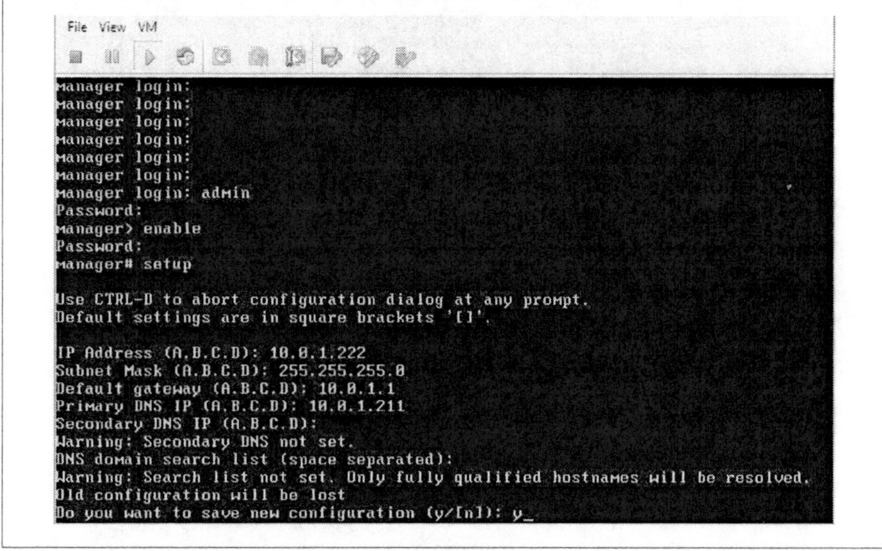

Figure 8-21. vShield Manager network setup

11. Open a browser and navigate to the IP address you assigned to the vShield Manager virtual machine. You will be presented with a login screen (Figure 8-22). Enter the username and password mentioned in step 8 on page 294.

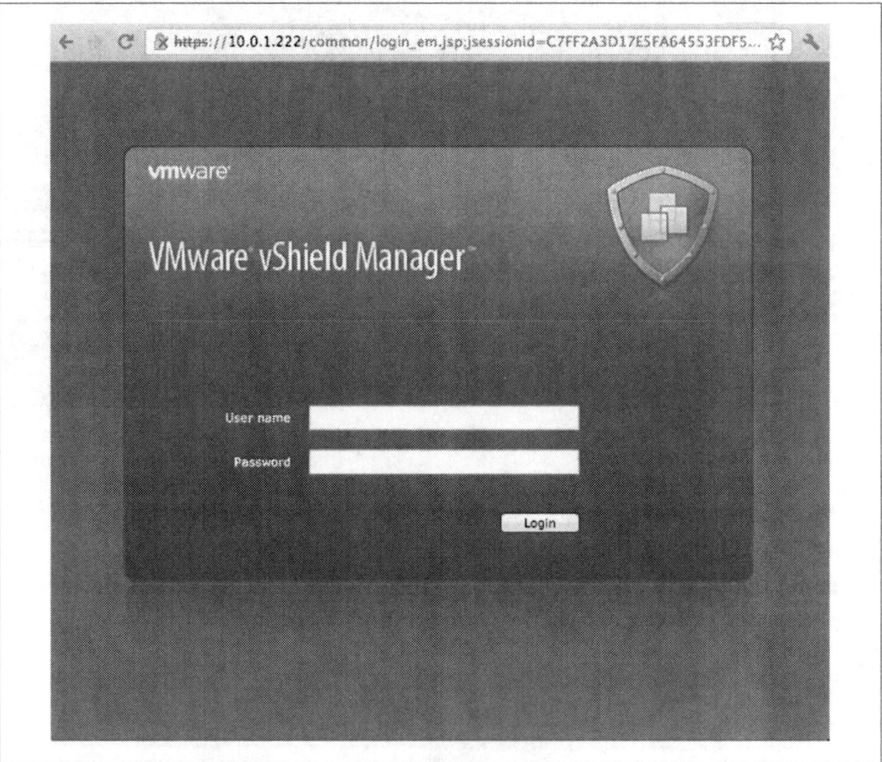

Figure 8-22. vShield Manager login

12. Once logged in to the vShield Manager interface, you will be presented with a configuration screen. To connect the vShield Manager to the vCenter server, enter the IP address, username, and password of your vCenter server and click the Save button (Figure 8-23).
13. Click the Register button under the vSphere Plug-in area to register the extension with the vCenter server.

Now vShield Manager is connected to your vCenter interface. This will allow you to proceed with the configuration inside of the vCloud Director interface.

Figure 8-23. Connect vShield to the vCenter server

8.7 Attaching vCloud Director to the vCenter Server

Problem

You have the vCloud Director software installed and need to attach it to the vCenter server so the vCloud Director can assign resources to virtual datacenters.

Solution

Attach the vCloud Director instance to the vCenter server.

Discussion

Attaching a vCenter server allows the resources to be available for use with the vCloud Director. Once attached, resource pools, datastores, and networks can be assigned to a virtual datacenter. In addition to providing the resources for the vCloud Director organizations, the vCenter will also hold the virtual machines and the related files for virtual machines to operate correctly.

1. Log in to the vCloud Director management URL: *https://ip_address*.
2. Click the Manage & Monitor tab, click vCenters in the left side pane, and click Attach New vCenter (Figure 8-25).

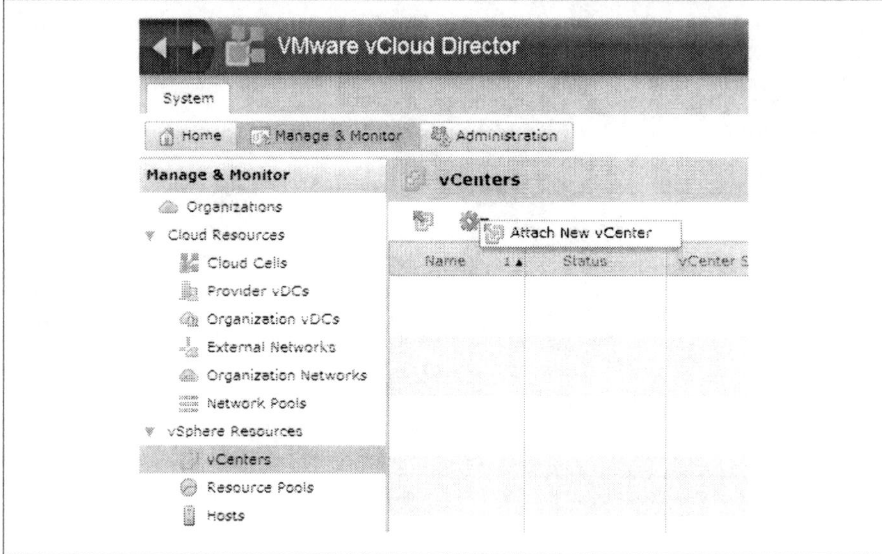

Figure 8-24. Attaching the vCenter server

3. Enter the information of the vCenter server to which you will be connecting.

   Host name or IP address
   : Denotes the vCenter server you wish to attach.

   Port number
   : The port number with which you will be connecting to the vCenter. This is set to 443 as default.

   User name
   : The administrator login for your vCenter server.

   Password
   : The administrator password for your vCenter server.

vCenter name
: The unique name you will be assigning to this vCenter server inside the vCloud Director.

Description
: An optional description.

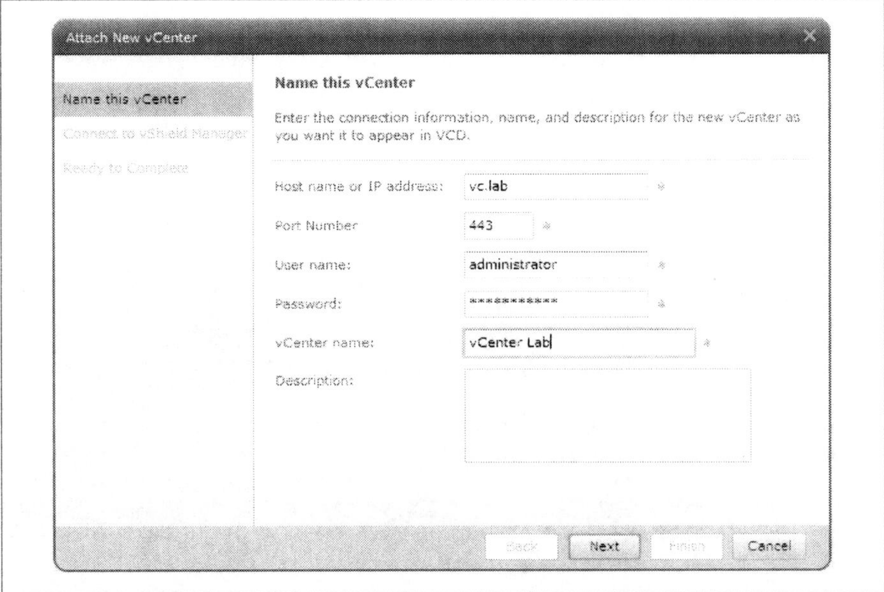

Figure 8-25. Connection information to attach to the new vCenter server

4. Click Next to continue the installation.
5. Enter the IP address, username, and password of the vShield Manager that will be used with the vCenter (Figure 8-26). It's important to note that each the vCenter being attached to the vCloud Director must have its own vShield Manager.
6. Click Next to save your choices (Figure 8-27). Review the settings, and once you are satisfied, click the Finish button to attach the vCenter server.

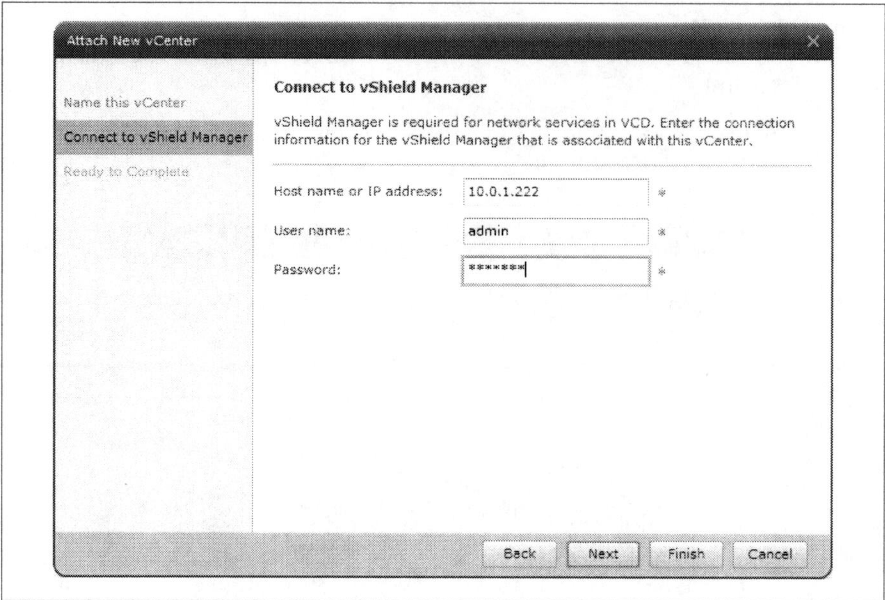

Figure 8-26. Selecting a vShield Manager

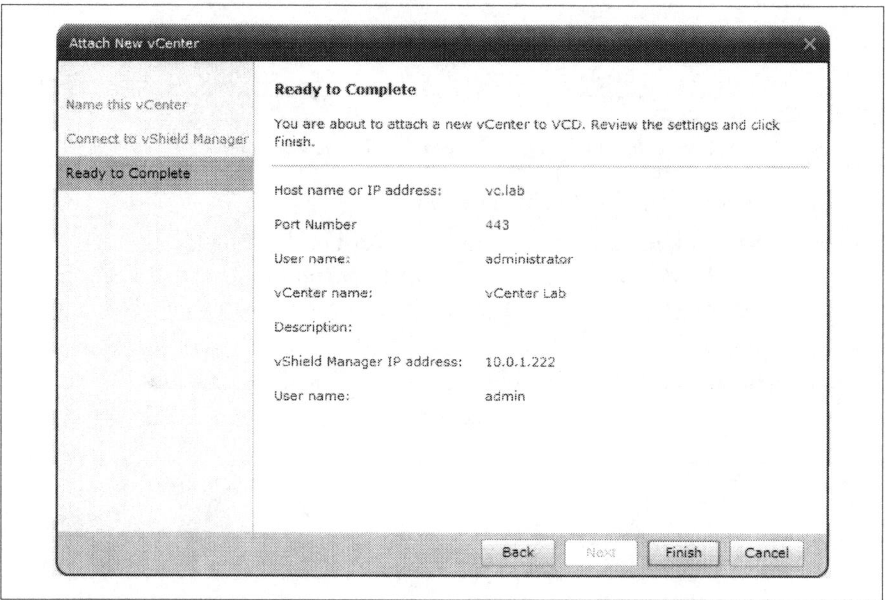

Figure 8-27. Reviewing the vCenter server

7. The vCenter server will now show up as active and enabled within the resources section of the vCloud Director, as shown in Figure 8-28.

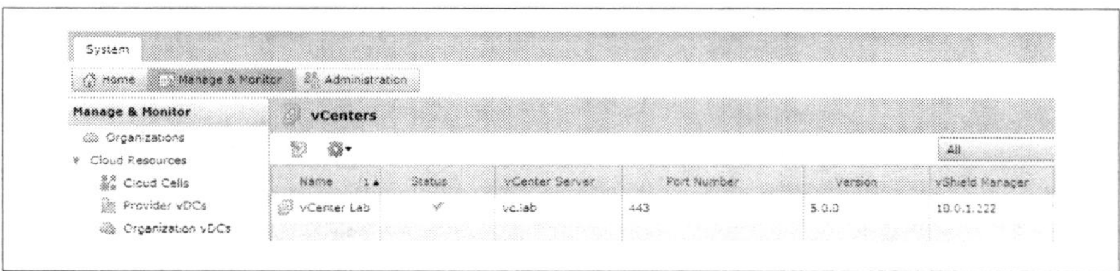

Figure 8-28. Active vCenter server

8.8 Creating a Provider Virtual Datacenter

Problem

You need to create a provider vDC so vCloud Director can allocate resources to organizations.

Solution

Enable a provider vDC and register the vSphere resources with the vCloud Director.

Discussion

Creating a vDC is the first step in allocating resources to the vCloud Director Cell. After you add a provider, storage, compute, and networking resources are presented to the vCloud Director for use. You can create multiple vDCs based on different business scenarios, such as geographic locations and features (HA, storage, compute) that can be allocated to different end users or business depending on their requirements.

1. Log in to the vCloud Director management URL: *https://`ip_address`*.
2. Click the Manage & Monitor tab and click the Provide vCDs link on the left side. Then click New Provider vDC (Figure 8-29).
3. Enter a name and description that indicate what this provider vDC is being used for (Figure 8-30). For example, if this vDC will have access to budget compute resources, Provider vCD Budget might be a good name. Select the latest supported hardware version. This will be hardware version 8 if you are running ESXi 5.0, and hardware version 7 if you are running ESX/ESXi, 4.x. Click Next.

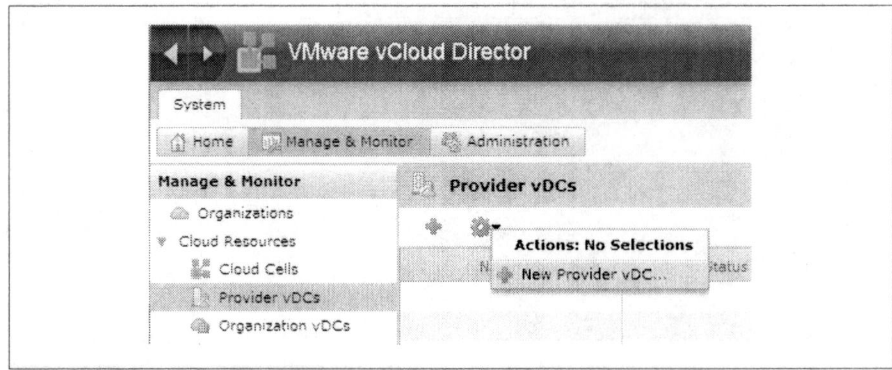

Figure 8-29. Create a new provider vDC

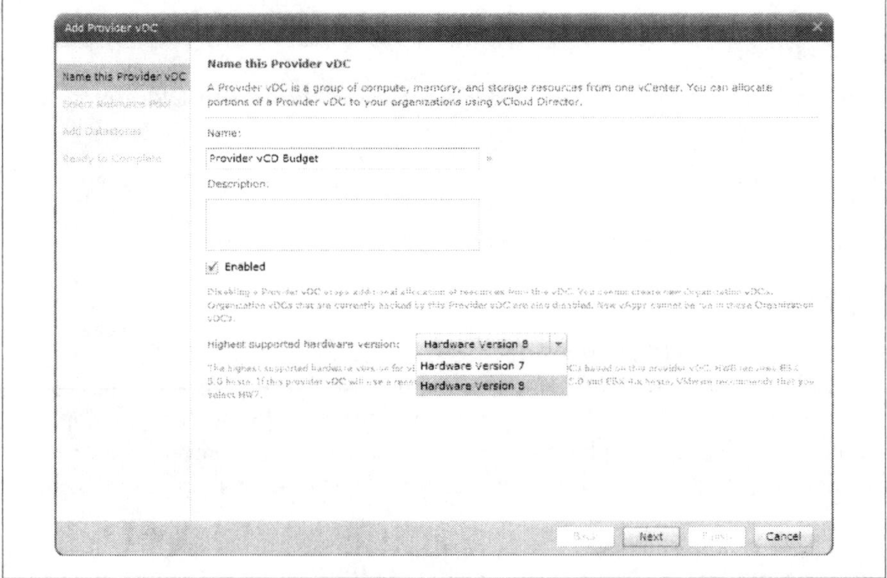

Figure 8-30. Naming the provider vDC

4. Select the vCenter server, Resource Pool, and VC Path. Additionally, select the external network you wish to use for this Provider vDC (Figure 8-31).

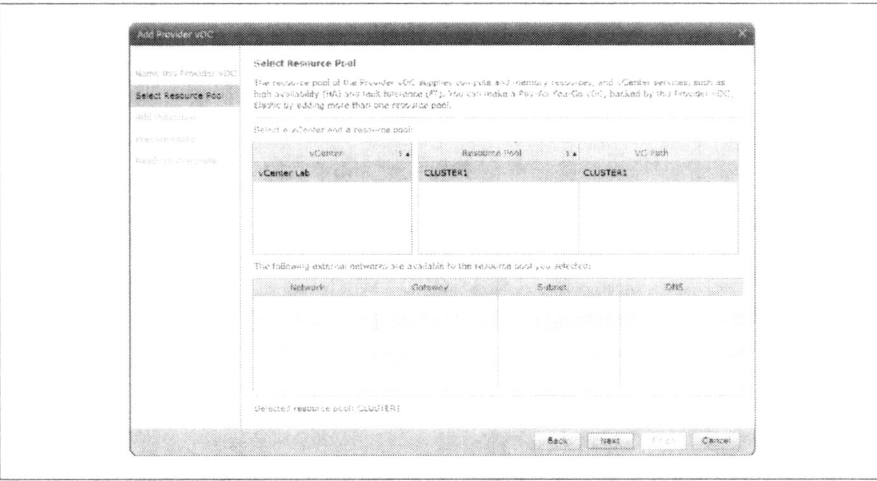

Figure 8-31. Provider vDC resource pool

5. Select one or more datastores to add to the datacenter and click the Add button (Figure 8-32). The datastores that are selected must be on a shared storage device such as NFS, Fibre Channel, or iSCSI. Do not add local storage devices here. In this example, we've added two datastores to our Provider vDC, `esx01_datastore_lun0` and `esx02_datastore_lun1`.

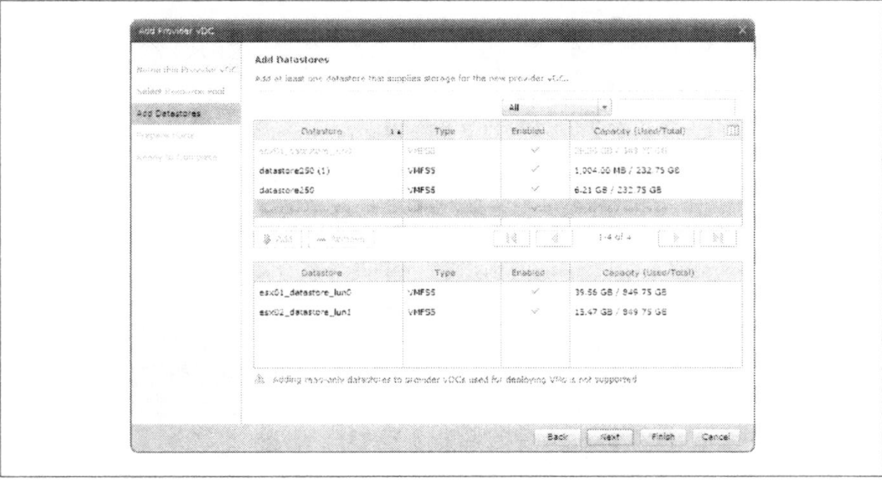

Figure 8-32. Provider vDC adding datastores

6. Enter the root username and password for the ESX/ESXi host(s) and click Next (Figure 8-33).

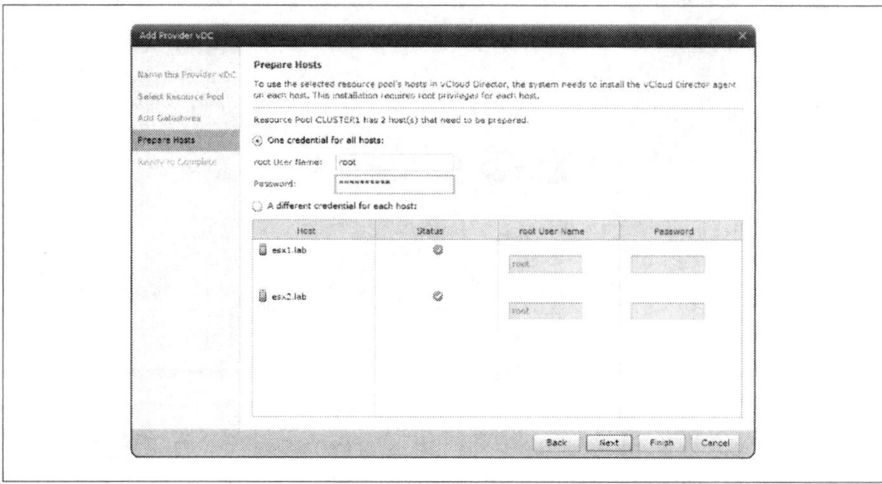

Figure 8-33. Provider vDC installing agent on ESXI servers

7. Click Finish to create the provider vDC (Figure 8-34). At this point you will see the ESXI servers in the vCenter server you attached go into maintenance mode, and agents will be installed on those hosts.

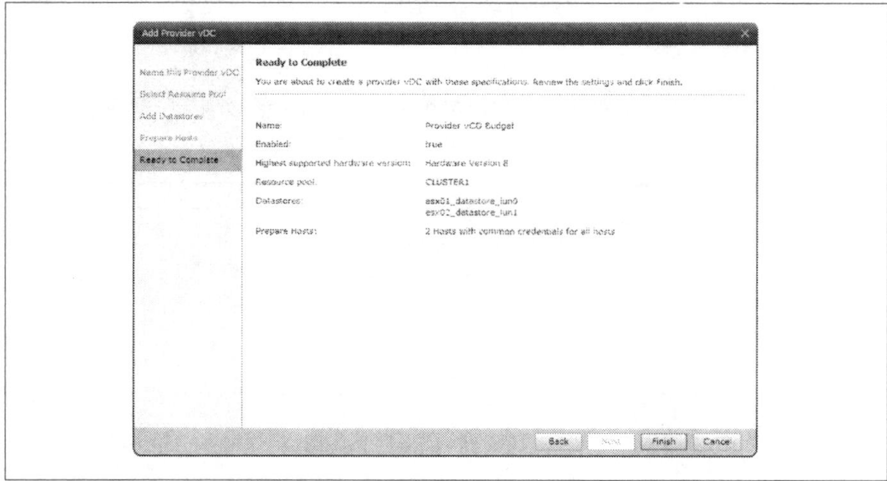

Figure 8-34. Provider vDC summary

8.9 Allocating External Network Resources

Problem

You need to assign external networks to the vCloud Director for use within provider vDCs.

Solution

Allocate the external networks for the vCloud Director to use.

Discussion

External networks are a logical network based on vSphere port groups. The external network provides the interface to the Internet for the virtual machines that reside inside different organizational networks. The external network is required if the organization has to connect to the Internet.

1. Log in to the vCloud Director management URL: *https://`ip_address`*.
2. Click the Manage & Monitor tab. Then click External Networks in the left side pane, and click Add Networks (Figure 8-35).

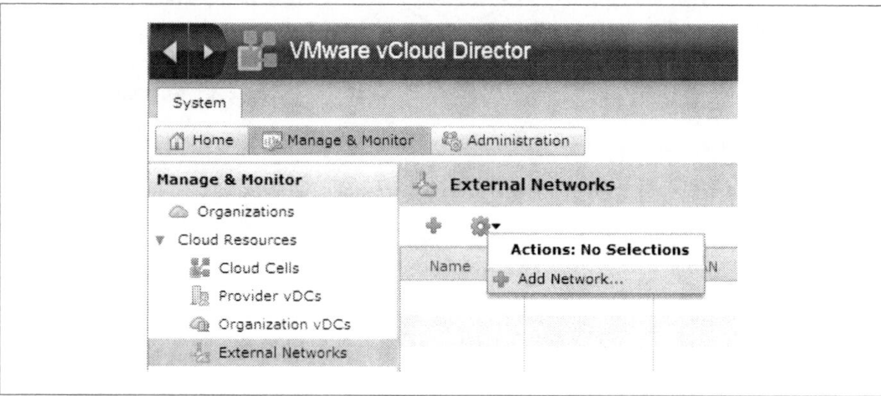

Figure 8-35. Adding an external network

3. Select a vCenter server and vSphere Network that will provide external access (Figure 8-36). Click Next to continue.

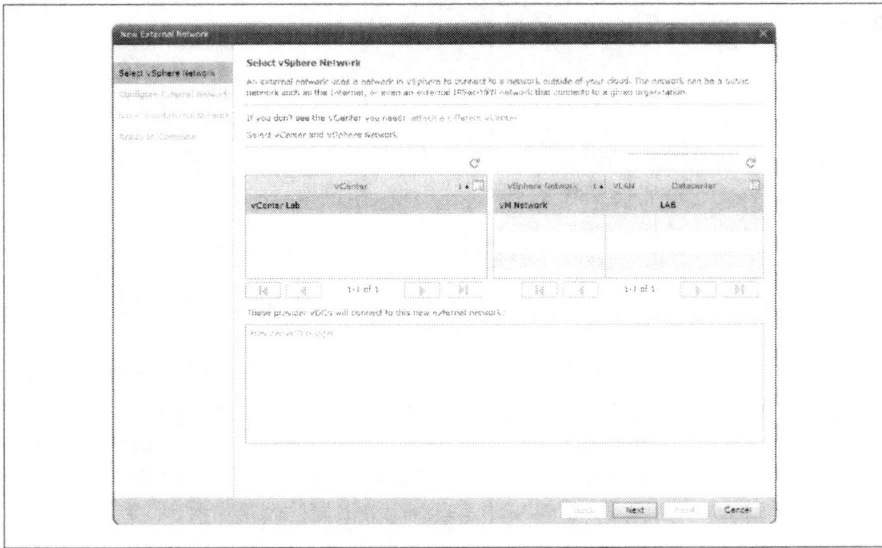

Figure 8-36. Adding vCenter and vSphere networks

4. Type the basic network settings: netmask, gateway, and DNS. Then assign a static IP range that this provider vDC will allocate to the organizations that are created with this provider vDC (Figure 8-37). Click Next to continue.

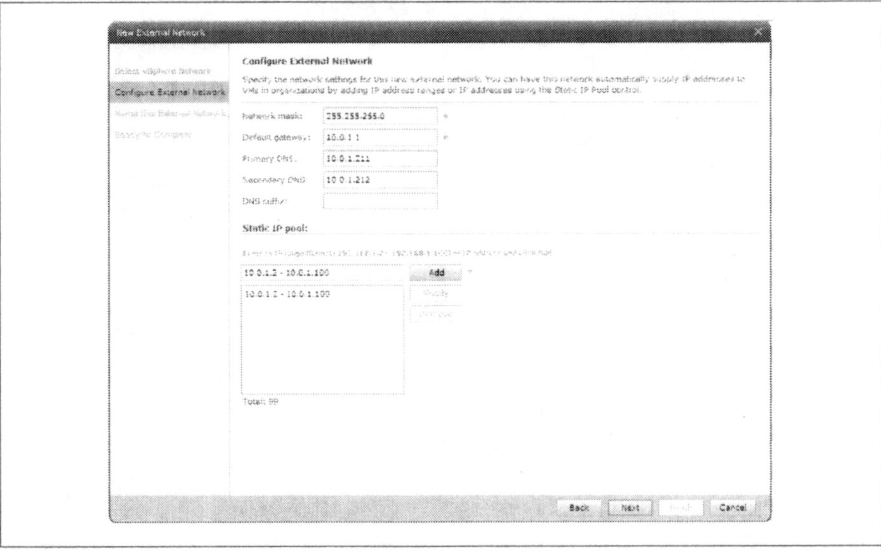

Figure 8-37. Configuring the external network

5. Type the name of the network and click Next to continue (Figure 8-38).

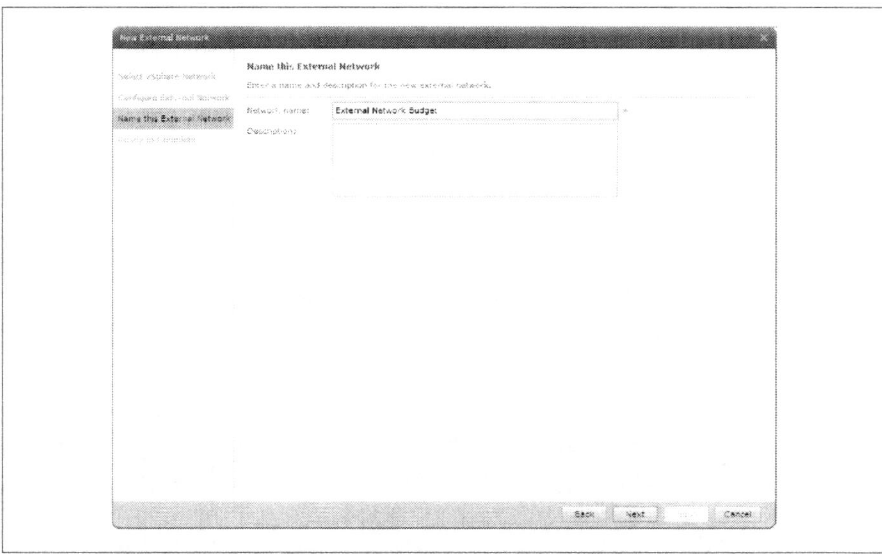

Figure 8-38. Naming external network

6. Review the network settings and click Finish (Figure 8-39).

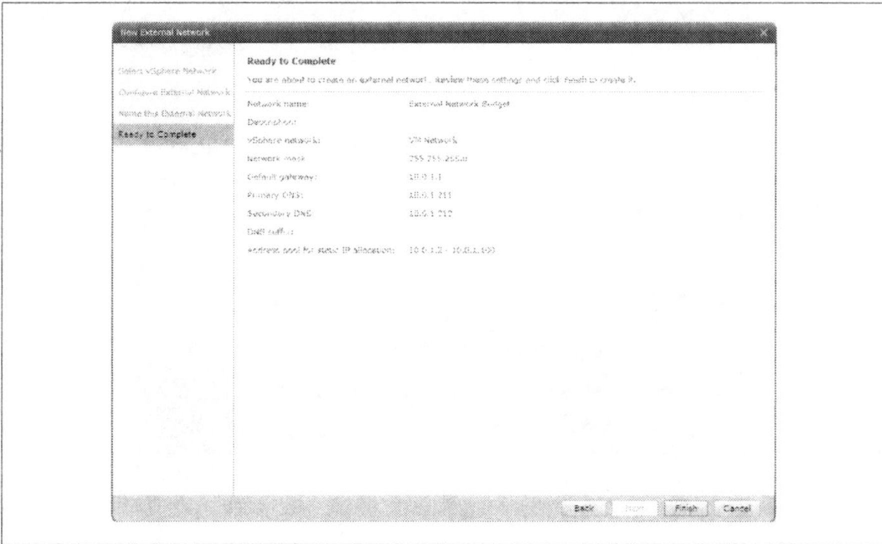

Figure 8-39. External network summary

8.10 Adding Network Pools for Virtual Datacenters

Problem

You need to add network pools to assign to organizational vDCs for internal network connectivity.

Solution

In this recipe, we will look at the steps required to add network pools to the vCloud Director. This will allow internal isolated networks within the vDCs.

Discussion

Network pools are a group of networks that are available for use within a organizational vDC to create vApp networks and simple or complex network configurations for the vDC. A network pool uses the network resources from vSphere, such as VLAND IDs, port groups, or the vCloud isolated networks. This allows vCloud Director to create NAT-based internal networks, assigning them to vDCs that will later be used in vApps when deploying virtual machines.

Each organization's vDC can have one network pool. However, multiple organizations can share the same network pool if required, giving additional flexibility within the vDCs.

To get started, follow these steps to add the network resources to the vCloud Director.

1. Log in to the vCloud Director management URL: *https://`ip_address`*.
2. Click the Manage & Monitor tab and then click Network Pools in the left side pane. Click Add Network Pool from the options (Figure 8-40).

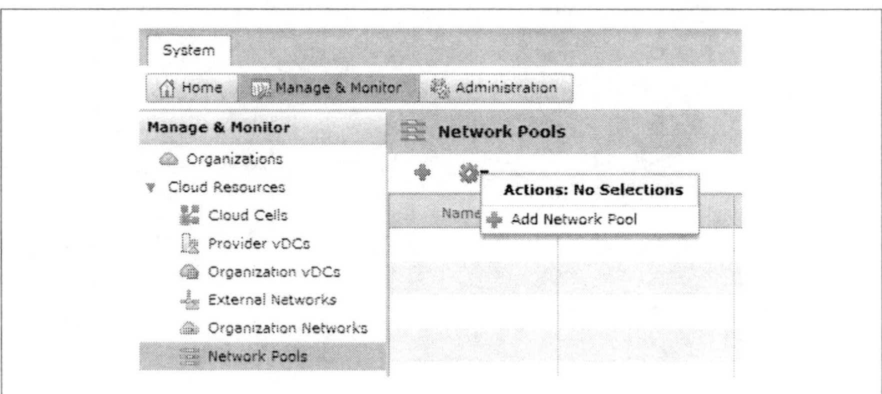

Figure 8-40. Adding a new network Pool

3. Select one of the following Network Pool options (Figure 8-41):

VLAN-backed
: This option provides the best security, scalability, and performance for organizational networks.

VCD network isolation-backed
: This option spans hosts and isolates traffic from other networks. This option is similar to VLANs, but it uses internal software to handle the separation of network space.

vSphere port groups
: Using this option will use network port groups and doesn't require vSphere Distributed Switches. These port groups must be isolated from all other port groups at the layer 2 level.

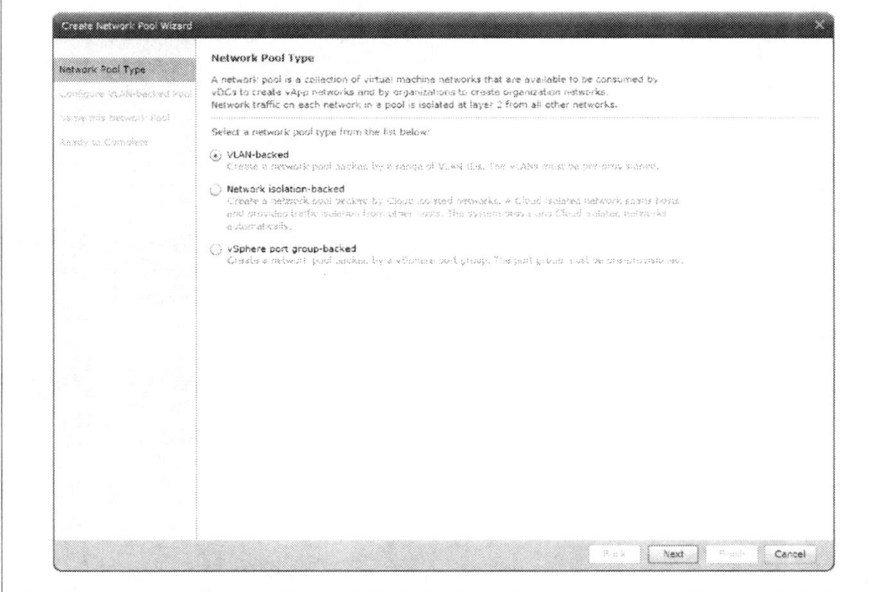

Figure 8-41. Network Pool type

4. Depending on which option was selected in the previous step, you will have multiple options:

    - If you selected VLAN-backed as your option, type a range of VLAND IDs, click Add, and select the vCenter Server and vDS switch (Figure 8-42). Click Next and continue to step 5 on page 311 in this recipe to complete the wizard.

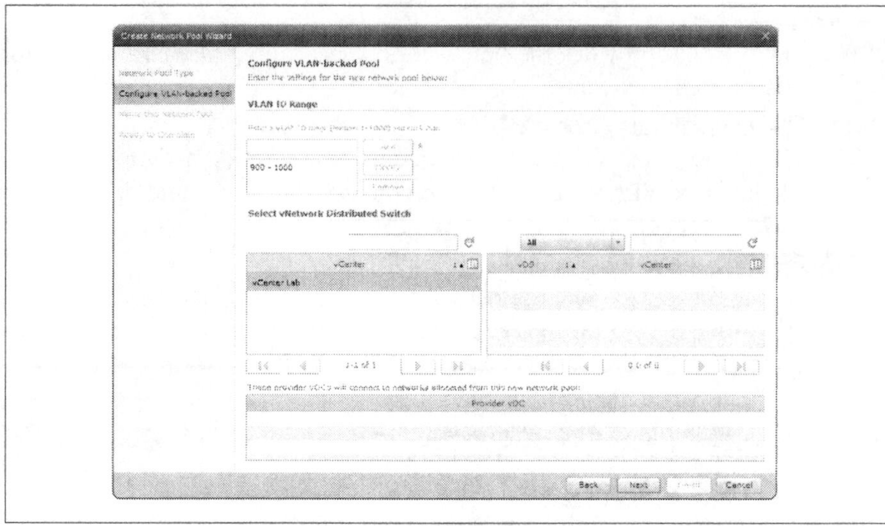

Figure 8-42. VLAN-backed Pool

- If you selected vCD Network Isolation, enter the number of VCD isolated networks and the VLAN ID. Select the vCenter server and vDC switch (Figure 8-43). Click Next and continue to step 5 on page 311 in this recipe to complete the wizard.

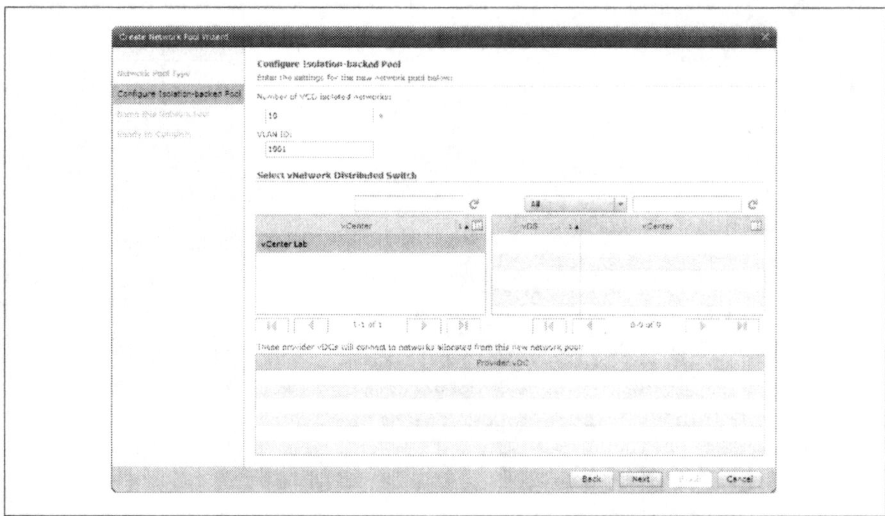

Figure 8-43. Isolation-backed Pool

- If you selected vSphere Port Groups, select one or more port groups from the list and click Add as (Figure 8-44. Click Next and continue to step 5 on page 311) in this recipe to complete the wizard.

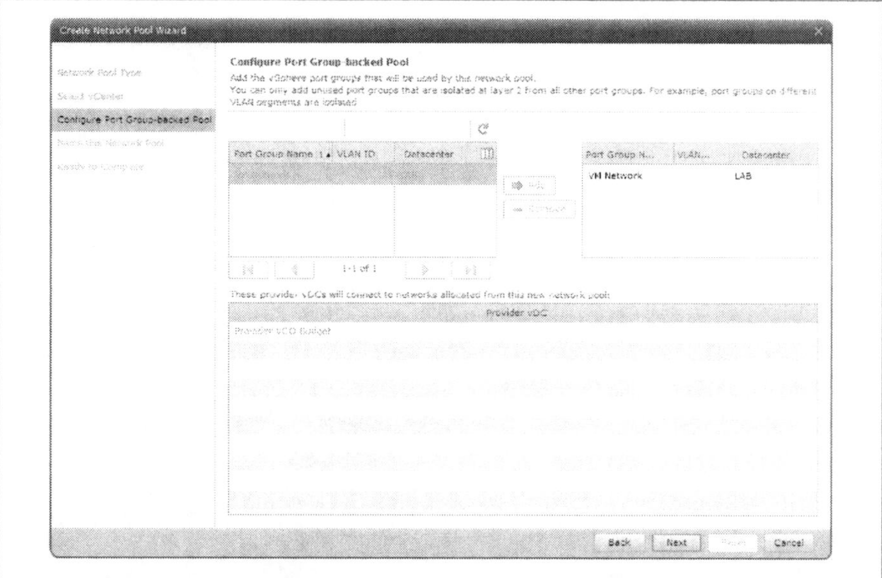

Figure 8-44. Port Group Backed Pool

5. Type a name for the network (Figure 8-45), and click Next.

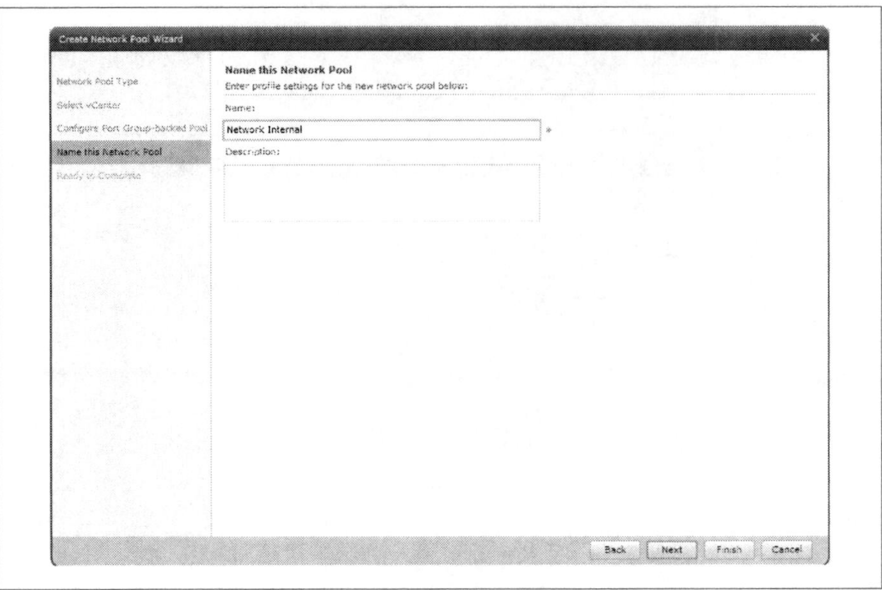

Figure 8-45. Network Pool name

6. Review the network pool settings and click Finish to complete the network pool addition.

CHAPTER 9

vSphere Storage Appliance

This chapter will discuss how to create a virtual SAN infrastructure that uses free and unused disk space on your ESXI servers. We will discuss the installation process, benefits, and limitations of the vSphere Storage Appliance.

9.1 What Is the vSphere Storage Appliance?

Problem

You wish to reclaim unused space on your ESXI servers and create a virtual SAN using the VMware Storage Appliance.

Solution

Deploy the vSphere Storage Appliance (VSA) on your vCenter server to create a VSA cluster and reclaim the disk space. The Discussion section discusses the benefits, features, and limitations of the VSA.

Discussion

The VSA is new in vSphere 5.0 and allows the SMB customer to use unused disk space on the ESXI servers and create a virtual SAN infrastructure to add more robustness to VMware's already highly redundant platform. The VSA is a virtual appliance that combines SUSE Linux Enterprise Server 11 and storage clustering services. The VSA virtual machine can run on either two or three ESXi hosts to create a unified storage platform.

At the time of this writing, using a VSA Cluster allows:

- Shared datastores for all ESXi hosts in the datacenter
- One replica of each shared data store across ESXi hosts
- vSphere vMotion and vSphere HA within the VSA cluster
- Hardware and software failover capabilities

- Replacement of a failed VSA cluster member
- Recovery of an existing VSA cluster

The VSA cluster will keep a replica of each volume inside the VSA cluster on another member of the cluster. This creates a highly redundant platform, so that failures of the VSA appliance don't entail massive amounts of downtime.

When building your VSA cluster, it's important to understand its disk layout. Let's take a look at the formulas that VMware has created to determine the amount of space available inside the VSA cluster.

VMware directly states: "VSA datastore capacity = hard disk capacity of an ESXi host / 4, Where hard disk capacity of an ESXi host = the total capacity of the hard disks that are installed internally on the ESXi host." The following examples are provided directly from VMware:

Example: Cluster with 3 ESXi Hosts with 8TB hard disk capacity per host w/ RAID 10

- Hard disk capacity per ESXi host = 8TB
- Total hard disk capacity of all ESXi hosts = 24TB
- VSA data store capacity = 8TB / 4 = 2TB
- Total VSA cluster capacity = 2TB * 3 hosts = 6TB

Example: Cluster with 3 ESXi hosts with RAID 5 and 8 disks (if using RAID 6, you will subtract another -1 on the total storage capacity per host line)

- Total storage capacity per host = (8-1) * 500GB = 3.5TB
- Capacity of a VSA data store = 3.5TB/2 = 1.75TB
- Total VSA cluster capacity = 1.75TB * 3 hosts = 5.25TB

These examples show that the replicas take up space.

It is possible to mix different drive sizes inside a VSA cluster. For example, if you have three ESXi hosts, two with 8TB and one with 6TB of space, ESXi will automatically take the lowest sized disk into consideration when calculating the space for the VSA cluster. It is important to keep this in mind so space is not wasted if it can be helped.

See Also

Recipe 9.2 , Recipe 9.3, Recipe 9.4

9.2 vSphere Storage Appliance Requirements

Problem

You want to know what you need in your environment to run the vSphere Storage Appliance.

Solution

The Discussion section lays out the requirements and the limitations of the vSphere Storage Appliance.

Discussion

The vSphere Storage Appliance has some strict limitations in its current 1.0 version. Table 9-1 summarizes the basic requirements needed to create a VSA Cluster.

Table 9-1. vCenter Server requirements for VSA

vCenter Server	Hardware requirement
CPU (processor)	Either a single dual-core 64bit processor or dual single-core processors
Memory	4GB minimum; increase to 8GB if you are running SQL on the same server
Disk (storage)	4GB minimum; allow for growth
Microsoft SQL versions	Roughly 500MB will be required for a small database; our suggestion is 2GB to ensure room for growth
Networking	Either a single gigabit or dual gigabit Ethernet connections

The ESXi Hosts in the VSA cluster must be configured identically. Additionally, the ESXi hosts must not be in a current HA cluster and cannot be running virtual machines. The VSA installer will create the networking and HA cluster when installing and configuring the VSA appliance (Table 9-2).

Table 9-2. VSA ESXi hardware requirements

ESXi Hosts (in a VSA Cluster)	Hardware requirement
CPU (processor)	Either a single dual core 64bit processor or dual single core processors; must be 2GHz or higher
Memory	6GB minimum, 24GB recommended, and a maximum of 72GB has been tested with VSA 1.0
Ethernet NICs	4 NIC ports must be available on each ESXi Host
Hard drives	2TB maximum capacity per hard disk with a 180GB limit per ESXi Host; disks must be all SATA or all SAS; they cannot be mixed; JBOD is not supported
Raid controllers	Any HCL supported RAID card in a 5, 6 or RAID 10 configuration
ESXi Hosts in VSA Cluster	A minimum of two ESXi Hosts per cluster with a maximum of 3 ESXi Hosts; you cannot add or remote ESXi Hosts to a VSA cluster once the cluster is created

Supported OSs:

- Windows Server 2003 Standard, Enterprise, or Datacenter 64-bit (SP2 required)
- Windows Server 2003 R2 Standard, Enterprise, or Datacenter 64-bit (SP2 required)
- Windows Server 2008 Standard, Enterprise, or Datacenter 64-bit
- Windows Server 2008 Standard, Enterprise, or Datacenter 64-bit SP2

- Windows Server 2008 Standard, Enterprise, or Datacenter 64-bit R2

Other required software:

- vCenter Server 5.0
- vCenter Server 5.0 Java Runtime Environment 1.6 (installed during vCenter Server 5.0 installation)
- vCenter Server 5.0 Tomcat 6.0.18 (installed during vCenter Server 5.0 installation)
- Windows Installer 4.5 or higher
- Microsoft .NET Framework 3.5 SP1
- Internet Explorer 7 or higher
- Latest version of Adobe Flash for Internet Explorer

When determining the number of virtual machines that can run inside the VSA cluster, keep the following in mind. vSphere HA will reserve around 33% of the CPU and memory resources in a three-member VSA cluster and 50% in a two-member VSA cluster. Because you are virtualizing the storage, vSphere needs to ensure that enough resources are available for the VSA appliances to offer good performance inside the HA cluster. Adding additional resources to the ESXI servers will allow a larger number of virtual machines inside the cluster.

9.3 Installation of the vSphere Storage Appliance

Problem

You wish to install the vSphere Storage Appliance to create a virtual SAN.

Solution

Install the vSphere Storage Appliance within the vCenter.

Discussion

The vSphere Storage Appliance can be downloaded from VMware's website. The installation is straightforward and should be performed on either the vCenter server or another Windows Server inside the network with access to the vCenter server. After installation, there will be a new plug-in added to vCenter that you will need to enable. Enabling it will then create a new tab on the datacenter inside the vCenter server.

1. Download the vSphere Storage Appliance from the VMware site. The appliance is going to be installed on your vCenter 5 Server. Double-click to launch the installation. Select the Language and click OK.
2. The vSphere Storage Appliance Installation Wizard starts. Accept the EULA and click Next.

3. The IP address and HTTPS port will be pre-filled if you are installing on the vCenter server (Figure 9-1). Otherwise, type in the IP address and HTTPS port of your vCenter server. Click Next.

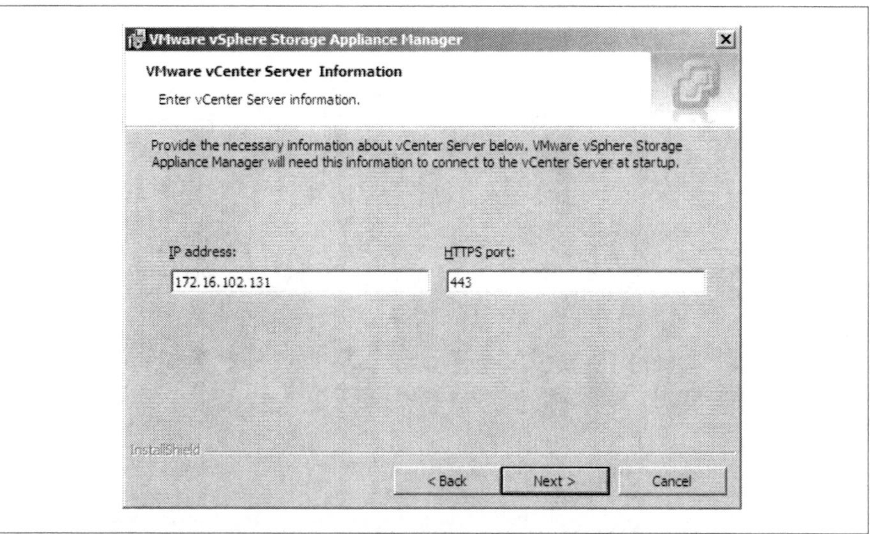

Figure 9-1. Storage Appliance Manager: vCenter Server information

4. Enter your vSphere Storage Appliance license key, or leave it empty to install in evaluation mode (Figure 9-2). Click Next.

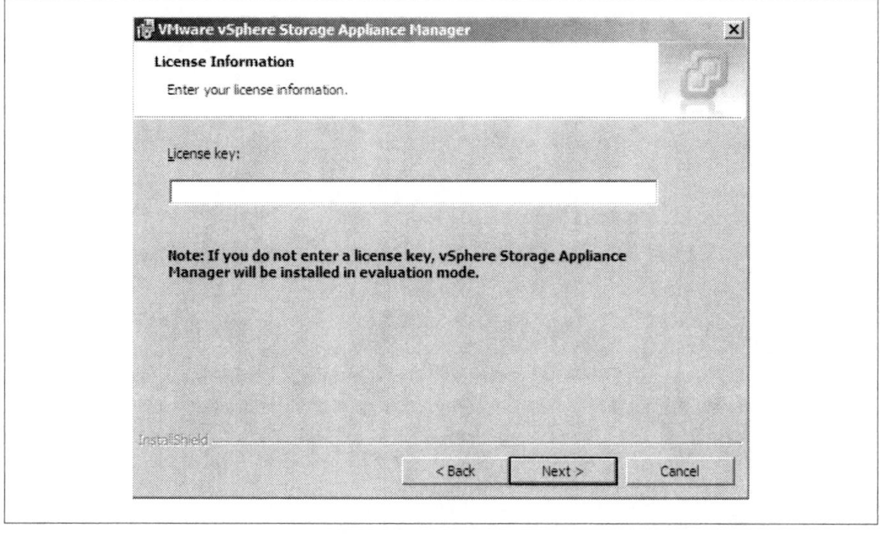

Figure 9-2. Storage Appliance Manager: license key

5. Click Next Install to begin the installation (Figure 9-3).

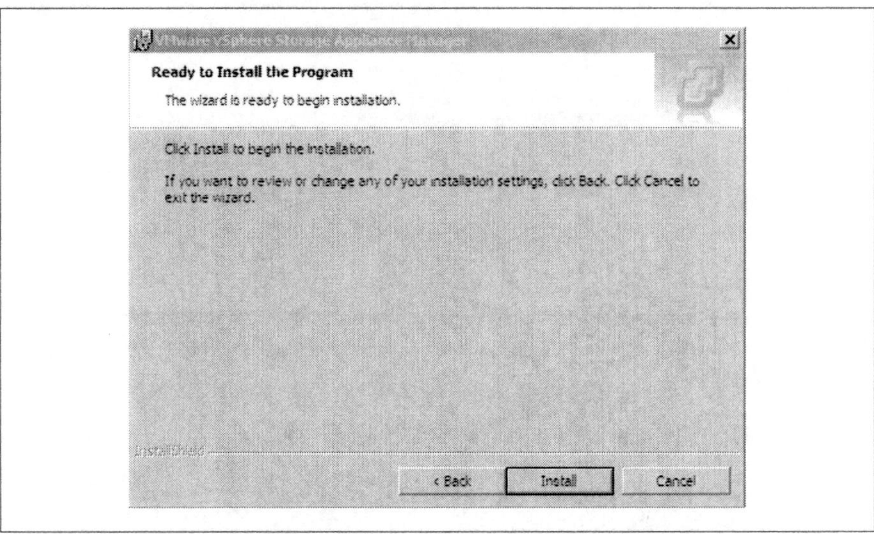

Figure 9-3. Storage Appliance: final installation

6. Once the installation completes, click Finish.
7. Next, log in to your vCenter server and click Plug-ins followed by Manage Plug-ins. The VSA Manager should be enabled (Figure 9-4). If it's not enabled, enable it now.

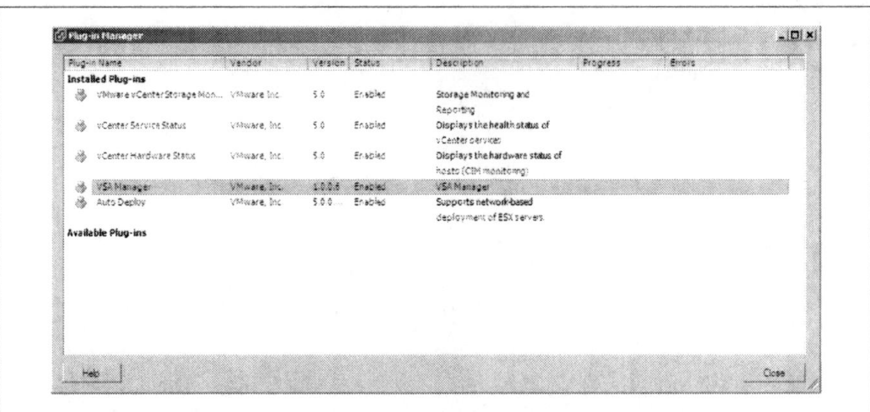

Figure 9-4. Storage Appliance: enable VSA Manager inside the vCenter server

9.4 vSphere Storage Appliance Cluster Creation Process

Problem

After installing the vSphere Storage Appliance, you need to configure your datacenters and hosts.

Solution

Following the simple steps in the configuration, you can enable the VSA.

Discussion

In Recipe 9.3, we installed the Storage Appliance Manager and enabled the plug-in inside the vCenter server. We can go ahead and build our configuration and VSA cluster at this time, assuming we meet the requirements in Recipe 9.2.

1. Open the vCenter, navigate to your datacenter, and click the VSA Manager tab. Click the Start VSA Installer link as shown in Figure 9-5. You will need to make sure you have Adobe Flash player installed on your server, because this tool requires it.

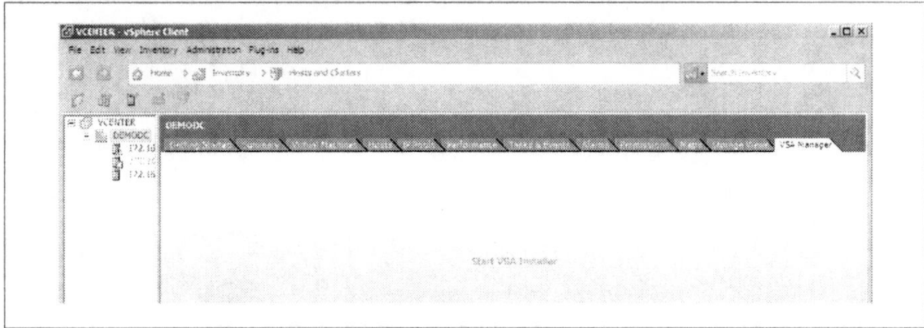

Figure 9-5. Create a VSA Cluster: datacenter tab

2. Next, you will see there are two options on the VSA Installer screen (Figure 9-6). Most of the time you will use New Installation. The other option, Recover VSA Cluster, should be used after you reinstall the vCenter from scratch or replace it without a migration.

New installation

This will install a new VSA cluster on the ESXi hosts you select during the installation process.

Recover the VSA Cluster

This will restore the VSA information and configuration back into the vCenter. This process will rescan the ESXi hosts for the VSA configurations and import them back into the cluster.

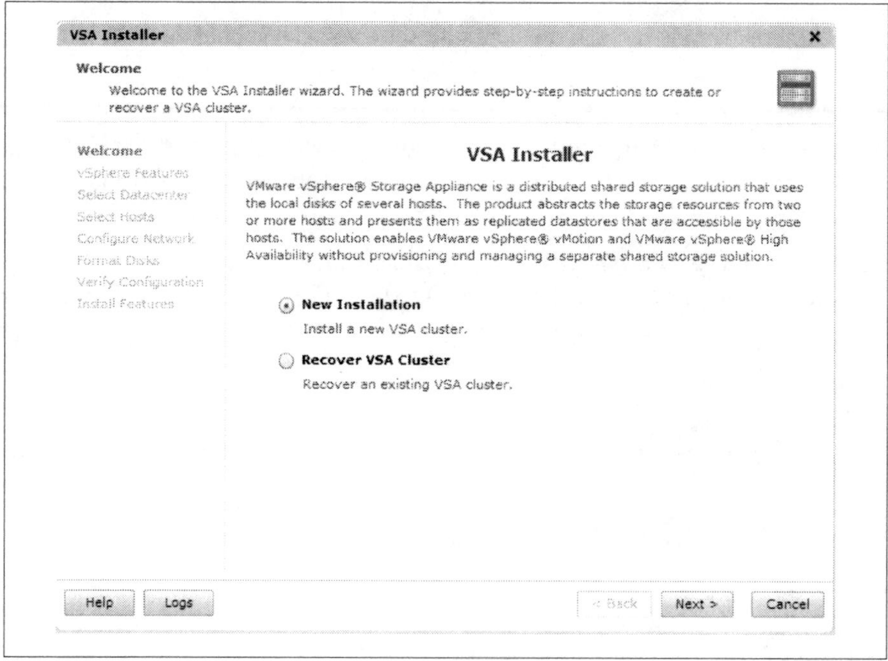

Figure 9-6. Create a VSA Cluster: main install screen

3. A summary of the VSA Install Wizard appears and will give you a overview of the installation process (Figure 9-7). Click Next to continue the installation.

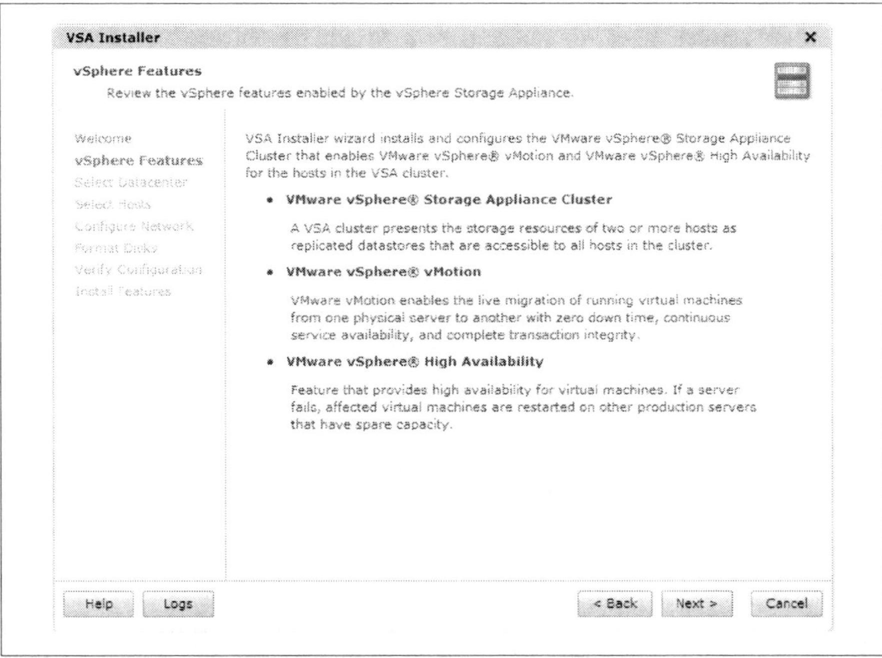

Figure 9-7. Create a VSA Cluster: installation summary

4. Next, select the datacenter where you wish to install the VSA cluster (Figure 9-8). If you have more than one datacenter, you must choose one to hold the VSA cluster. Click Next.

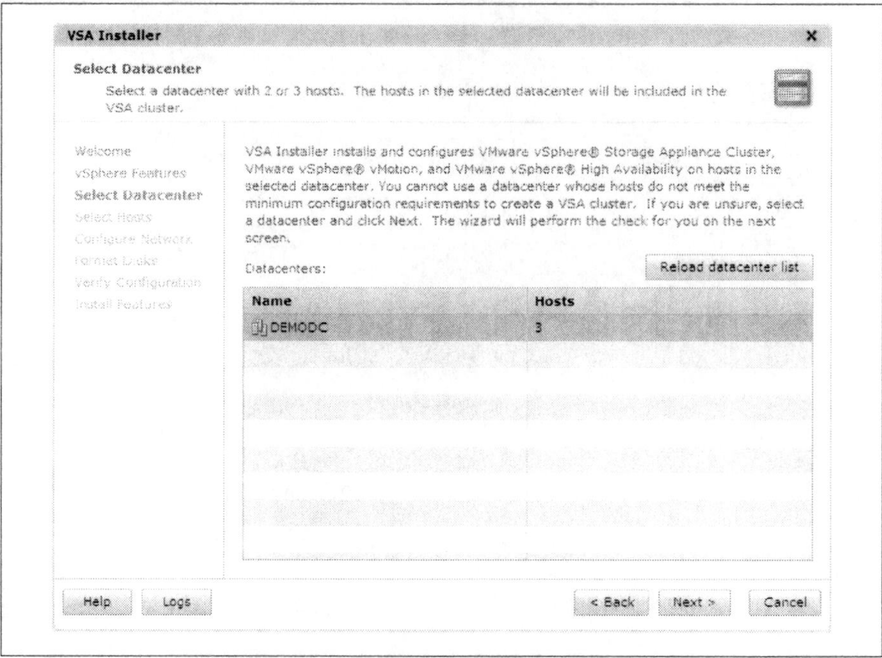

Figure 9-8. Create a VSA Cluster: select datacenter

5. Select the hosts to use for the VSA virtual machine (Figure 9-9). The status section will provide additional details that show you any issues regarding the configuration or provide information if that host doesn't meet the compatibility requirements of the VSA cluster. Once the hosts are selected click Next to continue the installation process.

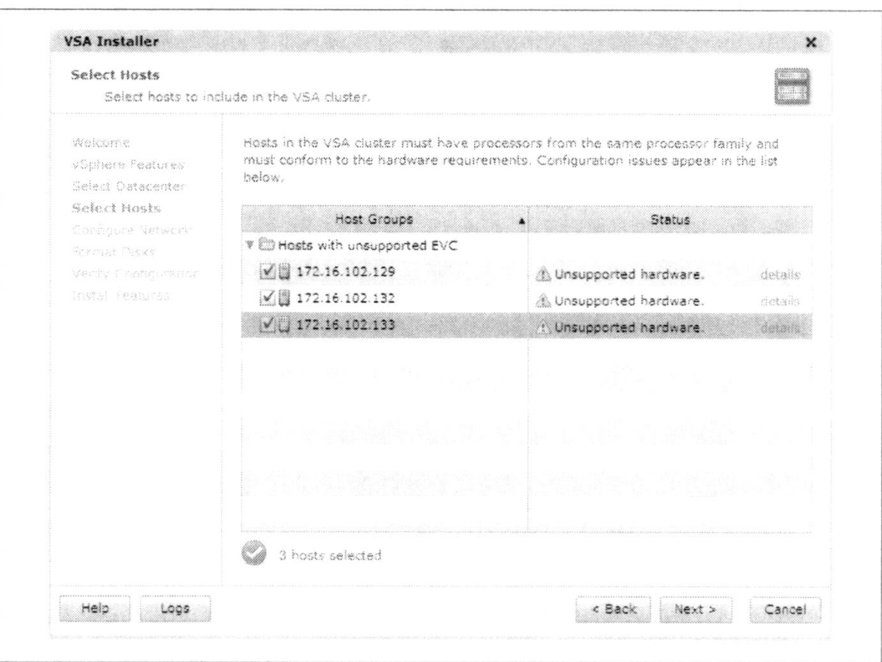

Figure 9-9. Create a VSA Cluster: select hosts

6. Enter the IP information for the VSA management network (Figure 9-10). This should be an IP address within the subnet where your ESXi Hosts reside. If you are configuring your VSA cluster with only two hosts, you will be required to enter another IP address. Once you enter the first IP address, the installer will autopopulate the additional IP addresses in sequential order, for example, 172.16.102.80, 172.16.102.81, etc. Click Next to continue the installation.

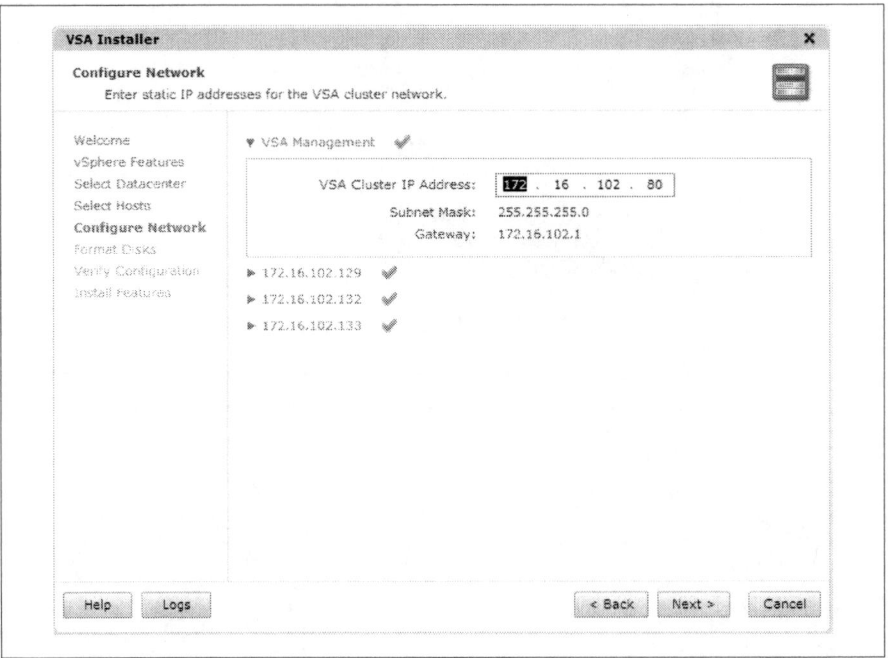

Figure 9-10. Create VSA Cluster: Configure Networking

7. Click the other ESXi Hosts and make sure their networking is correctly configured (Figure 9-11). The vSphere Feature IP address can be left to use DHCP if you choose. If unchecked, it will autopopulate with an IP address from the same subnet as the VSA Cluster IP address. Additionally, any VLAN information can be configured here as well.

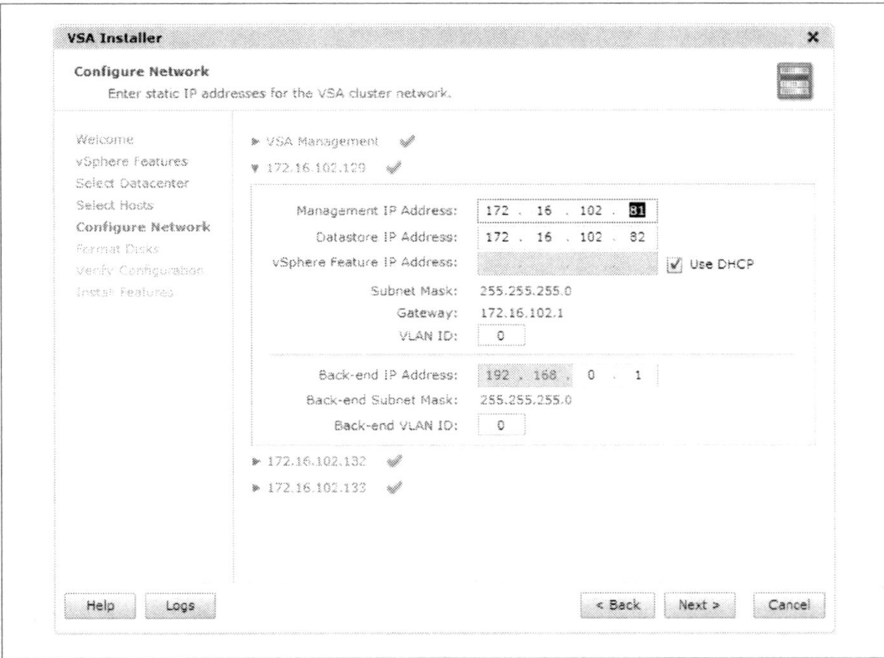

Figure 9-11. Create a VSA Cluster: network configuration on ESXi Host

Click Next to continue the installation.

8. The installation now asks how you want to format your storage (Figure 9-12). If you can, select the format the disks immediately option, this will save time and overhead on the ESXi hosts. However, if you wish to wait, you can select the Format disks on first access and they will be formatted later.

   Click Next to continue the installation.

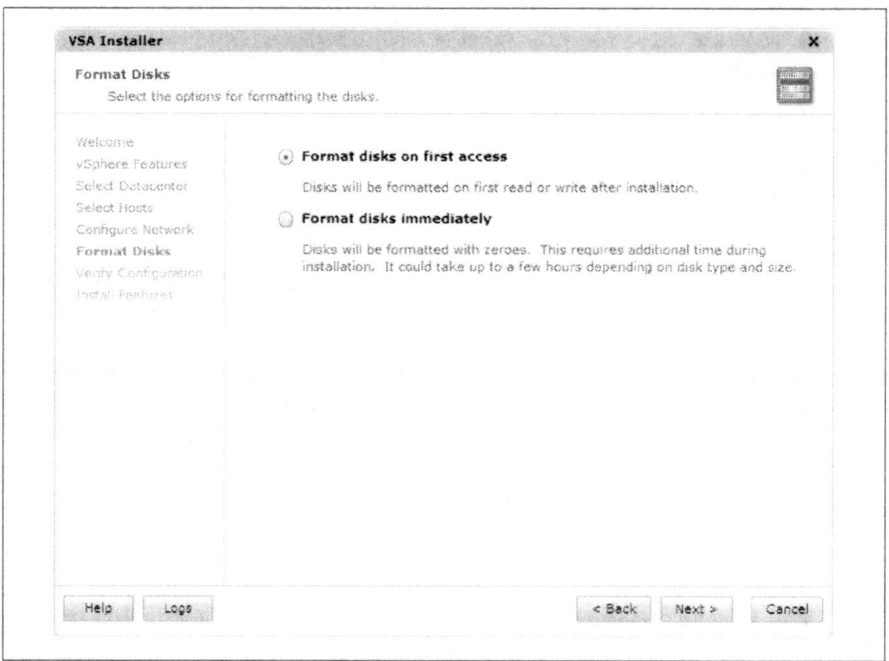

Figure 9-12. Create a VSA Cluster: select disk options

9. Review the summary of the installation and click Install (Figure 9-13).

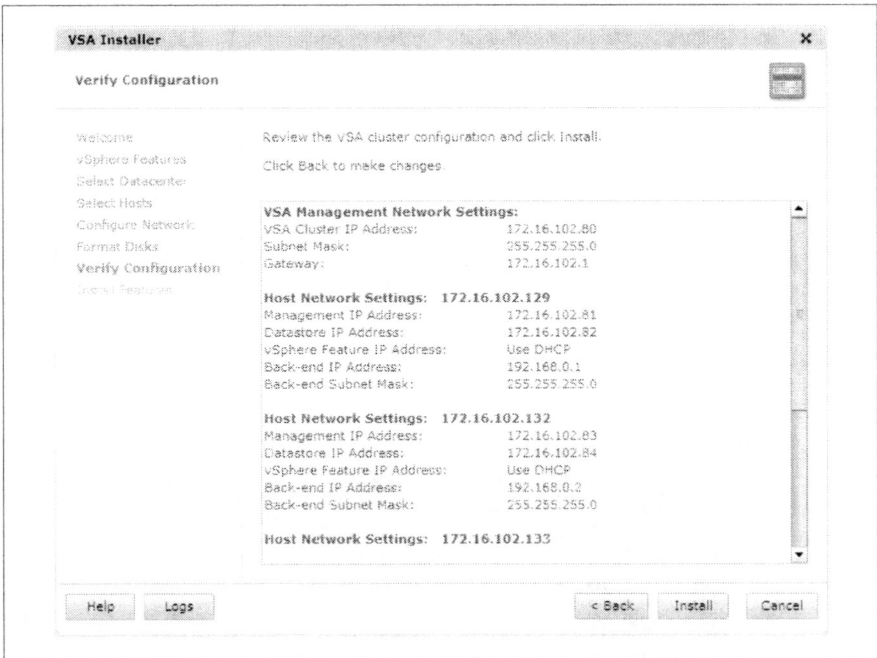

Figure 9-13. Create a VSA Cluster: installation summary

10. Once the installation starts, you will be prompted to accept the notice warning that the disks being used will be formatted and the content will be erased (Figure 9-14). Click Yes to accept and the installation will continue.

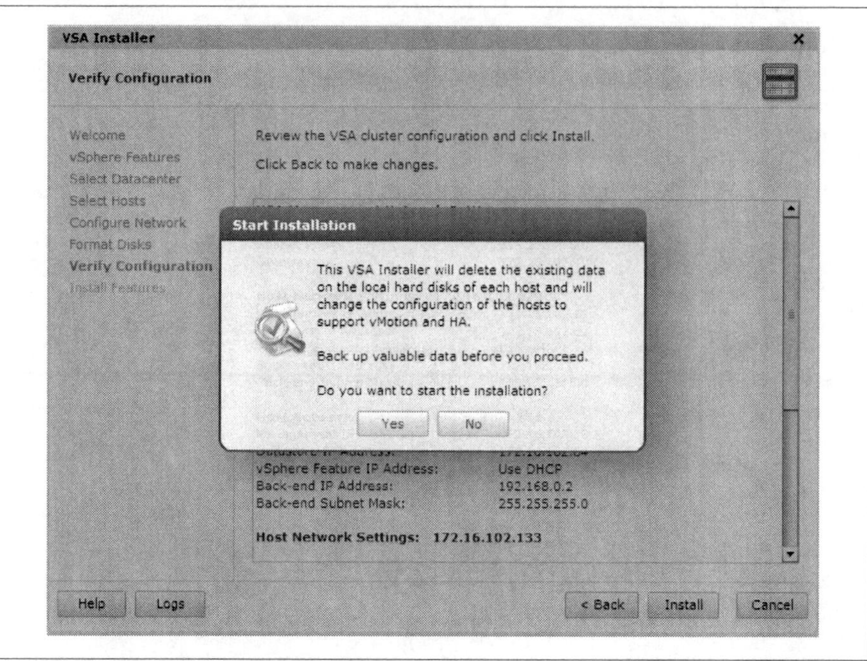

Figure 9-14. Create a VSA Cluster: local disk warning

11. The installer will begin creating the cluster and moving your ESXi Hosts into the new cluster as well as configuring the networking aspects of the VSA cluster (Figure 9-15). The time this takes can vary depending on the configuration and how you choose to format your disks. Any errors will be noted at the end.

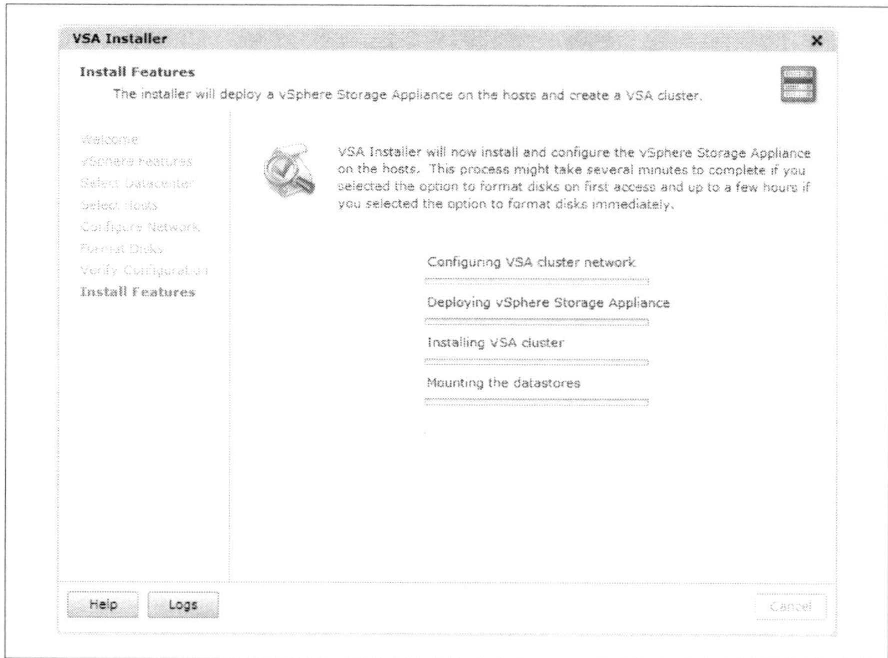

Figure 9-15. Create a VSA Cluster: installation processes

After the installer completes successfully, you will have access to the storage on the VSA Cluster immediately. Please see Recipe 9.1 for additional information and limitations on the vSphere Storage Appliance.

Index

Symbols

We'd like to hear your suggestions for improving our indexes. Send email to *index@oreilly.com*.

A

B

C

D

E

F

J

K

L

M

N

S

T

U

V

W

About the Authors

Ryan Troy has over 12 years of Unix/Linux system administration experience, working in diverse industries that range from web hosting to the newspaper industry. He has written articles for Linux Identity magazine and coauthored articles for Linux+ magazine. He is passionate about virtualization, specifically VMware's technologies. Ryan also founded the now-official Ubuntu Linux forums (http://www.ubuntuforums.org) in October 2004; he currently serves as technical administrator and chairman of the Ubuntu Forum Council. One of Ryan's latest projects has been to architect and build a virtualization infrastructure for a cloud provider, using VMware's ESXi and vCloud products.

Matthew Helmke is an active member of the Ubuntu Linux community. He coauthored O'Reilly's VMware Cookbook and Prentice Hall's *The Official Ubuntu Book*. He is also the author of Sams' *Ubuntu Unleashed*. Matthew got his first computer in 1981 (a TRS-80 Color Computer, the original in the silver case) and first used Unix in 1987 while studying Lisp on a Vax at the university; he has been a techno-geek ever since.

Colophon

The animal on the cover of *VMware Cookbook* is a leatherback sea turtle (*Dermochelys coriacea*). At four to eight feet in length, the leatherback turtle is the fourth largest reptile, behind certain species of crocodile. Most sea turtles have bony shells; however, the leatherback's shell is made of skin and oily flesh.

Leatherback sea turtles live as far north as the Arctic Circle and as far south as the Cape of Good Hope in Africa and the southernmost tip of New Zealand. They inhabit all tropical and subtropical oceans.

The turtle's diet consists almost entirely of jellyfish, and ecologists theorize that the turtle plays a key role in controlling jellyfish populations. Scientists also note that the leatherback turtle continues to be important to local ecosystems even after it dies: decomposing leatherback turtles often wash ashore and host various species of flies and beetles.

As with other sea turtles, leatherbacks begin their lives on land as they burst forth from the sand of their nesting beaches. Yet their lives are in danger even before they are born: birds and humans eat leatherback turtle eggs (in Malaysia, where the leatherback turtle is nearly extinct, the eggs are considered a delicacy). The danger doesn't end, however, once leatherbacks are born: birds, crustaceans, reptiles, and people will often eat newborn turtles before they reach the water. Once they reach the sea, the turtles become prey for some species of fish and cephalopods. Given all of their predators, very few leatherbacks reach adulthood; those that do usually have a life span of 30 to 50 years.

The cover image is from *Dover's Animals*. The cover font is Adobe ITC Garamond. The text font is Linotype Birka; the heading font is Adobe Myriad Condensed; and the code font is LucasFont's TheSansMonoCondensed.

CPSIA information can be obtained at www.ICGtesting.com
Printed in the USA
LVOW07s1935220814

400470LV00019B/377/P